# THE LIFE
# CHARLES DI(

BY
THOMAS WRIGHT

AUTHOR OF "THE LIFE OF WILLIAM COWPER,"
"THE LIFE OF EDWARD FITZGERALD,"
"THE LIFE OF WILLIAM BLAKE," ETC., ETC.

NEW YORK
CHARLES SCRIBNER'S SONS
1936

Printed in Great Britain

CHARLES DICKENS IN 1839

*By Daniel Maclise*
*National Portrait Gallery*

See page 134

# PREFACE

I BEGAN to collect materials for this work as early as 1893, for I was aware that a number of very important events relative to the life of Charles Dickens were not even alluded to by John Forster, whose biography had been received as the standard work on the subject. His work had many errors. It was re-edited, with useful notes, in 1928 by Mr J. W. T. Ley, but the text was not altered.

I was assisted in various ways by Dickens's intimate friends, Percy Fitzgerald and John Hollingshead. Others who helped me were Mr W. R. Hughes, author of *A Week's Tramp in Dickens Land*, whom I visited at Birmingham; Mr F. G. Kitton, to whom all Dickens students are deeply indebted; Mr S. B. Huffam, grandson of John Dickens's friend, Christopher Huffam; Mr W. S. Huffam, great-grandson of Christopher Huffam; Mr Hammond Hall, of the *Daily Graphic*; Mr Walter Wellsman, proprietor of Mitchell's Newspaper Directory; Mr C. Barrow, son of Thomas Culliford Barrow (Mrs John Dickens's brother); Mr R. Shiers, son of Mr Richard Shiers, tutor at Jones's School (the Mr Creakle's of *David Copperfield*); Miss Jessie Hepburn Starey, daughter of Mr S. R. Starey, who with Dickens's help established Ragged Schools (see §§ 64 and 65); Miss Lynn Linton, contributor to *All the Year Round*, who sold Gad's Hill Place to Dickens; Mr C. Burton; Mr Snowden Ward, author of *The Real Dickens Land*; the late Mr Robert Langton, author of *The Childhood and Youth of Charles Dickens*; and the late Mr Frank T. Sabin.

I have to thank for various kindnesses, Mr Walter Dexter, the gifted editor of the *Dickensian*; Mr A. W. Edwards, the very helpful honorary secretary of The

Dickens House, 48 Doughty Street, London; Mr T. W. Tyrrell, of Brondesbury; Mr F. J. Peplow, Borough Librarian of Deptford; Mr W. C. Edwards; Mr Ralph Straus; Mr Dudley Wright; Dr Holland Rose; Mr Selwyn Oxley; Mr K. Povey, of Queen's University, Belfast; Mrs Gabrielle Enthoven, of the Victoria and Albert Museum, South Kensington; Miss Helen Brown, also of that Museum; Mr E. W. Betts, Assistant Editor of the *Era*; Mr H. H. Harper, of The Bibliophile Society, Boston, U.S.A.; Mr G. F. Colcord (Mr Harper's Secretary); Mr S. P. Sabin, of Bond Street, London; Mrs Sarah Huffam, 20 Vrede Street, Cape Town; Mrs Gertrude Mary Estell, sister of Mr W. Stanley Huffam; and Mr Walter T. Spencer.

The book is very largely indebted to my friend, the late Canon Benham, to whom I was introduced on 24 January 1893, when he, as editor of Cowper's Poems in the "Globe" edition (Macmillan's) came to Olney in order to be present at the re-interment of the remains of Cowper's friend, the Rev. John Newton. I rarely afterwards visited London without calling on him at his home, 32 Finsbury Square.

In 1904 I resolved, unwisely, to issue my *Life of Charles Dickens* at once. I say "unwisely," because I could not then use the whole of my materials. I could not, for instance, include the portions relating to Miss Ellen Lawless Ternan.

However, the work was accepted by Mr Grant Richards, who had published my successful two-volume *Life of Edward FitzGerald*, and the agreement was signed on the 21st of June 1904. Before, however, further progress could be made Mr Richards's firm was found to be in difficulties. For long (and fortunately as far as concerned this book) everything was at a standstill. Eventually I bought back the copyright and resolved to put the work aside until the time should come when it would not be necessary to keep back anything. On 3 April 1934, after nearly thirty years had elapsed, I contributed to the *Daily Express* the article entitled *Charles Dickens began his Honeymoon*, in which the connection of Dickens with Miss Ternan was first made public. In so small a space as the page of a newspaper it was impossible, of course, to tell the whole story. Now that sixty-five years have passed since the death of Dickens there is no need to withhold anything whatever. The facts set down in this book take nothing from the genius of Dickens, nor should they deter a single person from having recourse to his amazing works. He was a great, a very great writer; he is, in the opinion of many of our best critics, the next greatest English writer to Shakespeare; he was a persistent philanthropist, he made the whole of the reading world his debtor. He erred. He suffered. He paid the full penalty for—to use the mildest term possible—his errors of judgment.

The article in the *Daily Express* had the results of proving to the public that most of the theories respecting Dickens's latter years were supremely ridiculous; and that his last books, *Great Expectations*, *Our Mutual Friend* and *Edwin Drood*, would have to be read in an entirely new light. This article was, to quote one of its critics, "the most important contribution to the biography of Dickens in this century," and his comment was generally endorsed by Dickens students.

All the references in this book are to the Crown Edition of Dickens's works.

In conclusion, I would not forget that in respect to these pages I have again and again been indebted to my wife who has helped by reading the proofs. She has been my right hand during the whole of my literary career, and the book has often benefited by her suggestions and her apposite criticisms.

THOMAS WRIGHT.

COWPER SCHOOL,
OLNEY, BUCKS.
16 *May* 1935.

# CONTENTS

## CHAPTER I

### 7 February 1812 to Spring 1823

PORTSMOUTH AND CHATHAM

| | | PAGE |
|---|---|---|
| 1. | PORTSMOUTH, 7 FEBRUARY 1812. CHRISTOPHER HUFFAM . | 23 |
| 2. | REMOVAL TO LONDON (PROBABLY IN 1814) AND THEN TO CHATHAM, 1817 . . . . . . . . . | 24 |
| 3. | THE DAME SCHOOL, 1817. . . . . . . | 26 |
| 4. | MICAWBER . . . . . . . . . | 27 |
| 5. | THE BROOK. MR GILES'S SCHOOL . . . . | 28 |
| 6. | CONVICTS AND BOATMEN AND GREAT SEA PORCUPINES . . | 30 |
| 7. | ROCHESTER . . . . . . . . | 30 |
| 8. | THE GLORIOUS GARRET . . . . . . | 32 |
| 9. | TOM-ALL-ALONE'S. GAD'S HILL . . . . . | 33 |

## CHAPTER II

### Spring 1823 to Christmas 1823

16 (LATER NO. 141) BAYHAM STREET

| 10. | "THE BLUE-EYED MAID" . . . . . . | 35 |
|---|---|---|
| 11. | THE ONE-LEGGED UNCLE . . . . . . | 36 |

## CHAPTER III

### Christmas 1823 to 28 May 1824

4 GOWER STREET NORTH TILL 24 MARCH
THE MARSHALSEA, 24 MARCH TO 28 MAY 1824

| 12. | GOWER STREET NORTH. JOHN DICKENS IS ARRESTED FOR DEBT, 20 FEBRUARY 1824 . . . . . . . | 38 |
|---|---|---|
| 13. | THE BLACKING WAREHOUSE . . . . . | 40 |
| 14. | A LEGACY. THE FAMILY LEAVE THE MARSHALSEA, 28 MAY 1824 . . . . . . . . . | 42 |

# THE LIFE OF CHARLES DICKENS

## CHAPTER IV

### June 1824 to November 1828

#### 29 (LATER 13) JOHNSON STREET

PAGE

15. Mr Creakle's School . . . . . . . 44
16. Lawyer's Clerk. Shorthand . . . . . 46

## CHAPTER V

### November 1828 to 1830

#### NO. 17 THE POLYGON, SOMERS TOWN AND DOCTORS' COMMONS

17. The Jarman Case. Traddles . . . . . . 48

## CHAPTER VI

### 1830 to January 1833

#### FITZROY STREET, FITZROY SQUARE (NEARLY THREE YEARS)

18. The Ross Family. Maria Beadnell. May 1830. "The
    Bill of Fare," May 1831 . . . . . . 53
19. Dickens tries to get on to the Stage. He becomes a
    reporter for the "True Sun." John Henry Barrow 56

## CHAPTER VII

### January 1833 to December 1834

#### 18 BENTINCK STREET (TWO YEARS)

20. Dickens comes of age, 7 February 1833. Maria Beadnell
    again, 18 March 1833. "Clari," 27 April 1833.
    Micawber anecdotes . . . . . . . 58
21. The Fetter Lane Old Curiosity Shop. "A Dinner at
    Poplar Walk" . . . . . . . . 64
22. On the "Morning Chronicle." Misery in Bentinck Street 66

## CHAPTER VIII

### December 1834 to 2 April 1836

#### NO. 13 AND NO. 15 FURNIVAL'S INN TO THE DATE OF HIS MARRIAGE

23. The "Evening Chronicle," 31 January 1835. "Sketches by
    Boz." Cruikshank . . . . . . . 70
24. Engagement to Catherine Thomson Hogarth, May 1835 72

# CONTENTS

PAGE

25. AINSWORTH. FIRST LETTER TO MACRONE, 28 OCTOBER 1835.
CRUIKSHANK . . . . . . . . . 75
26. THE KETTERING ELECTION, 18 DECEMBER 1835 . . 76
27. "SKETCHES BY BOZ," FIRST SERIES, FEBRUARY 1836. WHITE-
HEAD . . . . . . . . . . 79
28. "PICKWICK" NO. 1, 1 APRIL 1836 . . . . . 80

## CHAPTER IX
## 2 April 1836 to March 1837
### NO. 15 FURNIVAL'S INN TO DATE OF REMOVAL TO 48 DOUGHTY STREET

29. MARRIAGE, 2 APRIL 1836. . . . . . . 83
30. SUICIDE OF SEYMOUR, 20 APRIL 1836 . . . . 85
31. HABLOT KNIGHT BROWNE . . . . . . . 87
32. "SUNDAY UNDER THREE HEADS," JUNE 1836. THE "CARLTON
CHRONICLE," 6 AUGUST 1836 . . . . . 89
33. "THE STRANGE GENTLEMAN," 29 SEPTEMBER 1836, AND "VIL-
LAGE COQUETTES," 6 DECEMBER 1836 . . . . 92
34. "SKETCHES BY BOZ," SECOND SERIES, 17 DECEMBER 1836. FIRST
FRUITS OF HUMOUR. CRUIKSHANK'S PICTURES . . 95
35. DICKENS'S ELDEST SON BORN 6 JANUARY 1837. "PICKWICK"
CONTINUES TO RUN ITS VICTORIOUS COURSE . . . 97
36. ORIGINALS OF "PICKWICK" PERSONS . . . . . 98
37. THE LEATHER BOTTLE AT COBHAM . . . . . 101
38. PICKWICKIAN HUMOUR . . . . . . . 102
39. "BENTLEY'S MISCELLANY" AND "THE MUDFOG PAPERS,"
JANUARY 1837. "OLIVER TWIST," FEBRUARY 1837 . 104
40. "IS SHE HIS WIFE?", 6 MARCH 1837 . . . . 106
41. DEATH OF MARY HOGARTH, 7 MARCH 1837 . . . 108
42. JOHN FORSTER . . . . . . . . . 111

## CHAPTER X
## March 1837 to end of 1839
### 48 DOUGHTY STREET

43. GEORGE HENRY LEWES, 3 APRIL 1837, AND CHARLES MACREADY,
16 JUNE 1837 . . . . . . . . 113
44. DEATH OF JOHN MACRONE, 9 SEPTEMBER 1837. BROADSTAIRS,
SEPTEMBER 1837 . . . . . . . 115
45. "OLIVER TWIST" CONSIDERED . . . . . . 116
46. THE HUMOUR OF "OLIVER TWIST" . . . . . 119

PAGE

47. CRUIKSHANK'S CLAIM . . . . . . . 119
48. THOMAS GRIFFITHS WAINEWRIGHT. REV. WILLIAM GILES
   AGAIN . . . . . . . . . . 121
49. "NICHOLAS NICKLEBY" . . . . . . . 123
50. SHAW AND SQUEERS, 2 FEBRUARY 1838 . . . . 124
51. THE HUMOUR OF "NICHOLAS NICKLEBY" . . . . 129
52. HIS DAUGHTER MARY BORN 12 MARCH 1838. "MEMOIRS OF
   GRIMALDI," FEBRUARY 1838. MRS JENIWIN . . . 130

## CHAPTER XI

### End of 1839 to June 1842

1 DEVONSHIRE TERRACE, FIRST PERIOD, TO DATE OF HIS RETURN
AFTER FIRST VISIT TO AMERICA

53. "MASTER HUMPHREY'S CLOCK," FIRST No., 4 APRIL 1840.
   LANDOR . . . . . . . . . 135
54. "THE OLD CURIOSITY SHOP" . . . . . . 137
55. THE HUMOUR OF "THE OLD CURIOSITY SHOP" . . . 139
56. "BARNABY RUDGE," JANUARY 1841 . . . . . 140
57. "THE PIC-NIC PAPERS," 1 APRIL 1841. CHAUNCEY HARE
   TOWNSHEND'S MAGNETIC BOY. 21 MAY 1841. A VISIT TO
   SCOTLAND . . . . . . . . . 142
58. MR AND MRS BURNETT. A PAGE OUT OF BUNYAN. IN PRAISE
   OF IRVING'S "SKETCH BOOK" . . . . . . 145
59. FIRST VISIT TO AMERICA. 4 JANUARY 1842 . . . 148
60. THE CITY OF EDEN. NIAGARA, 26 APRIL 1842. MONTREAL,
   25 MAY 1842 . . . . . . . . . 151

## CHAPTER XII

### June 1842 to Spring 1847

1 DEVONSHIRE TERRACE, SECOND PERIOD. FROM HIS RETURN AFTER
HIS FIRST VISIT TO AMERICA TO HIS TEMPORARY RESIDENCE IN
CHESTER PLACE

61. DICKENS AND UNITARIANISM. "AMERICAN NOTES," 18 OCTOBER
   1842. THE TRIP TO CORNWALL, 28 OCTOBER 1842. REV.
   EDWARD TAGART, 20 NOVEMBER 1842 . . . . 155
62. "MARTIN CHUZZLEWIT," NOVEMBER 1842 . . . . 159
63. DICKENS AS A LETTER WRITER. A PEEP AT THE HOME LIFE 162
64. RAGGED SCHOOLS. MR S. R. STAREY, 24 SEPTEMBER 1843 164

# CONTENTS

PAGE

65. The Pencil Drawing of Dickens, Mrs Dickens and Miss Hogarth, 1843. Dickens meets again his old master, the Rev. W. Giles, 5 October 1843 . . . . 166
66. The "Christmas Carol," Christmas 1843 . . . 169
67. The Christiana Weller Idyll, 26 February 1844 . . 170
68. Stared in the Face by Ruin, 10 February 1844 . . 172
69. In Italy, 16 July 1844. "The Chimes," Christmas 1844. Landor . . . . . . . . . 173
70. The Three Fannys. Miss Kelly's Theatre. "The Cricket on the Hearth," Christmas 1845 . . . 175
71. The "Daily News," 21 January 1846 . . . . 176
72. To Switzerland, 31 May 1846 . . . . . 179
73. To Paris. "The Battle of Life," Christmas 1846 . 180
74. Victor Hugo . . . . . . . . . 183

## CHAPTER XIII

## Spring 1847 to November 1851

1 DEVONSHIRE TERRACE, THIRD PERIOD. FROM LEAVING CHESTER PLACE TO HIS REMOVAL TO TAVISTOCK HOUSE

75. Harold Skimpole. The Leigh Hunt and John Poole Benefit. 26 July 1847 . . . . . . 185
76. "Dombey and Son." Maclise's Portrait of Mrs Dickens 188
77. The Shakespeare House Fund . . . . . 190
78. Mrs Cowden Clarke . . . . . . . 191
79. The Actors at Birmingham, 6 June 1848, and in Scotland, 15 July . . . . . . . . . 192
80. Illness of Mrs Burnett, July. "The Haunted Man," Christmas 1848 . . . . . . . . 195
81. At Yarmouth, January 1849 . . . . . . 197
82. At the Isle of Wight, July 1849. The Mannings, 13 November 1849 . . . . . . . . 200
83. In Northamptonshire, 30 November 1849. Mrs. Gaskell, 31 January 1850. "Household Words," 30 March 1850 202
84. "David Copperfield." Last Number, November 1850. The Humour of "David Copperfield" . . . 204
85. Dickens's Admiration of Defoe. Thomas Adolphus Trollope . . . . . . . . . . 206

86. PERFORMANCES AT KNEBWORTH, NOVEMBER 1850. "A CHRIST-
MAS TREE," FIRST CHRISTMAS No. (1850) OF "H.W.". . 208

87. AT ROCKINGHAM AGAIN, JANUARY 1851 . . . . 209

88. WILKIE COLLINS ENTERS. THE GUILD OF LITERATURE AND ART 210

89. DEATH OF MICAWBER, 31 MARCH 1851. "A CHILD'S HISTORY
OF ENGLAND" . . . . . . . . 211

90. THE SPEECH AT GORE HOUSE, 10 MAY 1851. "MR NIGHTIN-
GALE'S DIARY," BY LEMON AND DICKENS. . . . 212

## CHAPTER XIV

## November 1851 to March 1856

TAVISTOCK HOUSE TO THE PURCHASE OF GAD'S HILL PLACE

91. DICKENS REMOVES TO TAVISTOCK HOUSE, NOVEMBER 1851.
"BLEAK HOUSE" COMMENCED. MRS GASKELL AND "CRAN-
FORD" . . . . . . . . . . 214

92. ORIGINALS OF CHARACTERS, ETC., IN "BLEAK HOUSE." THE
TYPE EVASION . . . . . . . . 217

93. THE GUILD COMPANY AT BIRMINGHAM. "WHAT SHALL WE
HAVE FOR DINNER?" "WHAT CHRISTMAS IS AS WE GROW
OLDER," SECOND CHRISTMAS No. (1851) OF "H.W."
"ROUND OF STORIES BY THE CHRISTMAS FIRE," THIRD CHRIST-
MAS No. (1852) OF "H.W.". . . . . . 221

94. AT BOULOGNE . . . . . . . . 224

95. TO SWITZERLAND WITH COLLINS AND EGG . . . 225

96. READINGS AT BIRMINGHAM 27 AND 29 DECEMBER 1853. "AN-
OTHER ROUND OF STORIES BY THE CHRISTMAS FIRE," FOURTH
CHRISTMAS No. (1853) "H.W." . . . . 226

97. "HARD TIMES," 1 APRIL TO 12 AUGUST 1854. "SEVEN POOR
TRAVELLERS," FIFTH CHRISTMAS No. (1854) "H.W." . 227

98. MRS WINTER (MARIA BEADNELL) FEBRUARY AND MARCH 1855 228

99. "THE LIGHTHOUSE" (BY COLLINS) . . . . 232

100. HE RETURNS TO PARIS. "LITTLE DORRIT," FIRST MONTHLY
PART, DECEMBER 1855. "THE HOLLY TREE INN," SIXTH
CHRISTMAS No. (1855) "H.W." . . . . 233

101. SCHEFFER, WARD, EGG, STANFIELD . . . . 235

102. FLORA AND MR F.'s AUNT. . . . . . 236

# CONTENTS

## CHAPTER XV

### 14 March 1856 to end of year 1857

TAVISTOCK HOUSE, SECOND PERIOD, AND GAD'S HILL PLACE, FIRST PERIOD

|  |  | PAGE |
|---|---|---|
| 103. | GAD'S HILL PLACE SECURED, 14 MARCH 1856 . . . | 239 |
| 104. | ELLEN LAWLESS TERNAN . . . . . . . | 241 |
| 105. | DANCING FEET . . . . . . . . | 243 |
| 106. | "THE FROZEN DEEP" COMMENCED 5 MAY 1856. "THE WRECK OF THE GOLDEN MARY," SEVENTH CHRISTMAS No. (1856) OF "H.W." . . . . . . . . . | 245 |
| 107. | "THE FROZEN DEEP," FIRST ACTED AT TAVISTOCK HOUSE, 6 JANUARY 1857. DEATH OF DOUGLAS JERROLD, 8 JUNE 1857 | 248 |
| 108. | "THE FROZEN DEEP" ACTED BEFORE THE QUEEN AT THE GALLERY OF ILLUSTRATION, 4 JULY 1857 . . . . | 250 |
| 109. | THE GATHERING AT MR OUVRY'S, 12 JULY 1857 . . | 251 |
| 110. | PREPARATIONS FOR ACTING "THE FROZEN DEEP" AT MANCHESTER. THE REHEARSALS WITH THE PROFESSIONAL ACTRESSES, 2 AUGUST 1857 . . . . . . | 252 |
| 111. | THE BRACELET . . . . . . . | 254 |
| 112. | "THE FROZEN DEEP" AT MANCHESTER, 21 AND 22 AUGUST 1857 | 255 |
| 113. | "THE LAZY TOUR," SEPTEMBER 1857 . . . . | 257 |

## CHAPTER XVI

### January 1858 to June 1860

TAVISTOCK HOUSE, THIRD PERIOD, AND GAD'S HILL, SECOND PERIOD

| 114. | SPEECH AT THE DINNER IN BEHALF OF THE HOSPITAL FOR SICK CHILDREN, 9 FEBRUARY 1858. . . . . . | 260 |
|---|---|---|
| 115. | THREE IN ERROR . . . . . . . | 262 |
| 116. | FIRST SERIES OF PAID READINGS, 29 APRIL 1858, IN ST MARTIN'S HALL . . . . . . . | 266 |
| 117. | THE SEPARATION, MAY 1858 . . . . . | 267 |
| 118. | "THE VIOLATED LETTER," 25 MAY 1858. . . . | 269 |
| 119. | THE ADDRESS IN "HOUSEHOLD WORDS," 12 JUNE 1858. THE EDMUND YATES ARTICLE, 12 JUNE 1858 . . . | 274 |

PAGE

120. LANDOR *IN TENEBRIS* . . . . . . . . 276

121. A PROVINCIAL TOUR . . . . . . . . 277

122. FIRST VISIT TO IRELAND, 27 AUGUST 1858 . . . 278

123. THE APOTHEOSIS OF MISS E. L. TERNAN . . . . 279

124. ESTELLA AND HELENA. THE FRITH PORTRAIT. "A HOUSE TO LET," NINTH AND LAST CHRISTMAS NO. (1858) "H.W." . 283

125. "ALL THE YEAR ROUND," 30 APRIL 1859. "TALE OF TWO CITIES" BEGUN . . . . . . . . 288

126. READING AGAIN AT PETERBOROUGH, 19 OCTOBER 1859. EXIT HABLOT K. BROWNE . . . . . . . 290

127. "THE HAUNTED HOUSE," FIRST CHRISTMAS NO. (1859) OF "A.Y.R." "THE UNCOMMERCIAL TRAVELLER," 1860. NEWMAN HALL . . . . . . . . 292

## CHAPTER XVII

### June 1860 to 9 November 1867

GAD'S HILL ALONE, FIRST PERIOD

128. MARRIAGE OF KATE DICKENS TO C. A. COLLINS, JULY 1860. DEATH OF ALFRED DICKENS, 27 JULY 1860 . . . 294

129. "GREAT EXPECTATIONS," "A.Y.R.," 1 DECEMBER 1860. THE HUMOUR OF "GREAT EXPECTATIONS" . . . . 296

130. ORIGINALS OF PERSONS AND PLACES IN "GREAT EXPECTATIONS" 301

131. SECOND SERIES OF PAID READINGS. DEATH OF ARTHUR SMITH, OCTOBER 1861. "TOM TIDDLER'S GROUND," THIRD CHRISTMAS NO. (1861) "A.Y.R." "SOMEBODY'S LUGGAGE," FOURTH CHRISTMAS NO. (1862) "A.Y.R." THE HOLOCAUST 303

132. DICKENS ON THE MORMONS. DEATH OF MRS HOGARTH, 5 AUGUST 1863. DEATH OF DICKENS'S MOTHER, SEPTEMBER 1863. "MRS LIRRIPER'S LODGINGS," FIFTH CHRISTMAS NO. (1863) "A.Y.R." . . . . . . . . 307

133. DICKENS AT THE FIVE BELLS, HATCHAM . . . . 308

134. THE STAPLEHURST ACCIDENT, 9 JUNE 1865. THE CHARACTERS IN "OUR MUTUAL FRIEND" . . . . . . 312

# CONTENTS

PAGE

135. DICKENS ON CLARE, 15 AUGUST 1865. THE CHÂLET, THIRD
SERIES OF PAID READINGS, GEORGE DOLBY. "DR MARI-
GOLD'S PRESCRIPTIONS," SEVENTH CHRISTMAS No. (1865)
"A.Y.R." . . . . . . . . . 317
136. MRS TERNAN RETURNS TO THE STAGE. MARRIAGE OF FRANCES
ELEANOR TERNAN, TO T. A. TROLLOPE, 29 OCTOBER 1866 . 319
137. "MUGBY JUNCTION." AT THE BRIDGE OF ALLAN. SECOND
VISIT TO IRELAND, 20 MARCH 1867. AT PRESTON, 25 APRIL.
HOGHTON TOWER, APRIL 1867. AT BLACKBURN, 26 APRIL.
"NO THOROUGHFARE," NINTH AND LAST CHRISTMAS No.
(1867) "A.Y.R." . . . . . . . . . 321
138. "HOLIDAY ROMANCE," JANUARY TO MAY 1868 . . . 324

## CHAPTER XVIII

### 9 November 1867 to 31 December 1869

GAD'S HILL ALONE, SECOND PERIOD TO THE END OF THE YEAR 1869

139. SECOND VISIT TO AMERICA, 9 NOVEMBER 1867. HIS BROTHER
AUGUSTUS. "GEORGE SILVERMAN'S EXPLANATION," 14
JANUARY 1868, MARCH 1868. HOME AGAIN, 26 APRIL 1868 326
140. LONGFELLOW IN ENGLAND, JUNE 1868. DEATH OF TOWNSHEND 332
141. FOURTH SERIES OF PAID READINGS, OCTOBER 1868 . . 334
142. IN SCOTLAND AGAIN . . . . . . . . . 335
143. IN IRELAND, THIRD VISIT . . . . . . . . 337
144. AT BLACKPOOL. "KICKING HIS HAT ABOUT," 21 APRIL 1869 339
145. "VERONIQUE" AND "VERONICA." PERCY FITZGERALD'S "AN
EXPERIENCE". . . . . . . . . . 341

## CHAPTER XIX

### The Year 1870

GAD'S HILL ALONE, THIRD PERIOD

146. FIFTH SERIES OF PAID READINGS, 11 JANUARY 1870 . . 343
147. "EDWIN DROOD," FIRST NUMBER, 1 APRIL 1870 . . 345
148. ORIGINALS OF CHARACTERS AND PLACES IN "EDWIN DROOD" . 346

|  |  |  |  | PAGE |
|---|---|---|---|---|
| 149. | THE NEWSVENDORS' DINNER, 5 APRIL 1870 | . | . | 348 |
| 150. | THE ACTING AT LADY FREAKE'S, 2 JUNE 1870. HIS WILL | | . | 351 |
| 151. | DEATH, 9 JUNE 1870 | . | . | 353 |
| 152. | LAST DAYS OF MRS DICKENS | . | . | 355 |

APPENDIX No. 1. SUMMARY OF DICKENS'S CHARACTER AND LIFE
                   WORK . . . . . . 357

    „    No. 2. DICKENS AS A TEXTUARY . . . . 360

    „    No. 3. HOW DID "EDWIN DROOD" END? . . 361

    „    No. 4. ATTEMPTS TO ANSWER THE QUESTION "HOW
                   DID 'EDWIN DROOD' END?" . . . 364

    „    No. 5. EVENTS SUBSEQUENT TO THE DEATH OF
                   DICKENS . . . . . . 366

    „    No. 6. THOMSON, HOGARTH, BARROW, JOHN DICKENS
                   AND CHARLES DICKENS FAMILIES . . 368

    „    No. 7. THE EARLY ILLUSTRATORS OF DICKENS . 370

    „    No. 8. "BOZ AND HIS PUBLISHERS" . . . 373

    „    No. 9. DICKENS COLLECTIONS . . . . 374

    „    No. 10. BIBLIOGRAPHY . . . . . 377

INDEX . . . . . . . . . . . 387

# LIST OF ILLUSTRATIONS

| | | |
|---|---|---|
| DICKENS, BY MACLISE . . . . . . | . *Frontispiece* | |
| DICKENS'S BIRTHPLACE. . . . . . | . *facing page* | 24 |
| CHRISTOPHER HUFFAM . . . . . . | ,, ,, | 25 |
| JOHN DICKENS . . . . . . . | ,, ,, | 28 |
| MRS JOHN DICKENS . . . . . . | ,, ,, | 29 |
| No. 11 ORDNANCE TERRACE . . . . | ,, ,, | 44 |
| WELLINGTON HOUSE ACADEMY . . . . | ,, ,, | 45 |
| THOMAS NOON TALFOURD . . . . . | ,, ,, | 50 |
| THE BARROW MINIATURE . . . . . | ,, ,, | 51 |
| MARIA SARAH BEADNELL AND AS MRS WINTER . . | ,, ,, | 54 |
| "MORNING CHRONICLE" OFFICE AND ST LUKE'S, CHELSEA | ,, ,, | 55 |
| THE DRUMMOND MINIATURE . . . . . | ,, ,, | 72 |
| MRS DICKENS, BY MACLISE . . . . . | ,, ,, | 73 |
| MRS DICKENS, BY MACLISE (HEAD AND SHOULDERS) . | ,, ,, | 80 |
| PORCH OF CHALK CHURCH . . . . . | ,, ,, | 81 |
| H. K. BROWNE . . . . . . . | ,, ,, | 92 |
| GEORGE CRUIKSHANK . . . . . . | ,, ,, | 93 |
| THE LEATHER BOTTLE, COBHAM . . . . | ,, ,, | 100 |
| COBHAM HALL . . . . . . . | ,, ,, | 101 |
| MARY SCOTT HOGARTH . . . . . . | ,, ,, | 108 |
| HER GRAVE . . . . . . . | ,, ,, | 109 |
| JOHN FORSTER . . . . . . . | ,, ,, | 114 |
| No. 48 DOUGHTY STREET . . . . . | ,, ,, | 115 |

19

# THE LIFE OF CHARLES DICKENS

DICKENS, BY SAMUEL LAURENCE . . . . . *facing page* 120

DICKENS, BY COUNT D'ORSAY (11 DECEMBER 1841) . ,, ,, 121

WILLIAM SHAW'S SCHOOL . . . . . . ,, ,, 124

WILLIAM SHAW'S GRAVESTONE . . . . . ,, ,, 125

DANIEL GRANT . . . . . . . . ,, ,, 132

No. 1 DEVONSHIRE TERRACE . . . . . ,, ,, 133

LAWN HOUSE, BROADSTAIRS . . . . . . ,, ,, 144

DICKENS, BY FRANCIS ALEXANDER . . . . . ,, ,, 145

DICKENS, MRS DICKENS AND MISS G. HOGARTH . . ,, ,, 166

BLUNDESTONE CHURCH . . . . . . . ,, ,, 167

FORT HOUSE, BROADSTAIRS . . . . . . ,, ,, 206

MISS GEORGINA HOGARTH, BY EGG . . . . ,, ,, 207

WILKIE COLLINS . . . . . . . . ,, ,, 210

TAVISTOCK HOUSE . . . . . . . ,, ,, 211

GAD'S HILL PLACE: FRONT . . . . . . ,, ,, 240

GAD'S HILL PLACE: BACK . . . . . . ,, ,, 241

MRS TERNAN AND LEWIS BALL . . . . . ,, ,, 244

SCENE IN "THE FROZEN DEEP" . . . . . ,, ,, 245

PLAY-BILL OF "ATALANTA" . . . . . ,, ,, 248

SCENE IN "ATALANTA" . . . . . . ,, ,, 249

PLAY-BILL OF "THE FROZEN DEEP" . . . . ,, ,, 252

INVITATION CARD TO MR OUVRY'S . . . . ,, ,, 253

DICKENS, BY WATKINS (QUILL IN HAND. SEATED AT DESK),
1858 . . . . . . . . ,, ,, 264

DICKENS, BY WATKINS (WAISTCOAT WITH CROSSES), 1858 ,, ,, 265

DICKENS, BY BAUGNIET . . . . . . ,, ,, 280

MISS TERNAN'S HOUSE . . . . . . ,, ,, 281

DICKENS, BY SCHEFFER . . . . . . ,, ,, 286

DICKENS, BY FRITH . . . . . . . ,, ,, 287

DICKENS, BY MASON . . . . . . . ,, ,, 292

# LIST OF ILLUSTRATIONS

DICKENS, BY LEHMANN (1861) . . . . . *facing page* 293

GRAVES OF THE COMPORTS . . . . . . ,, ,, 298

"TOM TIDDLER'S GROUND" (FROM THE "QUEEN," 21
   DECEMBER 1861) . . . . . . ,, ,, 299

JOHN HOLLINGSHEAD . . . . . . . ,, ,, 304

THE FIVE BELLS, NEW CROSS ROAD, LONDON . . ,, ,, 305

THE PRIOR'S GATEWAY, ROCHESTER . . . . ,, ,, 318

DICKENS, BY GURNEY (HEAD ONLY), 1868 . . . ,, ,, 319

DICKENS, BY GURNEY (FULL LENGTH), 1868 . . . ,, ,, 332

MISS GEORGINA HOGARTH, *c.* 1870 . . . . ,, ,, 333

DICKENS'S GRAVE IN WESTMINSTER ABBEY . . . ,, ,, 354

THOMAS AND MARY GIBSON (MARY WELLER) . . ,, ,, 355

# THE LIFE OF CHARLES DICKENS

## CHAPTER I

# 7 February 1812 to Spring 1823

## PORTSMOUTH AND CHATHAM

§ 1. *Portsmouth, 7 February* 1812. *Christopher Huffam*

OF the ancestry of Charles Dickens little is known, but Mrs Dickens his grandmother, housekeeper at Lord Houghton's seat at Crewe, was an adept at telling stories. His father, John Dickens, born in 1786, probably in London, became, at the age of 19, seventh assistant clerk in the Navy Pay Office at Somerset House with a salary of £80 per annum.

John Dickens's friendship with a fellow clerk, Thomas Culliford Barrow (son of Mr Charles Barrow, a lieutenant in the Navy and his wife Mary, whose maiden surname was Culliford), led to an intimacy with Thomas's sister Elizabeth; and four years later, on 13 June 1809 at the age of 23, he was married to her in the church of St Mary-le-Strand. In his nervousness after the ceremony, the future Micawber began to sign his name in the wrong place, leaving scanty room for that of his wife; but discovering the mistake, or as the result of a nudge from the Rev. J. J. Ellis, the curate, he started again higher up. Mrs John Dickens was a pretty little well-educated woman, with an extraordinary sense of the ridiculous, which was fortunate seeing the quixotic husband with whom she was linked. The witnesses of the marriage were Charles Barrow, Mary Barrow (father and mother of the bride) and a certain Sarah Barrow.

John Dickens on 24 June 1809, that is eleven days after his marriage, rented No. 387 Commercial Road, Landport, Portsmouth, and his tenancy continued just three years. He had natural ability, but he was hopelessly shiftless. As his income was then only £80 a year and the rent of the house was £35, probably even at that early period the Barrow family helped him. Certainly they helped later again and again, till at last they got heartily sick of him. In this house was born his first child Fanny (baptised 23 November 1810), and here also was born on 7 February 1812 the subject of these pages, who was baptised at St Mary's Kingston, by the name of Charles John Huffam—Charles after his grandfather Barrow, John after his father and Huffam after his godfather Mr Christopher Huffam, Rigger to King George the Third's Navy, Limehouse Hole, a gentleman with whom John Dickens's family were intimate and anxious to ingratiate themselves. In the parish register the name is incorrectly spelt "Huffham."

Christopher Huffam [1] was at this time 38 years of age. He and his wife were said to be the handsomest couple in London. Later he came under the notice of the Regent (afterwards King George IV) for fitting out a privateer against the French and was offered a knighthood, which he declined; but he accepted the position of First Gentleman-in-Waiting. Our portrait of him is from an oil painting by the Court Painter. On 24 June 1812 the Dickens family removed into Hawke Street, Portsea.

§ 2. *Removal to London (probably in 1814) and then to Chatham, 1817*

Later, possibly in 1814, the duties of Mr John Dickens necessitated his settling in London and he hired rooms in Norfolk Street (now Cleveland Street) Middlesex Hospital. Charles was at this time about five years old, and his father and mother sometimes took him to the house of Mr

---

[1] *Letters of S. B. Huffam, his grandson, and W. S. Huffam, his great-grandson, to T. Wright.* Christopher Huffam was born 23 August 1771. He died 29 April 1839.

THE BIRTHPLACE OF CHARLES DICKENS, LANDPORT, PORTSMOUTH
*Photo by T. W. Tyrrell*

See page 24

CHRISTOPHER HUFFAM
The godfather of Charles Dickens and the friend of his early years
*From an Oil Painting in the possession of*
*W. S. Huffam, Bromfield Road, Heaton Chapel*

See page 24

Christopher Huffam who resided at No. 12 (afterwards No. 5) Church Row, Limehouse. At Mr Huffam's the boy, who was a general favourite, used, mounted on the dining-room table, to recite little pieces of poetry. In 1816 was born to John Dickens a third child, Letitia. Subsequently, and apparently owing to Mr Huffam's influence, John Dickens was appointed to a clerkship in the Navy Pay Office, Chatham Dockyard, and the family removed, perhaps in 1817, to No. 2, afterwards No. 11, Ordnance Terrace, a good-looking three-storied house facing a hayfield.

Pickwick associated Chatham with soldiers, sailors, shrimps, dockyard men, oysters and tobacco. Marine-store dealers abounded there, though none, it is to be hoped, so unsavoury as the "dreadful old man" in a shocking flannel waistcoat at whose door sat for so many hours poor little David Copperfield. The most striking features of Chatham were its fortifications called "The Lines" and the extensive Dockyard, Chatham being a royal shipbuilding establishment. One of the Reviews held on the Lines was attended by Mr Pickwick, and it was here that he met the hospitable Wardle of Dingley Dell. Fort Pitt, in those days a Military Hospital, recalls the hostile meeting of Mr Winkle and Dr Slammer.

When the Dickens family settled in Chatham they were in comfortable circumstances, or might have been, for Mr Dickens's salary at the Navy Pay Office had increased to £200 a year, and in 1820 it was raised to £350; but Mr Dickens's easy, slipshod nature and lavishness of expenditure soon brought trouble. Then too the beer-glass and the punch bowl were too much in evidence. The youthful Copperfield exhibits a most unchildlike familiarity with strong drinks. Mrs Dickens's servant Mary Weller,[1] a smart young girl, besides having her name immortalised in *Pickwick*, is alluded to in *Sketches of Young Couples*. For a while Mrs Dickens had a second servant, Jane Bonny, a name used in *Nicholas Nickleby*.

---

[1] She married Thomas Gibson. In the *Rochester and Chatham Journal*, 28 April 1888, is a notice of her death. She was buried on 28 April in Chatham cemetery.

## § 3. *The Dame School*, 1817

With the Dickenses lived Mrs Dickens's widowed sister, Mrs Mary Allen. Charles, who was a weakly boy, early learnt to read from a primer of "fat black letters"; and, thanks to his mother and his Aunt Mary, made rapid progress. Subsequently he was sent to a Dame School situated over a dyer's shop in Rome Lane (later Railway Street) kept by a reverend old lady with hard knuckles who instilled into his mind "the first principles of education for ninepence a week" and was "wont to poke" his "juvenile head occasionally, by way of adjusting the confusion of ideas in which he was generally involved"—an old lady whom one cannot help associating with Mr Wopsle's great-aunt in *Great Expectations*. Indeed Philip Pirrip of that story, as well as David Copperfield, is largely Dickens himself. In 1819 while Charles was at this school, a book left the press which was destined to have a good deal of influence both on him and the reading world in general—Washington Irving's *Sketch Book*.

Charles and his sister Fanny often amused themselves with private theatricals, to which were generally invited their little next-door friends, Lucy and George Stroughill (pronounced Struggle) and another pair of small folk named Tribe, from The Mitre, a notable inn in Chatham High Street, which had "a bar that seemed to be the next best thing to a bishopric, it was so snug," [1] and boasted of having been patronised by Nelson. Charles was often a guest at children's parties given at The Mitre, where he used to recite with gusto " 'Tis the voice of the sluggard," and on one occasion, he and his sister Fanny sang there a popular duet, commencing "Long time, I've courted you, Miss."

Charles's chief friends, however, at this time were the Stroughills. George, "a frank, open and daring boy" who used to bring in his magic lantern, was the original of Steerforth in *David Copperfield*. In the company of Lucy, a peach-faced mite in a blue sash, Charles used to sit under the table and eat seed cake. He loved her to distraction, but that did not prevent him from loving to distraction

[1] *The Holly Tree.* Cr. ed., vol. 15.

Miss Tribe also. Another little playmate, Mary Ann Mitton,[1] he long after immortalised as Little Dorrit. Two other near neighbours at Ordnance Terrace were the Old Lady and the Half-pay Captain of *Sketches by Boz* "who took to breeding silk-worms, which he *would* bring in two or three times a day, in little paper boxes, to show the old lady, generally dropping a worm or two at every visit."

## § 4. *Micawber*

Charles Dickens, by his own account, had at home a poor sort of training; his mother, though saddled with so many children, did her best, but he was in after years indignant with his father whom he pitilessly caricatured, in the pages of *David Copperfield*, as Micawber. In circumstances that would make many a family feel rich, the Dickenses were continually straitened. John Dickens, however, was popular at Chatham, and indeed everywhere except among his own kin, who knew him only too well. Mr Thomas Wright, the head of the Navy Pay Office, described him as "a fellow of infinite humour, chatty, lively and agreeable."

On 29 January 1820 the long reign of George III ended and George IV ascended the throne. On 3 March that year a terrible fire broke out at Chatham, destroying thirty-eight houses and rendering many families homeless. Mr John Dickens, who was an active member of the relief committee, subscribed to the fund two guineas, and he was thanked in the Treasurer's report for his efficient and valuable services. He contributed an account of the fire to *The Times*.

When Charles was eight he was taken for a holiday to London where he saw Grimaldi the famous clown, whose antics delighted him, and whose Life [2] he was destined to write, or at any rate edit. At Ordnance Terrace two other children were born to John Dickens—Harriet, who died young; and, in 1820, Frederick, who inherited all the shiftless qualities of his father.

[1] He met her again at Rochester when he was a young man and told her he would write a book about her, and call it *Little Dorrit*. See § 100.

[2] *Memoirs of Joseph Grimaldi*, 2 vols. February 1838. Illustrated by Cruikshank.

## § 5. *The Brook. Mr Giles's School*

By Lady Day 1821 when Charles was nine the Barrow family had become thoroughly weary of John Dickens, who sank so low in the world that it was necessary to remove from the pleasant Ordnance Terrace to a mean little house, No. 18 St Mary's Place, next door to a Providence Baptist Chapel, which the family sometimes attended, in a thoroughfare called The Brook. The minister was a Rev. William Giles. Jane Bonny, one of the servants, was dismissed and other household expenses were cut down.

Dickens, then a handsome little fellow with light curly hair, and his sister Fanny were, after Charles had been taught the rudiments of Latin by his mother, sent to an academy in Clover Lane kept by William Giles, son of the minister of Providence Chapel, an accomplished and enthusiastic young man who had been ordained after receiving a first-class education at Oxford; and Dickens retained pleasant memories of him, and of a playmate Samuel Giles, his master's ten-year-old brother. He remembered too the delightful field adjoining with its two beautiful hawthorns. The boys were expected to wear white beaver hats—the headgear so conspicuous in *David Copperfield*. At the end of his first year there he recited at the breaking-up a piece called "Dr Bolus" and was rewarded with a prize.[1]

From an upper window in the side of the house in The Brook, could be seen the parish church and churchyard exactly as described in the sketch "A Child's Dream of a Star." Later, Mr Giles removed to a larger house at the corner of Rhode Street and Best Street, and Charles and Fanny continued to be his pupils.

On 11 December 1821 there was a wedding in the family, Mrs Dickens's sister Mary Allen having on that day married Dr Matthew Lamert (the Dr Slammer of *Pickwick*), surgeon at the Ordnance Hospital, and Charles and his sister Fanny were present at the ceremony.[2] John Henry Barrow, the bride's and Mrs Dickens's brother, was one of

[1] William Giles the younger died 30 September 1856. See § 48.
[2] For copy of entry in the Parish Register, see Langton, p. 52.

JOHN DICKENS
Father of Charles Dickens
*Engraved by Edwin Roffe after a Pencil Drawing*
*Lent by Frank T. Sabin*

MRS. JOHN DICKENS
Mother of Charles Dickens
*Engraved by Edwin Roffe after the Original Pencil Drawing*
*Lent by Frank T. Sabin*

the witnesses. Of him the family was proud. He contributed to *The Times* and other papers and wrote poetry. Mr and Mrs John Dickens were also witnesses.[1] After the marriage Mr and Mrs Lamert went to Ireland, and James Lamert, the doctor's son by a former wife, came to live at 18 St Mary's Place. James's passion for private theatricals made him popular there, and he and Charles, whom he sometimes took to the Theatre Royal at the foot of Star Hill, Rochester, became inseparable friends. Life through, Dickens was fascinated by the Stage.

St Mary's Place being nearer to the dockyard than Ordnance Terrace, Charles had increased facilities for becoming familiar with its features of interest. The Navy Pay Office was a plain building of red brick, with heavily barred windows and strong rooms lined throughout with iron, and Charles was impressed with the gravity upon it and its "staid pretence of having nothing worth mentioning to do." He loved to watch the rope-makers, the anchor-smiths (nine of them at once like "the Muses in a ring"), the block-makers and the gradual development of the huge men-of-war on the slips.

On St Clement's Day, 23 November, the dockyard blacksmiths used to get up a pageant in honour of their patron saint; and, headed by one of their party, masked as "Old Clem" and seated in a chair of state, they paraded through the town singing and collecting drink-money. From this custom was borrowed the refrain in *Great Expectations* "Beat it out, beat it out, Old Clem! with a clink for the stout, Old Clem." Dickens also recalled "the long files of convict labourers, who, guarded by soldiers, carried oak planks through the yard, the tall men bearing all the weight, while the short men walking in their places with their shoulders two or three inches below the plank contentedly carried nothing." The air of the place was "redolent of oak chips, oakum, tarred ropes and canvas."

[1] Letter of Robert Langton to T. Wright, 24 February 1896.

## § 6. *Convicts and Boatmen and Great Sea Porcupines*

Lying off the dockyard out on the black water was the "receiving ship," a hulk roofed like a Noah's Ark. To this "wicked" barque the convicts "with great numbers on their backs as if they were street doors," returned after their labours with the planks. When Pip, in *Great Expectations*, asked what hulks were he received as answer "prison ships right 'cross the meshes (marshes)." But allusions to convict life at Chatham bristle through this story, one of the most vivid being the account of how, in the old coaching days, convicts were removed from London; and how passengers on the box seat were disagreeably made aware of their presence, by feeling their breath on the back of their necks, and by their "bringing with them that curious flavour of bread-poultice, baize, rope-yarn and hearth-stone, which attends the convict presence." [1] Life through, Dickens's warmest sympathies were with creatures nautical; fishermen, boatmen and "great sea-porkypines" generally, which is not strange seeing that his father, his grandfather and his god-father were connected with ships and shipping and that his early boyhood was spent at a great Naval Depot.

## § 7. *Rochester*

Of Chatham, Rochester and Strood, which practically form one long town, for Strood is separated from Rochester only by the Medway, Dickens retained memories mostly pleasant; but he felt particularly drawn to quaint, dreamy, mediaeval and ecclesiastical Rochester. Dickens, however, was no antiquary and he seems to have endeavoured to keep himself free from its octopus arms. In *Pickwick* you may read how the stout and bird-like founder of the club leaned over the balustrades of Rochester bridge and admired the scenic beauties before him, how he and his friends visited the Bull inn; how the steed of the horsey Winkle drifted up Rochester street with its head towards one side of the way

---

[1] *Great Expectations*, Cr. ed., p. 174.

and its tail towards the other; and how the widow at Rochester enflamed the susceptible Tupman.

As the story advances Dickens gets his freedom, which he manages to keep through several subsequent stories till his arrival at that epic of the marshes, *Great Expectations*, the scenes of which are laid chiefly in Rochester city and Cooling village. Then he breaks away again, but at last in *Edwin Drood* he surrenders at discretion. It is "Cloisterham," and little beside, all through. The victory remained with the octopus. But there is little wonder that the spell of the old-world city was so potent. Nature and time have joined hand in hand to accomplish its glamour. The broad Medway, not a river but an arm of the sea, reflects in its waters the huge beetling walls of the castle keep whose worn and labyrinthine stairs carry to the topmost story whence one can peer giddily down into cavernous abysses, noisy with the coo of pigeons and the perpetual flapping of wings, or outward on to the cathedral, then with a spire; St Nicholas' Church; the vinery of the ancient monastery and the wilderness of roofs beyond. The cathedral alone is a dream to enchant a lifetime. One recalls its western front with its prodigality of crumbled sculptures; the nave with its vista of massive stone columns and contiguous rod-like shafts of dark marble; the triforium with its richly moulded arches; the choir with its effigies of saints and bishops; the crypt with its forest of dwarf supports and "lanes of light."

And Rochester High Street! One must see it by day and by night. By day, for fear of losing any of the minutiae of its rich feast of quaintnesses, its crumbling archways, old taverns, overhanging stories, its gables with woodwork and its Town Hall—to Dickens's childish eyes a sort of Aladdin's palace, though subsequently they were disenchanted. By night, because it is then fairyland absolutely. Artificially lighted, all the whimsicalities of the place stand out obtrusively. One would not be surprised to meet under this archway or that drooping story the Pied Piper of Hamelin, Dick Whittington, Richard Watts, who built the quaint house for Six Poor Travellers in Rochester High Street or any of Durdles "old uns." To picture the comparatively

31

recent Dickens there might require a nimble fancy, but the most matter-of-fact could conjure up in its street a John de Sheppey or a Bishop Merton.

## § 8. *The Glorious Garret*

In an upstairs room in the dingy little house in The Brook was a small collection of books.

"From that blessed little room," says Dickens, "Roderick Random, Peregrine Pickle, Humphrey Clinker, Tom Jones, The Vicar of Wakefield, Don Quixote, Gil Blas and Robinson Crusoe came out, a glorious host to keep me company. They kept alive my fancy and my hope of something beyond that place and time—they and the *Arabian Nights* and *The Tales of the Genii.*" [1]

The last, one of the many imitations of the *Arabian Nights*, was written in the middle of the eighteenth century by the Rev. James Ridley.[2]  To the hag in that work who used to hobble out of a chest and terrorise Abudah, the Bagdad merchant, Dickens refers in *The Uncommercial Traveller* No. 15 and in *The Haunted Man.*[3]

He consoled himself under his small troubles by impersonating his favourite characters in these stories.  He says, "I have been Tom Jones (a child's Tom Jones, a harmless creature) for a week together.  I have sustained my own idea of Roderick Random for a month at a stretch."  These books preserved long afterwards their fascination for him.  He is perpetually alluding to them or quoting from them.  He also had a "greedy relish" for volumes of voyages and travels, and went about the house with the centre-piece of an old set of boot lasts as a precaution against savages.  His adventures as a pirate are reflected in his story *A Holiday Romance.*[4]  At an early age he himself took to writing, and produced an *Arabian Nights* sort of tale, *Misar or The Sultan of India.*

[1] *David Copperfield*, Chapter 4.
[3] Cr. ed., vol. 14, p. 277.

[2] Published in 1765.
[4] *Ibid.*, vol. 15, p. 583.

## § 9. *Tom-all-Alone's. Gad's Hill*

His outdoor life at Chatham was equally pleasant. The soldiers were a perennial attraction, and he and his schoolfellows delighted to watch the reviews. Sometimes he and Fanny were taken by their father to Sheerness in an old-fashioned, high-sterned sailing yacht, the *Chatham*, or as it was more often called "the Navy Pay Yacht," a craft, pierced with circular ports, which dated from the Commonwealth. There were romps in the Fort Pitt Fields with Mary Weller and her sweetheart Thomas Gibson. There was rowing in summer and skating in winter. In the autumn he watched the sham fights and siege operations carried on at "Tom-all-Alone's" (a name utilised in *Bleak House*), which had attached itself to a sorrowful tenement built on a piece of waste ground by one Thomas Clark who had for twenty-five years towards the end of the eighteenth century lived in it solitarily as Robinson Crusoe.[1] Its site was afterwards occupied by the Convict Prison which in turn made way for Naval Barracks.

In 1822 another son had been born to John Dickens— Alfred Lamert, baptised 3 April in St Mary's Church, Chatham, and named after Dr Matthew Lamert. Indeed the lower John Dickens's fortunes got, the faster he peopled his house with children. Anybody could keep them. It was no business of his. If the Barrows wouldn't, others would. It was a Christian land, was it not! Some of the children very sensibly died, others very foolishly lived. Nobody could possibly keep a more ridiculous household or brew better punch. Nobody could have a kinder heart or a more senseless head. However, the inconsequence of the father was made up for by the competence of the son. "Even so," the moralist would comment, "yet each came to the same *Hic jacet*. Then does it so very much matter!"

At the top of the steep main road between Rochester and Gravesend, about two miles from the former, stood a gentleman's house called Gad's Hill Place. It was near

[1] See Kitton's *The Novels of Charles Dickens*, p. 140.

33

this spot that Shakespeare's fat roisterer robbed the travellers, an event commemorated by the name of a small wayside inn, the Sir John Falstaff, on the opposite side of the road. To the childish eyes of Dickens, accustomed to the meanness of the dingy little house in The Brook, Gad's Hill Place seemed almost a palace. Thither he often wandered; and his father, who abounded in precepts, noticing its fascination for his son, remarked one day, "If you are persevering and work hard you may some time come to live in it." Thirty-five years later this house became Dickens's. The boy, though small and delicate, was ambitious, but he was destined to draw his own portrait, for the youthful Pip in *Great Expectations* is certainly in a way the boy Charles Dickens.

## CHAPTER II

# Spring 1823 to Christmas 1823

16 BAYHAM STREET (LATER NO. 141)

§ 10. *"The Blue-eyed Maid"*

IN 1823, the sphere of John Dickens's duties having been transferred to Somerset House, it was necessary for the family to return to London. The night before they left Chatham Mr Giles, the schoolmaster, "came flitting in among the packing cases," says Dickens, "to give me Goldsmith's *Bee* as a keepsake, which I kept for his sake and its own a long time afterwards." To this book, indeed, Dickens owed almost as much as he did to Irving's *Sketch Book*. Charles, however, we are told, was after all left for a while with Mr Giles. In *David Copperfield*, Chapter 12, is a scene which, if we change Mrs Micawber to Mrs Dickens, seems to belong to this incident.

I think, as Mrs. Micawber sat at the back of the coach with the children [there were four, Fanny age 13, Letitia age 7, Frederick age 3, and the baby Alfred Lamert], and I stood in the road [probably with Mr. Giles] looking wistfully at them a mist cleared from her eyes, and she saw what a little creature I really was. I think so, because she beckoned to me to climb up . . . and put her arm round my neck and gave me . . . a kiss . . . I had barely time to get down again before the coach started, and I could hardly see the family for the handkerchiefs they waved.

John Dickens settled at No. 16 (afterwards 141) Bayham Street. The family were waited upon by a small slatternly servant girl from Chatham Workhouse. As there were no railways the boy was later sent by coach, Simpson's "Blue-

35

eyed Maid" (the Timpson's of "Dullborough Town.")[1]
He wore his white beaver hat and, "packed in damp straw,"
he was "forwarded, carriage paid like game," to the Cross
Keys, Wood Street, Cheapside.    There was no other inside
passenger, it rained hard all day and he munched his sandwiches in solitude and dreariness.

## § 11.  *The One-legged Uncle*

As it had been a step down from Ordnance Terrace to
The Brook, so it was another declension from The Brook to
Bayham Street; but, although the house was squalid and
although the neighbours were poor and dirty, nevertheless
Bayham Street was then pleasantly surrounded.    Indeed it
was almost in the country.    Hard by was "Mr Lever's
field," particularly inviting in hay-making time.    A delightful country walk led to Copenhagen House with its
rookeries.    A quaint little watchman's box stood close to
the "Mother Red Cap" tea gardens which were frequently
visited by the Dickens family.    The country round, in
short, was fine and open "with delightful views of far-
distant hills and vales" dotted about with lordly mansions.
Its dairies, dairy farms and "drinking wells" attracted
visitors from all parts of London; but the neighbourhood,
gradually becoming covered with brick and mortar, was
going down and the better class were leaving it.    At the
top of the street stood a row of almshouses, and Charles
liked to go up to them because from that spot he could see
the dome of St Paul's looming through the smoke.    As
always, the town attracted him more than the country.
The teeming life of the Strand and Covent Garden and the
narrow alleys of the great city gave him more delight than
river or tree.    The destined annalist of Tom-all-Alone's
and Bleeding Heart Yard preferred the rookeries of Seven
Dials to the rookeries of Copenhagen Fields.    Years after
he declared, "As I thought in the little back garret in Bayham

---

[1] See *The Uncommercial Traveller*, Cr. ed., p. 457.    In the parish rate
book for 8 October 1823 John Dickens appears at No. 16 Bayham Street and
also at No. 18.    In the next rate book No. 16 is marked "empty" because
at Michaelmas 1823 the family had removed to 4 Gower Street North.

Street of all I had lost in losing Chatham, what would I have given, if I had had anything to give, to have been sent back to any other school, to have been taught something somewhere." Similar words were used by the boy Pip in *Great Expectations*.

To the good nature and cheerfulness of the undersized slatternly maid of all work from Chatham we owe the Marchioness in *The Old Curiosity Shop*. On 9 April 1823 Fanny Dickens was by nomination of Thomas Tomkisson, a pianoforte maker in Dean Street, admitted as a pupil at the Royal Academy of Music, then recently established, and she, continuing her studies there till Midsummer 1827, became at last a well-qualified musician and singer.

The family, however, sank lower and lower. Next we hear of a composition with Mr Dickens's creditors. A sale followed. Charles's little bed, with a coal scuttle, a roasting jack and a bird-cage thrown in, went for a song.[1] How in after years Dickens derided the helplessness of his easy-going father the pages of *David Copperfield* bear witness. John Dickens was, as already said, kind-hearted and generous, but his self-indulgence and his fatal propensity to let things slide negatived all his virtues. Of Charles's attainments, especially the comic singing, he was even proud, but the boy was neglected, and, instead of being sent to school, was employed in looking after his little brothers and sisters, in cleaning shoes, and going "poor errands."

A small theatre made and painted for him by James Lamert, who had accompanied the family to Bayham Street, added brightness to his life, the monotony of which was occasionally broken by visits to his uncle, Mr Thomas Culliford Barrow, who lived over a bookshop in Gerrard Street, Soho. Mr Barrow was suffering from the effects of an accident to the left leg, which at last had to be amputated, and Charles was his "little companion and nurse."[2] Mrs Manson the proprietress of the shop also took notice of the boy and lent him books, among them being Colman's *Broad Grins*; and he tried to write little facetious pieces himself, though he was too shy to show them.

[1] *The Haunted House*, Cr. ed., p. 142.
[2] Letter of Dickens to Thomas Barrow, 31 March 1836.

CHAPTER III

# Christmas 1823 to 28 May 1824

4 GOWER STREET NORTH TILL 24 MARCH
THE MARSHALSEA, 24 MARCH 1824 TO 28 MAY 1824

§ 12. *Gower Street North. John Dickens is arrested for Debt, 20 February 1824*

THE family continued to visit Mr. Huffam, Charles's godfather, at No. 12 (afterwards No. 5) Church Row, Limehouse; and it will be remembered that many of the scenes in *Our Mutual Friend* are laid in that neighbourhood. There lived Lizzie Hexam and her father; and little Charles must often have passed that dropsical tavern, The Six Jolly Fellowship Porters, with its river frontage, "which was all but afloat at high water"; a tavern frequented by Riderhood and other waterside characters.

The idea then occurred to the Dickenses that the family fortunes might be retrieved by the establishment of a school for young ladies. Mrs Dickens had been well educated and it was believed that Mr Huffam, who had influence at Court and also an Indian connection, would be able to introduce pupils. So the bold removal was made to No. 4 Gower Street North (later 147 Gower Street). The tenancy was in Mrs Dickens's name; the rent being £50, and a large brass plate was affixed to the door announcing "Mrs Dickens's Establishment."[1] As John Dickens was heavily in debt and consequently did not possess fifty pence of his very own, let alone fifty

[1] The name of the tenant was from Michaelmas 1823 to Lady Day 1824 "Mrs Dickens." An extension of Messrs. Maple's furnishing premises now occupies the site of the house.

pounds, this was a beautiful instance of the powerfulness of his imagination. Charles was commissioned to go round delivering circulars. "Yet," he says, "nobody ever came to school, nor do I recollect that anybody ever proposed to come, or that the least preparation was made to receive anybody. But I know that we got on very badly with the butcher and baker; that very often we had not too much for dinner." At last, on 20 February 1824, John Dickens was arrested and taken to a debtors' prison—The Marshalsea (disguised in *David Copperfield* as the King's Bench) [1]—the whole family being in tears.

On the first visit of Charles to his father there were more tears, and Micawber pathetically adjured his son to take warning by the family circumstances "and to observe that if a man had twenty pounds a year and spent nineteen pounds, nineteen shillings and sixpence he would be happy; but that a shilling spent the other way would make him wretched." If aphorisms had been gold the elder Dickens would have been a second Crœsus. At home the struggle with poverty grew daily keener. The Barrow family, exasperated by the improvidence of John Dickens and his repeated calls upon them, had at last entirely severed their connection with him. Visits to the pawnshop became frequent. First Charles's beloved books had to go, then the furniture, piece by piece, till at last there was nothing left but a table, a few chairs and some beds. Even the great brass plate was taken off and carried away, "the man having no expectation of ever being paid for it"; [2] and the bankruptcy of Mr Christopher Huffam in 1824 destroyed all hope of help from that quarter. Mr Huffam had lost his money, Mr Barrow had lost a leg, John Dickens had lost his liberty, and Mrs Dickens had lost her furniture and her lodger, for James Lamert had left. The family were in a rare plight.

[1] It stood between St George's Church and London Bridge. It was demolished in 1856 when Dickens visited its ruins. See Langton, p. 69; *David Copperfield*, Chapter 7; *Catalogue of the Dickens Exhibition*, 1903, p. 29.
[2] *Our Mutual Friend*, Cr. ed., p. 28.

## § 13. *The Blacking Warehouse*

Where Lamert went is not clear, but he is next heard of as manager and part proprietor of a blacking manufactory, No. 80 Hungerford Stairs, carried on under the name of Warren, after a Mr Jonathan Warren, its founder. The devices of the firm (the most common of which was a cat gazing at its reflection in a boot) figure prominently among the advertisements of contemporary newspapers and magazines. To one of the devices there is an allusion in *Hard Times*, where Mr Bounderby brags that the only pictures he possessed when a boy were the illustrated labels of "a man shaving himself in a boot on the blacking bottles."

Perceiving how low the Dickens family had sunk, Lamert suggested that Charles should do something useful and try to earn a little—with the result that the boy was sent to commence life in the blacking warehouse,[1] a crazy tumbledown old structure overrun with rats. Dickens worked in a recess in the counting-house which was on the first floor looking over the coal barges and the river. He had to cover the pots of blacking first with oil paper and then with blue paper; to tie them with a string and then to clip the paper neatly all round. Finally he had to affix the label. Subsequently he worked downstairs with the other boys of the establishment. The name of one of them, Bob Fagin, was used in *Oliver Twist*. Another was Paul Green, "currently believed to have been christened Poll," a fiction transferred to Mr Tweedlepipe in *Martin Chuzzlewit*.

"No words," says Dickens, "can express the secret agony of my soul as I sank into this companionship; compared these everyday associates with those of my happier childhood; and felt my early hopes of growing up to be a learned and distinguished man crushed in my breast." As it was a long way to go home to Gower Street he used to take his dinner with him or dine at a Strand pudding-shop. Once he took his bread into the best dining-room in Johnson's *à la*

---

[1] The last house on the left-hand side of the way at old Hungerford Bridge, later Charing Cross Railway Bridge.

*mode* beef-house in Clare Court, Drury Lane, and magnificently ordered a small plate of *à la mode* beef to eat with it. The waiter stared while the food was being eaten and brought another waiter to look. "I gave him a halfpenny," says Dickens, "and wish now he hadn't taken it."

At last on 25 March 1824 the "encampment in Gower Street" broke up, Mrs Dickens joined her husband in the prison, and Charles was "handed over as a lodger to a reduced old lady in Little College Street,[1] Camden Town— a Mrs Roylance, whose acquaintance the family had made in their Bayham Street days, and who with a few alterations and embellishments" became Mrs Pipchin in *Dombey and Son*, where one may read of that ogress's mottled face, hook nose, hard grey eye and black bombazeen dress, worn out of respect for the memory of Mr Pipchin, who forty years previous had broken his heart in pumping water out of some Peruvian mines; and learn the secret of her management of children, which was "to give them everything they didn't like, and nothing that they did."

Though Charles mixed with the other boys and worked with them, he was treated by Lamert as one upon a different footing. They and the men always spoke of him as "the young gentleman." Sundays he and Fanny spent with their parents in the prison. All the time he was "miserably unhappy" and he felt keenly the separation from his parents and brothers and sisters; and when his day's work was done, going home "to such a miserable blank" as Mrs Pipchin's.

Later, owing to his tearful solicitations, he was removed from "Little College Street" and lodged in Lant Street (of Bob Sawyer fame) in the Borough with a family destined to be immortalised as the Garlands. To reach it he used to cross Blackfriars Bridge and pass down a turning off Blackfriars Road which had Rowland Hill's chapel on the one side and the likeness of a golden dog licking a golden pot over a door on the other—a street of dingy "low-browed old shops." He thought his new abode "a sort of paradise." Mr Garland was the little fat, placid-faced, kind-hearted old

---

[1] Later it became College Street West, and still later College Place, rebuilt in 1890.

gentleman in *The Old Curiosity Shop* with whom Kit lived after the departure of Little Nell. All the family—the stout good-humoured landlord, his quiet old wife, and their lame son—were very kind to Dickens, especially when he suffered from attacks of spasms, to which he was subject. As John Dickens's income still went on, the family lived more comfortably in the prison than previously. Their sharp little maid "The Marchioness," brought from Gower Street, still waited on them.

Charles portrays himself in a "poor white hat, little jacket and corduroy trousers," his chief treasure being "a fat old silver watch," a present from his grandmother Barrow before the blacking days. At dinner times he played on the coal barges with Fagin and "Poll," or strolled about back streets or under the "dark dismal Adelphi arches," [1] one of his resorts being a shabby wayside inn called The Fox-under-the-Hill, on the bench before which he remembered sitting eating sandwiches while he watched some coal-heavers dancing, as in *David Copperfield*. The boy was without hope. He was faced by impenetrable darkness.

§ 14. *A Legacy. The Family leave the Marshalsea*
*28 May 1824*

A considerable legacy, "some hundreds" from a relative, was the means of reinstating the elder Dickens. His debts were paid, and the family on 28 May, having quitted the prison, went to lodge in Little College Street with Mrs Roylance, so Charles (such is life!) had to renew acquaintance with the hook nose and bombazeen dress of the ogress Pipchin.

Just before the family left the prison occurred the scene described in *David Copperfield* of the signing of the memorial to the king. The occasion of the petition, however, which was drawn up by Mr Dickens, was not for the abolition of imprisonment for debt as in *David Copperfield*, but in order to the obtainment of a bounty for the prisoners so that they could drink the King's health on the approaching royal

[1] *Mrs Lirriper's Lodgings.* Cr. ed., p. 243.

birthday, which by the by was a long time ahead, the date being 12 August; but no pains were too great for John Dickens to take if it was a question of making preparation for something to drink.

Fanny Dickens, who had grown into a beautiful, attractive and lovable girl, with a sweet voice, had in the meantime made progress at the Royal Academy of Music; and when she gained a prize, probably at the end of 1824, the whole family attended at Tenterden Street to witness the presentation. Charles was not jealous of Fanny, whom he loved dearly, but when he reflected that he himself was "beyond the reach of all such honourable emulation and success" he cried bitterly, and that night, before creeping into bed, he prayed fervently that he might "be lifted out of the humiliation and neglect" into which he had fallen.

About this time the blacking business was removed to Chandos Street, Covent Garden. Dickens and Fagin, who for light's sake worked at one of the windows, were so dexterous at their occupation that people would stop to look at them. "Sometimes," says Dickens, "there would be quite a crowd there," and he continues, "I saw my father coming in at the door one day when we were very busy, and I wondered how he could bear it." Among the frequenters of the warehouse was the shabby genteel establishment poet from Seven Dials who became the Mr Slum of Mrs Jarley's Waxwork Show. There are allusions to Warren's and the blacking period in most of Dickens's works. Charles continued there about a year. One day a quarrel occurred between the elder Dickens and Lamert, violent words were used on both sides and the boy was removed. This was apparently in June 1824. At Midsummer of that year the family exchanged Little College Street for 29 (numbered later 13) Johnson Street,[1] between Seymour Street and old St Pancras Church, where they stayed till November 1828. The house is now demolished.

[1] In July 1824, according to the rate book the tenant was "Caroline Dickens," apparently a mistake for "Elizabeth Dickens," Dickens's mother. On 30 July 1827, she applied for "time to pay or relief." In January 1829 it was "empty."

CHAPTER IV

# June 1824 to November 1828

29 (LATER 13) JOHNSON STREET

§ 15. *Mr Creakle's School, June 1824*

JOHNSON STREET was the thoroughfare near the Veterinary College, Camden Town, where the Micawbers dwelt when Mr Traddles was their lodger.[1] An indescribable character of faded gentility that attached to the house made it unlike the other houses near, "though they were all built on one monotonous pattern." The inhabitants of the street appeared to have a propensity to throw any little trifles they were not in need of into the road—"a shoe, a black bonnet, an umbrella, a doubled-up saucepan." Indeed only a very lively imagination could mistake Johnson Street for Paradise.

Not only was Charles removed from Lamert's factory, he was sent, probably in June 1824, to a reputable school—Wellington House Academy, Granby Street,[2] Mornington Place, where, as a day scholar, he stayed nearly two years, that is till he was fourteen. The proprietor, Mr William Jones—the original of Mr Creakle in *David Copperfield*—though himself no scholar, had the wisdom to employ capable assistants—Mr Manville, who taught Latin (there is an unpopular Latin Master in *Holiday Romance*); Mr Taylor, a lame young man with a clerical appearance and a passion for the flute, who taught English; and a junior usher, Richard Shiers, who had been a pupil at the school.

Of the rod-loving, portly Jones, his heavy tread, and the

[1] *David Copperfield*. Cr. ed., vol. 4, p. 316.
[2] See *Our School*. Cr. ed., vol. 17, p. 374.

44

No. 11 Ordnance Terrace, Chatham

Home of John Dickens from about 1817 to Lady Day, 1821

*From a Photo by J. Graham*

See page 25

WELLINGTON HOUSE ACADEMY, GRANBY STREET, MORNINGTON PLACE
(Mr. William Jones's School)

Charles Dickens was at school here from June, 1824, to Easter, 1827

See page 44

yellow hackney coach in which he made vacation visits to parents, memory was retained by more than one who had felt his ready hand. The house faced a large dairy farm. The schoolroom, a detached timber structure, contained three rows of desks; and as the boys sat on each side of them, facing one another, there was every facility for interchange of trick and conversation when the teachers' eyes were off. Among the pupils were Harry Danson, Daniel Tobin, afterwards one of Dickens's amanuenses, Thomas Mitton, a lifelong friend of Dickens, Owen Thomas and three mulattoes named Key. A note written by Dickens to Owen Thomas in 1825 has been preserved. He tells "Tom" that he is quite ashamed at not having returned a certain "leg," whatever that was, and promises to send it by Danson. He is willing to sell his "clavis at a reduced price." The boys kept birds and mice in their desks and "the boys trained the mice much better than the master trained the boys." The description of this school which Dickens gives in *Household Words* 11 October 1851 was declared by Danson to be "mythical in many respects," and more especially in the compliments Dickens pays in it to himself. However, he won the Latin prize there, having been coached by Shiers, and as a token of gratitude he presented his tutor with a copy of the works of Horace.[1]

In 1840 a plaster cast of Shiers, who was then about 34 years old, was executed by M Charles Jacques, who became a distinguished artist. Mr Shiers died in 1850.[2] In a gibberish or lingo in use in the school Dickens took a delight. He also amused himself by mounting small theatres and by endeavouring with the aid of other boys to confuse old ladies who happened to pass, by pretending to be a beggar. John W. Bowden, who sat next to him for two years at this school, says: "He and I and others used to write short tales

---

[1] Letter of Mr R. Shiers, son of Richard Shiers, Dickens's tutor, to T. Wright, 18 July 1904. This book was exhibited at the Dickens Exhibition, March 1903.

[2] Letters of R. Shiers to T. Wright,. 18 July and 4 August 1904. Mr Shiers said, "I have a profile of my father cut in black paper, also a cast in brass (life size) of his face taken from the plaster cast."

D

on scraps of paper, pin them together so as to form booklets
and lend them to the other boys for the small charge of a
piece of pencil, &c. We also occasionally issued a small
morning newspaper containing comic advertisements and
scraps of news." There is a reminiscence of this period in
*Little Dorrit* where Dickens refers to the embellished cipher-
ing and copy books "where the titles of the elementary
rules of arithmetic diverge into swans, eagles, griffins and
other caligraphic recreations and where the capital letters
go out of their minds and bodies in ecstasies of pen and
ink."

§ 16. *Lawyer's Clerk. Shorthand*
*May* 1827 *to November* 1828

After leaving Mr Jones's, probably at Easter 1827,
Dickens became, it is said, a clerk in the office of Mr Charles
Molloy, whose office was until 1829 at 6 Symonds Inn,
Chancery Lane, and afterwards at 8 New Square, Lincoln's
Inn; but Dickens could have been with Mr Molloy only a
few weeks. Among the relatives of Dickens's mother was
an aunt, Mrs C. W. Charlton, who, with her husband, kept
a boarding house at 16 Berners Street, where Mrs Dickens
and her children frequently visited. Among Mrs Charlton's guests was Mr Edward Blackmore, junior partner of
the firm of Ellis and Blackmore, solicitors, of No. 1 Holborn
Court, Gray's Inn; and Dickens in May 1827, when he was
15, became, owing to Mr Blackmore's interest in him, a
clerk there; but he continued to board with his father in
Johnson Street. Among the other clerks in Holborn Court
was his schoolfellow Thomas Mitton, and they became still
faster friends. The firm removed soon after he joined it to
1 Raymond Buildings, where the clerk's office "on the
second floor looked out upon the street" and afforded
Dickens "an opportunity of dropping cherry stones from the
window on to the hats of passers-by." When not thus
pleasantly engaged he was occupied "in getting wills
registered, serving processes and carrying documents to and
from counsel's offices and the courts of law."

At Ellis and Blackmore's, where the pay was at first 13*s*. 6*d*. a week, raised in August 1828 to 15*s*., he stayed about eighteen months. His taste for theatricals continued to cling to him, and he, with a fellow clerk named Potter, frequented minor theatres and sometimes took parts. A petty cash book which he kept during his term of service with Messrs Ellis and Blackmore is still in existence.[1] Mr Ellis, an inveterate snuff-taker, is said to have been responsible for Mr Perker in *Pickwick*; while Mr Newman Knott, an impoverished gentleman who was frequently seen in the office, probably became "Newman Noggs." [2]

Coached by his uncle, John Henry Barrow, who was at this time a barrister of Gray's Inn and a reporter for *The Times* and the *Morning Herald*, Dickens began the study of Gurney's system of shorthand—Brachygraphy—his experiences with which are detailed in *David Copperfield*. He says:

"I bought an approved scheme of the noble art and mystery of stenography (which cost me ten and sixpence) and plunged into a sea of perplexity that brought me, in a few weeks, to the confines of distraction. The changes that were rung on dots, which in one position meant such a thing and in another position something else, entirely different; the wonderful vagaries that were played by circles; the unaccountable consequences that resulted from marks like flies' legs; the tremendous effects of a curve in a wrong place; not only troubled my waking hours, but reappeared before me in my sleep."

John Henry Barrow probably had another pupil, Dickens's father, who at any rate learnt shorthand somehow and became a competent reporter.

---

[1] Preserved in the Widener Library, Harvard University. 1st entry, 5 January 1828.
[2] F. G. Kitton, *Novels of Charles Dickens*. Ley p. 51.

CHAPTER V

# November 1828 to 1830

NO. 17 THE POLYGON, SOMERS TOWN AND DOCTORS'
COMMONS

§ 17. *The Jarman Case.   Traddles*

IN November 1828 the Dickens family removed from 29
Johnson Street to 17 The Polygon, Somers Town,
the site of which is now Clarendon Square.   This was
a classic spot [1] had Dickens but known it, for here resided
Godwin and Mary Wollstonecroft, and here on 10 September 1797 Mary Wollstonecroft died after giving birth to the
child who on 30 December 1816 (when Dickens was close
upon four) became the wife of Shelley.

The same month that the family removed to The Polygon,
Charles, having overcome the difficulties in shorthand, left
Ellis and Blackmore's and became a reporter for one of the
offices in Doctors' Commons, "a lazy old nook" near St
Paul's Churchyard—"a little out-of-the-way place where they
administer what is called ecclesiastical law, and play all kinds
of tricks with obsolete old monsters of Acts of Parliament."
A place that had to do with "people's wills and marriage
licences and disputes among ships and boats," and had to
punish hasty gentlemen who call ladies by unpleasant
names.[2]   Here (and it was the office of Spenlow and
Jorkins in *David Copperfield*) Dickens remained about two
years.

Doctors' Commons was approached by a little low archway in Knightrider Street.   When David Copperfield and

------

[1] See Cassell's *Old and New London*, i., 285.
[2] *Sketches by Boz.*  Cr. ed., p. 63.

his aunt called at Mr Spenlow's they were informed that Mr Spenlow was in court—the "Court of Arches," where the bewigged counsel wore red gowns and the proctors fur collars. Copperfield mingled with them and had never in all his life made one at such a "cosey, dosey, old-fashioned, time-forgotten sleepy-headed little family party." He called himself "a shorthand writer for the proctors; his duty being to take notes of cases on behalf of their clients. At one time he rented an office, No. 5 Bell Yard, which he shared with Mr Charles Edward Fenton, a proctor, for whom he reported cases. Facsimile pages of Dickens's transcript of a consistory court judgment delivered in November 1830 are printed in *Charles Dickens, Shorthand Writer*, by William J. Carlton. Dickens reported two judgments relative to a disturbance in the vestry room of St Bartholomew the Great.

Objection had been taken by some of the parishioners to the levying of a poor-rate, an altercation ensued and proceedings were instituted against Richard Wise and Samuel Bagster, two of the obstreperous ratepayers, by Charles Jarman, a churchwarden, who engaged, to act in his behalf, Dickens's co-tenant the proctor Charles Edward Fenton. Bagster, it seems, had called Jarman a liar. Wise had called him a "drunken churchwarden" and had used "other brawling expressions." The suits were heard separately in the Consistory Court. Judgment was delivered against each of the defendants on 18 November 1830. Wise was excommunicated for a fortnight, that is forbidden to enter the church for that period, and had to pay £35 costs. Bagster was let off more easily. Dickens's transcripts from his shorthand notes are still preserved among the archives of St Bartholomew's.

Of these cases, Jarman *v*. Bagster and Jarman *v*. Wise, Dickens made great fun in his article "Doctors' Commons" (*Sketches by Boz*) where Sludberry (Bagster), a sly-looking ginger-beer seller, impudently asks whether the Judge would be good enough to take off the costs and excommunicate him for life instead.[1] "It would be much more convenient to him," he said, as "he never went to church at all." As we

---

[1] *Ibid.* Cr. ed., p. 65.

shall see, Dickens had very much to do later with another Jarman.[1] Indeed he was destined to run—to his undoing —against members of the Jarman race during the whole of his latter days.

This was the period when David Copperfield took down the speeches of Traddles (Thomas Noon Talfourd apparently, who was then a parliamentary reporter to *The Times*). "My Aunt and Mr Dick," he says, "represented the Government or the Opposition" (as the case might be), "and Traddles thundered astonishing invectives against them. Standing by the table," with his finger in the page of a volume of parliamentary orations to keep the place, Traddles "would work himself into the most violent heats and deliver the most withering denunciations of the profligacy and corruption of my aunt and Mr Dick; while I used to sit, at a little distance with my notebook on my knee, fagging after him with all my might and main." This scene is illustrated by one of the cleverest Hablot K. Browne pictures. While at The Polygon, Dickens wrote an adaptation of one of Goldoni's plays, *La Vedona Scoeton*, described as *The Stratagems of Rozanza, a Venetian Comedietta, by C. J. H. Dickens*, that is, of course, Charles John Huffam Dickens. The handwriting of it is apparently that of Dickens's mother.

Harold Skimpole and his family (*Bleak House*) lived in The Polygon where there were at that time a number of "poor Spanish refugees walking about in cloaks, smoking little paper cigars." Mr Skimpole's house

"was in a state of dilapidation. Two or three of the area railings were gone; the water-butt was broken; the knocker was loose; the bell-handle had been pulled off a long time, to judge by the rusty state of the wire; and dirty footprints on the steps were the only sign of its being inhabited."

"It was in a dingy and not over-clean upper room that Mr Jarndyce, Richard and Ada found Mr Skimpole, who was not at all disconcerted by their appearance, but rose and received them in his usual airy manner."[2] Time was no

[1] See Chapter 15, § 104.    [2] *Bleak House.* Cr. ed., p. 476.

very truly yours
T. N. Talfourd

THOMAS NOON TALFOURD

See page 50

CHARLES DICKENS AT THE AGE OF 18 IN 1830
From the Miniature by his Aunt, Mrs. Janet Barrow
*Photo by T. W. Tyrrell*
*By permission of Frank T. Sabin*
See page 53

object there; Mr Skimpole could do nothing. His daughters could do nothing. Like the dogs in Dr Watts's *Moral Songs* it "was their nature to."

Old St Pancras Church near The Polygon figures in *A Tale of Two Cities*. Here Roger Cly the Old Bailey Informer was buried. The funeral over, Mr Cruncher and his companions went body-lifting. The church tower itself looked on like the ghost of a monstrous giant. "Father," said his son Jerry afterwards, "What's a Resurrection man?" "How should I know?" replied Mr Cruncher.[1] In St Pancras churchyard were buried Godwin and his wife. The monument to them still remains on the spot, but their bodies now rest at Bournemouth. In *Sketches by Boz* we read of the early clerk population of Somers Town fast pouring into the city.[2] Mr Lowton, the puffy-faced young man in *Pickwick*, seems to have lived there, for he had to pass "through The Polygon on the way to his duties."

At that time Dickens used, after studying the playbills, to go to some theatre nearly every night, never missing Charles Mathews whenever that comedian was to figure. On 8 February 1830, the day after his eighteenth birthday, Dickens commenced to read at the British Museum, one of his guarantors being Mr C. W. Charlton, whose wife, as already mentioned, was related to Dickens's mother. The Doctors' Commons position "was very uncertain"; but while Dickens was worrying about his future one of his aunts who had married and settled in Demerara came over to England on a visit and, as there seemed no probability of his finding a niche in England, he questioned her very closely as to the prospects for making headway in the West Indies.[3] She did not give any encouragement, but this episode suggested the allusions to the West Indies in *Barnaby Rudge*. Joe Willet lost his arm "at the defence of the Salwanners," and to the West Indies he would have returned but for the

---

[1] *A Tale of Two Cities*. Cr. ed., p. 466.
[2] *Sketches by Boz*. Cr. ed., p. 39.
[3] In a letter to Macrone in 1836, Dickens refers to a Mr Thomson "who has just returned to town prior to his departure for the West Indies." This was probably William Thomson, Mrs Dickens's uncle.

capitulation of Dolly Varden. In the mind's eye of Mr Willet, senior, the West Indies "were inhabited by savage nations who were perpetually burying pipes of peace, flourishing tomahawks and puncturing strange patterns on their bodies."

# CHAPTER VI

# 1830 to January 1833

FITZROY STREET, FITZROY SQUARE.    NEARLY THREE YEARS

§ 18. *The Ross Family.    Maria Beadnell.    May* 1830.
*"The Bill of Fare,"* May 1831

ABOUT this time Dickens's father, who, as already mentioned, had studied shorthand, obtained a post as Parliamentary reporter for the *Morning Herald*, and the family removed from The Polygon to Fitzroy Street.    Among those with whom the Dickenses were at this period intimate was Mr William Ross, who had two sons, John and William (afterwards knighted) the miniaturist, and three pretty daughters—Georgina, Janet and Thomasina.    Janet who, like her brother, was a miniaturist, married Dickens's uncle, Mr Edward Barrow, and in 1830 she painted a miniature of Dickens,[1] who was then 18. According to a family tradition, Dickens admired and wanted to marry Georgina,[2] but received no encouragement. She may have been the original of the eldest Miss Larkins [3] in *David Copperfield*.    In her album, Dickens wrote the verses entitled "The Ivy Green." [4]    John Ross is mentioned in a diary kept by Dickens in 1838, and in his letters to Thomas Beard and others.    The third sister, Thomasina, became a contributor to *Household Words*.

[1] She had a great reputation before her marriage.    Her work was praised by Benjamin West, who was engaged by Lord Carlisle of Castle Howard and other connoisseurs.

[2] *Dickensian*.    1 March 1934.    Letter from A. de Suzannet, p. 151.

[3] *David Copperfield*.    Cr. ed., p. 213.

[4] Set to music by Henry Russell, and then inserted in *Pickwick*.    See *The Real Dickens Land*, by Mr and Mrs Snowden Ward, p. 44.

*53*

In the spring of 1830 Dickens formed the acquaintance of Henry Kolle, a bank clerk, and later a quilt printer of 14 Addle Street, Aldermanbury. Misled by the pronunciation of Kolle's name, Dickens in his earliest letters to his friend spells it incorrectly Kollie; and in conversation he sometimes for fun called him Colly Cibber after the dramatist. In one of the earliest letters, written from North End (wherever that may be) Dickens invites Kolle to join him in a ride. He says "I can procure you an ''oss' which I have had once or twice since I have been here. I am a poor judge of distance, but I should certainly say that your legs would be off the ground when you are on his back."

Through Kolle, Dickens obtained an introduction to the family of Mr George Beadnell, whose brother John was manager of Smith, Payne and Smith's banking establishment, No. 1 Lombard Street.[1] George Beadnell, who was also connected with the bank, lived with his brother at No. 2 Lombard Street. He had, and the story is highly dramatic, three lovely daughters. Margaret, the eldest, was engaged to David Lloyd,[2] a tea merchant; Anne, the second, who had auburn curls, to Kolle.[3] With the youngest, Maria Sarah, Dickens fell violently in love. She was 19, he was 18. He speaks rapturously of her appearance, and he says there used to be a tendency in her eyebrows to join together. She was small in stature, and her friends called her "the pocket Venus."[4] Among her confidantes was Dickens's sister Fanny.

Maria, however, though flattered by his attentions, was less infatuated than he. Still they were often in each other's company and Dickens visited at Mr Beadnell's. Three undated letters to Kolle were written by Dickens from Fitzroy Street in 1830. In No. 1 he speaks of receiving

---

[1] The George and Vulture Tavern, Lombard Street, is referred to in *Pickwick*.

[2] Married 20 April 1831.       [3] Married 21 April 1833.

[4] "David Copperfield, a Reading," Henry Soterhan & Co., 1921. Dickens describes Flora as being "tall." Article by John Harrison Stonehouse, of Muswell Hill.

MARIA BEADNELL.
*"The Sphere,"* 20*th February,* 1909
*By permission of the Bibliophile Society*
*Boston, U.S.A.*
See page 54

MRS. WINTER, *c.* 1854
See page 231

ST. LUKE'S, CHELSEA, WHERE CHARLES DICKENS WAS MARRIED

*Photo by Lionel F. Gowing*

See page 83

ST. MARY-LE-STRAND, WHERE HIS PARENTS WERE MARRIED,
AND OLD "MORNING CHRONICLE" OFFICE

*Photo by Lionel F. Gowing*

"a bad five-shilling piece from a cab-driver." In No. 2 is an invitation to an informal party "for the purpose of knocking up a song or two." No. 3 is an invitation to Kolle to spend Christmas Day (1830) in Fitzroy Street.

Two undated letters of Dickens to Kolle written in January 1831 have also been preserved. In one he mentions that there has been a little sickness in the Dickens family and that they are going for a fortnight's change "to Mrs Goodman's next door to the old Red Lion" at Highgate. He asks Kolle to join him for a few hours. On 20 April 1831 Lloyd and Margaret Beadnell were married, and in May Dickens wrote, and recited at a dinner party given by the Beadnell's, a long metrical composition entitled "The Bill of Fare," containing many references complimentary to the family. Among those introduced are Dickens himself, Kolle, Maria, Anne and Maria's dog Daphne (to be immortalised as Jip) "who would eat mutton chops if you cut off the fat." Dickens was at best only a poor poet, but even he never penned anything less like poetry than "The Bill of Fare."

At 2 Lombard Street Dickens spent happy hours, and there was frequently music, for Anne, who sympathised with Dickens, was a skilful player on the lute; Maria played the harp, and was very seductive when, in her raspberry silk dress cut at the top into vandykes, she sang to it "Meet me by Moonlight alone"—as if anybody would want the least pressing to meet her in any light or anywhere—alone. Dickens contributed to the harmony by singing comic songs. He was in a state of perfect rapture. Her every movement was provocative of love.

Mr Beadnell, who was more familiar with the jingle of guineas than with the jingle of rhymes, found no fault with Dickens's atrocious verses, but he strongly objected to the young man's philandering with Maria, and he put every possible obstacle in the way. Nor was Mrs Beadnell, who always called him "Mr Dickin," to be won over, either. "The old gentleman," as Dickens styled him, became the Mr Spenlow of *David Copperfield* and the Mr Casby of *Little Dorrit*. Like Mr Pecksniff in *Martin Chuzzlewit* he had what Mr Joe Gargery called "architectooralooral" tastes, though he had never designed or built anything; but he had somehow learnt that Dickens's father had been imprisoned for debt. Kolle's chief business was to keep "the old gentleman" out of the way when Dickens and Maria were engaged in confidential talk. But Mr Beadnell didn't at all know his place. He *would* intrude in the most inconvenient moments and so would Maria's particular, saucy, and horrid friend, Marianne Leigh.[1]

§ 19. *Dickens tries to get on to the Stage. He becomes a reporter for the "True Sun." John Henry Barrow*

Dickens, who was still at Doctors' Commons, but who continued to have leanings towards the stage, made at this time a determined attempt to exchange reportership for the boards, and he offered his services to George Bartley, comedian and stage manager of Covent Garden Theatre. Bartley in reply said he was busy preparing for the production of Sheridan Knowles' comedy *The Hunchback* (billed for 5 April 1832) but would write again in a fortnight. The fortnight having passed, Dickens meant to present himself at the theatre, but a severe cold accompanied by inflammation of the face made attendance impossible.

Instead of trying again, he applied for the post of reporter to the *True Sun*, the first number of which had appeared on 5 March of 1832. The editor, Samuel Blanchard, having accepted him, he entered the gallery of the House of Commons as representative of that paper about a month after his 20th birthday.[2] The dramatic critic of the *True Sun* was John Forster, who became Dickens's intimate friend, as did another contributor of that paper, William Johnson Fox, orator and essayist, and afterwards M.P. Later, perhaps in August 1832, Dickens reported for the *Mirror of Parliament*, the office of which was No. 3 Abingdon Street, a periodical conducted by his uncle, John Henry Barrow, who had originated it in January 1828; but Dickens's connection

[1] Daughter of Mr and Mrs John Porter of Lower Clapton.
[2] Ley, p. 65. Carlton, p. 71.

with the blacking establishment was not quite severed, for he from time to time wrote puff verses for it.

John Henry Barrow's friendship indeed was of immense service to Dickens, Barrow being by far the ablest reporter of the day. Many years afterwards Mr W. E. Gladstone said from his place in the House of Commons, "At the time of the Reform Bill (which received Royal assent 7 June 1832), an attempt was made by a gentleman of the name of Barrow to produce verbatim reports of the debates in that House. He made it succeed, and for several years Barrow's record was far more of a mirror of Parliament than *Hansard's Debates*.[1] Those who corrected speeches at that time corrected from Barrow. "Barrow's work was done," Mr Gladstone further commented, "in the highest degree of perfection." But all the Barrows were gifted and would have continued to be good friends to the Dickenses if John Dickens's chronic improvidence and persistent appeals to them for money had not wearied them out.

[1] *Daily News*, 21 April 1877.

CHAPTER VII

# January 1833 to December 1834

18 BENTINCK STREET, MANCHESTER SQUARE.　TWO YEARS

§ 20. *Dickens comes of age, 7 February* 1833. *Maria Beadnell again.[1] "Clari," 27 April* 1833. *Micawber anecdotes*

EARLY in 1833 the Dickens family removed from Fitzroy Street to 18 Bentinck Street. Writing to Kolle on 5 January 1833 Dickens says: "The piano will most likely go to Bentinck Street to-day, and, as I have already said, we cannot accompany it, so that the piano will be in one place and we in another." The family expected to be settled in their new home "on Sunday week," and hoped to see Kolle on that day. Dickens still read at the British Museum, for his name reappears in the Reading Room books under date 2 February 1833 with his address 18 Bentinck Street. As he would come of age on 7 February it was decided to give a party on Monday, 11 February, that date being apparently the more suitable. It was to serve as a house-warming as well as to celebrate a birthday. Among those included was Mr Beard and the invitation ran as follows:

Mrs Dickens requests the pleasure of Mr Beard's company at an Evening party on Monday the 11th inst.　Quadrilles 8 o'clock.
18 Bentinck St., Manchester Square.

Kolle and his two brothers also received invitations. "I do not like," says Dickens, "after partaking so liberally of your hospitality to leave any one out."[2]　It would be

---

[1] *Beadnell Letters*, ed. by Payne and Harper (1929).　[2] *Ibid.*, p. 35.

interesting to know the names of the other guests. Dickens's sisters doubtless looked forward eagerly to the gathering. Fanny was 23, Letitia 17. Thomas Mitton and Henry Austin (who was then or soon after engaged to Letitia) were probably present. Both were of an age thoroughly to enjoy it.

The course of Dickens's love for Maria ran unsatisfactorily. Early in 1833 he proposed marriage, but he received little encouragement. By March of that year he had ceased to be welcome at Lombard Street, his prospects not being rosy enough to please the opulent father, but Kolle carried letters between Dickens and Maria, though her affection for her lover had gradually cooled. On 18 March 1833 Dickens wrote: "Our meetings of late have been little more than so many displays of heartless indifference on the one hand, while on the other hand they have never failed to prove a fertile source of wretchedness and misery," yet Dickens had, as he said, "throughout their intercourse acted fairly, intelligently and honourably." If he could execute any little commission for her he was happy, even if it was only to match a pair of blue gloves.

The breach was widened by the conduct of Marianne Leigh, who set herself the charitable task of embroiling the lovers and promoting misunderstandings between them— and it was a Mary Anne who was the source of the first quarrel between David Copperfield and Dora. Dickens in his misery then had recourse to Maria's sister Anne, who replied, "I really cannot understand Maria or venture to take any responsibility of saying what the state of her affections is." Dickens got on tolerably with the men folk, but all his love affairs were pitiable failures.

At this time he, though frequently at his father's in Bentinck Street, occupied rooms at 10 Norfolk Street, now Cleveland Street, Fitzroy Square. This is shown by a visiting-card left with his uncle, Mr Thomas Culliford Barrow, of the Admiralty.[1]

Dickens still frequented the theatre and in the hope of

[1] Letter of C. Barrow of Leamington (son of T. C. Barrow) to T. Wright.

becoming a professional actor himself, he took lessons with Robert Keeley, who later, with his wife, acted in several of Dickens's own plays. But the passion for theatricals gripped all the members of the Dickens family, father, brothers, sisters, cousins, all being stage-struck, and Dickens hired a hall for their performances. One of his play-bills is headed:

PRIVATE THEATRICALS.

STAGE MANAGER, CHARLES DICKENS.

SATURDAY EVENING.

APRIL 27TH, 1833.

Four pieces are announced to be played that evening, namely an Introductory Prologue, an opera called *"Clari,"* the favourite Interlude of *The Married Bachelor*, and a Finale entitled *The Farce of Amateurs and Actors*. *Clari*, by John Howard Payne, the play in which occurs the well-known song "Home, sweet home!", was first performed at the Theatre Royal, Covent Garden, in May 1823, and no doubt Dickens saw it acted in his boyhood.

On a "Monday morning" in the middle of April Dickens asks Kolle to spare an evening in order to paint "two pair of side scenes." "The time," he says, "is fast approaching and I am rather nervous. Thursday is a rehearsal of *Clari* with the band, and Friday a dress rehearsal," but Kolle was too busy sweethearting to attend the rehearsals regularly and Dickens, as stage manager, had later to admonish him. The next letter contained 14s. to be handed to Henry Bramwell, one of the cast, who afterwards became a judge and a peer of the realm. It was for cigars.

Of what happened when the rehearsals took place at 18 Bentinck Street, a good idea can be obtained from the article "Mrs Joseph Porter" in *Sketches by Boz*.[1] "The large dining-room, dismantled of its furniture and ornaments, presented a strange jumble of flats, flies, wings, lamps,

[1] Cr. ed., p. 323.

bridges, clouds, thunder and lightning, and various other messes included under the comprehensive name of properties." The compliments paid to one another by the actors and the mistakes they made are ludicrously described, and from time to time we hear the "Ting, ting, ting" of the prompter's bell, and the different noises made by piano and violoncello. From "Rose Villa, Clapham Rise" the fancy name for 18 Bentinck Street "the audience went home suffering from severe headaches and smelling terribly of brimstone and gunpowder."

Among the other players were Edward Barrow, Thomas Mitton, John Dickens (Dickens's father), Harry Austin, Miss Dickens (Fanny), Mrs Austin, Miss Letitia Dickens and a Miss Urquhart. In a letter to Miss Urquhart Dickens bemoans the great difficulty he and Mr Boston, the stage carpenter, were experiencing in making moonlight. Both Maria Beadnell and Marianne Leigh—the girl in the manger—were among the audience, but Marianne proved herself a greater nuisance than ever. She spoilt everything, and even when the play was over Dickens "could not get rid of her." She *would* be in the way, that she would!

In the meantime the marriage of Kolle with Anne Beadnell was announced to take place in May, and Dickens, realising that thenceforward he would be without anybody to smuggle letters into the Beadnell home, determined to make a final appeal to Maria. In a letter written apparently at the end of April 1833, he said:

"I will openly and at once say that there is nothing I have more at heart, nothing I more sincerely and earnestly desire than to be reconciled to you. . . . I have never loved and I can never love any human creature breathing but yourself. . . . The matter now, rests solely with you,"

which of course it didn't, owing to the interfering "old gentleman" and the ubiquitous and irrepressible Marianne Leigh. All the same, Dickens was terribly in earnest.

Maria answered coldly and reproachfully, yet he still adored her. Often when he returned from the House of

Commons at two or three in the morning he would wander past No. 2 Lombard Street only to look at the place where she was sleeping. And she, notwithstanding all, still loved him; at least, so she said, looking back, long after; while he, long after, thought he could have been intensely happy, life through, united to her; and for over twenty years he nursed this illusion, until indeed, as will be seen, another amatory illusion, which in its turn had to be abandoned, took its place. Still his passion for Maria did bear fruit, for, as he himself says, "It was the hope of winning her that led him to make the most desperate efforts to succeed in life."

This year 1833 Dickens wrote a travesty of Shakespeare's *Othello*—*The O'Thello*—one of the characters in it, "The Great Unpaid," being Dickens's father, who when his son became famous gave away the manuscript page by page as souvenirs.[1] It will be remembered that *Othello* was produced by the amateurs in *Mrs Joseph Porter*.

A few anecdotes concerning the Dickens family at this time have been preserved.[2] Dickens's sister Letitia being out of health and subject to fainting fits, went to stay with some girl friends for a change. She grew stronger but was still pale and delicate looking. Her father gave notice that he was coming to see how she was progressing. The girls, however, were not satisfied with their guest's complexion, which did not do sufficient credit to the pains taken about her health. It was therefore agreed that Letitia should be made to look more robust. So they squeezed geranium blossoms and rubbed the juice on her cheeks. Micawber arrived, wept for joy and "called upon Heaven to witness his everlasting gratitude to the house and its inmates who had restored a beloved daughter to health and happiness." Unfortunately the patient herself was so overcome that she went into hysterics and had to be led from the room.

One day at Bentinck Street somebody doubted whether the water in the kettle was boiling. Micawber

---

[1] A facsimile of a portion of *The Othello* is given in Langton, p. 106. A few pages of the MS. were in the possession of Mr F. T. Sabin.
[2] In *Temple Bar*.

uprose, and with pompous flourishes of action addressed the company. "My dears, you seem to have some doubt as to whether the water boils. Now by what test, what proof, can we ascertain whether it boils or not?" From across the table came the voice of one of his daughters, "Put your finger in it, pa."

When the time for Kolle's marriage drew near there was great excitement in the Beadnell family; and one day Dickens met Mrs Beadnell (who like her husband was stiff with him) and her three daughters in the street when they were on their way to the dressmaker's in St Mary Axe. They all wore green cloaks cut very round, and Dickens gallantly escorted them to the dressmaker's door, where Mrs Beadnell, anxious to get rid of him, said emphatically, "And now, Mr Dickin, we'll wish *you* good morning."

On Tuesday, 14 May 1833, Kolle, who still resided at 14 Addle Street, carried from Dickens to Maria a letter which dealt chiefly with Marianne's perfidy, but Maria's reply on 15 May could have afforded him little pleasure. He wrote again on Thursday, 16 May, and again, without waiting a reply, next day, when he enclosed a copy of an indignant letter which he intended to send to the mischief-making Miss Leigh.

On Saturday, 17 May, Kolle, whose wedding day was drawing near, gave a bachelor's supper. There was on the table "an extensive assortment of choice hock" and the wretched Dickens apparently drank too much, for in a letter written next day to Kolle he compares Kolle's most blest condition with the unhappy termination of his own love affair, adding "yesterday I felt like a maniac, today my interior resembles a lime-basket." In this letter to Kolle was enclosed another letter to Maria, which apparently never reached her, for Kolle's thoughts were monopolised with arrangements for his wedding, which took place on Tuesday, 21 May. Dickens, who was best man, called for the bridegroom at ten that morning and Mr and Mrs Beadnell were there of course. That was the last time Dickens met the family. The next news was that the inexorable "old gentleman" had packed Maria off to Paris; and thus ended for the time being, at any rate, an affecting romance.

Maria became the Dora of *David Copperfield* (1849) and the Flora of *Little Dorrit* (1855) though she was never so childish as in the first book or so tactless as in the second.

Among John Henry Barrow's friends was the afterwards well-known John Payne Collier, a reporter for the *Morning Chronicle*. They had been acquainted for six years and Barrow had presented Collier with a copy of his poem *Talavera* written in imitation of Sir Walter Scott. Ever ready to help his nephew, Barrow induced Collier to give Dickens a letter for the editor of that paper. "I myself," he said, "taught my nephew shorthand." In order to be better acquainted with Dickens, Collier on 27 July 1833 invited him to dinner. Dickens, who was at that time young-looking, having "no vestige of beard or whiskers," gladly accepted, and after dessert "sang two comic songs." Collier gave the recommendation, but it was unsuccessful.

A little later, Collier wrote in reference to Dickens:

> I observed a great difference in his appearance and dress; for he had bought a new hat and a very handsome blue cloak, with black velvet facings, the corner of which he threw over his shoulder *a l'Espagnole*. . . . . We walked together through Hungerford Market where we followed a coal-heaver, who carried his little rosy but grimy child looking over his shoulder. Dickens bought some cherries, and as we went along he gave them one by one to the little fellow without the knowledge of the father.[1]

§ 21. *The Fetter Lane Old Curiosity Shop. "A Dinner at Poplar Walk"*

In company with a friend named Wiffin, a gold-and-silversmith's apprentice, Dickens used to frequent a circulating library kept at No. 24 Fetter Lane by a printer and curio-dealer named Haines. The house was very ancient, and its tarnished silver, foxed and tattered engravings, cracked paintings and old china may have got reflected in *The Old Curiosity Shop*. After Dickens became famous, Haines often recalled his pleasant face, his habit "whenever he laughed of throwing up his upper lip" and his passion for

[1] Carlton, p. 101.

sensational novels which he would carry away by the pile. On one occasion at Haines's Wiffin fulminated against Fenimore Cooper because in his tale *Red Rover* the English had been abused, the American extolled. Dickens championed Cooper and, the dispute having waxed warm, strengthened his argument by flinging the copy of *Red Rover* at Wiffin's head.

Ambitious to see himself in print, Dickens at the end of 1833 wrote a sketch which he entitled "A Dinner at Poplar Walk." One evening in November, at twilight, he stealthily and with fear and trembling made his way up Johnson's Court, Fleet Street, and dropped his manuscript into the letter box of the *Monthly Magazine* edited by Captain Holland.[1]  To his inexpressible joy it appeared in print, and he tells us how on the occasion he walked down to Westminster Hall and turned into it for half an hour, because his eyes were so dimmed with happiness and pride that they could not bear the street. The piece subsequently appeared in *Sketches by Boz* under the title of "Mr Minns and his Cousin." Its merit is small, but Mr Budden's dog, as the forerunner of many more comic creations, deserves honourable mention. On Tuesday, 3 December, Dickens sent a copy of the article to Kolle, asking him to beg Mrs Kolle's criticism of it.[2]  Mrs Kolle, it will be remembered, was Anne Beadnell, so Maria may have heard of it too.

Encouraged by his success Dickens wrote other sketches which from time to time appeared in the same periodical. The one in the August number for 1834 was the first that had the signature of Boz, the nickname of his youngest brother, Augustus, then aged 7, whom in honour of *The Vicar of Wakefield* he had dubbed Moses, changed to Boses and ultimately to "Boz."

One of the most notable characteristics of Dickens was his gift for pouncing upon suitable or at any rate striking names for his characters. He had seen the importance of this even when engaged on his first sketch in which we are treated to

[1] Captain Holland was editor of the *Monthly Magazine* from November 1833. See *Dickensian* (article by Walter Dexter), 1 March 1934.
[2] *Beadnell Letters*, p. 63.

such curiosities as Mr Minns and Mr Budden. Balzac used to say that names which were invented never imparted life to imaginary characters, while those which had belonged to real persons endowed the personages in a book with vitality. Dickens agreed with him. He was always on the look out for real and striking names. If he happened to be in Rochester, Rochester names were sure to creep into his books; if at Broadstairs, Broadstairs names. Twenty of the names given to his characters appear in the list of mayors of Rochester.

§ 22. *On the "Morning Chronicle." Misery in Bentinck Street*

As already related, John Henry Barrow had unsuccessfully tried to get his nephew on to the *Morning Chronicle.* Later this paper changed hands, having been secured by Mr (afterwards Sir) John Easthope,[1] and two co-proprietors under whom it became a Whig organ. Joseph Parkes, a Whig agent engaged in behalf of the new owners, Thomas Beard as stenographer, and asked him to recommend another able shorthand writer. He at once named his friend Dickens, who commenced duties with a salary of £5 a week. This would probably be in August 1834 when he severed his connection with the *Mirror of Parliament.* The Whig *Morning Chronicle* and the Tory *Times* were continually at loggerheads and each discharged insulting epithets at the other, a state of affairs that probably suggested the Pott and Slurk episode in *Pickwick.*

In time, Dickens made such strides that among the eighty or ninety reporters in the gallery he occupied the very highest rank, not merely for accuracy in reporting but for marvellous quickness in transcribing. His duties, however, were not confined to the gallery. They took him all over the country. He flew about in the old coaches, just before they were displaced by railways, and he put up at old inns while they were still in their glory. He speaks of having to

---

[1] £690 was recently (June 1934) paid in London for a series of letters written by Dickens to Sir John Easthope.

charge the *Morning Chronicle* again and again for "break-downs" and for all sorts of other catastrophes "fifty times in a journey"; for broken hats, broken luggage, broken chaises, broken harness. He believed he had been upset in almost every sort of vehicle known in this country. In one of his letters to Henry Austin, he writes, in allusion to a prospective journey in a gig through Essex, "It strikes me I shall be spilt before I pay a turnpike. I have a presentiment I shall run over an only child before I reach Chelmsford." Apparently Dickens was present, in his capacity as reporter for the *Morning Chronicle*, at the parliamentary by-election which took place at Ipswich on 25 and 26 July 1834. If his discomforts were many abroad they were no pleasanter nearer home. "He wore out his knees," he said, "by writing on them on the back row of the gallery of the old House of Commons;" and his feet "by standing to write in a preposterous pen in the old House of Lords," where the reporters used to be huddled together like so many sheep.

In the autumn of 1834 a great banquet was offered by the citizens of Edinburgh in honour of the Prime Minister, Earl Grey, on his retirement from office. The *Morning Chronicle* sent two reporters, Beard and Dickens. They travelled by sea and reached Edinburgh on 13 September. A temporary pavilion had been erected on Calton Hill, and some 2,800 persons assembled to do honour to the distinguished statesman. The joint report of Beard [1] and Dickens occupies eleven columns of the *Morning Chronicle* of the 17th and 18th.[2]

Shortly after this event, Dickens took lodgings in Cecil Street so as to be near the office of the paper, 332 Strand, almost opposite Somerset House. The members of the staff were expected to meet at the office between 10 and 11 each morning in order to receive instructions from Black. The people in Cecil Street, he tells Kolle, attended on him

---

[1] In Count de Suzannet's Library at Lausanne is a "poem" of "48 verses" entitled "A Fable (not a gay one)" composed by Dickens in 1834 for the album of Miss Ellen Beard. The *Dickensian*, 1 March 1934, p. 112.

[2] Reprinted in the *Dickensian*, No. 233, 1 December 1934, pp. 5–10.

most miserably so he "gave them warning" and was for a time unable to fix "on a local habitation"—that is to say apartments near the *Chronicle* office.   He is next heard of in rooms at 1 5 Buckingham Street, Adelphi, the chambers rented by David Copperfield from Mrs Crupp, which admitted of a peep at the river.   At times when acting as a reporter he could be found in the well of Lincoln's Inn Hall, "where the Lord High Chancellor sat in his High Court of Chancery," "a foggy glory round his head, softly fenced in with crimson cloth and curtains."   This hall was the scene of the interminable trial of Jarndyce v. Jarndyce in *Bleak House*.   It was while acting as a reporter that Dickens acquired that almost uncanny understanding of court work which he utilised when dealing with the Bardell v. Pickwick case.

Of the life in Bentinck Street at this time we get insight from the collection of letters preserved by Mr Frederick Ouvry, who became Dickens's solicitor.   In one, Dickens says: "On waking this morning I was informed that my father had just been arrested by Shaw and Maxwell, the quondam wine people."   Dickens fears it is an awkward business and really has no idea of the extent of his father's embarrassments.   "I have not yet been taken," he continues, "but no doubt that will be the next act in this domestic tragedy."   To be under danger of arrest was the elder Dickens's chronic position.   At such times he would disappear from home.   "I own," writes his son on one occasion of the sort to Thomas Mitton, "that at present his absence does not give me great uneasiness, knowing how apt he is to get out of the way when anything goes wrong."

Letter after letter reveals how Micawber was draining his son.   Dickens is even not above borrowing four shillings as he wanted to give money to his father, who, by the by, was at the same time borrowing from Thomas Beard to say nothing of other Thomases who were weak enough to listen to him.   It speaks volumes for Dickens that he was able to rise, dragged to the earth by the terrible family burden. His environment indeed could scarcely have been worse, but happily in respect to man the determining forces are within not outside him. Certainly they were not outside Dickens, which was fortunate, considering the "damnable shadow" [1] cast in all those early years by his father.

[1] *Dickens-Kolle Letters*, p. 82.

## CHAPTER VIII

# December 1834 to 2 April 1836

§ 23. *The "Evening Chronicle,"* 31 *January* 1835.
*"Sketches by Boz,"* February 1836.  *Cruikshank*

THIS same month, December 1834, Dickens moved
from his father's house and took chambers at No. 13
Furnival's Inn, Holborn—"the three pair back."
Furnival's Inn, entered through a low tunnel-shaped archway, was then new and smart-looking having just been
rebuilt by Mr Peto, the contractor whose statue stood in the
middle of the square.  On the site of Furnival's Inn are
now the buildings of the Prudential Insurance Company.
Dickens, who paid £35 5s. for his rooms, occupied them for
twelve months.

In January 1835 there was a General Election, and
Dickens, in order to report for his paper, travelled in a gig to
Ipswich.  Two short paragraphs about the occurrences
appeared from his pen in the *Morning Chronicle* for 6 and 7
January.  He then went on to Sudbury, and a column
about the events there appeared in that paper on 7 January.
It is contended that Sudbury and not Ipswich is the original
of Eatanswill in *Pickwick*.  But Exeter (see p. 72) also has
claims.  So, as we shall find (see p. 76), has Kettering.
Those who favour the claims of Ipswich point out that one
of the candidates was a Mr, afterwards Sir, Fitzroy Kelly—
which certainly suggests Horatio Fitzkin, Esq.

From Sudbury Dickens went in this same gig on a dark

night and in a torrential rain [1] to Bury St Edmunds, also for the needs of the *Morning Chronicle*. Up to this time his contributions to the *Monthly Magazine* had been voluntary, for the editor, Captain Holland, an old soldier of Bolivar, the hero of South America, was unable to make any payment. But as it happened, the proprietors of the *Morning Chronicle* were just then about to issue an evening paper, and Mr John Black, the editor, placed the new venture in the hands of their music critic, Mr George Hogarth, a Scotchman, formerly of Edinburgh. Mr Hogarth, influenced by Black, asked Dickens to furnish a sketch for the first number and further suggested that he should write a series of papers something after the style of those that had appeared in the *Morning Chronicle*. Mr Hogarth, who was destined from that time onward to figure conspicuously in Dickens's life, had in his earlier days been Sir Walter Scott's law agent, and was personally acquainted with most of the literary characters of the day. He is mentioned in Christopher North's *Noctes Ambrosianae*.

Dickens replied to Mr Hogarth's letter on 20 January 1835. He was willing to fall in with the suggestion but he hoped "to receive something for the papers" beyond his ordinary pay as reporter. The response was a prompt increase of salary from five to seven guineas. The first sketch, "Hackney Coach Stands," appeared on 31 January 1835. The series, which consisted of twenty sketches, pleased Mr Black, and his encouragement sent Dickens forward in a rare heat. "It was John Black that flung the slipper after me," he used to say, "dear old Black! my first hearty out-and-out appreciator."

About this time Dickens arranged to write for Mr Tegg, the publisher, a work to be called "Sergeant Bell and his Raree Show," the price to be £120, but the arrangement fell through. Mr James Grant, "the military novelist," who had succeeded Holland as editor of the *Monthly Magazine*, having written to ask Dickens's terms, received answer that he could not accept less than half a guinea a page. The attendance of his sister Fanny at the Royal Academy of

[1] *Sketches by Boz.* Cr. ed., vol. 5, p. 348.

Music was the means of bringing him into touch with John Pyke Hullah, the musical composer, and letters passed between them.[1]

In the spring of 1835 Lord John Russell, who had accepted office in the new Melbourne Ministry, offered himself for re-election as member for South Devon. Beard and Dickens proceeded straightway to Exeter. The principal meeting was held in Castle Yard on 1 May in the midst of a lively fight maintained by all the vagabonds in that division and "under such a pelting rain" says Dickens, "that I remember two good-natured colleagues who chanced to be at leisure held a pocket handkerchief over my note-book, after the manner of a state canopy in an ecclesiastical procession." Even then he could not have proceeded had not another friend offered a shoulder as a writing-desk. He was made still further uncomfortable owing to the unreliability of the platform on which he was seated, and which indeed collapsed before the meeting ended. However, the report was sent off that night, and it appeared in the columns of the *Morning Chronicle* next day, a remarkable achievement, as the railway had not then reached Exeter.

In a letter to Kolle written in March or April 1834, Dickens thanks him for purchasing a lottery ticket. He also hopes to place in Kolle's hands the manuscript of the *O'Thello*, and he mentions facetiously what he will do with the money if his ticket wins a prize. It seems that the winner could have the value in "money or freehold houses" —but that is all we hear about the venture. Later a little Miss Kolle appeared on the scene and Dickens became godfather. "I shall be at Ball's Pond Chapel" (in Islington) he says, "on Sunday next at half-past two precisely."

## § 24. *Engagement to Catherine Hogarth, May* 1835

By this time, May 1835, Dickens had fallen in love with Catherine Thomson, eldest daughter of Mr George Hogarth; and his engagement present to her took the form of his portrait on ivory, painted by Miss Rose E. Drum-

[1] See the *Dickensian*, vols. 29 and 30.

CHARLES DICKENS AT THE AGE OF 23 IN 1835

From the Miniature by Mrs. Rose Emma Drummond
given to Miss Catherine Hogarth by Charles Dickens
when they were engaged

*Photo by T. W. Tyrrell*

See page 72

PAINTING OF MRS. CHARLES DICKENS BY MACLISE, *c.* 1846

It belonged to Mrs. Perugini

*Photo by T. W. Tyrrell*

See page 73

mond, a skilful miniaturist,[1] who became the original of Miss La Creevy in *Nicholas Nickleby*. Miss Hogarth's second name was taken from that of her maternal grandfather, George Thomson, the friend of Burns and the correspondent of Beethoven and other composers. Of Thomson, the Hogarths were proud. Helen, George Thomson's daughter, and Catherine were life-long friends. The Hogarths included her name in that of their youngest daughter, Helen Isabella. Burns's letters to Thomson are well known.

Catherine was very pretty and she knew it, and rather *petite*, with heavy-lidded large "blue eyes." The nose was a little retroussé, the mouth small, round and red-lipped. She had a pleasant smiling expression, notwithstanding a sleepy nonchalant look. There was about her a somnolent voluptuousness suggestive not of the north, whence she came, but of the south. Her portrait by Maclise shows a graceful attractive figure, with long dark hair, touching her shoulders, and flowers at her bosom. When animated she was charming. But she was petulant and capricious. Dickens was satisfied that she had culture, as might be expected from the daughter of so gifted a father, for along with one of his early letters to her he sent a volume containing the *Life of Savage*. After begging her to read it attentively he says, "if you do, I know from your excellent understanding you will be delighted." As regards her sisters, each of whom was to figure in Dickens's life, Mary Scott (named after her grandmother [2]) was 15, Georgina 7, Helen Isabella 3.[3] Mary was destined to be immortalised as Little Nell in *The Old Curiosity Shop*.

Owing to Catherine's petulance the courtship was

[1] Cf. "In the times when you used to pay two guineas on ivory and took your chance pretty much how you came out." *Mrs Lirriper's Lodgings.* Cr. ed., vol 15, p. 233. The portrait is reproduced in Carlton's *Charles Dickens, Shorthand Writer*, p. 130. See § 24.

[2] Robert Hogarth, Mrs Dickens's grandfather, who died 3 October 1819, aged 77, married Mary Scott. George was their eldest son.

[3] Hogarth's daughters: Catherine Thomson, born 19 May 1815; Mary Scott, born 26 October 1819; Georgina, born 22 January 1827, died 19 April 1917; Helen Isabella, born in 1833, died 1 December 1890.

attended with storms, and in a letter written in May 1835, only three weeks after they had become engaged, Dickens writes, "The sudden and uncalled-for coldness with which you treated me just before I left last night, both surprised and deeply hurt me." "Not once or twice, but again and again," she had betrayed what he called "a sullen and obstinate temper." He complains that she had used him like any other toy that suited her humour for the moment. All the same, he is "warmly and deeply attached" to her; and in a later letter he says: "I have never ceased to love you for one moment since I knew you."

The time for their marriage drawing near, he invited her to breakfast with him and he sent his love to her sister Mary, adding, "I rely on her characteristic kind-heartedness and good nature to accompany you." The lovers frequently met, but not frequently enough for Dickens, who writes, "I have not seen you, you know, dearest, since seven o'clock yesterday morning. It seems an age." Sometimes Dickens's brother Frederick took messages to Catherine, carried black-currant jam to cure her throat, and did other small services. Micawber continued to cause trouble. "I have only this moment returned," Dickens says, "from accompanying father to Cold Bath Fields." What actually took place is not recorded, but the elder Dickens was always in difficulties, and the journey to that prison could not have been a pleasant experience for either of them.

Later, Dickens and Catherine got on better together, she was his "dearest Life" and his "dearest mouse," and he sends her kisses innumerable, but at times she is distrustful of him and he again feels hurt. Another bond between Dickens and George Hogarth was their enthusiasm for Sir Walter Scott's novels. Dickens several times refers to them, and in a letter to the artist Cattermole he eulogises *Peveril*, *A Legend of Montrose* and *Kenilworth*, which he had just been reading "with greater delight than ever." His occasional indebtedness to Scott was pointed out by Mr H. Walters in the *Dickensian*, 1 March 1934.

Dickens's first series of sketches in the *Evening Chronicle* finished on 20 August 1835 with "Our Parish." After an interval of about twelve months he commenced a second series for the same paper. Of the four sketches which he then supplied, three were printed in the morning edition as well: "Meditations in Monmouth Street," "Scotland Yard," "Doctors' Commons," and "Vauxhall Gardens by Day." On 27 September 1835 appeared a sketch by him in *Bell's Life in London*, a popular sporting journal, the title being "Seven Dials," the first of a series of twelve, all of which were subsequently included in *Sketches by Boz*. They were signed "Tibbs."[1] The editor of *Bell's Life*, Mr Vincent Dowling, is said to have been the first to discern Dickens's genius for character sketching.

§ 25. *Ainsworth. First letter to Macrone, 28 October 1835. Cruikshank*

Sometime this year Dickens heard from Harrison Ainsworth, whose *Rookwood* (in which Dick Turpin so conspicuously figures) had been issued by John Macrone, a young publisher. A friendship sprang up between the two writers; and Ainsworth introduced Dickens not only to Macrone but also to George Cruikshank who had illustrated *Rookwood*. About the same time Dickens became friendly with Edward Buller, afterwards Lord Lytton, who was already famous as the author of *Paul Clifford* (1830), *Eugene Aram* (1832), and *The Last Days of Pompeii* (1834). Indeed he and Ainsworth were, just before the rocket which was Dickens went up, the two most popular novelists of the day. *Rookwood* and *Paul Clifford*, glorifications of the highwayman, no doubt suggested the far more healthy and realistic *Oliver Twist*.

Dickens's first recorded letter to Macrone, whose house of business was 3 St James's Square, is dated 28 October 1835, and a little later Macrone agreed to publish Dickens's articles in book form with the title *Sketches by Boz*. The correspondence between them dealt chiefly with this work and with Dickens's difficulties with Cruikshank who was

[1] Mr Tibbs was the proprietor of the Boarding House in *Sketches by Boz*.

75

illustrating it.[1]  Cruikshank and his brother Robert, who were "cradled in caricature," had in early life worked together in a studio in Dorset Street where they patronised not only the pencil but also the boxing gloves, an unlucky tap from which one day twisted George's nose, which remained awry the rest of his life.  In the picture "Public Dinners" Cruikshank introduced himself and Dickens among the wand bearers; and nobody could mistake the hooked and twisted nose.  After his marriage he resided in Amwell Street.  His animal spirits were amazing, he was pugnacious, he loved adventure and he drank to excess; but later he forswore the bottle and became one of the most doughty champions of temperance.

On 9 November 1835 Dickens and Beard were at Newbury on a further reporting expedition.  From the George and Pelican there Dickens wrote on Sunday morning, 8 November, to Thomas Fraser, sub-editor of the *Morning Chronicle*, mentioning various arrangements he had made in conjunction with another paper, the *Herald*.  The same day he and the *Herald* man made for the Bush Inn, Bristol, so as to be present at a dinner to Lord John Russell which was to take place a little later.

§ 26. *The Kettering Election, 18 December 1835*

On 18 December, Dickens's duties took him to Kettering,[2] which was in the throes of an election.  He tells Macrone that during his absence Mr Hogarth would read the proofs of *Sketches by Boz*.  In the postscript of a letter to Catherine, written from the White Hart, Kettering, he says, "Damn the Tories!  They'll win here I am afraid!"  The two chief newspapers of the county were the *Northamptonshire Mercury* (Whig) and the *Northamptonshire Herald* (Tory) and their editors weekly insulted each other after the manner of Mr Pott of the *Eatanswill Gazette* and Mr Slurk of the *Eatanswill Independent*.

[1] See the *Dickensian*, March 1934, p. 135.
[2] The *Dickensian*, Spring 1934, p. 138.

As already stated, it had generally been assumed that "Eatanswill" in *Pickwick* is Ipswich or Sudbury.[1] Dickens may however have had this north Northamptonshire election most in mind. He says:

"The noise and confusion here this morning—which is the first day of polling—is so great that my head is actually splitting. There are about forty flags on either side, two tremendous bands, one hundred and fifty constables, and vehicles of every kind, sort and description . . . conveying voters to the Poll; and the voters themselves are drinking and guzzling and howling."

On 23 December occurred a riot. He says:

"Such a ruthless set of bloody-minded villains I never set eyes on. . . . . All agricultural places at election times are as bad; but beastly as the electors usually are, these men are superlative blackguards."

The nomination took place at Kettering on 15 December. Dickens and the reporter for the *Globe* were on the ground at an early hour. The Tory candidate was Mr Thomas Philip Maunsell, the Whig Mr William Hanbury. The supporters of Mr Hanbury were all on foot. Perfect order and good humour existed until the arrival of a body of horsemen in Mr Maunsell's interest, who rode in upon the people, and endeavoured to force their way to the front of the hustings. The pedestrians, to avoid being trampled upon, seized the reins of the horses, and endeavoured to force them back. The horsemen having resisted with large sticks and heavy riding-whips, a scene of indescribable confusion ensued.

When the disorder was at its height,

and before missiles had been thrown by the Buff party, a certain John George produced a pistol and levelled it at a person in the crowd. His hand was arrested by some member of his own party, and cries of "Seize him!" "Carry him off!" "Constables, do your duty!" were immediately raised. . . . It is worthy of remark, observes the *Northamptonshire Mercury*, that not one speaker on the Conservative side made the slightest allusion to, or expressed any regret for, this disgraceful proceeding. We heard Mr Maunsell

---

[1] See the *Dickensian*, vol. 3, No. 5, p. 133.

(the Conservative) himself appealed to on the hustings. His reply was that the other (Buff) party had taken the ground first.

"It will hardly be credited," says Dickens, "that the pistol was a double-barrelled one, and was *loaded*." The result of the poll, declared on 26 December, was as follows:

Thomas Philip Maunsell (Tory) . . 1,841
William Hanbury (Whig) . . . 1,247

Majority . . . . 594

Mr Maunsell, when offering thanks, said:

"I must be allowed to refer to a paragraph which appeared in the columns of a morning paper on Saturday last. I mean the *Morning Chronicle*, for the editor of that print has had the hardihood and impudence to declare that the electors of this division, the 1841 honest and independent electors who have done me the honour of supporting me by their votes on this occasion, were 'the most brutal, the most drunken, and most ignorant set of electors in the kingdom.'"

—a passage written no doubt by Dickens. Mr Maunsell was chaired, flags were waved, and his supporters shouted themselves hoarse crying "No Popery!" "Church and State!" and "Mr Maunsell the farmers' friend!"

At Christmas 1835 Dickens removed from No. 13 Furnival's Inn to No. 15, where he occupied the "three pair floor south," for which he paid £50 a year. On 7 January 1836 he tells Macrone that he has been invited to Cruikshank's house in order to see the plates (for *Sketches by Boz*). He says he is highly gratified with Ainsworth's appreciation of "A Visit to Newgate"[1] in that work, and wonders whether his new friend has also seen "The Black Veil."[2] He still kept in touch with Captain Holland, for in a letter to Macrone on 15 *January* 1836 he says, "Captain Holland invited himself here tomorrow night to take a glass of grog and some oysters. Will you meet him? I shall be most happy to see you in my new quarters."

[1] Cr. ed., vol. 5, p. 147.    [2] Cr. ed., vol. 5, p. 279.

§ 27. *"Sketches by Boz," First Series, February 1836.*[1]
*Whitehead*

The notice of *Sketches by Boz* in the *Evening Chronicle*
from the pen of Hogarth gave Dickens great pleasure, and
later referring to an article in the *Morning Post* on 12 March
he says it "is as good as Hogarth's." *Sketches by Boz*, the
first of Dickens's works, owed its origin partly to Goldsmith's *Bee*, but chiefly to Washington Irving's *Sketch Book*,
though there is little comparison between Irving's charming
vignettes and delicate humour and the crude productions of
his English imitator. Dickens, however, was only a
beginner. In a minor degree he was influenced by Theo-
dore Hook, who at the tables of the aristocracy delivered
himself of his witticisms—chiefly puns; but that glittering
life, though Hook had not reached 50, was fast hurrying to a
close.

Later, Dickens formed the acquaintance of the unfortunate poet, dramatist and novelist, Charles Whitehead, and
a friendship which proved to be of the utmost importance to
Dickens sprang up between them. Whitehead had undertaken for Messrs Chapman and Hall the editorship of a
"Library of Fiction" (announced 26 March 1836) and he
invited Dickens to contribute to it, with the result of "The
Tuggses at Ramsgate" and "A Little Talk about Spring"
which were subsequently included in *Sketches by Boz*.

Whitehead was tall and dark complexioned. His hollow
chest and stooping gait betrayed the close student. The
diffidence of his manner struck the most casual observer.
Many a man with half his genius but with abundance of
confidence has floated buoyantly where he sank. He first
appeared as an author in 1831 with the *Solitary*, a poem that
won the admiration of Dante Gabriel Rossetti. It was
followed in 1834 by the *Autobiography of Jack Ketch* and
*Lives of English Highwaymen*, sensational works which
passed through many editions. He later obtained fame as

[1] *Sketches by Boz* finally appeared in 2 vols. with 16 illustrations by
Cruikshank early in February 1836. See *Dickensian*, Spring 1934,
p. 139.

the author of *Richard Savage*.[1] For some time he and Dickens were on the warmest terms of friendship, and Dickens, who praised highly Whitehead's works, was considerably influenced by them. This friendship led to Dickens's acquaintance with Robert Seymour and Robert William Buss. The former illustrated "The Tuggses at Ramsgate," the latter "A Little Talk about Spring."

Seymour, who was educated in his father's workshop as a pattern draughtsman, was ambitious, and had, for the purpose of study and quiet, hired a room at the top of Canonbury Tower, a well-known Islington pile. Finding, however, the impracticability of pursuing high art, he turned from it to the less entrancing, but more remunerative, occupation of designer on wood and caricaturist; but though he left his tower he continued to reside in Islington.

## § 28. *Pickwick*, 1 *April* 1836

Early in 1836 Seymour was employed in illustrating with sporting plates a little book for Messrs Chapman and Hall, and he proposed to do a series of Cockney plates of a superior character to be issued monthly. Mr Chapman, favouring the idea, requested Whitehead to write the letterpress. Whitehead declined on the ground that he was unequal to the task of producing the copy with sufficient regularity, but recommended his friend Charles Dickens, who when approached by Mr Hall with the offer of £14 for each monthly part at once closed with it. This publication was *The Pickwick Papers*. The name Pickwick was taken from that of a well-known coach proprietor of Bath—Moses Pickwick, said to have been a foundling left in Pickwick Street and brought up in Corsham Workhouse. In Whitehead's *Jack Ketch* a humorous allusion is made to the possibility of the author producing "his more mature experience under the unambitious title of *The Ketch Papers*." This passage and conversations with Whitehead seem to have given Dickens the idea of calling his work *The Pickwick Papers*.

[1] *Richard Savage* appeared in serial form in *Bentley's Miscellany*, 1841–2.

MRS. CHARLES DICKENS BY MACLISE
*From "Charles Dickens by Pen and Pencil" by Frank T. Sabin*

CHALK CHURCH WITH FIGURE OF THE MONK

Over the porch was a quaint stone carved figure representing a monk in a stooping position holding a vase. Dickens, who was interested in this queer carving, used, whenever he passed it, to raise his hat or give it a friendly nod as to an old acquaintance

*Photo by Lionel F. Gowing*

See page 83

The first public announcement concerning it was made by means of an advertisement in *The Times*, 26 March 1836:

The Pickwick Papers.—On 31st of March will be published, to be continued monthly, price one shilling, the first number of the *Posthumous Papers of the Pickwick Club*, containing a faithful record of the Perambulations, Perils, Travels, Adventures and Sporting Transactions of the corresponding members. Edited by Boz. Each monthly part embellished with four illustrations by Seymour. Chapman and Hall, 186 Strand, and of all booksellers.

The proposed book, indeed, was to be a record of the adventures of a Nimrod Club, the members of which were to go out shooting, fishing and so forth, getting themselves into difficulties through their want of dexterity. Dickens, however, did not like the idea of writing letterpress to suit a series of pictures. "It would be infinitely better," he said, "for the plates to arise naturally out of the text"; moreover, it would give him freer range. His views were deferred to, the first sketch was written, and from its proof sheets Seymour made his drawing of the club and its founder, not, however (according to one account) as we now know him, but a long thin Pickwick. Dickens, it is said, suggested a fat man instead, and described a friend of Edward Chapman's at Richmond, named John Foster, "a fat old beau, who *would* wear, in spite of the ladies' protests, drab tights and black gaiters." Then Seymour produced the present engaging and bird-like figure perched upon a chair, with his left hand under his coat-tails and his right raised—the great man eloquent.

This piece of good fortune having come to Dickens, he thought he might safely venture on marriage, and Catherine Hogarth and her sister Mary, with a view to preparing the home, spent much time at Furnival's Inn. After a whole day there they would return by the last bus to their father's at Chelsea. On 31 March Dickens wrote to his uncle, Thomas Culliford Barrow, informing him that owing to the success of *Pickwick* he was able to get married earlier than at first supposed possible.

"I have therefore," he says, "fixed Saturday next for my marriage with Miss Hogarth—the daughter of a gentleman who has recently distinguished himself by a celebrated work on Music. There is no member of my family to whom I should be prouder to introduce my wife than yourself."

John Dickens had been "excluded" from Thomas Barrow's house. Therefore there had for some time been little intimacy between Dickens and his uncle. This Dickens regretted and he adds, "Nothing that has occurred to me in my life has given me greater pain than thus denying myself the society of yourself and aunt." [1]

The first number of *Pickwick* appeared on 1 April 1836 and Dickens was paid for that and the second number at once as he required the money for the wedding. The publishers, who were not over sanguine as to the success of the undertaking, ordered at first only 400 copies to be stitched. Eventually 1,500 copies of each of the first five numbers were sent out on sale or return. The reception was discouraging. When, however, No. 6 appeared, introducing Samuel Weller, the sale proceeded by leaps and bounds, and thenceforward Dickens's literary career was dazzling beyond compare.

In the Bardell against Pickwick scene, Sam is asked "Do you spell it with a V or a W," the reply being "I spells it with a V"; and the elder Weller in the gallery exclaims "Quite right too Samivel! Put it down a we, my lord," and the name on the signboard of The Marquis of Granby was at first printed "Veller" though later "W" was substituted. A Mr Thomas Weller once kept the Granby Head in Chatham High Street. One presumes therefore that Tony Weller's inn, The Marquis of Granby, was at Chatham, not Dorking.

[1] J. W. T. Ley's ed. of Forster's *Life of Dickens*, p. 18.

## CHAPTER IX

# 2 April 1836 to March 1837

NO. 15 FURNIVAL'S INN FROM THE DATE OF HIS MARRIAGE,
2 APRIL 1836, TO HIS REMOVAL TO 48 DOUGHTY STREET

§ 29. *Marriage to Miss Catherine Thomson Hogarth,
Saturday, 2 April 1836*

LICENCES to marry without the publication of banns were in those days granted at Doctors' Commons, and Dickens, who knew all the ins and outs of that place and how to go to work, took out a licence. The wedding ceremony was performed at St Luke's Church, Chelsea, on 2 April 1836, Dickens's friend, Thomas Beard, acting as best man. Dickens was a little over 24, Catherine just over 21.

"The wedding breakfast," wrote Henry Burnett, who became husband of Fanny Dickens, "was the quietest possible. The Hogarth family and Mr Beard comprised the whole of the company. A few common, pleasant things were said, and healths drunk, with a few words—yet all passed off very pleasantly, and everybody seemed happy, not the least so Dickens and his young wife. She was a bright, pleasant bride, dressed in the simplest and neatest manner."

Recalling the event long after, Burnett said of Dickens:

"I can see him now helping his young wife out of the carriage after the wedding and taking her up the steps of quiet, intellectual, unobtrusive Mr Hogarth in the Fulham Road, then standing opposite orchards and gardens extending as far as the eye could reach."

The honeymoon was spent "at Mrs Nash's,"[1] Chalk,

[1] Not at the cottage at the corner of Thong-lane as some supposed. The tenant of this cottage was in 1836–37 a Mrs Craddock.

five miles from Rochester; and for their early married life they settled at 15 Furnival's Inn. Mrs Dickens's sister Mary resided with them.

The Henry Burnett mentioned was a serious young man who had been brought up by a devout grandmother and had in his boyhood come under the influence of Mr Richard Knill, afterwards famous as a missionary. When Knill started for India (he went afterwards to Russia) he said to the little boy: "Now, Henry, I am going away, and may never see you again. I want you to make me one promise, and that is, that you will pray for me every day as long as you live, if I am alive." The boy promised, and never for a single day omitted his prayer for Mr. Knill.[1] Henry, who had a remarkable voice, learnt music at Brighton, and once sang, on a table, a solo before King George the Fourth, who, a sufferer from gout, had been wheeled into the room, covered from head to foot with flannels and bandages.

Like Fanny Dickens, he studied at the Royal Academy of Music, and it was there he first met her. On quitting the Academy, he fulfilled engagements at the Theatre Royal, Edinburgh, and elsewhere. Braham the great tenor singer used to say, "If I can't come, send for Burnett, he will do as well." But the theatrical life Burnett never liked. Those were the days

> When John Braham could sing,
> Ere he docked off the A from his name.[2]

Dickens, owing to his ebullient high spirits, was apt to indulge in practical jokes both at Furnival's Inn and at the Hogarth house in Chelsea. Once when the Hogarths were sitting quietly in their parlour he, "dressed as a sailor, jumped in at the window, danced a hornpipe, whistling a tune, jumped out again, and a few minutes afterwards walked gravely in at the door, as if nothing had happened, shook hands with all, and then at the sight of their puzzled faces burst into a roar of laughter."

Dickens refers to his taste "for doing something fantastic

[1] *Memories of the Past*, by Rev. James Griffin.
[2] John Braham [i.e. Abraham] 1774-1856.

84

and monkey-like," which on all occasions had strong posses-sion of him,[1] in *The Old Curiosity Shop*, for when depicting Quilp he was drawing partly on himself. See § 52 *re* Mrs Jeniwin.

Mrs Dickens loved the country, and could have lived in Chalk for ever: Dickens loathed it. The town and the town alone had attractions for him, but occasionally in their early married life he, to please her, revisited that village and spent a few days at Mrs Nash's.

### § 30. *Suicide of Seymour*, 20 *April* 1836

Although there had been correspondence between Dickens and Seymour, Dickens had to this time never seen his associate. They were destined to meet only once—on a day in April, when Seymour brought to Furnival's Inn an etching of the Dying Clown which was to be one of the four illustrations of the second number. Some alterations having been suggested, Seymour on the following evening worked late and carried them out. Next day he destroyed himself. Henry Burnett says: "Just at the time of poor Seymour's death it was my privilege to be once or twice a week at the home of Dickens; and I well remember the consternation, disappointment and anxiety the melancholy news caused to the young writer."

Of the four plates which Seymour was to produce for the second number, only three were finished, consequently his contribution to *Pickwick* consisted of only seven plates:

(1) Mr·Pickwick addressing the Club.
(2) Scene with the Cabman.
(3) The Sagacious Dog.
(4) Dr Stammer's Defiance of Jingle.
(5) The Dying Clown.
(6) Pickwick at the Review.
(7) Winkle and the Refractory Steed.

The spirited picture of Mr Pickwick at the Review, running after his hat, with Mr Wardle in the barouche and

[1] Cr. ed., vol. 7, p. 60.

the Fat Boy asleep on the box, is a worthy companion to "Mr Pickwick addressing the Club," but the rest are less excellent.

In 1849, Mrs Seymour, widow of the artist, endeavoured to prove by means of a pamphlet that the credit of the conception of *Pickwick* belonged less to Dickens than to her husband. She said that the artist first conceived the idea of *The Pickwick Papers* in the summer of 1835, and would but for a severe illness have written as well as embellished the book. Dickens in reply averred that Seymour never originated, suggested or in any way had to do with, save as illustrator, "an incident, a character (except the sporting tastes of Mr Winkle) a name, a phrase or a word to be found in *The Pickwick Papers*.

This is true, and yet, in a sense Seymour was the originator of *Pickwick*. Mr Thomas Butler Gunn says that he remembers the figure of Pickwick in some comic etchings by Seymour, published by Chapman and Hall, some years before Dickens's *Pickwick* appeared. Seymour introduced it also in one of his threepenny sketches, in which he drew Mr Winkle and the Fat Boy. And Seymour probably did, as his wife declares, plan the writing of a humorous work to accompany the plates. But that is all. Seymour may have planned a sort of *Pickwick*, but he was utterly incapable of producing anything like the work that Dickens executed. He was without literary ability.

A successor to Seymour was found in Robert William Buss, who had illustrated one of Dickens's contributions to *The Library of Fiction*—"A Little Talk about Spring and the Sweeps." [1] Buss produced two plates for *Pickwick*:

The Cricket Match.

Tupman and Miss Wardle in the Arbour, the Fat Boy looking on.

Both, however, were speedily suppressed, and copies of *Pickwick* containing them are rare. They were reproduced in *Dickens and his Illustrators* (Dickens Fellowship Publications No. 2). It will be noticed that in "The Cricket

---

[1] This sketch appeared in *Sketches by Boz* as "The First of May," but Buss's plate gave place to one by Cruikshank.

Match" Buss introduced a farcical incident not in the text, the ball knocking off the hat of one of the fielders. The difficulty had been that Buss did not understand the process of etching, consequently he had put the plates into the hands of a professional engraver. Had time permitted he would himself have cancelled these plates and issued fresh ones, for by dint of practice he afterwards attained proficiency in the art.

## § 31. *Hablot Knight Browne*

However, instead of giving Buss another chance, the publishers cancelled the engagement and looked out for a successor. Among the applicants for the post was William Makepeace Thackeray, who called at Dickens's chambers with specimens of his work. Another applicant was John Leech. The successful candidate, however, was Hablot Knight Browne, a young artist who had just been awarded a Society of Arts Medal for a large and original etching of "John Gilpin"; and a more suitable choice could scarcely have been made. Some of Browne's early plates are signed "Nemo," but later he adopted the well-known pseudonym of Phiz. For Buss's plate "The Cricket Match," was substituted Browne's design, depicting Mr Wardle and his friends under the influence of "the salmon" and for "Tupman and Miss Wardle in the Arbour" another plate representing the same scene; Browne's first real success, however, was the plate depicting Pickwick's introduction to Sam Weller in the yard of the White Hart. As Mr F. G. Kitton says: "Whereas Seymour, so to speak, invented Mr Pickwick, so Browne had the honour of being the first to bring before us the pictorial presentment of the imperturbable Sam, who is here seen in the act of polishing boots."

Sam's special kind of facetiousness is as old as Theocritus, perhaps older. When Gorgo and Praxinoe (Idyll 15) are trying to squeeze into the palace Praxinoe cries, "Come, wretched girl! Burst through. Well done! We are all inside, as the man said when he shut in his bride." The germ, however, out of which grew in Dickens's mind the apt, original and spicy personality of Sam Weller, was probably a two-act farce entitled "The Boarding House; or, Five Hours in Brighton," by Samuel Beazley, first performed in London on 27 August 1811. In it a militia-man, Simon Spatterdash, delivers himself of a number of queer comparisons, such as "I am down upon you, as the extinguisher said to the rushlight." "Let everyone take care of themselves, as the jackass said when he was dancing among the chickens."

Thanks to Samuel Vale, a comic actor of the Surrey Theatre (so well-known to Dickens as a boy), who took the part of Spatterdash, witticisms of this kind became popular and formed part of the stock-in-trade of every London wag. As a humorist, however, Dickens, in narrating the adventures of Sam, gradually developed. He threw off Spatterdashism as Thackeray discarded the poor humour derived from false spelling. We do not laugh at "No, no, reg'lar rotation, as Jack Ketch said when he tied the man up," but when we come to the trial with Mr Justice Stareleigh writing something down "with a pen without any ink in it" and to the medical student chapter with Mr Bob Allen drinking from a funnel with a cork in the narrow end, and all that sort of thing, it is different, and the most stolid bubbles over. In short, the humour of *Pickwick* has three stages: (1) Seymourian burlesque, (2) Spatterdashism, (3) The full-flavoured, indigenous, genial and satirical humour of Dickens.

The popularity of *Pickwick* was unprecedented in the history of fiction. The whole nation laughed over it, talked about it, quoted it. A "profane story" current at the time has often been repeated. A clergyman, it is said, had been administering ghostly consolation to a sick man, and apparently with beneficial effect, but no sooner had he got out of the room than he heard the sick man ejaculate, "Well, thank God, *Pickwick* will be out in ten days anyway!" The publishers made £15,000 profit in three years by the sale of the work in numbers alone, and they presented Dickens at different times with cheques amounting to £3,000 in addition to the stipulated payments. *Pickwick* being a success, Dickens gave up reporting. He says, "I left the reputation behind me of being the best and most rapid reporter ever known. . . . I daresay I am, at this present writing, the best shorthand writer in the world."[1] This, said his friends, was probably the truth.

In May 1836, Mrs Kolle (Anne Beadnell) was near her end, though she had been married only three years. A little before her death she wrote some touching verses entitled *Farewell Bequests*. She leaves her father, to "whose high and stainless reputation" she refers, her diamond ring; to her mother a locket containing one of her auburn curls; to her "sister" her lute, and other gifts to her brothers. Dickens doubtless condoled with Kolle at the time; and when, long after, Maria sent him a copy of these verses he was deeply affected (see § 121). Before the end of the month poor Anne was dead. She left a daughter named after her, Anne. A few years later, Kolle married again.[2]

§ 32. *"Sunday Under Three Heads," June* 1836.
The *"Carlton Chronicle,"* 6 *August* 1836

Early in 1836 was introduced into the House of Commons by Sir Andrew Agnew a bill in which not only all work but also all recreation was prohibited on the Sunday. This provoked Dickens to produce a booklet, *Sunday Under Three Heads: As it is; As Sabbath Bells would make it; As it might be,* with four pages of illustrations by Hablot Knight Browne. It was published by Chapman and Hall, 186 Strand, in June 1836. A reproduction in facsimile was issued in 1884 by J. W. Jarvis and Son, 28 King William Street, Strand. The Dedication, a caustic production, is to Dr Bloomfield, Bishop of London, who "had contemplated Sunday recreations with . . . horror."

The pen-name used by Dickens was *Timothy* Sparks, and it is not without interest that the freelance clergyman,

---

[1] *Letters of Charles Dickens,* 2nd ed., 1880, vol. 1, p. 438.
[2] Kolle died in 1881. His widow, Mrs J. S. Kolle, sold his letters in February 1890.

Timothy Richard Matthews, of Bedford, who frequently carried his activities into London, was by far the best known preacher of the day. Indeed, he was the only one who just then emitted "sparks." Moreover, he was a familiar figure in the Chelsea, Walham Green and Fulham neighbour-hoods, so well-known to Dickens in his courting days.

With much of the booklet, which advocated rational enjoyment of the Sunday, few persons would now dis-approve, but "Timothy Sparks" goes out of his way to throw ridicule both on preacher and worshipper, whether in the fashionable church or the crowded dissenting chapel. Though a clergyman of the Church of England, Matthews preached latterly in Nonconformist places of worship, con-sequently Dickens supposed him to be a Dissenter. No doubt he had Matthews particularly in mind when he wrote, "He grows warmer as he proceeds with his subject and his gesticulation becomes proportionately violent. . . . The congregation murmur their acquiescence in his doctrines; and a short groan occasionally bears testimony to the moving nature of his eloquence." The booklet is a mixture of common sense, unfairness and caricature. However, it did good, for Sir Andrew's impossible bill was thrown out on 18 May 1836 by a majority of 32, and it was never reintroduced into the House. Matthews, besides being the foremost preacher of his day, is also remembered as being the intimate friend of John and Edward FitzGerald.[1]

In *Sunday Under Three Heads,* Dickens attacks all religious bodies, but his antipathy to the Dissenters is particularly marked. They had greatly offended him by their leaning to Sabbatarianism. From this booklet we know how he thought Sunday should be spent. We also know how Nonconformity in those days regarded such doctrines. In *Memories of the Past,* by the Rev. James Griffin, occurs the following reference to Henry Burnett who, with his wife, Dickens's sister, Fanny, worshipped under Griffin at Rusholme Road Chapel, Manchester. "The evenings of the Sunday were usually spent at the house

[1] See *Life of Edward FitzGerald,* 1904, by Thomas Wright; also *Life of the Rev. Timothy Richard Matthews,* 1934, also by Thomas Wright.

of Mr Dickens in a manner which, though strictly moral was not congenial with his feelings." Dickens was aware that in the eyes of Burnett and religionists of the same way of thinking he stood condemned. This to some extent explains how it is that when he depicts the Dissenting minister he is as pitiless as he is unjust. The intemperate preacher in *Sunday Under Three Heads* was only the precursor of the greasy, hypocritical Stiggins in *Pickwick*, the prophesying Melchisedech Howler, formerly of the West India Docks, but "discharged on suspicion of screwing gimlets into puncheons" of *Dombey and Son*; the oily Chadband of *Bleak House* and the yellow-faced Verity Hawkyard in *George Silverman's Explanation*.[1]

Yet there were eloquent and fervent Nonconformist ministers in those days, the cultured Binney, hymn-writer and philanthropist, the pithy and impressive Jay, the erudite Halley, the saintly Angell James. Rowland Hill, eccentric but valiant for truth, was filling Surrey Chapel, the tall figure with black locks of the apostolic Edward Irving, "so tall that it seemed as if it would never finish rising," was well known in Regent's Square. But Dickens saw only one side of the picture. In 1836 he was drawing the hypocritical Stiggins, in 1868 the blasphemous Hawkyard. One denomination alone he spared—the Unitarians. Them, moreover, he eulogised, life through. The style of the pamphlet bears a remarkable resemblance to that of Washington Irving. The description of the cricket match might have been taken bodily from the *Sketch Book*.

In July 1836 Dickens tried to place his brother Frederick in Macrone's office. "If," he wrote to Macrone, "you will give him a stool, he shall sit himself upon it forthwith," but Frederick never did any good there or indeed any good anywhere, life through. He was his father's own son—a chip of the old Micawber. On 6 August 1836 appeared in the *Carlton Chronicle* an article by Dickens headed *Leaves from an unpublished volume by Boz (which will be torn out once a fortnight) The Hospital Patient*. The second article, *Hackney Cabs and their Drivers*, appeared on 17 September. Two

[1] Cr. ed., vol. 15, p. 615.

other of his sketches were printed in this periodical during October, but they were lifted without permission from the *Morning Chronicle*.[1]

§ 33. *"The Strange Gentleman,"* 29 *September* 1836; *and "Village Coquettes,"* 6 *December* 1836

In 1836 terminated finally Dickens's connection with the gallery of the House of Commons. Among his friends was John Pritt Harley, a comedian, who won laurels as Launcelot Gobbo, and who on account of his equable temper and merry disposition was a general favourite both on and off the stage. At Harley's request, Dickens wrote a farce *The Strange Gentleman*, founded on his sketch "The Great Winglebury Duel."[2] *The Strange Gentleman*, first performed 29 September 1836, at St James's Theatre, sets forth like Goldsmith's comedy, which no doubt suggested it, the mistakes of a night; the various characters arriving at an inn with different objects being led into a series of misconceptions as to one another's identity. Dickens, who was in after years ashamed of this production, used strong language when questioned concerning it, and devoutly wished it to be forgotten. However, it ran for seventy nights, Dickens received £150 for it, and Braham the tenor singer, manager of the theatre, was satisfied. A poor play, it contains one respectable jest. When asked respecting the health of the Strange Gentleman, Tom the waiter said, "He was very boisterous half an hour ago, but I punched his head a little, and now he's uncommon comfortable."

A month earlier Dickens's friend, John Pyke Hullah,[3] had set to music a portion of an opera, to be called "The Gondolier," and it occurred to him that he and Dickens might profitably join forces. Dickens "in a fit of damnable

---

[1] The *Dickensian*, 1 March 1934, p. 111. Article by Mr Walter Dexter.

[2] *Sketches by Boz*. Cr. ed., p. 305.

[3] John Pyke Hullah 1813–1884, the pioneer of music for the people. His life, written by his wife, appeared in 1886. For letters of Dickens to him, see the *Dickensian*, 1933.

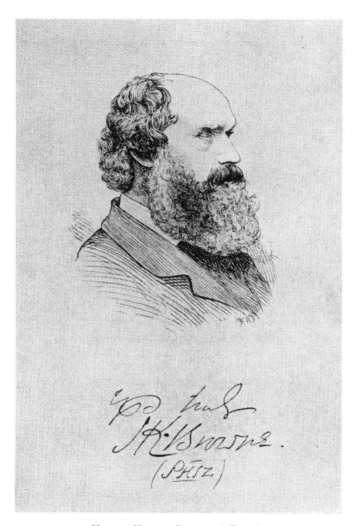

HABLOT KNIGHT BROWNE ("PHIZ")

See page 87

GEORGE CRUIKSHANK

*Engraved by D. J. Pound from a Photo by C. Watkins*

See page 95

good nature" (whether for £150 or not is unrecorded) agreed to do the writing part, desiring only that Hullah would drop the Venetian idea, observing "while I am at home in England, I am in Venice abroad indeed." So the title was changed to *The Village Coquettes*. It was accepted by Braham, to whom we are told Mr Hogarth had spoken highly of Dickens's literary work, and played for the first time on 6 December 1836 at the St James's Theatre, the piece itself and the words of the songs being by "Boz," the music by John Hullah. Of this play, the presentation of which was assisted by an "impolitic and injudicious band of clacquers" (paid applauders), Dickens was also afterwards ashamed. "If," he said, "in an exhibition of bluster, caught from his friend Landor," I thought there was a copy of it in my house and I could not destroy it in any other way, I would burn down that part of the house which contained it. He wrote in similar strain to Hullah as late as 8 May 1866.

All the same, it would be folly for the student of Dickens to disregard these early ventures. *The Village Coquettes* took its title from two village girls, Lucy and Rose, who, led away by vanity, coquetted with men above their station (Lucy with Squire Norton and Rose with a certain Honourable Sparkins Flam) and flouted their humble though faithful lovers. Before too late the girls discover their error.

On the same evening, 6 December 1836, was played [1] for the "59th time" *The Strange Gentleman*. On this occasion, as earlier, the Strange Gentleman was John Pritt Harley. Others who took parts were a Miss Rainforth, a Miss Julia Smith,[2] a very plump lady, and Madame Sala, mother of George Augustus. Squire Norton's song in *The Village*

[1] For facsimile of the play-bill see the *Dickensian*, 1 December 1833, p. 16. On the same play-bill *The Savage Gentleman* is announced to be performed for the 50th time.

[2] For coloured portraits of her (as Mary Wilson) and Miss Kitty Smith (Fanny Wilson) see *The Savage Gentleman*, privately printed by W. Miller, 43 Spelman Street, London, E.1. This work also contains a coloured portrait of J. P. Harley.

*Coquettes*, sung by Braham and addressed to Lucy, quite upset the painfully modest Miss Rainforth and the equally modest Miss Julia Smith, to whom were assigned the parts respectively of Lucy and Rose, especially the verse,

> A Winter's night has its delight,
> Well warmed to bed we go:
> A Winter's day, we're blithe and gay
> Snipe shooting in the snow.

Dickens writing to Hullah said:

> I . . . cannot consent to give up (what I consider) the best verse in the best song in the whole piece.   If the young ladies are especially horrified at the bare notion of anybody's going to bed, I have no objection to substitute for the objectionable line,
>
> > Around, old stories go.
>
> But you may respectfully signify to Cramer's that I will see them d—d before I make any further alteration . . .   We ought not to emasculate the very spirit of a song to suit boarding schools.[1]

Eventually the bashful ladies gave way, and Miss Rainforth and the over-plump Miss Julia Smith endured (not without blushes) the declaration,

> Well warmed to bed we go.

A two-columned notice of the play which appeared in the *Examiner* of 11 December was probably written by John Forster.   The clacquers at the close of the play screamed loudly for Boz, who appeared, bowed, smiled, and disappeared; and left the audience in perfect consternation because he had neither Mr Pickwick's corporation nor Mr Tupman's large circular eyes; and the critics in the gallery considered that they had not received their money's worth because he lacked the jaunty air of Sam Weller.   The first run of the piece ended on 24 December.   On 11 April and subsequently Mr Henry Burnett (described as "of the Theatre Royal, Edinburgh") sang in place of Mr Braham. This was Burnett's first appearance on a London Stage.[2]

[1] Maggs's Catalogue, No. 551, p. 57.
[2] See the *Dickensian*, December 1833, p. 19.

§ 34. *"Sketches by Boz," second series, 17 December 1836. First Fruits of Humour. Cruikshank's Pictures*

Early in 1837 Macrone published a second series of *Sketches by Boz*, the preface being dated 17 December 1836. The work, which was in one volume, was also illustrated by Cruikshank. What a tyro Dickens was at the time in the art of writing is evinced by his shocking habit of commencing a would-be comical sketch by stating that something funny was coming. He makes a preamble about the amusing things that are to follow and then frequently says nothing that provokes even a smile. Furthermore, he calls people vulgar, ignorant, selfish, shrewd, simple, mean, lazy. Later, when he became more of an artist, his characters required no labelling. Yet there are distinct indications that he was already beyond the ordinary run of writers; for the book is not without its scintillations of genuine humour— of that unforced sort in which he outdistanced all his contemporaries. For instance:

*The Governess at Astley's.* Then it was providentially discovered that one of the little boys was seated behind a pillar and could not see, so the governess was stuck behind the pillar and the boy lifted into her place.

*No formality.* Three or four chairs were pulled out of their places, and a corresponding number of books carefully upset, in order that there might be a due absence of formality.

*Scrubbing.* The second floor was scrubbed and washed and flannelled till the wet went through to the drawing-room ceiling.

*A Pin in the Baby.* It is not fever, as I apprehended, but a small pin, which nurse accidentally stuck in his leg yesterday evening.

The boy of thirteen in the chapter entitled "Criminal Courts" is the prototype of the "Artful Dodger." The Parish Beadle blossomed into Mr Bumble. The story entitled "The Black Veil" had the honour to be praised by Edgar Allan Poe. Though there are clever touches in *Sketches by Boz*, yet it is owing to the pencil of Cruikshank rather than to the pen of Boz that one at the present day turns to this book, which by Cruikshank's plates is not merely saved—it is immortalised. "Monmouth Street,"

"The Pawnbroker's Shop," "The Broker's Man," to mention only a few, are unforgettable. It is only fair, however, to note that Cruikshank was a man in his prime, his age being 44, while Dickens was only 24.

Mary Hogarth used to accompany Dickens when he called at 3 St James's Square to see Macrone. The following unpublished letter, written by John Strang, who was acquainted with both Dickens and Macrone, contains interesting references to Mary, to Ainsworth and to Dickens himself. It is written to Macrone and dated 2 January 1837.

I have read also *Rookwood*. It is a powerful piece of limning. It has given me a very high notion of Ainsworth not only as a painter and a poet, but as a philosopher. He does not content himself with looking mainly at the surface of humanity, but likes to discover the secret springs of human action. I see you and he are about to give the Public an account of the Lions of London. Our acquaintance "Boz" seems also not to be sleeping. His name appears to irradiate at least three publishers' lists. How does his pretty little sister-in-law get on? She is a sweet, interesting creature. I wonder some two-legged monster does not carry her off. It might save many a yonker losing his night's rest.

Macrone had in his office a number of busts of distinguished persons, including one of himself, presented to him by Mr Strang. Apparently he had one also of Mr John Sadleir, M.P., the original of Mr Merdle in *Little Dorrit*. At any rate another friend of Macrone's, J. R. Slater, asks for a cast of it. He says Mr Angus Fletcher, a maker of busts, who resides at Oxton near Tadcaster "expects to get a commission from Leeds for one."[1] With Fletcher Dickens, who dubbed him "Kindheart," formed a friendship and they were often in each other's company. Another writer whom Dickens met at Macrone's and with whom he formed a friendship was Mr William Jerdan.[2]

[1] The W. C. Edwards Collection of Unpublished Letters written to Macrone.
[2] William Jerdan, 1782–1869. It was he who seized Bellingham, the murderer of Spencer Percival, in the lobby of the House of Commons, 11 May 1812. He published his autobiography in 1852–3 and *Men I have known* in 1866.

§ 35. *Dickens's eldest son born 6 January 1837.*
*"Pickwick" continues to run its victorious course*

On 6 January 1837 was born Dickens's eldest son,
christened Charles Culliford Boz, Charles after his father,
Culliford after the maiden surname of his grandmother—
Mrs Charles Barrow.   Month after month *Pickwick* had
been running its victorious course.   Its success was amazing.   It outdistanced anything done by Dickens's contemporaries Ainsworth and Lytton.   Nothing so original in the
way of fiction had for many years left the press.   Yet it owed
something to its predecessors.

The influence of Washington Irving, so conspicuous in
Dickens's earlier work, is in this book scarcely noticeable.
Apparently, however, Mr Winkle owed his name to the
more famous sportsman Rip Van Winkle; and Gabriel
Grub, with his fondness for Hollands and his reappearance
after ten years, seems to be the same old friend slightly
disguised.   Pickwick has more indebtedness to Smollett
than to Irving.   He has his Sam, just as Roderick Random
had his Strap and Peregrine Pickle his Pipes.   Apparently
Mr Pickwick would not have got into the Fleet, and Sam
would not have acted as he did, had not their predecessors
Peregrine Pickle, Hatchway and Pipes undergone certain
well-known experiences in that prison.   The rollicking
humour of Smollett found a sympathiser in Dickens, and
many of the scenes in *Pickwick* are in the Scotchman's rough-
and-tumble style.   To Fielding he is less indebted; but if
Dickens imitated the virtues of his great predecessors he
imitated also their vices.   "That punctual servant the sun,"
for example, is precisely the style of Fielding's inflated intro-
ductions, and he followed Fielding in the vicious habit of
inserting wheels within wheels.   In *Pickwick* there are no
fewer than eight interpolatory stories, all dull, and none
having any particular connection with the text.   Here and
there are reminders of Sterne.   Dickens admired Sterne
and declared that he knew every word of *The Sentimental
Journey*,[1] but Sterne's delicate touch he never acquired.

[1] *The Holly Tree Inn*, Christmas No., 1855.   Cr. ed., vol. 15, p. 24.

Resemblances have also been traced between *Pickwick* and *Don Quixote*. Pickwick, like the Spaniard, sallies forth to redress grievances. Sam, like his prototype Sancho, is always ready "with a quaint and homely common-sense view to contrast with the flighty visions of his master." Mr Percy Fitzgerald in his *Pickwickian Manners and Customs* points out some interesting parallels between Pickwick and Boswell's *Life of Johnson*, one of Dickens's favourite books. Johnson and Pickwick had the same christian name, both founded clubs, both had devoted followers, and curiously it is mentioned in Boswell that Johnson had a friend named Weller. Both Johnson and Pickwick frequented the Borough. Against Mrs Bardell and Mr Wardle can be set Mrs Thrale and the hospitable Rev. John Taylor. Boswell's story of the unlucky gentleman who died from a surfeit of crumpets is served up with embellishments in *Pickwick*. Winkle often suggests Boswell, and he is treated by Pickwick with as great rudeness as was Boswell by the ponderous Samuel.

In a little work, *The Law and Lawyers of Pickwick*, Mr (afterwards Sir) Frank Lockwood, Q.C., points out that Dickens, who at one time intended to pursue a legal education, and had kept a term or two at one of the Inns of Court, presents us in *Pickwick* with three types of the practising solicitor or attorney, namely Mr Perker, Messrs Dodson and Fogg and Mr Pell; and, after remarking that the Trial chapter in Pickwick is meant for broad fun amounting to burlesque and nothing more, he goes on to say that the remarkable forensic effort of Sergeant Buzfuz stands to-day as perhaps the best-known speech ever delivered at the Bar. Mr Lockwood also points out that many of the reforms in our legal administration were brought about in part by the humour, courage and industry of Dickens.

## § 36. *Originals of Pickwick Persons*

Among those who read *Pickwick* and spoke proudly of Dickens's fame was the portly schoolmaster, Mr William Jones, of Wellington House memory. He died shortly after, and was buried in the churchyard of old St Pancras, only, however, to be resurrected by his old pupil and enshrined in *David Copperfield* as Mr Creakle. In *St Pancras Notes and Queries* (article No. 71) is an account of Mr Jones's school by John Leighton, F.S.A., who was there ten years after Dickens left, that is just before Jones's death.

The inscription on the tomb ran:

Sacred to the memory of

Mr William Jones,

for many years master of a respectable school in this parish, who departed this life on the 20th day of January 1836, aged 50 years. The inflexible integrity of his character and the social and domestic virtues which shadowed his private life, will long be cherished in the recollection of all those who knew him.

So carefully has *Pickwick* been studied that even its errors have been tabulated. Here are a few:

(1) When Winkle had his embarrassing experience with Mrs Dowler and the sedan chair in Royal Crescent, Bath, he afterwards "tore round the crescent hotly pursued by Dowler," he kept ahead and "the door was open as he came round the second time." But it was not possible to tear "round" Royal Crescent.[1] When anybody got to the end of it he had to turn and retrace his steps.

(2) In Chapter 2, Mr Jingle, talking in 1827, relates how he took part in the Revolution of 1830.

(3) In Chapter 52, Mr Weller, senior, signs himself "Tony Veller" and his second wife leaves in her will the bulk of her property to "Tony Weller," but previously, in Chapter 33,[2] Mr Weller, senior, gives the latest bulletin about his second wife and adds "signed upon oath, S. Veller Esquire, senior." Dickens evidently started out with the intention of making father and son possess the name of Samuel and afterwards forgot all about it. But in the way of being responsible for anachronisms and forgetfulnesses Dickens sinned in good company—that of Shakespeare and Cervantes.

[1] See plan, Snowden Ward, p. 100.    [2] Cr. ed., vol. 1, p. 360.

The following notes on the originals of the personages in
*Pickwick* are of interest:

*Bardell, Mrs.* A Mrs Ann Ellis who kept an eating-house
near Doctors' Commons.

*Buzfuz.* Mr Sergeant Bompas, an eminent counsel at the
time.

*Dodson, Fogg, Ramsey, Wicks, Bullman.* These names were
to be seen on shops in Camberwell Green and neighbourhood in those days.

*Jingle.* Mr Potter, clerk at Ellis and Blackmore's.

*Joe the Fat Boy.* James Budden, whose father kept the Red
Lion, Chatham.

*Nupkins.* Mr Laing, the London magistrate. Also
figures in *Oliver Twist*.

*Old Nobs.* Moses James Nobs, the last of the mail-coach
guards.

*Stareleigh.* Mr Justice Sir Stephen Gazelee who died in
1839.

*Weller, Senior* (Tony). Old Chumley who drove the stage
daily from Rochester to London. Mrs Lynn Linton
describes him in the *Fortnightly Review*, November
1885.

*Weller, Junior* (Sam). Job Baldwin, whose grave is in the
churchyard of Rainham, is held by some to have been
the original of Sam Weller. Canon Benham, however
(*Dickens and Kent*), expressed himself as doubtful about
the story and Mr Matz (*Dickensian*, September 1907)
"was inclined to the Sam Vale identification." [1]

In 1827 had died Frederick Augustus, Duke of York, and
the event reminded the public of that prince's connection
with Mary Anne Clarke. He was accused in the House of
Commons of giving promotion to officers on the recommendation of Mary Anne, whose courage and sauciness at
the time became a proverb. Dickens had evidently read the
"Minutes of Evidence in the case as to Mrs Clarke and
H.R.H. the Duke of York" published in 1809,[2] for four of

[1] See § 31.
[2] When the Duke of York died, in 1827, interest in the case was
revived.

THE LEATHER BOTTLE, COBHAM

*Photo by J. Graham, 17 Ordnance Terrace, Chatham*

See page 101

COBHAM HALL

*Photo by J. Graham, 17 Ordnance Terrace, Chatham*

See page 101

the characters in *Pickwick* have names taken from those of the witnesses examined in that *cause célèbre* before the committee of the House of Commons, Mrs Mary Anne Clarke, Colonel Wardle, M.P., Mr William Dowler and Mr Thomas Lowten. Sam's mother-in-law was the quondam relict and sole executrix of the dead-and-gone Mr Clarke.[1] Was not Mr Wardle the genial occupier of Manor Farm, Dingley Dell? Who does not know the blustering coward Captain Dowler, the captain's blushing wife and puffy-faced young Lowten, clerk to Mr Perker, Pickwick's attorney.

## § 37. *The Leather Bottle at Cobham*

Of the places mentioned in *Pickwick*, one, the Leather Bottle at Cobham, calls for special mention. After the return of the Pickwickians to Dingley Dell with the runaway Miss Wardle, Mr Tupman fled from an odious world and buried himself at Cobham.

Mr Pickwick, and his other two friends, then bade adieu to the Wardles, procured at Muggleton a conveyance to Rochester and thence made their way on foot to Cobham. Their walk lay through a deep and shady wood whence they emerged upon an open park and in sight of a picturesque Elizabethan house—Cobham Hall, the seat of Lord Darnley. Having been directed to the Leather Bottle, a clean and commodious village alehouse, the three travellers entered and at once enquired for a gentleman of the name of Tupman. A stout country lad opened a door at the end of the passage and the travellers entered a long low-roofed room, furnished with a large number of high-backed, leather-cushioned chairs of fantastic shapes. The walls were embellished with a great variety of old portraits and roughly coloured prints. At the upper end of the room was a table, covered with a white cloth and loaded with a roast fowl, bacon, ale and etceteras. At the table sat Mr Tupman, looking as unlike a man who had taken his leave of the world as possible.

After Mr Tupman had finished his dinner, the four

[1] Cr. ed., vol. I, p. 292.

friends walked in the churchyard, where the disconsolate lover was prevailed upon to abandon the idea of a life of solitude; and shortly after, Mr Pickwick made the archæological discovery which turned out to be nothing more wonderful than "Bill Stumps, his mark."

The Leather Bottle stands much as it did when Mr Pickwick visited it, for although it once caught fire, the "low-roofed room" to which all Dickens lovers pilgrimage fortunately escaped injury. To this quaint little inn Dickens came again and again, and Cobham village always had pleasant memories for him. As to where Muggleton was, Dickens students differ. Some favour Maidstone, and Maidstone was certainly "a corporate town," but Canon Benham (*Dickens and Kent*) is certain that it was not Maidstone. Mr W. R. Hughes hesitatingly suggested Town Malling, which, however, has never been "a corporate town." Mr Leonard Miller, who knew every inch of North Kent, writing on 21 March 1898, says as to these towns: "There is at least one fatal objection to every place that can be named." Mr H. Snowden Ward, *The Real Dickens Land*, says, "Almost certainly the place depicted as Manor Farm, Dingley Dell, was Cob Tree Hall, Sandling, near Maidstone."

## § 38. *Pickwickian Humour*

In an earlier paragraph it was mentioned that the humour of *Pickwick* is of three kinds (see § 31). The first two, Seymourian burlesque and Spatterdashism, may be dismissed without another thought; but of the third kind, the real Dickensian brand, a few examples may be given, though it must be borne in mind that their richness is of necessity partly lost by their severance from the context:

*Their Occupation.* What are these lads for? enquired Mr Pickwick abruptly. He was rather alarmed; for he was not quite certain but that the distress of the agricultural interest, about which he had often heard a great deal, might have compelled the small boys, attached to the soil, to earn a precarious and hazardous subsistence by making marks of themselves for inexperienced sportsmen.

It appears, however, that they were there only to start the game.

*Making believe.* And sure enough my father walks arter him, like a tame monkey behind a horgan, into a little back office, vere a feller sat among dirty papers and tin boxes, making believe he was busy.

*Mr Justice Stareleigh.* The silence woke Mr Justice Stareleigh, who immediately wrote down something with a pen without any ink in it, and looked unusually profound, to impress the jury with the belief that he always thought most deeply with his eyes shut.

*The Dirtiest One.* "I don't rightly know which is your brother, Miss," replied Sam. "Is it the dirtiest vun o' the two?" "Yes, yes, Mr Weller," returned Arabella, "go on. Make haste, pray."

*Sam is obliging.* "It may seem very strange talkin' to me about these here affairs, Miss," said Sam with great vehemence, "but all I can say is, that I'm not only ready but villin' to do anythin' as'll make matters agreeable; and if chuckin' either o' them Sawbones out o' winder 'ull do it, I'm the man."

*Pickwick* has its flaws, but everything can be forgiven for its abundant flow of humour. We turn once more to its pages—the shadows pass before us—Mr Pickwick, his three friends, the facetious Sam, his ample father, the Fat Boy, the dissipated medical students, Mrs Bardell, Messrs Dodson and Fogg, and a long line of minor personages, enough to people a village. Again we sit round the rousing fire at Dingley Dell, again we philander with the spinster aunt in the honeysuckle bower; again we find our lost friend at The Leather Bottle, again we take part in the spirited contest at Eatanswill—again we eat buttered muffins with Mrs Weller; again we travel with "Sawyer, late Nockemorf" waving a crimson silk pocket-handkerchief—the rag-tag of Bristol in our wake; and finally we settle down to the enjoyment of a well-earned retirement in the pleasant suburb of Dulwich. After which we refresh our memory once more with Phiz's wonderful pictures.

It is sometimes forgotten that Dickens attempted a sequel to *Pickwick* [1]—a fragment which was used as a kind of introduction to *Master Humphrey's Clock*. Pickwick and

[1] Cr. ed., vol. 15, p. 465.

the two Wellers are revived, and a third Weller is added, Sam's little boy. But it was a dreary failure, and Dickens very wisely after a few pages gave the trio Christian burial. Several other men of prominence had by the time that *Pickwick* was becoming famous been drawn into the Dickens circle. One was Sergeant (afterwards Judge) Talfourd, who revised for his friend the scene Bardell *v.* Pickwick. To him the work was dedicated. Another was the artist Daniel Maclise. Among those who received presentation copies of the *Pickwick Papers* as they came out was Mary Hogarth. No. 1 is inscribed "Mary Hogarth from hers most affy. Charles Dickens," and each of the numbers 2 to 14 is similarly autographed.[1]

## § 39. *"Bentley's Miscellany" and "The Mudfog Papers," January* 1837. *"Oliver Twist," February* 1837

Dickens next made arrangements to write for Mr Macrone a novel to be entitled "Gabriel Vardon, the Locksmith of London," and it was advertised in December 1836, among that publisher's "Books preparing for publication." Dickens and Macrone, however, could not come to terms, so the book was withdrawn from him and put, as will be presently seen, into the hands of another firm. In *Barnaby Rudge* Gabriel Varden (spelt with an "e") is one of the characters.

At the end of 1836 George Hogarth introduced Dickens to Richard Bentley of New Burlington Street, successor to the publisher Henry Colburn.[2] Bentley was short, pinkfaced, heavily whiskered and bristly haired. He had a strong character and was daring in his plans, which usually succeeded. It was this smart business-like quality that drew Dickens to him. No one advertised more brilliantly than Dickens when he was about to publish a new story. His orange-coloured bills printed in red and black, six feet long, were seen everywhere.

[1] *The First Editions of Charles Dickens*, by John C. Eckel. Chapman and Hall, 1913.
[2] Henry Colburn's widow married Dickens's friend John Forster.

Bentley had in mind a new magazine and he appointed Dickens editor at £20 a month, increased later to £30. At first they thought of calling it *The Wit's Miscellany*. Bentley told Barham, whose *Ingoldsby Legends* were to appear in the new venture, of the proposed change. "Instead of *The Wit's Miscellany*," he said, "I have determined to call it *Bentley's Miscellany*." "Would not that be going to the other extreme!" remarked Barham slyly. Bentley,[1] however, could appreciate a jest, and the Magazine made its bow on 2 January 1837.

Dickens's contribution to the first number consisted of "The Public Life of Mr Tulrumble," the opening sketch of a series which received the name of *The Mudfog Papers*— skits upon the Royal Association, supposed to meet at Mudfog (Chatham). The adventures are recorded of a wealthy coal merchant of that town—Mr Tulrumble, who while absent in London at the Lord Mayor's banquet, learns that he has been elected Mayor of Mudfog. Brimful of the Lord Mayor's Show he determines to have a similar celebration in his native town. The fun which, however, is feeble, is intermingled with an account of Mr Tulrumble's efforts to work a reformation in the morals of the town.[2] In the February number was commenced the story *Oliver Twist*. To the third number George Hogarth contributed an article on Beaumarchais, for he too had a nimble pen—Dickens's contributions being, besides the continuation of *Oliver Twist*, "The Pantomime of Life" and "Some Particulars concerning a Lion."

In February 1837 Dickens, his wife (this time Mary Hogarth accompanying them) again spent a few days at Mrs Nash's cottage, Chalk. His principal object seems to have been to renew acquaintance with his youthful haunts. He had invited Beard to stay with him there from Saturday,

[1] For articles on Bentley, see the *Dickensian*, vol. 3, February and March 1907. They are by Percy Fitzgerald.

[2] To *The Mudfog Papers* Cruikshank contributed three drawings: "Ned Trigger in the Kitchen at Mudfog Hall," "The Tyrant Sowster" and "The Automatic Police Officer." See the *Dickensian*, vol. 2, May 1906, p. 122.

25 February to Monday, 27 February. On the Saturday
he, Mrs Dickens, Mary and Beard set off "to Chatham to
inspect the fortifications," and they had "a snug little dinner
together" at The Sun. On the Sunday, Dickens was
engaged to dine at the Marine Barracks, so he was obliged
to leave Beard "for a few hours with the ladies and the
cigars."

§ 40. *"Is She His Wife."* *First performed* 6 *March* 1837

By this time Dickens had written a third burletta *Is She
His Wife.* In a letter to John Pritt Harley he said he would
be willing "to sell to Mr Braham the acting copyright" for a
hundred pounds, and this was apparently what Hullah paid
for it. The play was performed at St James's Theatre on
6 March 1837, the principal part, Felix Tapkins, a flirting
bachelor, being taken by Harley, the part of Mrs Peter
Limbury by Madame Sala, mother of the better-known
George Augustus.

The interesting feature of the play is the fact that it
throws light on Dickens's private life. Mr Lovetown is
Dickens, Mrs Lovetown, Mrs Dickens. They had already
begun the bickering which eventually ended so sadly.
Here are some citations:

*Mrs Lovetown:* "I wish, Alfred, you would endeavour to assume
a more cheerful appearance in your wife's society. If you are perpetually yawning and complaining of ennui a few months after
marriage, what am I to suppose you'll become in a few years!"

*Mr Lovetown:* "The fact is, my love, I'm tired of the country—
green fields and blooming hedges and feathered songsters are fine
things to talk about, and write about, but I candidly confess I prefer
paved streets, area railings and dustman's bells after all."

*Mrs Lovetown:* "How often have you told me that blessed with
my love you could live contented and happy in a desert." (As he
pays no attention to her she continues.) "Have you heard what
I have just been saying, dear."

*Mr Lovetown:* "Yes, love."

*Mrs Lovetown:* "And what can you say in reply?"

*Mr Lovetown:* "Why really, my dear, you've said it so often that
I think it quite unnecessary to say anything more about it." (*Aside*)

I could put up with anything rather than these petty quarrels. "I repeat, my dear, that I am very dull in this out-of-the-way villa—confoundedly dull, and horribly dull."

*Mrs Lovetown:* "If you took any pleasure in your wife's society, or felt for her as you once professed to feel, you would have no cause to make such a complaint."

*Mr. Lovetown:* "If I did not know you to be one of the sweetest creatures in existence, my dear, I should be strongly disposed to say that you were a very close imitation of an aggravating female."

*Mrs Lovetown:* "That's very curious, my dear, for I declare that if I hadn't known you to be such an exquisite, good-tempered, attentive husband, I should have mistaken you for a very great brute———"

*Mr Lovetown:* "My dear, you're offensive."

*Mrs Lovetown:* "My love, you're intolerable."

*(They turn their chairs back to back.)*

This was written the year of Dickens's marriage, with recollections of the bored period of the honeymoon in the out-of-the-way village of Chalk, and the eagerness with which Dickens returned to the sights and sounds of the beloved Town. Mrs Dickens also recalled her life at Chelsea which was then as we have seen almost country. A writer in the *Mirror* in 1833 refers to its avenues of limes and chestnut trees. It was remarkable for its tulip gardens and nurseries, but "proverbial for its dulness." The blushing Miss Sophy Wackles (*Old Curiosity Shop*) lived at Chelsea and the bashful Mr Cheggs who stole her from Dick Swiveller was a market gardener.[1] *Is She His Wife* reflects the bickerings that thus early disturbed the peace of Dickens's married life.

Mr Felix Tapkins in the play is also a lover of the country where on a fine summer's evening "the frogs hop off the grass plot into the sitting-room . . . and the stables are close to the dining-room window. . . . The horse can't cough but I hear him." Here again we gave recollections of the farm house at Chalk and the amenities of Chelsea. In short, anybody may have the country if Dickens can have the town. Later Mrs Lovetown says to her husband, "How little did I think when I married you, six short

[1] Cr. ed., vol. 7, p. 53.

months since, that I should be exposed to so much wretchedness." And *Is She His Wife* was written just six months after Dickens's marriage.

But the town would have been endurable enough to Mrs Dickens if her husband had been more considerate and accommodating, and had been less outrageously eulogistic of her sister Mary (for he had already begun this excessive praise); but hearing a sister's virtues trumpeted in season and out of season, with never a word for those of a wife, would have made any place to any woman difficult to endure.

As late as 10 August 1848 Dickens was writing from Broadstairs: "Mrs Dickens being in an *un*interesting condition, has besought me to bring her out of that stagnant air of London for two months, and here we are accordingly." Later, Dickens produced another play, a farce entitled *The Lamplighter* [1] written in 1838 but never acted. In 1841 he converted this farce into a humorous narrative called *The Lamplighter's Story*. [2] The four burlettas mentioned were the only plays written entirely by Dickens. Long after he collaborated heavily with Mark Lemon in *Mr Nightingale's Diary*, 1855, and with Wilkie Collins in *The Frozen Deep*, 1857, and *No Thoroughfare* in 1867. A book entitled *The Plays and Poems of Charles Dickens* (2 vols.) was issued in 1882 by Mr Richard Horne Shepherd, but was withdrawn a few weeks after publication owing to copyright difficulties.

## § 41. *Death of Mary Hogarth*, 7 *March* 1837

Dickens's adoration of Mary Hogarth—the expression is not too strong—was the commencement of his marital ruin. She was not pretty, she was even plain, as anybody can see from her portrait by Phiz. Personally indeed she was far less attractive than his wife. The portrait shows her hair in hard curves, and the face entirely lacks the winsome-

---

[1] Dickens's plays, *The Strange Gentleman*, No. 466; *The Village Coquettes*, No. 467; *Is She His Wife*, No. 470; *The Lamplighter*, also No. 470, are included in Dicks' Standard plays.
[2] Included in Ward Lock & Co.'s book *The Mudfog Society*.

MARY SCOTT HOGARTH

*From a Painting by H. K. Browne ("Phiz"), 1837*

*Photo by T. W. Tyrrell*

See page 108

GRAVES OF MARY HOGARTH AND GEORGE THOMSON, THE FRIEND
AND CORRESPONDENT OF BURNS, KENSAL GREEN CEMETERY

*Photo by Lionel F. Gowing*

See pages 108 and 216

ness of Mrs Dickens as revealed in the Maclise portrait. The difference in their ages was not great, Mrs Dickens being 22, Mary 17. But Mary was gentle and engaging in manners. Her health was delicate. She was dazzled by the genius of her gifted brother-in-law. He exhausted the vocabulary in her praise. He lived in the light of her smiles and the odour of the incense she offered. Mrs Dickens was not of a jealous disposition, but she resented, as would any wife, being relegated to the background, and so soon too.

Then came a thunderclap. On Saturday night, 6 March 1837, Dickens and his wife, Dickens's father and mother and Mary were at the St James's Theatre. On their return to Furnival's Inn, Mary was suddenly taken ill and she died at five o'clock on the Sunday afternoon in Dickens's arms. The blow came upon Dickens like a park of artillery. He declared that he never could or would separate his spirit from hers. He records his "deep and severe" distress in a letter written on the Sunday night to Edward Chapman of Chapman and Hall and on 8 March to a friend, George Cox, who was associated with him when he was producing *The Strange Gentleman*.[1] To the latter he said, "A sister of Mrs Dickens, a young and lovely girl, who has been the grace and ornament of our home for the whole time of our marriage, died here yesterday."

His wail of anguish is heard for years. Such was the shock to him that he could not continue his work. The publication of *The Pickwick Papers* was suspended for two months. *Oliver Twist* was also interrupted. She lies in Kensal Green Cemetery, and on her tombstone is the epitaph written by Dickens:

> Young, beautiful and good
> God in His mercy numbered her
> With His angels at the early age
> Of seventeen.

He hoped to be buried beside her, and long after he could write, "I don't think there ever was love like I bear

---

[1] In an earlier undated letter Dickens speaks of a likeness of Cox to be done by H. K. Browne as an illustration to *The Strange Gentleman*.

her." Reading this and remembering that he possessed a delightful, if capricious wife, one pardonably loses, notwithstanding Dickens's marvellous gifts as a writer, all patience with him. Mrs Hogarth on 26 October 1837 sent him as a present a chain made of Mary's hair. Had Mary lived to that day she would have been 18. After expressing the sorrowful pleasure he would take in wearing it, and how highly he would prize it, he said: "I have never had her ring off my finger day or night, except for an instant at a time, to wash my hands, since she died. I have never had her sweetness and excellence absent from my mind so long."

After describing her later as "the gentlest and purest creature that ever shed a light on earth," he continues: "I wish you could know how I weary for the three rooms in Furnival's Inn and how I miss that pleasant smile and those sweet words which, bestowed upon our evening's work, in our merry banterings round the fire, were more precious to me than the applause of a whole world would be. I can recall everything she said and did in those happy days, and could show you every passage and line we read together." In a fragment of a diary which is now preserved at South Kensington, he writes under date 1 January 1838: "A sad New Year's Day in one respect, for at the opening of last year poor Mary was with us." Of the apotheosis of Mary Hogarth in that threnody, *The Old Curiosity Shop*, we shall speak later.

The following notice appeared in *Bentley's Miscellany* on 1 June. "Since the appearance of the last number of this work the editor has to mourn the sudden death of a very dear young relative to whom he was most affectionately attached and whose society had been for a long time the chief solace to his labours." This paragraph would alone have shown how affairs had been going on in his home. It was right of him to be attached to Mary Hogarth, but surely "the *chief* solace of his labours" should have been his own wife, who certainly in spite of the unevenness of her temperament was really attached to him, and could, had Dickens been more tactful, have been a veritable helpmate.

It was mentioned earlier that a copy of *The Pickwick*

*Papers* Nos. 1 to 14 is in existence with Dickens's autograph inscription to Mary Hogarth on each number, No. 14 being the May issue.[1]   As Mary Hogarth died on 7 March the April and May numbers must have been in Dickens's hands *before* that date.   The fifteenth part has the signature of George Hogarth.   The remaining twenty parts were given to Miss R. T. Walker, an intimate friend of Mary.[2]   In May 1837 Dickens went for a change of scene to Collins's Farm, North End, Hampstead,[3]—a house, now called "Wyldes," which had been the home of John Linnell and one of the haunts of William Blake.

## § 42.  *John Forster*

About this time Dickens first met, in the house of Harrison Ainsworth, the man of letters who was destined to become his biographer, John Forster.   An honest, good-hearted, high-minded soul, of the same age as Dickens, Forster, who had massive features, a solemn countenance and a broad intellectual forehead, had just before attracted notice by a series of vigorous political articles in the London *Examiner*, and as a rising man he was worth knowing.

To his superiors he was oleaginous, with his equals pompous, with his inferiors haughty.   A cabman once referred to him as "the harbitary gent."   His high and mighty style both in speaking and writing have often been ridiculed, and no one made more fun of him than Dickens did.   However, he was a creditable essayist and he wrote subsequently valuable biographies of Sir John Eliot, Oliver Goldsmith and Landor.   W. P. Frith, who met him later, said: "On casual acquaintances his brusque manner produced a very unfavourable impression; but when he became better known it was evident enough that the rough exterior concealed a generous heart as well as a refined mind."

[1] See § 38.
[2] In the *Dickens Encyclopædia*, by Arthur L. Hayward (Routledge, 1924), are portraits of Mary Hogarth and John and Elizabeth Dickens (Dickens's father and mother).
[3] He wrote from Collins's Farm to Beard on 17 May.

Dickens was described by a pen of that period as having "a youthful look, a capital forehead, a shaven face and 'eyes wonderfully beaming with intellect.'" People marked the eager, restless, energetic appearance of each several feature, that seemed to tell so little of the student or writer of books, and so much of the man of action and business in the world. Visits to the chambers of Forster, jaunts to Chelsea to see the Hogarths, attendance at publishers' and shopping expeditions through Holborn in company of his wife are the principal events of this period that have been recorded.

CHAPTER X

# March 1837 to end of 1839

48 DOUGHTY STREET

§ 43. *George Henry Lewes, 3 April* 1837, *and Charles Macready,* 16 *June* 1837

THE agreement for the renting of No. 48 Doughty Street is dated 3 April 1837. It was taken for three years, and the fixtures mentioned in the Inventory are valued at Forty-four pounds seven shillings.[1] Dickens seems to have lived for a short time in Upper Norton Street, for an undated letter to Mr E. Chapman, written on paper with the watermark 1837 commences "Furnival's Inn, I mean Upper Norton Street," but in March we find him settled at 48 Doughty Street—now a Dickens Museum.

Among those who made his acquaintance in this house was George Henry Lewes, the friend of George Eliot— "Ape Lewes" as Carlyle called him, from the plainness of his face, which had not been improved by an attack of small-pox. Lewes, a scholar and an enthusiastic lover of books, called by request of Dickens at 48 Doughty Street. He entered the house aglow with anticipation. But when he caught sight of the bookshelves, his spirits sank like lead —for he could see "nothing but three-volume novels and books of travel, all obviously presentation copies from authors or publishers"; with none of the treasures of the bookstall, each with its history, and all giving the collection its individual physiognomy. "A man's library," he says, "expresses much of his hidden life. I did not expect to

[1] Maggs's Catalogue, No. 525.

113

find a bookworm, not even a student, but nevertheless this collection of books was a shock." Then Dickens entered the room and his sunny presence amply compensated for the poverty of his library. Lewes, however, was "more impressed with Dickens's fullness of life and energy than with any sense of distinction." That "library" improved somewhat, but to the last it was a sorry collection; of the name of library quite unworthy. Dickens rarely bought a book, and to most of the masterpieces of literature, excluding the greater playwrights and works of fiction, he was to the day of death indifferent.

On 16 June 1837 he first met Charles Macready, and they became the greatest of friends. Though cultured, Macready had an ungovernable temper, as the actors and actresses associated with him knew to their cost. His motto was Seneca's *Inveniet Viam Aut Faciet* (Find a way or make one), and he is remembered for his striking impersonations of Shakespearian characters. Indeed at the time *Pickwick* appeared, he was recognised as the most gifted member of his profession.

To Dickens's comic burletta *Is She His Wife* reference has been made (see § 40). As already stated it was first acted on 6 March 1837, when the part of Mr Felix Tupkins, the principal character, was taken by Harley. One evening when this play was acted, Harley appeared after it in the character of Mr Pickwick and sang a comic song, attributed to Dickens, about a whitebait dinner.

A little later, Dickens heard that John Macrone, the young publisher to whom he had sold his *Sketches by Boz*, intended to issue those sketches in monthly parts and in the style of the *Pickwick* numbers. To this Dickens objected, and in order to prevent it he arranged with Chapman and Hall to acquire the copyright jointly with himself and Forster at the high figure of £2,250. The Memorandum of Agreement between Chapman and Hall and Macrone for the repurchase of both series of *Sketches by Boz*, which is dated 17 June 1837, is in Macrone's handwriting, the purchase being completed on 24 June. Dickens's first letter to Forster from 48 Doughty Street, written at the end

JOHN FORSTER

See page 111 *et al*.

**48 DOUGHTY STREET**

The Home of Charles Dickens, 1837-1839

*Photo by Catherine Weed Ward*

See page 113

of March, informed him that the dinner to celebrate the first anniversary of the publication of *The Pickwick Papers* was to be held on the following day, Saturday, at the Prince of Wales Hotel in Leicester Place. The letter of invitation to another of the guests is preserved in the Dickens Museum, 48 Doughty Street.

§ 44. *Death of John Macrone, 9 September* 1837.
*Broadstairs, September* 1837

In the meantime, Dickens had obtained release from his contract to write the novel *Gabriel Vardon* (*Barnaby Rudge*) for Macrone, and had come to an arrangement respecting it with Chapman and Hall. When Macrone died[1] on 9 September 1837, his affairs were found to be in confusion, and his widow and children were left unprovided for. A little later, Dickens, pitying Mrs Macrone, edited for her benefit, as we shall see (§ 57) the sketches entitled *The Pic-nic Papers*.

In September 1837 Dickens and his wife stayed at Broadstairs, the delightful Kentish watering-place to which he so often returned, and which is so intimately associated with his name. Perched upon its lofty white cliffs, Broadstairs looks down upon a bewitching toy semicircular bay, partly embraced by an old-fashioned pier that did duty long before seaside frequenting became the vogue. The old town consists mainly of three streets, which zigzag from the railway station to the sea, namely High Street, Albion Street and York Street, the last of which used at the sea end to be defended from privateers—the ancient pest of the place—by a flint gate, built in 1540, the archway of which still remains, a picturesque object, reminding of a time when it was still more picturesque, with its portcullis and drawbridge and spike or two above for the rogue's head of any French "swab" the valiant harbour-master might have the good luck to secure.

Several old taverns adorn the town, notably the Neptune's

[1] The Letters of Dickens to Macrone were published in the *Dickensian*, Nos. 230, 231, spring and summer, 1934.

Hall, which has resounded with the mirth and been saturated with the tobacco fumes of old salts ever since the devil-may-care buccaneering days; and an ancient chapel is shown—"St Mary's Shrine at Bradston" (old name for Broadstairs) so old and so venerated that mariners when passing used reverently to lower their topsails.   On the north of the bay stands a conspicuous edifice, with one side semicircular, Fort House, also called "Bleak House," where Dickens, for a time, later resided.   During his first visit to Broadstairs, however, he settled himself in a modest little house in the High Street, then No. 12, afterwards altered to No. 31.   It had a brick front and flint sides.   The front which had two windows, one above the other, was painted white above and chocolate below.   There was another window at the end facing the sea.   Dickens enjoyed immensely this first visit and got fun out of the strollers on the sands taking their walks in buff slippers, and stout gentlemen on the pier "looking at nothing through powerful telescopes for hours."[1]

Of Dickens's London habits later we get many a pleasant glimpse.   He often took horse exercise, his idea of complete enjoyment being "a fifteen-mile ride out," with Forster, "ditto in, a lunch on the road, and a wind-up dinner in Doughty Street," or a brisk walk over Hampstead Heath, with a red-hot chop and a glass of good wine," at Jack Straw's Castle.   For a time his brother Frederick lived with him.   In a Doughty Street letter to Beard, undated except as to the year, Dickens speaks of sitting for his portrait to George Cruikshank, and consequently unable to see anybody, George being a very exacting "subject."

## § 45. "Oliver Twist" considered

All the while, *Oliver Twist* (see §§ 39 and 41) had been steadily progressing.   This work, though in parts raw and tentative—for Dickens was feeling his way to the story pure and simple—will always attract, owing to the masterly character of Fagin and Cruikshank's unforgettable series of plates.   Oliver, the lad who gives the book its title, is an

[1] See *Our English Watering Place.* Cr. ed., vol. 17, p. 219.

insipid, colourless mortal, but Fagin looms as large in the book as does Satan in *Paradise Lost*. Dickens and Cruikshank together have constructed one of the most forcible and original characters in literature.  Was anything more realistic ever drawn than the picture entitled "Oliver introduced to the respectable Old Gentleman," where Fagin is looking off from the frying pan,[1] unless it is the one representing Oliver's reception by Fagin and the boys.[2]  How awful is the representation of Fagin in the condemned cell![3]  In the grotesque and the terrible, Cruikshank has no peer.

The main idea of *Oliver Twist* was, no doubt, borrowed from Smollett's *Humphry Clinker*,[4] though, as stated in the preface, Dickens had set himself the task to depict the thief and his associates as they really existed—to paint them in all their deformity and in all the squalid misery of their lives. He owes something to Defoe.  Indeed the prefaces of *Oliver Twist* and *Moll Flanders* are in precisely the same vein.

To return to Smollett, Humphry is a workhouse boy, put out apprentice.  He is reduced to want.  He attracts the attention of Mr Bramble, who takes him into his service. He turns out to be Mr Bramble's natural son.  Oliver Twist is also a workhouse boy, put out apprentice.  He falls among thieves, attracts the attention of Mr Brownlow, who becomes his friend.  He finally turns out to be the son of a young lady, Agnes Fleming, and heir to a fortune of which a rascally half-brother, Monks, has sought to deprive him.

When Dickens had killed Nancy, he read the chapter to Mrs Dickens, and the "unspeakable state into which it put her" caused him to augur well.  Then he despatched Sikes. What he should do with the Jew he was uncertain.  And when that "out-and-outer," to use Dickens's phrase, was sent to his own place, there remained Charley Bates.  For him Talfourd pleaded earnestly, with the result that this young gentleman was induced to migrate to Northamptonshire, where in time he became a successful grazier.

[1] Cr. ed., facing p. 52.  [2] *Ibid.*, facing p. 96.  [3] *Ibid.*, facing p. 329.
[4] *Humphry Clinker* is certainly Smollett's best.  I am rather divided between *Peregrine Pickle* and *Roderick Random*, both extraordinarily good in their way.  Letter of Dickens to Frank Stone 30 May 1854.

In *Oliver Twist*, Dickens began the noble work which he continued all his life, of exposing the most hateful evils of his day.   Here the heartless parochial system is held up to opprobrium, and Bumbledom will probably to all time be the most convenient term for pompous and asinine petty official tyranny.   Mr Bumble indeed ranks among the characters of the story only after Fagin.   Dickens, like Defoe, never makes vice attractive; but, unlike Defoe, he brings his ill characters to bad ends.   In real life, as everybody knows, vice is frequently triumphant.   The plot of *Oliver Twist* is feeble and improbable, and Mrs Oliphant who complains of the "absurdly melodramatic story of Oliver's birth" calls Monks an impossible villain.   The most unreal passage, however, is that describing the parting of Oliver and Little Dick.   It is improbable that any mortal boy since the world began ever said to another mortal boy, "I am very glad to see you, dear," or troubled about angels, or asked another boy to kiss him.

Mr R. H. Gooch, a friend of Cruikshank, says [1]: "I have often sat in Cruikshank's parlour which numbered among its visitors the burglar Sikes.   His first name, it seems, was Bill, though his surname has not come down to us."   "Jaw away, Bill," Dickens would say, and Dickens took shorthand notes while Cruikshank did the sketching.   Both Nancy and Oliver were also veritable characters and used to make their way to this room.

The London of *Oliver Twist* is chiefly that to the north of what is now the Holborn Viaduct.   When Oliver came from Barnet, he and the Artful Dodger crossed from the Angel at Islington into St John's Road, and thence proceeded to the house of Mr Fagin near Field Lane.   Mr Brownlow's pocket was picked near Clerkenwell Green; and the police court to which Oliver was taken was situated in Hatton Yard, an affluent of Hatton Wall, Mr Fang being the notorious Mr Laing.   Another portion of the London of *Oliver Twist* is the district of Bermondsey called Jacob's Island—the scene of the death of Sikes.   Jacob's Island was enclosed by Jacob Street (north of the island), George

[1] Letter to Thomas Wright.

118

Row (east), London Street (south) and Mill Street (west). Through Mill Street ran formerly Folly-ditch crossed by wooden bridges.

## § 46. *The Humour of "Oliver Twist"*

Some of the satire in *Oliver Twist* is biting enough. For instance:

*Our Tender Laws.* What a noble illustration of the tender laws of England! They let the paupers go to sleep!

*Mr Bumble's Button.* The die is the same as the parochial seal—the Good Samaritan healing the sick and wounded man. . . . I put it on, I remember, for the first time, to attend the inquest of that reduced tradesman who died in a doorway at midnight.

*Earning a halfpenny.* When Oliver, dog-tired, begged of the coach passengers, they told him to wait till they got to the top of the hill and then let them see "how far he could run for a halfpenny."

As examples of the simply humorous, we may notice:

*A foolish action.* "Wipe your eyes . . . and don't cry into your gruel; that's a very foolish action, Oliver!" It certainly was, for there was enough water in it already.

Then there is the exclamation of Mrs Sowerberry after she, Charlotte and Noah had beaten Oliver till they were weary. "Oh, Charlotte, what a mercy we have not all been murdered in our beds!" How cleverly Dickens in Chapter 12 takes off the doctor, and what a capital scene is that of Oliver before Mr Fang! How amusing too is the description of the courtship of Mr Bumble and Mrs Corney, though it is equalled by that of the degradation of Mr Bumble who in retreating "boxed the ears of the boy who opened the gate for him."

## § 47. *Cruikshank's Claim*

As the honour of having originated *Pickwick* was claimed for Seymour, so that of having created *Oliver Twist* was insisted upon by Cruikshank; and the two cases are curiously analogous. Cruikshank's version was as follows. He said that he had strongly advised Dickens to write the life of a London boy, and offered himself to supply all the characters, which a large experience of London life would be easy to him; also that the suggestion that the boy should fall among thieves and be saved by his honesty and good disposition, came from him.

An enquiry was about that time being made in the parish of St James's, Westminster, as to the cause of the death of some of the workhouse children who had been farmed out. To this enquiry Cruikshank drew Dickens's attention, telling him that if the matter were taken up many a workhouse child might be saved from injury and death. He wished Dickens to make Oliver a pretty boy, so as to attract the ladies. To this Dickens agreed, and, adds Cruikshank, "If anybody will take the trouble to look at my representations of Oliver he will see that the appearance of the boy is altered after the first two illustrations."

Again, according to Cruikshank, the well-known portraits of Fagin, Sikes and Nancy, were drawn before Dickens commenced *Oliver Twist*, and he declares that if Dickens had not seen them the story would not have been written. In short, Cruikshank's claim is summed up in "My drawings suggested the text, rather than his strong individuality my drawings." He might also have added that the originals of Sikes and some of the other characters were interviewed by Dickens in his parlour. But even conceding all this, the text of *Oliver Twist* remains none the less Dickens's. At the same time, just as in the early chapters of *Pickwick* we move in a Seymourian atmosphere, so in *Oliver Twist* the atmosphere is decidedly Cruikshankian.[1]

Cruikshank tells us how he hit upon the figure of Fagin in the condemned cell. He had been pondering it many days and could not satisfy himself. He thought the task hopeless, but one morning when he was sitting up in bed,

---

[1] See also the *Dickensian*, vol. 2, No. 5, May 1906, for article on Cruikshank by W. A. Fraser, p. 117. On p. 119 is a reproduction of the cancelled Cruikshank plate of *Oliver Twist*, "Rose Maylie and Oliver Standing at her Knee."

CHARLES DICKENS BY SAMUEL LAURENCE, 1838

*Photo by T. W. Tyrrell*

See page 123

CHARLES DICKENS BY COUNT A. D'ORSAY, 16TH DECEMBER, 1841

with his hand covering his chin, and the tips of his fingers between his lips, the whole attitude expressive of disappointment and despair, he saw his face in a cheval glass which stood on the floor opposite to him. "That's it," he involuntarily exclaimed, "that's just the expression I want." And so he became

> The man who drew
> The awful Jew.

As previously said, the idea of writing a work on the lines of *Oliver Twist* was probably suggested by the success of Bulwer's *Paul Clifford* (1830) and Ainsworth's *Rookwood* (1834). But as the popularity of *Oliver Twist* had eclipsed that of Ainsworth's earlier work, so a new story, *Jack Sheppard*, which Ainsworth in January 1839 commenced in *Bentley's Miscellany*, while Dickens was still its editor, threw for the moment *Oliver Twist* into the shade, and Ainsworth's "Little Burglar" became the lion of the day, indeed old West-enders used to tell how enthusiastic readers raided Willesden churchyard and carried off bit by bit a grave-rail said to be Sheppard's. After 1839, however, Dickens had really no rival under the head of popularity. In March 1839, he yielded the editorship of the *Miscellany* to Ainsworth. For *Oliver Twist* Dickens received £750. Speaking of him at this time Thomas Adolphus Trollope [1] says, "Of the general charm of his manner I despair of giving any idea to those who have not seen or known him. He warmed the social atmosphere wherever he appeared with that summer glow which seemed to attend him. His laugh was brimful of enjoyment."

### § 48. *Thomas Griffiths Wainewright.* *Rev. William Giles again*

Among the prominent literary men of the twenties and thirties, was Thomas Griffiths Wainewright, who wrote

---

[1] T. A. Trollope, brother of Anthony Trollope. He married for his second wife Frances Eleanor Ternan, sister of Dickens's friend Ellen Lawless Ternan. See Chapter 17, § 136.

under the pen-name of "Janus Weathercock" and lived in handsome rooms in Great Marlborough Street, where Hazlitt and other prominent men of letters had been his guests. Dickens, too, was occasionally there.

Wainewright, who had some £200 a year, outran his means, and in 1824 committed a forgery. Between 1829 and 1831 occurred the mysterious deaths of his uncle, his sister-in-law (Helen Frances Phœbe Abercromby), his mother-in-law and one of his acquaintances, all of whom he is said to have removed by strychnine. He had insured Miss Abercromby's life for £18,000, and twice he endeavoured to obtain the money, but without success. For a while he lived in France, but in 1837 he ventured to return to England. Upon his landing, however, he was arrested, not on the charge of murder, but upon that of forgery, and lodged in Newgate. During his incarceration there, Dickens and his friend Macready happened to go over the prison, when Dickens, chancing to look through an eyelet hole of one of the cells where were four prisoners, distinguished, to his horror, the wretched man who had once been his acquaintance, and who had held so respected a position in the literary world.

Sentenced to transportation for life, Wainewright spent the rest of his days in Tasmania, where he died in 1852. He was never publicly charged with murder. He is the Slinkton of Dickens's *Hunted Down* and, with some alterations, the Blandois of *Little Dorrit* (see § 102) and the Jonas of *Martin Chuzzlewit*. He is also the subject of Oscar Wilde's brilliant essay, "Pen, Pencil and Poison." [1]

In October 1837 *Pickwick* was finished (part 20 being the last), and the work was then brought out in volume form and dedicated to Talfourd. The event was celebrated by a dinner at the Prince of Wales in Leicester Square, Talfourd, Forster, Ainsworth, Jerdan, Macready and the publishers being present.

---

[1] For a detailed account of Wainewright see the *Dickensian*, vol. 2, pp. 291 and 334. On p. 293 is a portrait of Miss Abercromby. See also Wainewright's *Essays* edited, with a memoir, by W. C. Hazlitt 1880, and our Chapter 13, § 102. Cr. ed., vol. 15, p. 563.

In October 1837 Dickens was at Brighton where he read and got absorbed in Defoe's *History of the Devil* and practically finished *Oliver Twist*. Sergeant Ballantine, writing under date 10 January 1838 says: "Evening party at Levien's. Met Boz—looks quite a boy. His sister (Fanny) was there, she sang beautifully, is pretty, and, I should think, clever."

On returning from Brighton to 48 Doughty Street, Dickens heard from his old schoolmaster, the Rev. William Giles, who had started an academy at Barton Hall near Manchester. Accompanying his letter was a silver snuff-box with the inscription "To the inimitable Boz." Dickens when replying sent him copies of *The Pickwick Papers* in volume form, *Sunday Under Three Heads* and *Sketches of Young Gentlemen*. "Accept with them," he said, "all the warm and earnest wishes for your happiness and prosperity, which a vivid remembrance of your old kindness and excellence can awaken."[1] This year Dickens's portrait was drawn by Samuel Laurence.[2] A bust of him taken by a sculptor named Joseph, of Charlotte Street, Fitzroy Square, about the same time never got beyond the clay state.

## § 49. *"Nicholas Nickleby"*

In February 1838, Dickens commenced a new story, *Nicholas Nickleby*, the most humorous and on the whole the most pleasing of his novels. It has all the vivacity, piquancy and humour of *Pickwick*, and more buoyancy than the serious *David Copperfield*; for *David Copperfield* is serious despite the joviality of Micawber and the innocences of Mr Dick. The reason for its excellence is obvious, Dickens was at the summit of his fame, domestic trouble had not yet left its serious print upon him, and he was in roistering spirits.

[1] See *Charles Dickens and his First Schoolmaster*, by Arthur Humphries. Manchester, 1926. During part of the time that the Rev. W. Giles lived at Barton Hall he undertook the pastoral oversight of a Baptist cause at Eccles. After residing at Barton Hall until 1837 or 1838, he removed to Manchester and established an academy at 38 Ardwick Green.

[2] Laurence died in 1884. For account of him see *Charles Dickens by P.O.P.*, vol. 1, p. 21. There are three portraits of Dickens by Laurence.

Mr Mantalini, Mr Crummles, John Browdie, the Kenwigses—what entertaining company they are! The two tiresome interpolatory tales, "The Five Sisters of York" and "The Baron of Grogswig," can be skipped.

The first number appeared in April 1838, and the sale reached nearly 50,000. As Dickens had been out of town when *Pickwick* commenced, so he contrived to be out of it when *Nickleby* made its bow, and it was the same with subsequent works, whenever possible; for he was not without a tincture of superstition. On this occasion the Star and Garter at Richmond was the place chosen.

His idea of Do-the-boys Hall was derived from a law case which brought to light the scandalous state of some cheap schools in the north; and in February 1838 he and Hablot Knight Browne made a journey into Yorkshire for the express purpose of investigating. As a fellow passenger they had a very queer old lady, the mistress of a Yorkshire school, who produced "a long letter which she was carrying to one of the boys from his father, containing a severe lecture (enforced by many texts of scripture) on his refusing to eat boiled meat," and who drank brandy and water till she was insensible.

The travellers arrived at the George and New Inn, Greta Bridge, late on 31 January 1838, and started off next morning in a postchaise for Barnard Castle four miles off, round about which were "all the schools and a dozen old abbeys besides." They put up at the King's Head, and made enquiries respecting the educational establishments. Among those questioned was a watchmaker named Humphreys, just inside whose door hung a conspicuous clock which took Dickens's fancy, and which later suggested to him the name for the publication—*Master Humphrey's Clock.*

§ 50. *Shaw and Squeers.* 2 *February* 1838

The school Dickens and Browne decided to visit was situated at Bowes. It was conducted by a one-eyed gentleman named William Shaw and his wife Bridget. He had

WILLIAM SHAW'S SCHOOL.—DOTHEBOYS HALL.

*Photo by E. Yeoman, Teesdale Studio, Barnard Castle*

See page 124

GRAVESTONE OF WILLIAM SHAW, THE ORIGINAL OF
MR. SQUEERS IN "NICHOLAS NICKLEBY"

*Photo by E. Yeoman, Teesdale Studio, Barnard Castle*

See page 127

200 pupils and seven assistants. The house was a hand-some one. They had land and 20 cows, and the boys are said to have been well fed and healthy. When Dickens and Browne presented themselves, Shaw, who seems to have assumed that they had come in order to pick holes, haughtily snubbed them and they were obliged to return without seeing over the premises. Then apparently someone directed them to a former usher of Shaw's, who poured into the eager ears of the two visitors the tale which suggested the school and family of Mr Squeers. Had Dickens known that the usher was a man of bad character who had for that reason been dismissed, he would probably have been more charitable to the unfortunate Shaw. But the mischief was done, and Shaw was a ruined man.

A correspondent of the *Newcastle Weekly Chronicle*, "J.M.R.," May 1889, a native of the Barnard Castle district, says:

*Nicholas Nickleby*, a study in untruth, broke the hearts of two very decent people, and sent them to their grave before their time (Bridget Shaw died just 13 months after the last number of *Nicholas Nickleby* appeared). The book (as far as the school aimed at was concerned) was a terrible libel. In the second edition, Dickens protests that he meant no particular school. This may pass with outsiders; but those who knew the district are aware that, like Dickens's picture of the school, and like his letters about the Rev. Thomas Binney (see § 63) his protest lies on the cloudy side of truth. Anyone over fifty who has read the book and who knows the district can see a dozen finger posts in the novel directly pointing at one school. "Squeers," says Dickens, "had only one eye." This alone would show who was meant as there was only one schoolmaster near Greta Bridge with only one eye.

The picture drawn of the school was as far from the truth as it well could be. In Dickens's novel, Nicholas was the only usher. Do-the-boys Hall contained about 40 scholars. They were bleary-eyed, hair-lipped and deformed. This picture was made to do duty for a school where the scholars numbered 200 and where the teachers were seldom fewer than seven. The charge of feeding the boys on cattle that had died a natural death, the brimstone and treacle farce, the frozen pump story—all these and a heap of other novel furniture were simply so many artistic untruths.

The writer goes on to describe the scholars as being in reality "perfectly healthy young scamps" and the master as a "kindly good-hearted fellow" though "just a shade hasty in his temper." "Fanny Squeers," we are further told, "was one of the sweetest and kindest of women. Every word, every glance of her eye or motion of her hand bespoke a kindly heart. She suffered her undeserved martyrdom in silence."

Corroborative evidence of the identity of Squeers is afforded by Dickens's notebook where under 2 February 1838 he entered the following: "Shaw, the schoolmaster we saw to-day, is the man in whose school several boys went blind some time since from gross neglect. The case was tried and the verdict went against him." The case referred to was the charge of cruelty brought on 30 October 1832 against Shaw by parents of children who had been his pupils. The charge of starving the boys broke down but Shaw was found guilty of carelessness and neglect.[1]

To sum up, Shaw was certainly the original of Squeers, and it is equally certain that six years before he had been punished for neglecting his pupils. The evidence, however, is that subsequently he conducted his school on far better principles, and even came to be respected. It is therefore regrettable that Dickens made Squeers so closely resemble the original.

The following is one of Mr Shaw's advertisements taken from contemporary issues of *The Times*:

Education—By Mr Shaw, at Bowes Academy, Greta Bridge, Yorkshire. Youth are carefully instructed in English, Latin and Greek languages. Writing, Common and Decimal Arithmetic, Book-keeping, Mensuration, Surveying, Geometry. Geography and Navigation, with the most useful branches of the Mathematics, and provided with Board, Clothes, and every necessity, at 20 guineas per annum each. No extra charges. No vacations. Further particulars may be known on application to Mr J. Metcalfe, agent, 38 Great Marylebone Street. Mr Shaw attends at the *George and Blue Boar*, Holborn, from 12 to 2 daily.

That Shaw was respected in the Bowes district at this

[1] See *Charles Dickens and the Yorkshire Schools* by Cumberland Clark, 1918.

126

time may be assumed from the fact that after his death in
1850, his neighbours placed a stained-glass window in the
village church to his memory.

The inscription on his tombstone runs:

In
Memory of
WILLIAM SHAW
Who died January 10th, 1850
and of BRIDGET SHAW, wife of
the above, who died Nov. 1, 1840
aged 56 years.
Also WILLIAM SHAW their son
who died Oct. 21st, 1837
Aged 24 years.

The daughter, "Fanny Squeers," is said to have been
buried in the same grave. A similar story issued at the
present day would certainly invite heavy damages for libel.

When dealing with *Pickwick*, we noticed indebtednesses
in that work to *Don Quixote*. In *Nicholas Nickleby* the
influence of Cervantes is also discernible. The meeting
between Squeers and his wife may be compared with that of
Sancho Panza and Teresa.

"How is my Squeery?" said the lady in a playful manner, and very
hoarse voice.

"Quite well, my love," replied Squeers. "How's the cows?"

"All right, every one of 'em," answered the lady.

"And the pigs?" said Squeers.

"As well as they were when you went away."

"Come, that's a blessing," said Squeers, pulling off his great coat.
"The boys are all as they were, I suppose?"

Now take Cervantes.[1]

Upon the noise of his arrival, Sancho Panza's wife made haste
hither to enquire after her good man for she now knew that he had
gone as squire to the knight. As soon as ever she set her eyes upon
him the first question she asked him was whether the ass was well.
Sancho answered that he was come back in better health than his
master.

---

[1] Book IV, chapter 52.

The original of Mrs Nickleby was, to an extent, Dickens's mother. In a letter to Mr R. Lane, Dickens wrote: "Mrs Nickleby herself, sitting bodily before me in a solid chair, once asked me whether I really believed there ever was such a woman!" Kate Nickleby was Dickens's sister Fanny, and Nicholas was her husband, Mr Henry Burnett. The brothers Cheeryble were the Brothers Grant, manufacturers and merchants of Manchester and Ramsbottom. Of these brothers—William, Daniel and John—the last being probably the original of Tim Linkinwater—some account may be read in Smiles's *Life of James Nasmyth.*

According to the American comedian, Davidge, the original of Vincent Crummles was an old English actor named Davenport, the "Infant Phenomenon" being his daughter Jean. Davidge was in Davenport's company about 1837. He says: "The Infant Phenomenon was a buxom English lass of 12 or 14 with stout legs and a florid complexion. She always wore short dresses, pantelettes and neat slippers; her hair was in braids down her neck, and she looked no more than 9." When in a small town Davenport would pick out a lodging where passers-by would be numerous. He would dress her up and make her sit dancing a big doll at the window, and "the people would stand in groups open mouthed in wonder at the baby who played with her doll in the morning and trod the boards at night as Macbeth." On a Sunday the family would form "in procession with prayer books in their hands and the vanity of earthly joys in their faces" and go to church, contriving to arrive just after everybody else was seated, marching up the aisle in a style of pure melodrama, thus attracting the attention of all to the phenomenon.

In reference to the Bow allusions in *Nicholas Nickleby* Mr B. W. Matz in a letter to the *Daily News* on 21 July 1906 pointed out that "the gentleman in the next house" who made love to Mrs Nickleby must have been an inmate of Byas's Private Lunatic Asylum, which formed part of the Grove Hall Estate. He said Byas's Asylum was for well-to-do patients, and "the mad gentleman" is described by one of his keepers as well-to-do. "The estate was surrounded by a high wall and back gardens of some cottages abutted on to this wall, exactly as did the garden of the Nicklebys' cottage. The mad admirer of Mrs Nickleby first paid his addresses to her from the top of the wall." At the time the book was written the district was entirely rural.

§ 51. *The Humour of "Nicholas Nickleby"*

The humour of *Nicholas Nickleby* is of the finest quality, and the letter of Miss Squeers has often been pointed to in proof:

"My Pa," we read, "requests me to write to you, the doctor's considering it doubtful whether he will ever recouver the use of his legs, which prevents his holding a pen." "When your nevew that you recommended for a teacher had done this to my pa and jumped upon his body with his feet and also langwedge which I will not pollewt my pen with describing, he assaulted my Ma with dreadful violence, dashed her to the earth and drove her back comb several inches into her head. A very little more and it must have entered her skull."

Who can help smiling when Newman Noggs had trimmed himself up a little, "his coat presenting the phenomena of two consecutive buttons, the supplementary pins being inserted at tolerably regular intervals," or when Crummles "with one very bushy eyebrow stuck on crooked over his left eye," and the fellow eyebrow and the calf of one of his legs in his hand "embraces Nicholas cordially?" The sudden arrival of Nicholas among the Kenwigses also creates comical scenes enough. "Suppose it should be an express sent to say that his property has all come back again?" "Dear me," said Mr Kenwigs, "it's not impossible. Perhaps in that case we'd better send up and ask if he won't take a little more punch." How good too are Mr Mantalini and Mr John Browdie. But the book literally coruscates with fun, and, unlike that in *Pickwick*, none of it has since evaporated. It is as droll reading to-day as it was when its 50,000 subscribers shook their sides in the summer of 1838.

At the time Dickens wrote *Nicholas Nickleby*, he was a dapper little being of 24, delighting in crimson velvet waist-

coats, multi-coloured neckties with two breastpins joined
by a little gold chain, and yellow kid gloves. A perfect
toucan for colour, he, even late in life, often wore as much
jewellery as the proprietor of a travelling menagerie. For
this novel he received £3,000 and after five years the copyright was to revert to the author. At the conclusion of the
story, however, the delighted publishers presented him
with "an honorarium of £1,500 over and above the sum
nominated in the bond." Finally the work appeared in
book form with 39 illustrations by "Phiz" and a portrait of
Dickens, engraved by Finden from the painting by Maclise.
(See § 52.) It must not be overlooked that the book
abounds in aphorisms as well as humour. In connection
with poor tired Nicholas's and Smike's trudge up Hind Head
we learn that "the hill has not lifted its face to Heaven yet,
that perseverance will not gain the summit of at last"—a
pronouncement that loses none of its force, although,
hundreds of years before, Periander of Corinth had said the
same in different words and although half the copybooks in
schools tell us that "Labor Omnia Vincit," which though it
doesn't, has cheered millions.

§ 52. *His daughter Mary born* 12 *March* 1838.
*"Memoirs of Grimaldi." Mrs Jeniwin*

On 12 March 1838, Mrs Dickens gave birth to a second
child, a daughter, who was named Mary (Mamie). To
signalise the occasion, Dickens and Forster "rode out
fifteen miles on the Great North Road" and dined at the Red
Lion in Barnet. As already shown, Dickens's married life
had not been an ideal one, but soon after this event the
trouble between him and his wife became intensified. In a
letter to Forster written long after, he fixes the date when
the differences became really serious. He said, "What is
now befalling me I have seen steadily coming, ever since the
days you remember when Mary was born."
The truth is he never went out of his way to please his
wife. He never made enough of her. Indeed he put
others before her, consequently he was never to her Great

Apollo. If he had done his bit in the world, had not she, she asked herself, as mother and manager of his household, also done hers! The poet Wither, over 200 years before, thus neatly described the situation. "If she be not fair to me, what care I how fair she be." Change "she" to "he" and you have precisely Mrs Dickens's attitude to her husband at this time. When these outbreaks occurred at Doughty Street, Mrs Dickens had recourse to her mother, Mrs Hogarth, whose portrait Dickens drew as Mrs Jeniwin in *The Old Curiosity Shop*. Quilp was, in a sense—in his love for monkey tricks, for instance—Dickens himself as seen by the eyes of Mrs Hogarth; and the word-conflicts between that comical dwarf and Mrs Jeniwin, or something like them, certainly took place in real life. As for Mrs Dickens, she was an affectionate, if slightly irascible woman, whose weaknesses (men having none) should have been allowed for. A little tact and restraint, merely, would have met the case.

During this year (1838) Dickens edited for Bentley *The Memoirs of Joseph Grimaldi*. In the famous clown he had long been interested; but, according to D. G. Rossetti, though the work was undertaken by Dickens, most of it was done by his father. If so, we have one book from the pen of Micawber. However, the editor of the *Grimaldi*, whoever he was, took little pains. It was done badly though revised by Whitehead; and it sold badly, most of the copies being purchased as remainders.

Among the publications of 1839 was a booklet issued by Chapman and Hall entitled *Sketches of Young Ladies*, by E. Caswall, who used the pseudonym of "Quiz." Each essay purported to describe the idiosyncrasies of young femininity. Dickens, not to be behindhand, then produced anonymously *Sketches of Young Gentlemen* in which he made fun of the opposite sex. Later he issued a second collection of papers entitled *Sketches of Young Couples*, similar in treatment to its predecessor; but he was afterwards proud of neither. The same year he attempted to insure his life, application being made to the Sun Society. The sum was to be £1,000. The application, however, was unsuccessful.

Later he took out policies in the Eagle and National Provident Institution. Another event of 1838 was the hiring by Dickens of a country retreat—Elm Cottage—at Twickenham, where he stayed several months, entertained his friends Talfourd, Maclise, Forster, Ainsworth and Jerrold, and wrote part of *Nicholas Nickleby*.

In an undated letter which had the water mark of 1838, Dickens when writing to J. P. Harley, breaks into rhyme:

> Two aunts and two uncles, a sister and brother
> Dine with us next Thursday will you make another?

These were probably his uncles John Henry Barrow and Edward Barrow, their wives, his sister Fanny and his brother Fred. At the end of October 1838, Dickens and Browne were at Leamington whence they started in a post-chaise for Kenilworth, which delighted him on account of its connection with Sir Walter Scott. Thence they journeyed first to Warwick Castle, which possessed for him no very great attraction beyond a fine view and some beautiful pictures, and afterwards to Stratford-on-Avon, where they visited Shakespeare's birthplace. From the Lion Hotel, Shrewsbury, he wrote on 1 November to Mrs Dickens, describing his experiences. The letter ends, "God bless you, my darling. I long to be back with you again and to see the sweet Babs," and it is signed "Your faithful and most affectionate Husband."

Dickens does not seem to have made much use of his experiences during this journey till years later when he was writing *Dombey and Son*. Mrs Skewton lived at Leamington; and Mr Dombey, Mrs Skewton, Edith, Mr Carker and Major Bagstock visited Warwick Castle with which the major was terribly bored, while Mrs Skewton "was in such ecstasies with the works of art" that she could do nothing but yawn (they were such perfect inspirations). From Shrewsbury the travellers proceeded to Chester whence they returned to London.

In February 1839, Dickens relinquished his connection with *Bentley's Miscellany*. And it was well, for his hands were far too full. Indeed the brain reels as we think of his

DANIEL GRANT, ONE OF THE ORIGINALS OF THE CHEERYBLE BROTHERS
*Photo of a Sketch from Life by The Rev. T. Kilby*
*By permission of Mrs. Ada Moore Duffield, only possessor of the copyright and of the original Pencil Drawing*

See page 128

1 DEVONSHIRE TERRACE

The Home of Charles Dickens, 1839-1851

*Photo by Catherine Weed Ward*

See page 135

multitudinous labours at this period. In March 1839 he took for his father and mother what he calls a "beautiful little thatched white house, 'Mile End Cottage,'" at Alpington, a village near Exeter; and thenceforward he supported them. In a letter to Forster 5 March (1839) he says: "If they are not pleased with it I shall be grievously disappointed . . . there is a beautiful little room over the parlour . . . and there is a splendid garden." To Thomas Mitton he wrote: "I do assure you I am charmed with the place . . . I don't think I ever saw so cheerful and pleasant a spot."[1]

On 30 March 1839 a dinner was given to Macready on the occasion of his retirement from the management of the Covent Garden Theatre. The Duke of Cambridge presided. Of the speech which Dickens then made, Macready said, "It was most earnest, eloquent and touching. It took a review of my enterprise at Covent Garden and summed up with a eulogy of myself that quite overpowered me." Mrs Cowden Clarke, who was present, was much struck by Dickens's "superlatively handsome" face, his "rich wavy locks of hair and his magnificent eyes." But she noticed most his "remarkably observant faculty"—his "perpetually discursive glances at those around him, taking note as it were of every slightest peculiarity in look, or manner or speech or tone" that characterised each person.

Some time this year appeared the mock prophetic piece of doggerel entitled *The Loving Ballad of Lord Bateman* which was sung by Cruikshank at a dinner of the Antiquarian Society, and issued by Charles Tilt of Fleet Street. Mrs Ritchie (Thackeray's daughter) attributes the ballad to Thackeray and the notes to Dickens. (See *Harper's Magazine*, vol. 25, p. 124, which reproduces Thackeray's droll illustrations.) On 29 April died that good friend of the Dickens family, Mr Christopher Huffam. At the end of October was born to Dickens another daughter, who was christened Kate Macready, the second name being taken, of course, from that of the famous actor.

[1] There is an illustration of it in Snowdon Ward's *Real Dickens Land*, p. 113.

During the year, Maclise painted the fine portrait of Dickens which forms the frontispiece to *Nicholas Nickleby*. Of the original, which now hangs in the National Portrait Gallery, Thackeray said, "As a likeness it is perfectly amazing; a looking-glass could not render a better facsimile." Charles Dickens the younger agreed with him, though he commented, "It was impossible for the painter quite to catch the brightness and alertness which, in so remarkable a degree, distinguished his sitter." The picture originated from a remark made by one of the guests, William Jerdan, at a dinner given at the Albion in Aldersgate Street to celebrate the completion of *Nicholas Nickleby*. Jerdan, who knew that Mrs Dickens longed to possess "a portrait of her husband," hinted in a speech that this was a desideratum. Dickens's publishers thereupon commissioned Maclise to paint it. Miss Georgina Hogarth told Mr J. W. T. Ley that it had only one rival—the portrait made in 1836 by Samuel Laurence. However, there he sits with his abundant hair and shaven chin, his right hand holding a pen, his left pressed upon his manuscript—a literary Count D'Orsay, for everybody who was anybody in those days wished to look a little like that handsome and immaculate dandy.

# CHAPTER XI

# End of 1839 to June 1842

§ 53. *"Master Humphrey's Clock."*  *Landor*

AT the end of 1839 Dickens, who, owing to a growing family, required a larger home, removed from 48 Doughty Street to No. 1 Devonshire Terrace, Regent's Park—a handsome house, with a large garden shut out from Marylebone Road "by a high brick wall, near the York Gate of Regent's Park."  *Nicholas Nickleby* finished, he resolved to try a fresh form of publication, his idea being a venture on the lines of Addison's *Spectator* with the revived Pickwick Club to take the place of Sir Roger and his friends.  The result was *Master Humphrey's Clock* with illustrations chiefly by George Cattermole and H. K. Browne.  One of them was by Samuel Williams, another by Daniel Maclise.

*Master Humphrey's Clock* was issued in 88 weekly numbers at threepence each and in 20 monthly parts, the price varying from a shilling to one and threepence.  The first number appeared on 4 April 1840 and nearly 70,000 copies were sold, but the public did not take kindly to the new form of publication, which is not surprising, seeing that the re-suscitated Pickwick and Sam Weller were, as already mentioned, hopeless failures; consequently when Dickens in the fourth number commenced *The Old Curiosity Shop* the Master Humphrey apparatus was abandoned.  After the new story had run its course, Master Humphrey was for the moment revived, but merely to introduce a second story, *Barnaby Rudge*, at the conclusion of which the clock gave a few uncertain ticks and then stopped for ever.

At the end of February 1840, while Dickens was writing *The Old Curiosity Shop* he with a few friends visited Walter Savage Landor at Bath. Expelled from Rugby and rusticated at Oxford, Landor, who at different times had quarrelled with his father, his wife, his Welsh tenantry and most of his neighbours, reminds us of that Antipodean wasp which, if cut in two, fights—so great is its pugnacity—the head with the tail. His imposing and leonine appearance, and the strength of his will, led Carlyle to call him "the unsubduable old Roman." His intimate friends, however (including Dickens, who drew upon him subsequently for Mr Boythorn in *Bleak House*), sincerely loved him, though they stood in awe of him.

It was during this visit to Bath that there arose in Dickens's mind the idea of Little Nell, the original of whom, as everybody knows, was Mary Hogarth, whose death Dickens continued to deplore. With Landor Little Nell was a favourite, and he once declared with tremendous emphasis, half in earnest, half in jest, that he never in his life regretted anything so much as his neglect to purchase the house which Dickens had hired at Bath, No. 35 St James's Square. "I would have burnt it to the ground," he said, "to the end that no meaner association should ever desecrate the birthplace of Nell"—following up his declaration, after a short pause, with a thundering peal of laughter. To the end Landor remained a big, wayward, spoilt, unpractical but cultured, noble and fascinating child. With age his appearance grew more leonine than ever, but the characters which time imprinted on his face were "those not of his transient bursts of fury, but of his habitual moods of lofty thought and tender feeling." In September 1840 Dickens and his wife were at Broadstairs again and their friend Angus Fletcher ("Kindheart") stayed with them most of the time.[1] Fletcher, who was eccentric, behaved very oddly, and visitors mistook him for Dickens who,

[1] Ley's *Forster*, pp. 161, 163.

hearing their comments, begged Fletcher to moderate his "insane gambolings."

## § 54. *"The Old Curiosity Shop"*

Regarded simply as a character in a novel, Little Nell fails to create interest, indeed the "smear of white"—Mrs Oliphant's expression—can scarcely be called a character at all unless ghosts, angels and other impalpables come under this category; but regarded as the apotheosis of Mary Hogarth, she rivets attention. Dickens once made the infelicitous remark that it was a pity the lives of other distinguished authors were not as great a blank to us as the life of Shakespeare. Were we not intimately acquainted with the inner life of Dickens, one book of his, and that containing the character he most cherished—would by now have ceased to be read as a whole. We should be satisfied with selections—chiefly those relating to the Marchioness and Dick Swiveller. Dickens's contemporaries, however, were moved by the grandiloquent account of Nell's death and burial; and even by the sing-song of such sentences as "And now the bell—the bell she had so often heard," etc. Nevertheless, infelicitous as is the language in which these thoughts are expressed, the death and burial of Little Nell were to Dickens himself terrible realities. He said, as the book drew to a close, "Nobody will miss her like I shall. It is such a very painful thing to me but I really cannot express my sorrow. . . . I can't preach to myself the schoolmaster's consolation, though I try. Dear Mary died yesterday, when I think of this sad story——" one more instance of Dickens's incorrigible persistence in the habit of self-pity.

As George Eliot observes, "Dickens can copy Mrs Plornish's colloquial style (in *Little Dorrit*) with the delicate accuracy of a sun-picture, but he scarcely ever passes from the humorous or external to the emotional and tragic without becoming as transcendent in his unreality as he was a moment before in his truthfulness." However, as already stated, Dickens's contemporaries were moved by little Nell's story—some of them even to tears. Macready begged him to spare her life, and observed that he was cruel. "He blushed," said Macready, "and men who blush are said to be either proud or cruel; he is not proud and therefore"— as Dickens added—"the axiom is false."

Lord Jeffrey could not help "sobbing terribly" over the book; Washington Irving was "deeply touched" by its "exquisite and sustained pathos," and Daniel O'Connell, after groaning, "He should not have killed her! He should not have killed her!" indignantly threw the book out of the window, unable to read more. Interest at the present day, however, centres not on Little Nell, but on Messrs Codlin and Short, Mrs Jarley, the Marchioness and Dick Swiveller —not forgetting Mr Quilp. Several houses have claimed to be the original of *The Old Curiosity Shop*, but it was probably the one already alluded to as situated in Fetter Lane (see § 21). We are told at the end of the story that when Kit took his children to the street where Nell had lived, he found that "the old house had long been pulled down."

According to a writer in the *Daily Graphic*, the originals of Codlin and Short were a pair of Punch and Judy men named Tom Willis and "Tubby" (so nicknamed from his shortness and fatness) whom Dickens and Mark Lemon came upon at Englefield Green just outside Windsor Old Park. Throwing himself on the grass, Dickens called for a performance, adding, "No cutting anything out, mind." Both he and Lemon heartily enjoyed it, shouting: "Go it, Devil; go it, Punch," when these heroes fought. After the finish the two friends *would* have the curtain rung up, and all the company appear, while Dickens played the pipes and Lemon the drum. Dickens gave a sovereign, and would not let Lemon pay half, because he said it was his "bespeak." Subsequently Willis and Tubby "opened" at Egham races, when a seedy old man and a little girl in a plain stuff dress came up and the girl said, "May we stay next you, sir, 'cos we're afeard of the gypsies and people!" On "Cup day" the child held the hat and among the onlookers was Dickens, who afterwards enquired concerning her and the old man. "Be kind to them, Tubby," said he, "and don't let your sulky friend (meaning Willis) be cross with them, neither."

The pair who were supposed to have "run away from some-body" stayed with the showmen ten days and then vanished for ever. Dickens subsequently sent Tubby a silver collar for the dog, with the inscription, "To Toby, from his friend and admirer, Charles Dickens."

The old archway referred to in Chapter 27 of *The Old Curiosity Shop*, where Nell saw Quilp, was probably the venerable Carmelites Archway in Much Park Street, Coventry—hence the chimes would be those of St Michael's, and the picturesque old church, the scene of Nell's burial, was possibly that of Tong in Shropshire, which is still famous for its splendid and quaint carvings and magnificent monuments. To the prototypes of the Marchioness, the Garland family and Mrs Jarley's poet, we referred on pp. 41 and 43. Edward FitzGerald was so taken with *The Old Curiosity Shop* that he made of the story of Little Nell and her wanderings with her grandfather a short abstract which he called *The Nelly-ad*.[1]

## § 55. *The Humour of "The Old Curiosity Shop"*

As samples of the humour of *The Old Curiosity Shop* we may take the following:

*Kit's Writing Lesson.* How when he did sit down he tucked up his sleeves and squared his elbows and put his face close to the copy-book and squinted horribly at the lines—how from the very first moment of having the pen in his hand, he began to wallow in blots, and to daub himself with ink up to the very roots of his hair—how, if he did by accident form a letter properly, he immediately smeared it out again with his arm in his preparations to make another.

*Swiveller's Hat.* Mr. Swiveller placed his hat upon the desk, and taking from his pocket a small parcel of black crape, applied himself to folding and pinning the same upon it, after the manner of a hatband. Having completed the construction of this appendage he surveyed his work with great complacency, and put his hat on again—very much over one eye, to increase the mournfulness of the effect.

---

[1] The whole of the *Nelly-ad* is printed on pages 147–190 of *A Fitzgerald Medley*, edited by Charles Ganz. Methuen, 1933. The manuscript is in the Library of Trinity College, Cambridge.

*Orange-peel and water.* "Did you ever taste orange-peel and water?"—Mr Swiveller replied that he had never tasted that ardent liquid.—"If you make believe very much, it's quite nice," said the small servant, "but if you don't, you know, it seems as if it would bear a little more seasoning, certainly."

The incidents of the dog playing the Old Hundredth, and Swiveller practising on his flute, and the conversation respecting the "Sip of Beer" are also in Dickens's best vein; but the Marchioness and Dick Swiveller are choice company whenever they appear.

In August Dickens ran down to see his father in Devonshire, taking his work with him. In September he was again at Broadstairs, installed in a small villa called Lawn House, where he finished the first volume of the *Clock*, and the next month he returned to Devonshire Terrace, which became the scene of a series of social gatherings with his friends Maclise, Macready, Talfourd, Landseer, Rogers, Sydney Smith, Bulwer (Lord Lytton) and others. Dickens reckoned his profits from the sale of *The Old Curiosity Shop* at about £10,000.

On 3 October 1840 was first performed at the Theatre Royal, Covent Garden, a comedy by Dickens's old enthusiasm Charles Mathews,[1] *Past Two O'clock in the Morning*, in which a Mr Newpenny (Dickens's friend, Mr Keeley) is disturbed at night by a stranger (Mr C. Mathews) who makes a great noise, knocking. For the sake of peace Mr Newpenny asks the stranger in, with the result of farcical occurrences. This play greatly took Dickens's fancy, and he later often acted in it, after altering it to his taste.[2]

### § 56. *"Barnaby Rudge," First No. January* 1841

*The Old Curiosity Shop* was finished on 17 January 1841, and in the following week appeared the first number of *Barnaby Rudge*, of which Dickens had already written a goodly portion. Though usually a rapid writer, yet there were often times when he could do nothing. On Friday, 29 January 1841, he says: "I didn't stir out yesterday, but

[1] Mathews died 28 June 1835.    [2] See §§ 60 and 70.

sat and thought all day; not writing a line; not so much as
the cross of a t or the dot of an i." But the time was not
wasted, for he says, "I imaged forth a good deal of
*Barnaby* by keeping my mind steadily upon him."

As an historical tale *Barnaby Rudge* is valueless, the riot-
ing portions wearying us as much as the Nellyan wanderings
and obsequies of *The Old Curiosity Shop*, but Dolly is
exquisite. Round the charming, though coquettish, daughter of the locksmith all the interest circulates. Gabriel
Varden, Mrs Varden, and Miggs, are life itself; and
Dickens was rarely more successful than in his delineation
of the rare old Maypole and its phlegmatic landlord, Joe
Willet, whose dying words, by the by, though not much
light in this case is let in "through chinks that time has
made," are better remembered than those of many a mighty
potentate or respected divine. "I'm a goin', Joseph," said
Mr Willet, turning round upon the instant, "to the 'Salwanners,' and immediately gave up the ghost."

The original of the Maypole at Chigwell is the King's
Head, a fine old inn opposite the churchyard, the room
upstairs with huge bay window being the one in which
passed the conference between Mr Haredale and Sir John
Chester. There is, of course, no resemblance between the
King's Head and the enormous and stately Elizabethan
incongruity by Cattermole which forms the frontispiece to
*Barnaby Rudge*. That, as Charles Lamb would have said,
was only the artist's fun. Mr Chester is meant to be Lord
Chesterfield, author of the immortal *Letters to his Son*. Let
no man, however, suppose that Mr Chester is much like his
original, or neglect to study the famous letters because
Dickens has caricatured—we might almost say maligned—
their author.

Humour is not very conspicuous in *Barnaby Rudge*.
Some of it circulates round Grip the raven who, however,
is not an unqualified success; still he is at times entertaining
and his remarks, "I'm a Polly," "I'm a kettle on," "I'm a
Protestant kettle," light up several dull scenes. The
original of Grip died while *Barnaby Rudge* was being
written. Dickens whimsically described the incident to

Forster in a letter accompanied with an enormous black seal. "Towards eleven he was so much worse that it was found necessary to muffle the stable knocker. At half-past, or thereabouts, he was heard talking to himself about the horse . . . and to add some incoherent expressions which are supposed to have been either a foreboding of his approaching dissolution, or some wishes relative to the disposal of his little property, consisting chiefly of half-pence which he had buried in different parts of the garden. On the clock striking twelve he died." The children exhibited only moderate regret. "He bit their ankles."

In one of his letters Dickens records Grip's last words, which were "Hello, old girl!" and he speaks of being thrilled when reading in manuscript an account written by Lady De Lancey of scenes she had witnessed at Waterloo. He says: "After working at *Barnaby Rudge* all day . . . I went at it about ten o'clock. If I live for 50 years I shall dream of it every now and then from this hour to the day of my death. . . . It is a striking proof of the power of that most extraordinary man Defoe that I seem to recognise in every line of the narrative something of him." [1] Dickens was as full of life in Devonshire Terrace as he had been in Furnival's Inn and Doughty Street. Private theatricals sometimes engaged his attention, and for exercise he on wet days had recourse to battledore and shuttlecock.

§ 57. *"The Pic-nic Papers." Chauncey Hare Townshend's Magnetic Boy. A Visit to Scotland*

Early in 1841 the publisher Henry Colburn of Marlborough Street, who had some sort of connection with Richard Bentley, proposed to issue a work to be called *The Pic-nic Papers* for the benefit of Macrone's widow, who, as already stated, had been left poorly off, and it was arranged that Dickens should be the editor. Colburn, however, interfered, accepting or rejecting papers without consulting Dickens, who for a whole year angrily resisted what he called "this indecency in Mr Colburn," consequently there

[1] *Century Magazine*, April 1906. See also Chapter XIII, § 103.

were delays, which Mrs Macrone wrongly believed to be the fault of Dickens. Eventually Dickens, for the lady's sake, gave way to Colburn, but declined to have anything further to do with the publication. Thus ended the quarrel between two well-intentioned men. However, Mrs Macrone received £300 as the result of the venture. Dickens's own contribution to *The Pic-nic Papers* was *The Lamplighter's Story*, founded on his farce *The Lamplighter*. *The Pic-nic Papers* appeared that year, Colburn being the publisher. *The Lamplighter's Story* contained an illustration by Cruikshank, "The Blowing up of the Crucible," the last drawing done by him for Dickens's work. It is reproduced in the *Dickensian* May 1906, vol. 2, No. 5, p. 121.

Among the subjects that next attracted Dickens, were the mesmeric investigations made by Dr Elliotson [1] and these brought him into touch with that enthusiastic student of Animal Magnetism, the Rev. Chauncey Hare Townshend, a wealthy clergyman who had seceded from the Church of England on account of his inability to agree with some of its doctrines, Mr Townshend had brought over from Belgium a young German lad, Alexis, who had mesmeric and clairvoyant gifts, which for a while astonished London Society. Dickens, Mrs Dickens, Maclise and Cruikshank went together one evening to see him. Fanny Kemble,[2] who was present on one of the occasions when Alexis was exhibiting his powers in a drawing-room, says (21 May 1841) "his clairvoyancy consisted principally in reading passages from books presented to him while under the influence of the mesmeric sleep into which he had been thrown by Mr Townshend, and with which he (and his eyes were bandaged) was previously unacquainted." When Mrs Dickens held her Geneva watch behind his head he read the name of the maker in a moment. "The results," continues Fanny Kemble, "were sufficiently curious, though probably neither marvellous nor unaccountable." We were

[1] At Christmas 1860 Dickens presented to Dr Elliotson a copy in full morocco of *The Uncommercial Traveller*. Dr Elliotson was consulted by Mrs Burnett during her illness. See § 73.

[2] *Records of Later Life*, by Fanny Kemble, vol. 2, p. 77.

all of us sceptical. After an exhibition of clairvoyance given by Alexis, Mr Townshend would exclaim, "There now, you see that?" To which one of the audience replied with the most imperturbable phlegm, "Yes, I see it, but I don't believe it." To the Countess of Blessington Dickens writes 2 June 1841: "Have you seen Townshend's magnetic boy? If you get him to Gore House, don't, I entreat you, have more than 8 people. . . . He fails in a crowd, and is *marvellous* before a few. . . . I am a believer in earnest."

Mr Townshend, who was a poet, with antiquarian tastes, had the penetration to see genius in the earlier work of John Clare. Indeed he had visited Helpston, near Peterborough, in 1821 on purpose to meet the peasant poet, and was very much astonished at Clare's humble surroundings. He was able to interest Dickens in Alexis, but not in Clare in whom Dickens, indifferent to rural delights, could see nothing to admire. Percy FitzGerald always thought that Mr Townshend was drawn upon for the character of Cousin Feenix in *Dombey and Son*. "Townshend," he says, "had all the gentle amiability and softness of Cousin Feenix with a sort of old-fashioned simplicity and aristocratic bearing." Besides indulging in antiquarian research, which led him to be the occasional butt of Dickens, though they were to the last most intimate friends, Townshend devoted his life to disseminating his religious opinions.

For some time Dickens had been planning a visit to Ireland, but in March 1841 Lord Jeffrey wrote declaring that the people of Edinburgh considered that nothing so good as Little Nell had appeared since Shakespeare's Cordelia, and urged him to come northward to receive an ovation. So Dickens, who loved ovations, put off Ireland, and on 22 June made for Scotland instead,[1] taking Mrs Dickens with him. Sir William Allen, R.A., squired him about, and Mrs Dickens went with Miss Allen to see the house in which she was born. Then followed a grand dinner with Wilson (Christopher North) "a mountain-looking fellow in the chair"—a brilliant affair. The Lord

[1] He was then writing *Barnaby Rudge* and he took the portion on which he was engaged with him. So parts of the story were written in Scotland.

LAWN HOUSE, BROADSTAIRS
Occupied by Dickens in 1840
*Photo by Swaine & Co., 4 High Street, Broadstairs*
See page 140

CHARLES DICKENS, FROM PAINTING BY FRANCIS ALEXANDER
Done for J. T. Fields, 1842

*Photo by T. W. Tyrrell*

See page 150

Provost, the Council and the Magistrates voted their guest the freedom of the city, and the parchment scroll conferring it became one of the most valued ornaments of his study.

On Sunday, 14 July, he proceeded to Stirling, and thence to Callendar, where, however, he sighed for London and the Devonshire Terrace battledore and shuttlecocks. He wants to dine again in a blouse with Forster and Maclise; and he feels the merits of his man Topping "more acutely" than he had ever done. Angus Fletcher ("Kindheart"), who then joined them, conducted them through the Trossachs. After visiting Loch Earn, Glencoe and other spots of interest they returned, via Inverary, Glasgow and York, home to Devonshire Terrace, battledore and shuttlecocks and Topping—reaching London on 17 July. In August 1841 Dickens was again at Broadstairs whence he wrote to Cattermole on the 19th giving instructions respecting the *Barnaby Rudge* illustrations. On 12 September, for instance, he requests him "to design a sword duel between Mr Haredale and Mr Chester and to make other pictures."

§ 58. *Mr and Mrs Burnett. A Page out of John Bunyan.*
*In praise of Irving's "Sketch Book"*

By this time Mr and Mrs Burnett (Dickens's sister Fanny) had settled at No. 3 Elm Terrace, Higher Ardwick, then a pleasant suburb of Manchester, where they continued to teach music and singing. One day they entered Rusholme chapel, the minister of which was the Rev. James Griffin. The service over, they followed Mr Griffin into the vestry and after introducing themselves, they expressed a wish to have an interview with him "in reference to their religious concerns."

Mr Burnett said he had for some years been engaged as an opera singer, but he had abandoned the stage "and desired to spend his life in far other scenes and associations than those of the theatre." His mind and his wife's, he said, "were chiefly intent on spiritual things."

"I was brought up," followed Mrs. Burnett, "in the Established Church, but I regret to say, without any serious ideas of religion.

145

I attended Divine Worship as a duty, not as a privilege. I feel the necessity of a Saviour, and am fully persuaded that Jesus Christ is in every way the Saviour I require. Sometimes I have doubts and fears, but I am encouraged in His blessed Word to rely on His gracious promises. While reading it, I seem to hear Him speaking to me individually." [1]

The knowledge that her parents paid little attention to Christian exercises often troubled her, and when her father and mother were coming to visit her she said to her husband, "Now, Henry, don't omit family prayer morning and evening during their stay with us. They have never been used to it, but that should not prevent us from continuing our usual habits; it should rather induce us to be firm in maintaining them."

Mr and Mrs John Dickens stayed with the Burnetts many months. When one looks at the old picture of "Micawber" with his everlasting bottles and his come-day-go-day air, and then at this where he and his wife sit listening to their daughter's serious converse, one seems to be reading, not a chapter from *David Copperfield*, but a page out of John Bunyan. Burnett's enthusiasm for the religious leaders under whose influence he had come and for their teaching irritated Dickens, who became more and more antagonistic towards the Nonconformist ministry.

While *Pickwick* was appearing, a letter had reached him from Lewis Gaylord Clark, an American author, with congratulations on account of its merits and success. A correspondence ensued, and from it came to Dickens the idea of visiting America. Clark was a "genial vampire" who ran the *Knickerbocker* without paying anybody except in the shape of puffs, flattery, honeyed politeness, drinks and oyster stews. He was cultured, however, and through him Dickens became a correspondent of Washington Irving.

"I should love," wrote Dickens to Irving, recalling the *Sketch Book*, "to go with you—as I have gone, God knows how often—into Little Britain, Eastcheap, Green Arbour Court, and Westminster Abbey. It would make my heart glad to compare notes

---

[1] *Memories of the Past*, by James Griffin, 1883, pp. 165–210.

with you about that shabby gentleman in the oilcloth hat and red nose, who sat in the nine-cornered back parlour of the Masons' Arms; and about Robert Preston and the tallow chandler's widow, whose sitting-room is second nature to me; and about all those delightful places and people that I used to walk about and dream of in the daytime, when a very small and not over-particularly-taken-care-of boy."

The advantage of going to America then appeared, by steady looking at it, so great that Dickens persuaded himself that it was a matter of imperative necessity. Not so Mrs Dickens, however, for, says he (13 September), "Kate cries dismally if I mention the subject." She didn't want to be separated so long from her children.

In October 1841 Mrs Dickens lost two of her relatives, her grandmother Catherine Thomson, wife of George Thomson, the friend of Burns, and her brother George Hogarth. Mrs Thomson died at Brompton on 18 October, while on a visit to her daughter Mrs Hogarth. George Hogarth, who was only 20, died six days afterwards, apparently in the same house. So there were two funerals in the family in one week. Both Mrs Thomson and George Hogarth were buried in Kensal Green Cemetery in adjoining graves.[1] The death of George reminded Dickens again of the loss of Mary Hogarth, and when the grave was reopened to receive the remains of George he drove over before the funeral to look at her coffin. His distress, he tells us, was so great that for days he could not bear to leave his room and he was depressed for over a month. To Mary's tombstone were then added the words:

THIS IS ALSO THE GRAVE
OF HER BROTHER
GEORGE HOGARTH
WHO DEPARTED THIS LIFE
OCTOBER 24TH, 1841
AGED TWENTY
LIKE HER
HE WAS TAKEN ILL AND DIED
IN ONE NIGHT.

[1] See also §§ 91 and 146.

147

A jaunt is next chronicled to the White Hart at Windsor with Mrs Dickens, her sister Georgina and Forster. Some pleasant conversations with Landor in London followed and then came the eventful 4 January on which Dickens and his tearful wife were to start for America in the *Britannia*. They took with them Mrs Dickens's maid Anne. Their four children Charles aged 4, Mary 3, Kate 2 and Walter Landor some 9 months, were left with Mr and Mrs Macready.

§ 59. *First Visit to America.* 4 *January* 1842

The voyage was a stormy one. There was a smiting rain, the wind blew great guns, and the vessel was all but lost. "I never expected to see the day again," says Dickens, "and resigned myself to God as well as I could." Mrs Dickens "suffered the utmost terror all the way." The oldest salts had never experienced such weather. The eighty passengers rolled about the deck like disturbed bottles.

Just before reaching Halifax harbour, the ship struck. All was dismay. The pilot lost his head, the passengers were in terror. Everything was in the most intolerable confusion and hurry. Rockets were thrown up, blue-lights burnt and other signals of distress made. However, at last Halifax was reached, and the passengers presented the captain with a valuable piece of plate as an acknowledgment of his skill in saving the vessel.

Mrs Dickens, writing to Fanny Burnett on 30 January 1842 said:

"You cannot imagine what a dreadful voyage we had. . . . I was nearly distracted with terror, and don't know what I should have done had it not been for the great kindness and composure of my dear Charles. It was very awful. . . . I trust, dearest Fan, that you and yours are well. Charles joins me in most affectionate love to yourself and Burnett, and kiss your dear little ones from Aunt Kate."

Referring to her own children she says "God grant that the darlings are well—how my heart yearns for them."

When they were safely landed there came a breathless man, shouting like a maniac, as he tore along, the name of Dickens. It was the Speaker of the House of Assembly, and he dragged Dickens, who, to the American eye appeared "a middle-sized somewhat fleshy person, with a slightly aquiline nose," to the house of Lord Falkland the Governor, and thence Heaven only knows where. The crowds cheered him in the streets. Judges, law officers and bishops welcomed him. He was placed in a great elbow chair by the Speaker's throne in the House of Assembly.

At Boston a dozen editors with bundles of newspapers under their arms assailed him, shaking hands like madmen. Crowds poured in and out of his lodgings every day. People lined the streets when he went out. "They cheered, oh how they cheered!" There were invitations of all kinds —balls, dinners, assemblies without number. There were public dinners to him. Authorities from nearly all the States wrote to him. "It is no nonsense, and no common feeling. It is all heart." Never, to use his own words, "was a king or emperor so cheered and followed by crowds," but in the midst of all his triumph he remembers the "sweet lost Mary" Hogarth. He says, "I feel something of the presence and influence of that spirit which directs my life, and through a heavy sorrow, has pointed upward with an unchanging finger for more than four years past."

At Boston he met Dana, Felton, Dr Channing, Longfellow and Bancroft. Thence he proceeded to Newhaven, visiting jails and deaf and dumb asylums, and shaking hands with people by the thousand. Even when in bed he snuffed incense, for choristers serenaded him under his window, but Mrs Dickens would have preferred to hear the crooning of her baby.

They arrived at New York amid the acclaims of multitudes and Dickens hired a splendid suite of rooms at the Carlton Hotel. After dinner Washington Irving came in, with open arms, and stayed till ten at night. The ball got up in Dickens's honour was light, glitter and glare beyond description. Among the friends whom Dickens met at

149

New York was David Cadwalder Colden. Mrs Colden's sister was the wife of Lord Jeffrey.[1]

While he was at Boston, a bust of him was made by Henry Dexter, a young sculptor, and Mrs Dickens declared herself delighted with it.[2] Then, too, Dickens's portrait was painted by the Boston artist, Francis Alexander, who, on learning that Dickens needed a secretary, recommended his pupil George W. Putnam. Dickens was accompanied by Putnam during the rest of the American visit, and always refers to him as "Q" or my "Boston Friend."[3] Everywhere the famous novelist was the hero, but there was a fly in the ointment.

At one of the great public dinners in his honour he spoke in advocacy of International Copyright; but this provoked newspaper attacks; and the man who had just before been lauded as a deity was denounced as a mercenary scoundrel, compared with whom Colt—a notorious murderer—was an archangel. On 6 March he and Mrs Dickens were at Philadelphia, but they found railway travelling a terrible ordeal. The windows of the cars were closed and the heat from the charcoal stove was intolerable. But all the American institutions were furnaces—chapels, theatres, prisons, private houses. The prison arrangements were shocking. At Richmond the buying and selling of slaves made his heart ache.

He then purchased an accordion and regaled the ladies with "Home, sweet Home." It made him pleasantly sad and he often thought of his "dear, dear children, in England," while Mrs Dickens at all times thought of nothing else. From Washington the travellers proceeded to Baltimore, reached on 22 March. Everywhere Dickens carried in his great-coat pocket a Shakespeare given to him by Forster. "What an unspeakable source of delight," he says, "that

[1] The letters of Dickens to Mr and Mrs Colden appeared in No. 233 (1 December 1834) of the *Dickensian*.
[2] For picture of one of the casts from it, see the *Dickensian*, 1 December 1833.
[3] In 1870 Putnam wrote two articles for the *Atlantic Monthly*, "Four Months with Charles Dickens during his First Visit to America."

book is for me." From Baltimore they went by canal to Pittsburgh where they stayed three days.

§ 60. *The City of Eden. Niagara, 26 April* 1842. *Montreal, 25 May* 1842

The canal ran for the most part by the side of the Susquehana and Iwanata rivers. The scenery was perfection. The stifling cabin was awful. Dickens rose every morning at half-past five and plunged his head into half-frozen water. He jumped from the boat to the towing-path and walked five or six miles before breakfast, keeping up with the horses. The Americans, who preferred to sit shivering round the stove, evinced astonishment. The canal wound its way through deep sullen gorges. To them succeeded swamp and morass where the frogs so croaked at night that there seemed to be millions of phantom teams with bells an enormous distance off. They passed by a number of new settlements and detached log-houses. The appearance of these erections was "utterly forlorn and miserable. Scarce in one of them were the windows whole. Old clothes and paper were stuffed into the broken glass." These scenes of misery and desolation suggested the city of Eden in *Martin Chuzzlewit* and the character of Mark Tapley.

He likened Pittsburgh to Birmingham. While there he met a little man, D. G. D'Almaine, whom he had known ten years before in London and who had become a portrait painter. In the company of D'Almaine and Putnam he held forth on the subject in which he had recently been so interested—"Animal Magnetism." He said he thought he could exercise the influence, though he had never tried. He then began to practise on Mrs Dickens. He says: "In six minutes, I magnetised her into hysterics, and then into the magnetic sleep. I tried again next night. . . . I can wake her with perfect ease; but I confess (not being prepared for anything so sudden and complete) I was on the first occasion rather alarmed."

From Pittsburgh they steamed, 1 April 1842, to Cincinnati, reaching it on 4 April, and on the way sat and counted the days before which they should be home. At Cincinnati, a beautiful city with pretty villas and gardens, they were introduced to a hundred and fifty first-rate bores. At the next city, Louisville (6 April) occurred a disquieting incident. Dickens had taken apartments in the Galt House, the landlord of which, Throckmorton, was a person of character and influence, the intimate of Clay, Crittenden and other notable Americans. Dickens had not been in the house long before Throckmorton visited him and politely offered his services in introducing him to the first families of Kentucky.

"Sir," enquired Dickens, "are you not the publican who keeps this inn?"

"Yes, sir."

"Then, sir, when I have need of your services, I will ring for you!"

The American narrator of the story assures us (untruthfully, no doubt) that "the next moment the distinguished novelist was half-way out of the window." The story is sometimes told as a sample of Dickens's conceit and haughtiness. That in America, as in England, he occasionally showed himself to disadvantage is probable; but on the occasion referred to there was perhaps some excuse. When he remembered the hundred and fifty bores to whom he had so recently been introduced, he must have chafed at the idea of encountering a hundred and fifty more.

From Louisville they went by steamer on the Ohio to its junction with the Mississippi and thence also by steamer to St Louis which they reached on 10 April. At St Louis, a lady, with the idea of uplifting Mrs Dickens, complimented her upon her voice and manner of speaking, assuring her that she would never have suspected her of being Scotch, or even English. Certainly Mrs Dickens needed all the uplifting she could get, for to her the journey was a prolonged agony. "You recollect her propensity," writes Dickens to Forster [1] (24 April 1842). "She falls into, or out of, every coach or boat we enter; scrapes the skin off her legs; brings great sores and swellings on her feet; chips

[1] Ley's *Forster*, p. 265.

152

large fragments out of her ankle-bones; and makes herself blue with bruises." This characteristic of Mrs Dickens was shared by Tilly Slowboy (in *The Cricket on the Hearth*).[1] It is observed of that young lady's legs "that there was a fatality about them which rendered them singularly liable to be grazed; and that she never effected the smallest ascent or descent, without recording the circumstance upon them with a notch as Robinson Crusoe marked the days upon his wooden calendar." Charity, however, forbids us to assume that Mrs Dickens when in England, had been, like Miss Slowboy, in the habit of holding the baby (Walter Landor) upside down or of crying "Ketcher, ketcher" to it, or of "performing cow-like gambols round that all-unconscious Innocent," or that she used to "hand it round to everybody in succession as if it were something to drink." [2]

After leaving St Louis, Dickens and his wife returned to Cincinnati, whence they journeyed to Niagara Falls, reached on 26 April. While at Niagara he entered into conversation with some of the inhabitants respecting International Copyright. "If," said he, "you steal English books you will naturally have no literature of your own." "We don't want one," was the reply. "Why should we pay for what we can get for nothing? Dollars, banks and cotton are our books, sir."

At Montreal on 25 May Dickens and Mrs Dickens took part in some private theatricals for the benefit of a charity. Dickens was stage manager. "And didn't I come Macready over them!" he asks. "Oh no! by no means!" The pieces were Thomas Morton's farce *A Roland for an Oliver*,[3] in which Dickens was "Alfred Highflyer"; Mathews's *Past Two O'clock in the Morning* [4] in which he distinguished himself as Mr Snobbington (in a wig obtained

---

[1] Cr. ed., vol. 15, p. 167.     [2] *Ibid.*, p. 200.
[3] For copy of play-bill, see Ley's *Forster*, p. 276.
[4] *Past Two O'clock in the Morning* was first performed at the Theatre Royal, Covent Garden, on Saturday, 3 October 1840, when Mr Keeley was Mr Newpenny, the Stranger Mr C. Mathews. As altered by Dickens the Stranger becomes Mr Snobbington.

from New York) and John Poole's *Deaf as a Post* in which he was "Gallop" and Mrs Dickens "Amy Templeton."

Speaking of the Mr Snobbington part, Dickens says, "I really do believe that I was very funny." On the play-bill which he sent home he put eight exclamation marks after Mrs Dickens's name, commenting, "But only think of Kate playing! and playing devilish well!" "The pieces indeed went with a roar" all through. This was pleasant, but the pleasantest of all was the prospect of Home! The return journey to England (they steamed out of New York harbour on 7 June) was accomplished without event, and one evening at the end of June 1842, a hackney coach carrying Dickens and his wife rattled up to Devonshire Terrace. Four little children hurried out of the house, and their father, too eager to wait till the gate opened, kissed them between the bars. Mrs Dickens was equally excited.

To celebrate the return, a dinner was arranged at Greenwich. Talfourd, Beard, Forster, Monckton, Milnes (Lord Houghton), W. B. Procter, Maclise, Stanfield, Captain Marryat, Barham (of *Ingoldsby Legends*), Thomas Hood, and George Cruikshank took part. On the way home Cruikshank, to the great amusement of the others, stood on his head in Beard's phaeton and sang comic songs.

## CHAPTER XII

# June 1842 to Spring 1847

§ 61. *Dickens and Unitarianism. "American Notes,"* 18
*October* 1842. *The Trip to Cornwall* 28 *October* 1842.
*The Rev. E. Tagart*

WHEN in America Dickens attended the services of Dr Channing and other eminent Unitarian Ministers, and he met Longfellow, Jared Sparks, Bancroft, Adams and other prominent Unitarians. After his return to England he worshipped for a few Sundays in Essex Street Chapel under the Rev. Thomas Madge. The leading features in the Unitarian creed are, in the words of Dickens's friend, W. J. Fox, "Belief in the supremacy of God the Father and in the humanity and divine mission of Jesus of Nazareth." [1]

Dickens did not believe in the Virgin Birth of Christ, and, as might be expected, this is made evident in *The Children's New Testament, An Abstract of the Narrative of the Four Gospels for the use of Juvenile Readers*, which he began a little later and finished in June 1846—the work which was first published 5 March to 17 March 1934, in the *Daily Mail*. Speaking of Jesus in the opening paragraphs he says, "His father's name was Joseph," and subsequently where Joseph is referred to he is spoken of as "Christ's father." Christ is usually alluded to as "Our Saviour," and he defines Christianity as "To do good

[1] *Collected Works of W. J. Fox,* vol. 1, pp. 89, 196, 205.

always—even to those who do evil to us. It is Christianity to love our neighbour as ourself, and to do to all men as we would have them do to us. It is Christianity to be gentle, merciful and forgiving." [1]

As the Rev. Clement E. Pike [2] points out, Dickens was first attracted to Unitarianism owing to the attitude of the denomination to rational and innocent amusement. In his *American Notes* [3] he says: "The peculiar province of the pulpit in New England (always excepting the Unitarian minority) would appear to be the denunciation of all innocent and rational amusements." Dr Channing indeed made a deeper impression on Dickens than did any other preacher.

As soon as Dickens could settle down after his return home he commenced his Impressions of America. In August he was at Broadstairs reading Tennyson on the sands and writing his book, and in September he was back in London where he visited William Hone of the *Every Day Book* who was on his death-bed at Tottenham. Hone died on 8 November 1842.[4]

The book *American Notes* appeared on 18 October. For the philanthropic institutions of Massachusetts and other states he has unstinted praise. He says, "I sincerely believe that the public institutions and charities are as nearly perfect as the most considerate wisdom, benevolence and humanity, can make them." He gives an account of a visit which he and Mrs Dickens made to the Perkins Institution, and Massachusetts Asylum for the Blind at Boston. He was particularly affected by the sight of one of the inmates, Laura Bridgman, who was blind, deaf and dumb; destitute of smell; and nearly so of taste—a fair young creature with every human faculty . . . and but one outward sense—the sense of touch. She was 12 years of age; and he tells how in spite of great difficulties she was taught many things. He says, "She never seems to repine, but has all the buoyancy and gaiety of childhood."

When Dickens offered his hand she rejected it, but she

[1] See also § 80.  [2] *Unitarian Monthly*, February 1912.
[3] Cr. ed., vol. 13.  [4] For the letter, *re* his funeral, see § 63.

retained Mrs Dickens's with evident pleasure, kissed her, and examined her dress with a girl's curiosity and interest. He also gives an account of a poor boy of 13, Oliver Caswell, who was also deaf, dumb and blind. It was all so pathetic, especially when Laura came in and Dickens, who made motions with his fingers, saw the two together. Dickens has references in several of his books to the deaf and dumb, but he was always interested in charitable institutions. His sympathy for the deaf and dumb is shown in other of his books. Very affecting, for instance, is his story of Sophy in *Dr Marigold* [1] (you couldn't produce a deafer or a dumber)—the poor child whom the tender-hearted cheap-jack left in the Deaf and Dumb Establishment. It is gratifying to know that in England at the present day the Deaf, Deaf-blind, and Hard of Hearing are well cared for. The Guild of St John of Beverley, for instance, the headquarters of which are at Ealing, superintended by Mr Selwyn Oxley, sees that in this respect our own country is not behind the States.

*American Notes*, which appeals chiefly to the humanitarian, contains four designs by Marcus Stone. It has little to attract those who read solely for amusement or who are in search of literary merit. Macaulay said of the book, "It is impossible for me to review it, I cannot praise it, and I will not cut it up. I cannot praise it, though it contains a few lively dialogues and descriptions; for it seems to me to be on the whole a failure. It is written like the worst parts of *Humphrey's Clock*. What is meant to be fine is a great deal too fine for me, as the description of Niagara." But if he would not praise it he would not attack it, because he had eaten salt with Dickens, and secondly, because Dickens "is a great man, and a man of real talent." Macaulay's opinion is very generally endorsed.

Just before the appearance of this book Longfellow visited England, and he, Dickens, and Forster visited, among other spots, Dickens's dear old Rochester—storming the castle strongholds in something the same

[1] Cr. ed., vol. 15, p. 281.

L

fashion as did fighting men in the Middle Ages; over-leaping gates and barriers, defying the custodian, who was insolent, and threatened the terrors of the law, and working their will among the ruins. To-day no such desperate valour is necessary, for Rochester Castle, stand-ing amid beautifully kept grounds, is at all times open to the public. The friends also, under the guidance and protection of two prison officials, made a tour by night through the most dangerous parts of London—visiting the haunts of tramps, thieves, and harlots.

Longfellow left on 21 October 1842, and a week later Dickens, in the company of Stanfield, Maclise and Forster took a trip to Cornwall. "I think," says Dickens, "of opening my new book (*Martin Chuzzlewit*) on the coast of Cornwall, in some terrible, dreary iron-bound spot," but he changed his mind. The jaunt turned out all that was hoped. Historical scenes were visited, earthy old churches and strange ocean caverns explored. Four such boon companions, it seems, never were. "Laughter!" says Dickens, "I was choking and gasping and bursting the buckle off the back of my stock all the way." For Dickens had not lost his boyishness at 30. Nor had Forster, grandmotherly as was his usual manner. Cer-tainly he was not grandmotherly in physique. He clambered to the top of the Logan stone, and they rocked him. But he was ever their leader in deeds of daring. He piloted them over the waterfall of St Wighton, he perched like Ariel on the tip-top stone of the Castle of St Michael's Mount, and capered up the difficult path to Tintagel like a he-goat among his own rocks; and so after the most rollicking three weeks that four merry men ever wasted, they returned to London. There was laughter enough, but all the same it seems a little forced.

The journey over, Stanfield and Maclise finished the sketches made in the most romantic of their halting-places. Stanfield's was the Logan Stone with Forster perched at the top; and Maclise painted for the Academy from one of his a picture called "A Girl at the Waterfall," which included a portrait of Miss Georgina Hogarth, who wasn't there. Georgina was then nearly 16, that is to say, close on the age reached by Mary Hogarth when she died. Dickens used to say that his attachment to Miss Hogarth originated partly from her resemblance in appearance and character to Mary. So eager was he to possess Maclise's picture that he bought it under a feigned name before the Academy opened, "and steadily refused to take back the money, which Maclise, on discovery of the artifice, pressed upon him."

On 20 November 1842, Dickens attended the Chapel in Little Portland Street,[1] the leading West End place of worship of the Unitarians, in order to hear the Rev. Edward Tagart [2] preach a funeral sermon on Dr Channing, who had died on the 2nd of October. After the service, Dickens entered into conversation with Mr Tagart, and finding that their views on religion tallied, he took sittings in the chapel. He and his family attended regularly for five years. After 1847 when the differences between him and his wife had become acute, he worshipped there alone. His religious views never materially changed. He always regarded Jesus Christ reverentially as the Great Master whose precepts were misconstrued, whose lessons were perverted.[3] Dickens's intimate friends, Forster, William Johnson Fox, and Mrs Gaskell, were Unitarians; and among Fox's addresses is a sermon delivered to prove that "the spread of Unitarianism is a blessing to society." Dickens's friendship with Tagart continued till that minister's death in 1858.

## § 62. "Martin Chuzzlewit," November 1842

Up to the time of his return from Cornwall, Dickens had done nothing of the proposed new story, but in November (1842) he set about it in earnest, and after

---

[1] The Rev. Dr Martineau was for many years minister there.

[2] See §§ 61 and 68.

[3] See the article, "A Memorable Unitarian," February 1912 (Centenary of Dickens's birth) in the *Unitarian Monthly*, by the Rev. Clement E. Pike; also the *Dickensian*, June 1934, p. 216. The former has a portrait of Dickens lent by Chapman and Hall.

waverings among Chuzzleton, Chuzzleboy, and other titles, he finally decided upon Chuzzlewit, and opened in a Wiltshire village, near Salisbury. The object of the story, to use Dickens's words, was "to show how selfishness propagates itself, and to what a grim giant it may grow from small beginnings."

*Martin Chuzzlewit*, though it begins atrociously—the first chapter, which is all about nothing, being a model of bad writing—is one of the best of Dickens's novels. Mr Pecksniff—"the moral Pecksniff," the man "who never ceases to be laughable and yet never ceases to be loathsome," is one of Dickens's greatest creations. "He was a most exemplary man: fuller of virtuous precept than a copybook. Some people likened him to a direction post, which is always telling the way to a place, and never goes there." We know his daughters—the grave and prudent Charity and the skittish and artless Mercy— better than our next-door neighbours. A house called St Mary's Grange at Alderbury, two miles from Salisbury, has been pointed out as the residence of this world-famous family. Mark Tapley is surely one of the most original characters ever invented, and Ruth is not, perhaps, so very bad, as angels go.

Mr Augustus Moddle, the youngest gentleman at Mrs Todger's boarding-house who sighed for Mercy Pecksniff, and was entrapped into an engagement with her sister Charity, is of the minor characters one of the best. Jonas is almost as repulsive as Sikes—though far more cleverly drawn. What a capital chapter is that (the 27th) which describes the interview of Jonas with Mr Tigg Montague, of the Anglo-Bengalee Disinterested Loan and Life Insurance Company!

Mrs Gamp has been over-rated. Her lingo irritates. Professor Ward, and many others, however, exhaust the vocabulary in her praise, and Mr Gissing ranks her with Dame Quickly and Juliet's nurse. The midwife in Richardson's "Pamela" was Mrs Harris, and it has been suggested that Mrs Gamp's friend was a reminiscence of her.

Among those fascinated by *Martin Chuzzlewit* was Sir Richard Owen, the famous anatomist. Under date 3 May 1844, Mrs Owen writes in her diary: "After a hard day's work, R. deep in *Martin Chuzzlewit*. My father came in before going to the Royal Society and talked to R. without mercy; but R., whose thoughts and attentions were so entirely given up to Mrs Gamp and Jonas, could only answer at random. As soon as my father was gone we laughed over Mrs Gamp until bed-time." The fame of Mrs Gamp has led Dickens students to overlook the merits of her rival, Mrs Prodgit, who in her "black bonnet of large dimensions" figures in "Births, Mrs Meek, of a son," [1] a *Household Words* article in which Mrs Hogarth (Mrs Bigby) also seems to figure.[2]

If Dickens had in *American Notes* chastised the Americans with whips, in *Martin Chuzzlewit* he chastised them with scorpions. Referring to the account of the "New York Sewer," Professor Ward remarks: "Satire in such passages as these borders too closely on angry invective; and neither the irresistible force, nor the earnest pathos of the details which follow, can clear away the suspicion that at the bottom lay a desire to depreciate."

The following may be given as samples of the humour of *Martin Chuzzlewit*:

*An Editor.* The captain . . . took a cordial leave of his friend the colonel, and hurried away to despatch the champagne: well-knowing that if he failed to conciliate the editor of the Rowdy Journal, that potentate would denounce him and his ship in large capitals before he was a day older; and would probably assault the memory of his mother also, who had not been dead more than twenty years.

*Mr Fips.* They occupied the two chairs, and Mr Fips took the office stool, from the stuffing whereof he drew forth a piece of horse-hair of immense length, which he put into his mouth with a great appearance of appetite.

*The Mat.* An old mat, worn into lattice work which, being useless as a mat (even if anybody could have seen it, which was

---

[1] Cr. ed., vol. 17, p. 247.          [2] *Ibid.*, p. 248.

impossible), had for many years directed its industry into another channel, and regularly tripped up every one of Mr Fips's clients.

Dickens's humour at its best is delicious, but it often tails off into silliness.  Where is the fun in the colloquy between Mark Tapley and Pinch (chapter 5) where Pinch asks, "Why don't you wear a waistcoat?"  What could be flatter than the would-be humorous account of "The Dragon" in chapter 3.  Yet even the minor characters display genius—Mr Nadgett, for instance, and the old woman called Tamaroo, though they are only sketches.

*Martin Chuzzlewit* is well illustrated with forty pictures by Phiz, whose rendering of Pecksniff has been considered to resemble Sir Robert Peel.

§ 63. *Dickens as a Letter Writer.  A Peep at the Home Life*

In the spring of 1843 Dickens spent a holiday with Mr Charles Smithson (Thomas Mitton's partner) at Easthorpe Hall near Malton, Yorkshire.[1]  It was in March 1843, while Dickens was holidaying at Cobley's Farm, Finchley, that he wrote parts of *Martin Chuzzlewit*.

On 2 March 1843, Dickens wrote the unfortunate letter [2] to Felton with its ludicrous account of the conversation between the Rev. Thomas Binney and Cruikshank at Hone's funeral.  The letter was in shockingly bad taste, for Binney, one of the most prominent figures in the religious world, was a metaphysical preacher of amazing power and would be remembered if only as the author of "Eternal Light," and other hymns.  He was tall in stature, with a lofty intellectual forehead which seemed "piled up story upon story of brain built each over the other."  An article appeared in the *Evangelical Magazine* denying Dickens's statements.

---

[1] Smithson died in 1844 and Dickens attended his funeral on Good Friday.

[2] Letters, 2 March 1843, to Professor Felton.  Hone died 8 November 1842.

Dickens, however, did not particularly shine as a letter writer, the well-known work so shockingly edited by Miss Georgina Hogarth and his eldest daughter being one of the dreariest epistolary collections ever published. The style is affected and stilted, almost the only topics the writer waxes eloquent over being cold punch, brandy cocktails and sherry cobblers. It is, however, nothing but fair to say that his unpublished letters and the deleted portions of the published ones are much more lively and attractive.

After his return from America, Georgina Hogarth had become practically head of his household; unconsciously, for her intentions were certainly good, usurping the place that should have been Mrs Dickens's, and so she continued until his death. Mrs Dickens, being a wife, naturally resented being continually put in the background, with the result of more family jars.

Two notable dinners are next to be recorded, one at Greenwich to John Black, who had "thrown the slipper," [1] and the other at Richmond to Macready, who was just about to start for America. In August, Dickens was at Broadstairs again, performing an "insane match" against time by walking on a hot broiling day eighteen miles in four hours and a half—one more instance of his attempts to weary himself and so to escape from the recollection of home broils. He generally occupied his time by writing "in a bay window in a one pair" from nine to one. At one he bathed, and after lunch he walked a dozen miles or so or lay on his back on the sand reading. Early in October he was in Town again, and there might have been heard in Lincoln's Inn Fields at night—Forster's quarters—sound as of "men laughing, together with a clanking of knives and forks and wine-glasses."

Charming descriptions have been preserved of him with his children at this time.[2] Seated in an American rocking-chair, he used to sing to Charles (age 5), Mary (age 4), and Kate (age 3), comic songs and ditties including "The Loving Ballad of Lord Bateman," the

[1] See § 23.    [2] *Windsor Magazine*, Christmas 1934.

favourite being the song about Guy Fawkes who reached
London by crossing over Vauxhall Bridge,

> That is he would have come that way
> To perpetrate his guilt, sir,
> But a little thing prevented him
> The bridge it wasn't built, sir.

It is pleasant to see him with the children about him
or on his knees, thus amusing them with dramatic action
while all join in the chorus which was never right unless
the affecting "fol de riddy oddy" came into it somewhere.

One recalls, too, his charming Fairy Tale, "The Magic
Fishbone," embedded in *Holiday Romance*,[1] for he must
have looked back on his own Devonshire House days
when he made the pretty story which lets us peep behind
the scenes in an industrious home—the women-folk with
rag-bag and scissors, the baby tumbling down and bump-
ing herself and screaming herself black in the face, while
Mrs Dickens is busy as busy can be, stitching and snipping.
We see the little girl with tucks in her frock "to admit
of being let out" and her doll which, in a lovely world
of make-believe, is not a doll at all but a born duchess
with flaxen curls and a set smile; and surely that was a
real cook who "ran away with her own true love, a very
tall but tipsy soldier."

## § 64. *Ragged Schools and Mr S. R. Starey, 26 September* 1843

About this time a number of persons of influence, and
among them the philanthropic Miss Burdett Coutts (later
the Baroness Burdett Coutts), were interesting themselves
in the valuable institution of Ragged Schools, a movement
which, since its commencement (some twenty years previous)
by the good shoemaker, John Pounds, had gradually been
spreading its ramifications throughout the country; and
Dickens joined heartily with Miss Coutts in lending help
in various ways. By the year 1843 there was a sprinkling
of these schools in London; and among the most indefatigable of the teachers was a lawyer's clerk named Samuel

[1] Cr. ed., vol. 15, p. 595.

Roberts Starey,[1] who laboured in that unsavoury spot, Field Lane, Holborn—the London slum in which Dickens had located the house of the "Awful Jew." Every other tenement was a "thieves' kitchen," the resort of the scum of the earth. Mr Starey and his coadjutors were often pelted with filth. Many a time he returned from teaching covered with mud from head to heel. Their windows were broken with rotten vegetables. On one occasion Master Bates, the "Artful," and friends rushed upstairs to the apartment, overturned the forms, blew the lights out, danced, and sang obscene songs on the forms, assaulted the teachers and then dropped from the window into the yard beneath. On another—the evening on which the girls were taught—William Sykes, Esq., and party made their appearance and skittishly smashed the door in, dashed upstairs all among the girls and women, and broke up the chairs and tables. Then there was a general rush to the stairs, and "the screaming, swearing, and uproar as the mob fell pell-mell over one another was awful."

"After one such night at Field Lane, four of us," says one of the teachers, "walked as far as Gray's Inn Road, and, pausing by a lamp-post at the corner of Guildford Street, we there in our helplessness offered prayer to God in a few earnest words for strength, and begged Him, as the work was His, to sustain it and us, and give us His blessing. Feeling strengthened, we encouraged each other, and there and then promised each to stick to the work through thick and thin." Into these slums no policeman dared enter alone. Some of the teachers—"the fair-weather men"—fell off, but the majority bravely persevered.

Dickens, who kept himself well posted in the work of this courageous band, had frequent interviews with Mr Starey, and several times corresponded with him on the subject. In the letter of 24 September 1843, written after a visit to the Field Lane school, he suggests "that

[1] Letters of S. R. Starey to Thomas Wright. S. R. Starey died in November 1904. See *Christian World*, 24 November 1904.

the boys should have an opportunity of washing themselves before beginning their tasks," and he asks Mr Starey to "ascertain at about what cost a washing-place—a large trough or sink—with a good supply of running water, soap, and towels, could be put up," and whether in the event of his procuring funds for this and other improvements, Mr Starey would see any objection to expressly limiting teachers to confining their questions and instruction to the broad truths of religion. He concludes, " I set great store by this question, because it seems to me of vital importance that no persons, however well-intentioned, should perplex the minds of these unfortunate creatures with religious mysteries that young people with the best advantages can but imperfectly understand." This letter is also interesting as being one of the earliest instances of the mention of the term "Ragged School," which had been suggested a short time previously by Mr Starey.

§ 65. *The pencil-drawing by Maclise of Dickens, Mrs Dickens and Miss Hogarth. Dickens meets again the Rev. W. Giles*

In 1843, Maclise made the well-known pencil-drawing of Dickens, Mrs Dickens and Miss Hogarth. It has often been reproduced, in Kitton's *Dickens*, for instance, p. 114, and, though only a sketch, it is a very remarkable study of the three figures. Dickens has a confident and conquering look with firm lip, bright eye and steadfast gaze; Mrs Dickens with her *retroussé* nose, closed lips and well-outlined face, is as pretty as in the later portrait by Maclise, but she had a downcast, meditative and almost sad look, which tells its own story. Miss Hogarth, on the other hand, who, there, is not nearly so good-looking as Mrs Dickens, is perky with lips partly open and a retreating chin. The picture is a vivid biography in pencil of all three. Maclise has drawn in each case, not only the face but the character—the attitude of each, at that moment, to actual life. The picture is startling indeed owing to

CHARLES DICKENS, MRS. DICKENS AND MISS HOGARTH
Pencil Drawing by Maclise, 1843
*Photo by T. W. Tyrrell*

See page 166

BLUNDESTONE CHURCH, SUFFOLK

Blundestone is the "Blunderstone" of "David Copperfield"

*Photo by Catherine Weed Ward*

See page 198

its profound and even wizardly truthfulness and the artist's gift of seeing into the soul. Georgina's look is that of one who is appreciated and knows it, Mrs Dickens's that of one who is unappreciated and knows it.[1]

On Wednesday, 4 October, Dickens visited Manchester in order to preside at the opening of the Athenæum, and stayed with his sister, Mrs Burnett, at No. 3 Elm Terrace, Higher Ardwick. Close by in that suburb resided his old school-fellow, Samuel Giles, with whom the Rev. William Giles,[2] the Chatham schoolmaster (his brother), was staying. Dickens (accompanied, no doubt, by his sister) called on him, and subsequently letters passed between them. Occasionally when at Manchester Dickens stayed with the Rev. William Gaskell and Mrs Gaskell at 84 Plymouth Grove. The address at the Athenæum was delivered on 5 October [3]—Cobden and Disraeli being also among the speakers—and Dickens returned to London next day.

Early in 1844 Dickens's interest in the Ragged School movement was renewed, and on 1 February 1844, he wrote to ask Mr Starey for any little facts or details concerning it which might benefit the design. After a while the idea began to be mooted that it would be advisable to weld the schools of London into one body, and on 11 April 1844, Mr Starey called a meeting at his father's house, 17 Ampton Street. To this invitation three responded, Messrs Locke, Moulton, and Morrison, who with Mr Starey composed the "Immortal Four," who laid the foundation of the Ragged School Union, by adopting a resolution to call a general meeting of superintendents and teachers for the purpose of forming a central committee of Ragged Schools. At the next meeting forty persons were present. On 5 July nineteen

---

[1] Of the portrait of Dickens himself in this sketch, his eldest daughter says in a letter to F. G. Kitton that it is to her mind "the most beautiful of all the portraits. It is the likeness which goes through all the best portraits throughout his life." *Charles Dickens by P. and P.*, vol. 2, p. 47.

[2] Rev. William Giles died 30 September 1856.

[3] See *Dickens's Speeches*. Hotten's ed., p. 74.

schools were recognised as associated with the new Union, and at this meeting the name "The Ragged School Union was formally adopted." Towards the end of the year Lord Ashley (Earl Shaftesbury) became President, and under his fostering care the small twig speedily became a great and wide-spreading tree. The abominable Field Lane was swept away when the Holborn Viaduct was formed.

How necessary these labours of Starey, Dickens and others were may be judged from an article in the *Quarterly Review* for 1847 [1] (vol. 79).

We have penetrated, the writer says, alleys terminating in a cul-de-sac long and narrow like a tobacco pipe, where air and sunshine were never known. The children sit along these depositories of death, or roam through the retired courts in which the abomination of years has been suffered to accumulate. They receive no education religious or secular. A short time ago, the night having set in, we were passing through a dark street to the inspection of a school, when a gentleman of the company was addressed with, "How are you, there?" He looked at the lad who turned from him with evident displeasure saying, "I thought you were Teacher. If you had been I would have shaken hands with you." This may be a small fact in itself, but it is a mighty one to show the power of sympathy over these Arabs of the Metropolis."

Dickens's interest in the Ragged School movement soon made itself felt in his novels. It led to the creation of Mr Casby, Mr Pancks, Mrs Plornish and the Bleeding Heart yard of *Little Dorrit*; and to poor ignorant Jo's slouching figure in *Tom-all-Alone's*,[2] which *Bleak House* was at first intended to be called.

Says Jo, " 'I don't know nothink.' Jo lives—that is to say Jo has not yet lived—in a ruinous place known to the like of him by the name Tom-all-Alone's. It is a black, dilapidated street, avoided by all decent people." The ignorance of the brickmaker's family in the same story was equal to Jo's.

"Ain't my place dirty? Yes, it is dirty—it's naturally dirty and it's nat-rally onwholesome; and we've had five dirty and onwhole-

---

[1] Also *Edinburgh Review*, April 1847.
[2] *Bleak House*. Cr. ed., vol. 10, p. 175.

some children. . . . Have I read the little book what you left? No, I ain't read the little book wot you left. There ain't nobody here as knows how to read. . . . How have I been conducting myself? Why I've been drunk for three days; and I'd a been drunk four, if I'd a had the money." [1] "It must be a strange state," says Dickens, "to be like Jo. . . . To see people read, and to see people write, and to see the postman deliver letters, and not to have the least idea of all that language—to be, to every scrap of it, stone-blind and dumb."

### § 66. The "Christmas Carol," Christmas 1843

Christmas 1843 saw the first, as it certainly is the best, of Dickens's Christmas Books, "that incomparable, entire, and perfect chrysolite poem," as one admirer styled it, the *Christmas Carol* (1843). The others are:
*The Chimes.* 1844.
*The Cricket on the Hearth.* 1845.
*The Battle of Life.* 1846.
*The Haunted Man.* 1848.
There was no Christmas Book for 1847.

The *Christmas Carol* contains some autobiographical touches. Scrooge's little sister has the same name as Dickens's sister—"Fan"—and the shapes that at the bidding of the spirit arose before Scrooge were the heroes of the beloved books of the Golden Garret days—Ali Baba, Robinson Crusoe, with his parrot, Friday, and others. All hearts warm to Tiny Tim, and we are always anxious for the welfare of the rest of the Cratchits, including certainly the impatient two who crammed spoons into their mouths "lest they should shriek for goose before their turn came to be helped."

The revival of the observation of Christmas is largely due to Washington Irving and Charles Dickens. The honour may be fairly divided between them. *Bracebridge Hall* came first, and was no doubt the prototype of the scenes at Dingley Dell, but Dickens's work had a far greater vogue than Irving's, and his influence was no doubt greater too. There is no prettier story of a poor man's Christmas extant

[1] Cr. ed., vol. 10, p. 86.

than that of Bob Cratchit's in the *Christmas Carol*. True pathos, which, as we have said, occurs but rarely in Dickens's works, is more in evidence in the *Christmas Carol* than elsewhere.

The writing of this story excited its author to the highest pitch. Says Forster: "He wept over it, and laughed, and wept again, and walked thinking of it fifteen and twenty miles about the back streets of London," and when it was over "he let himself loose like a madman."

For 7 February 1844 (on which date "dear Kate," to use Miss Hogarth's reference in a letter to Beard, was expected "down again" after the birth of little Francis Jeffery), a cosy dinner was planned—Forster and Beard to be the only guests, but that could not have been a singular occasion, for when was "dear Kate" not "down again" after the arrival of some little Francis Jeffery or other!

§ 67. *The Christiana Weller Idyll, 26 February* 1844

In February 1844 Dickens consented to take the chair at a soirée to be held in the Mechanics' Institution, Liverpool, and the committee sent him a bank order for twenty pounds in payment of the expenses contingent on his visit to that city. He did not like to accept the money, and on the 21st he wrote to a friend asking for advice. He said, "Now, what in the name of goodness ought I to do? I am as much puzzled with the cheque as Colonel Jack (in Defoe's novel) was with his gold." However, he got over the difficulty by returning the money.

The soirée took place on Monday, 26 February, and Dickens appeared in a white-and-black or Magpie waistcoat, leading members of the audience to enquire, "What is it? Is it a waistcoat? No, it is a shirt!" But more amusement was caused when he announced the name of the pianist as Miss Christiana Weller. With the beauty and talent of Miss Weller he was greatly struck. During the evening he could hardly take his eyes from her face. He was introduced and asked permission to call on her. He wrote glowingly to her on the 27th, "Let me congratulate

you with my whole heart on your brilliant achievements last
night. Nothing could have been more successful, graceful,
charming—triumphant in every particular. I felt a pride
in you which I cannot express."

When this episode in Dickens's life was first revealed in
the *Tribune*, 3 February 1906, Victorian-minded people
were foolishly indignant; but it is surely no disgrace, it is
even a beautiful trait in human nature for the male heart,
whatever its age or position, to be fluttered by the sight of
female beauty. Indeed, female beauty would, one presumes, be chagrined were its charms to prove ineffective.
Certainly life would be a duller affair were it otherwise; but
it is necessary for that same male heart to be severely on its
guard. Dickens was then severely on his guard. It is
true that on discovering her to be an admirer of Tennyson,
he sent her the two-volume edition of that poet's works; but
that was all, though possibly it would not have been all if
he had not introduced Miss Weller to his friend T. J.
Thompson who had come to Liverpool on purpose to be
present at the soirée. Thompson fell in love with her. In
Dickens's words (sent to Miss Weller) Thompson "fell
desperately, madly, irretrievably in love there, which was so
perfectly natural (the circumstances of his case being quite
uncommon, and his provocation enormous) that I could not
find it in my heart to remonstrate with him for his folly.
Indeed I rather encouraged him in it than otherwise."
Æsop libelled the fox when he made him say, after failing
to reach the grapes, "They are sour." What he actually
did was to go, generously, and tell a younger and more
lissom fox all about them.

The idyll had as its sequel the marriage of Thompson and
Miss Weller. Their elder daughter, who became Lady
Butler the battle painter, died in October 1933 at the age of
86. Their second daughter, Alice, who married Mr
Wilfrid Meynell is, as poet and essayist, well known to
fame. The letters that passed between Dickens and Miss
Weller first appeared in the *Tribune* for 3 February 1906,
and afterwards in the *Dickensian* for 1916. An amusing
story told by Mr Desmond MacCarthy, evidently belongs

to this period. One day when Dickens was sitting dejectedly at lunch, one of his children explained pityingly in a whisper to a guest, "Poor papa is in love again."

## § 68. *Stared in the Face by Ruin*, 10 *February* 1844

To Dickens's surprise and disappointment there was a considerable falling off in the sales of *Chuzzlewit*. Instead of 50,000 purchasers, as with *Pickwick* and *Nickleby*, and 70,000 with its successors, *Chuzzlewit* attracted at first only 20,000, and subsequently only 23,000. The hint from his publishers that on account of this declension a reduction might be made in the payments caused Dickens to take offence, and he resolved to exchange Messrs Chapman and Hall for Messrs Bradbury and Evans, to whom, in consideration of an advance of £2,800, he then assigned a fourth share in whatever he might write during the ensuing eight years. He also resolved to go abroad with a view to improving his health, invigorating his mind, varying and extending his observation, and lowering his expenses, for his family was large (five at the time) and calls were made upon his purse by thriftless and ne'er-do-well relations, sometimes to such an extent as to throw him almost into a fever. He even declared that he had grave thoughts "of keeping his whole menagerie in Italy three years."

The *Chuzzlewit* trouble was followed by a disappointment in the results in the sale of the *Christmas Carol*. Dickens had set his heart and soul upon getting £1,000, but the probabilities were that he would have no more than half that amount. His "year's bills, unpaid," he spoke of as "terrific." He was almost at his wits' end. "Do come soon," he writes to Forster, 10 February 1844, "as I am very anxious to talk with you. I am not afraid, if I reduce my expenses; but if I do not I shall be ruined past all mortal hope of redemption."

To add to his embarrassments, his father and mother were entirely dependent upon him. Then, too, his brother Frederick was chronically and cheerfully in difficulties. Of indigent relatives, indeed—parents, brothers, sisters, brothers-in-law, sisters-in-law, cousins—he had a choice and sufficient assortment. If a year passed without some fresh one being left entirely or partially on his hands, "Poor Papa" evinced surprise. So when his face betrayed dejection, it was not necessarily because he was in love again.

When in 1844 the Little Portland Street congregation acknowledged the value of the Rev. Edward Tagart's services by a handsome present of plate, Dickens, who was one of the subscribers, wrote the inscription graven on the chief piece.[1] In it he described Unitarianism as "the religion which has sympathy for men of every creed, and ventures to pass judgment on none." This was in 1844, and in his last year he asked his children "to try to guide themselves by the teaching of the New Testament in its broad spirit and to put no faith in any man's narrow construction of its letter. Among Dickens's kind actions at this time was the writing of a preface to a collection of stories by a poor carpenter, John Overs. He also exerted himself to obtain help for Mrs Overs and her children after her husband's death. The book was entitled *Evenings by a Working Man*, the publisher being T. C. Newby.

§ 69. *In Italy, 16 July 1844. "The Chimes,"
Christmas 1844. Landor*

Having let his house in Devonshire Terrace, Dickens, after a brief residence at 9 Osnaburgh Terrace, set out with his "menagerie" or his "caravan" as he sometimes called it, for Italy, via Marseilles. The party, consisting of Mrs Dickens, Miss Hogarth, Charles (7), Mary (6), Kate (5), Walter (3), the baby, Francis Jeffery under 1, two nurses and Louis Roche, whom he called the "brave courier," lumbered into Genoa on 16 July 1844.

At the Villa Bagnerello, and subsequently at the Palazzo Peschiere, he lived as idly as he liked, feasting his eyes on green vineyards and deep blue skies. He was not idle long, however, for it was at the Peschiere that he wrote his story, *The Chimes*. He had heard the Genoan chimes, at mid-

---

[1] Ley's *Forster*, p. 236. See also §§ 61 and 68.

night, but, says he: "Let them clash upon me now from all the churches and convents in Genoa, I see nothing but the old London belfry I have set them in."

As in Devonshire Terrace, in Yorkshire, as indeed everywhere he went, he dreamt of Mary Hogarth. In the Genoa vision she wore "blue drapery as the Madonna might in a picture by Raphael." In November, leaving Mrs Dickens and Miss Hogarth at Genoa, he travelled to Parma and Venice. He declares that the wildest visions of the Arabian Nights are nothing to the piazza of St Mark. "The gorgeous and beautiful reality of Venice is beyond the fancy of the wildest dreamer." On 16 November he was at Cremona and on the 20th at Milan, where Mrs Dickens and Miss Hogarth spent a few days with him. He then returned, via Fribourg, Strasburg and Paris, to England, leaving his "menagerie" in Italy.

On 2 December he read at Forster's House, 58 Lincoln's Inn Fields, his Christmas book *The Chimes* to an audience including Forster, Maclise, Douglas Jerrold, Carlyle, Laman Blanchard, William Johnson Fox, Stanfield and Frederick Dickens. To commemorate the event, Maclise drew the well-known picture which represents Saint Dickens in the middle of the group, reading, with a halo round his head. 58 Lincoln's Inn was the residence of Mr Tulkinghorn in *Bleak House*. A few days later Dickens returned to Genoa.

As the hero of the *Christmas Carol* is Tiny Tim, so the hero of *The Chimes* is Trotty Veck, who by long waiting at the church door struck up, Quasimodo-like, a sort of friendship with the bells, "fancying discouragement or patronage in their Chime." *The Chimes* is much inferior to the *Christmas Carol*, but its author's motive was the same, namely, to help and cheer the poor and down-trodden.

With the illustrations to the Christmas Books Dickens was disappointed.

On 30 January, leaving Miss Hogarth and the children at Genoa, Dickens and his wife went to Rome for the Carnival. Miss Hogarth joined them at Naples; and they returned to Genoa via Rome and Florence, not, however, before he had visited Fiesole in order to meet Landor. With Mrs Landor whom he met (Landor was away) he was much taken, and he mentioned to Forster how agreeable she was. This being some time after reported to Landor, that demonstrative gentleman exclaimed with an interruptive roar: "And the Lord forbid that I should do otherwise than declare that she was agreeable to everyone but ME!" When at Florence Dickens called on Mrs Trollope and her son Thomas Adolphus, both of whom lived frequently in Italy and, as we shall see, the visit had an interesting result.

On 25 February 1845, that is while Dickens was away in Italy, his old love Maria Beadnell married Henry Louis Winter, a prosaic business man; but as it afterwards transpired, she had not forgotten Dickens, and she followed with interest his meteoric career. In her home life she was reasonably happy; happy with Dickens she could never have been. However, she preserved his letters to her, and it gave her pleasure to recall that she had once, by him, been furiously loved.

On 9 May he wrote from the Palazzo Peschiere, Genoa, to Maclise an amusing letter announcing the marriage of his cook, his "good-looking cook" to the cook of the governor of Genoa. He also tells of a public hanging, which he was afraid to witness knowing that he would be horrified. His man Roche went, however, and was sorry afterwards, the sight being so dreadful.[1]

§ 70. *The Three Fannys. Miss Kelly's Theatre.*
*"The Cricket on the Hearth," Christmas* 1845

In these days people still talked of the three Fannys: Fanny Kemble, Fanny Kelly and Fanny Ternan. Of the last we shall speak later. Fanny Kemble acted in *Macbeth* and *King Lear* with Macready, who pinched her black and blue in the one and raged the stage like a tiger in the other. Miss Kelly, who possessed a theatre (in Soho) of her own, was less favoured, for who would not gladly be pinched black and blue by so famous an actor!

[1] Letter, the *Dickensian,* 1 December 1833, p. 39.

In the summer of 1845 Dickens and several of his friends decided to hire Miss Kelly's theatre for a night and to give an amateur performance. Stanfield was the scene painter, the play chosen being Ben Jonson's *Every Man in his Humour*. The first performance took place on 21 September. It was so great a success that they decided to give a second performance in a larger theatre, St James's, for some charitable object. Dickens as Captain Bobadil covered himself with glory, and a painting of him in that character was made by Charles Robert Leslie, R.A.[1] Jonson's play was followed by Mathews's farce *Past Two O'clock in the Morning*. Besides Dickens, Lemon, Forster, Jerrold and Leech took parts.

The Christmas story for 1845, *The Cricket on the Hearth*, should have been entitled "Dot," who is one of the most attractive of Dickens's heroines. It is very pleasant to remember heavy, honest John Peerybingle, Tilly Slowboy, "the doll of a baby," the man with "Glass" in bold characters on his back, and the toy merchant. "I wrote this story," says Dickens, "to awaken some loving and forbearing thoughts never out of place in a Christian land." *The Cricket on the Hearth*, dramatised, at Dickens's special request, for the Keeleys, was produced at the Lyceum in December 1845. Mr J. W. T. Ley tells us that on 11 January 1846 versions of this Christmas book were being acted at twelve London theatres. On 3 January 1846, was performed at the Soho Theatre, for Miss Kelly's benefit, Fletcher's comedy *The Elder Brother*; Forster, Dickens and Dickens's brothers Frederick and Augustus being in it. It was followed by Peake's farce *Comfortable Lodgings*, in which both Forster and Dickens figured.

## § 71. *The "Daily News,"* 21 *January* 1846

The unhappiness in Dickens's home had become, as years went on, more and more accentuated. Dickens was injudicious and Mrs Dickens was not conciliatory. She continued to resent, as any wife would, the constant placing

[1] Reproduced in Kitton's *Dickens*, p. 408.

before her of the virtues of the dead Mary Hogarth. Tributes to his wife are absent from his letters, while tributes to Mary Hogarth crowded them. Her ring was never off his finger. He was always dwelling on her sweetness and excellence. Everywhere he dreamed of her. Then, too, Miss Georgina Hogarth was all the while taking the lead, occupying the place in the house that ought to have been Mrs Dickens's. The breach was continually widening. Nearly all writers on Dickens have assumed that his restlessness was the cause of the trouble between him and his wife. This was not so. It was the other way about. It was the difference with his wife that caused the restlessness. To Forster, long after, he admitted "one happiness I have missed in life and one friend and companion I have never made." He could find no relief except in hysterical action after hysterical action.

A few years later, he wrote in *David Copperfield* (pub. in 1849): "There can be no disparity in marriage like unsuitability of mind and purpose. . . . It would have been better for me if my wife could have helped me more, and shared the many thoughts in which I had no partner." How could she help him! At the time these words were being printed, she had had eight children in thirteen years, that is thereabouts one every eighteen months. She never had time to get over one confinement before she was expecting another. The poor woman was never at rest. She deserved more consideration.

After No. 8 there were two more children. When the tenth arrived, 13 March 1852, he wrote to Cerjât, "My wife is quite well, after favouring me (I think I could have dispensed with the compliment) with No. 10." Elsewhere he refers to his "tons of children." But the person to be blamed was surely not Mrs Dickens, but Dickens himself. In those days, however, it was a standing jest against a woman if she had a huge family and was therefore so often, to use Dickens's phrase, in an "*un*interesting state." It never seemed to occur to anybody that if there was to be a jest at all, it should, in fairness, be at the expense of the man. Dickens's own pages are full of witticisms directed against the over-fruitful wife, the most conspicuous being the picture of Mrs Micawber with the perpetual twins. But it was an ungallant age; and Dickens was no worse in this respect than so many of his contemporaries.

We spoke of his hysterical actions. Among them was the preparation for founding a daily newspaper for the conducting of which his disqualifications were so patent that his friends, prominently Forster, urged him to give up the idea. However, he would not be gainsaid, and the result was the *Daily News*. Its price, as an advertisement in *Punch* announced, was to be fivepence. It was to be a morning newspaper of Liberal politics and thorough independence, scientific, commercial, and Parliamentary intelligence was promised, and among the writers of its leading articles were to be some of the most distinguished men of the day.

Forster, although he had tried to dissuade Dickens from starting the new daily paper, consented to hold a place on its staff. Others of Dickens's colleagues were W. J. Fox, the Anti-Corn Law orator, Douglas Jerrold, Mark Lemon, and Charles Mackay. Mr George Hogarth, Dickens's father-in-law, was musical and dramatic critic; Mr John Dickens (Dickens's father) had the management, in other words the ill-management, of the reporting staff.

The printing machines having been christened with bottles of wine, after the manner of naming ships, a dummy paper was produced (on Saturday night, 17 January) a few copies of which have been preserved. The first real number appeared on Wednesday, 21 January, and among its contents was the first instalment of a series of papers by Dickens —"Travelling Letters," subsequently republished as *Pictures from Italy*. The work, however, proved eminently distasteful to him, and on 9 February, "tired to death and quite worn out," he resigned the editorship, having held it only about three weeks. He subsequently contributed occasionally in its columns—one of his effusions being an infliction in verse, the "Hymn of the Wiltshire Labourers." In a letter to Madame de la Rue, written from Devonshire Terrace, 17 April 1846, he explains why he severed his connection with the *Daily News*. He said he was not satisfied with the business managers of the newspaper, who he believed would be the ruin of what might otherwise have been a very fine property, so he "walked bodily" out of the concern.

He then spoke of going abroad for a year, adding, "I have engaged to produce a new story (*Dombey and Son*) in twenty monthly parts, and I think I could write it more comfortably and easily abroad, than at home.[1] . . . I shall publish early next month a little volume called *Pictures from Italy*." [2]   On Saturday, 16 May, his brother Albert Lamert was married.

Dickens was succeeded in the editorial chair of the *Daily News* by his friend Forster, whose appearance and mannerisms at this time are vividly set before us in Lady Bulwer's spiteful novel *Cheverley*, where the "harbitary gent" appears as Fuzboz.   He is represented "as a very ugly and noiseless likeness of the great tragedian Macready," whom he tried to imitate . . . even to his handwriting.   Another writer,[3] referring to Forster's habit of imitating Macready, observes: "I remember being in this way rather overpowered at my first interview with him.   I had called on him by appointment and he had kept me a few minutes waiting. Then he strode into the room, and striking an attitude exclaimed in a tragic tone: 'It is with infinite regret that I have caused you this delay.   Believe me' (and here he placed his hand upon his heart) 'I feel it sensibly.' "   That the good qualities of "Fuz," by which name Carlyle, taking his cue from Lady Bulwer, designated Forster, far outshone his faults is, however, admitted by all except the most savage of his detractors.

## § 72. *To Switzerland*, 31 *May* 1846

On 31 May 1846, Dickens, his wife, Miss Hogarth, with Anne, their maid, and Dickens's invaluable servant Roche, quitted England for Switzerland, via Ostend, Worms, and Strasburg.   On 8 June they were at Bale, on 11 June at

[1] Maggs's *Catalogue*, No. 525.
[2] Published in 1846.   Illustrated by Marcus Stone and Samuel Palmer.
[3] Author of "The Carlyles and a Segment of their Circle"—*Bookman*.

Lausanne.  For his residence he chose "a doll's house"—
with a balcony and a stone colonnade in front—called
Rosemont, a spot worthy of its name, for it was smothered
in roses.  The room he made his study looked on to the
lake and mountains—"the Simplon, the St Gothard, Mont
Blanc, and all the Alpine wonders piled there in tremendous
grandeur."  To his circle of friends he here added a
Mr de Haldimand,[1] to whom he wrote many letters, Mr
Haldimand's sister and a Mr and Mrs de Cerjât.

Settled in Lausanne, Dickens prepared for work, but
first of all he sent to London for blue ink, quill-pens and a
pair of bronze frogs fighting a duel which always stood on
his writing-desk, accessories apparently necessary to inspiration.  By 28 June he had finished his *History of the New
Testament*, the work already referred to which was published
in 1934, by the *Daily Mail*, with the title of *The Life of Our
Lord*.  He also went on with *Dombey and Son*, but he made
little headway with it, his attention being partly taken up
with preparation for his next Christmas venture, *The Battle
of Life*.

§ 73. *To Paris.  "The Battle of Life," Christmas* 1846

He got a good deal of pleasure out of his experiences in
Italy.  The country fêtes or gatherings of the peasantry
greatly amused him.  The people "waltzed and polka'd
without cessation, they sang and clinked their cups in drinking booths, and shot with rifles for prizes."  The fondness of
the Swiss for gunpowder was constantly tickling Dickens's
fancy; and he describes a farmer and his friends celebrating
a wedding by firing off guns all the day and all the night
afterwards.  But amid this enjoyment one need especially
Dickens missed—the streets of London, those fascinating
mazes in which he had so often found inspiration.

In August he visited the Castle of Chillon, inseparably
associated with Bonivard and Byron, and entered the

---

[1] At one time an M.P.  He lived at Lausanne, where Dickens met him
in 1846.  Dickens's fifth son, born 18 April 1847, was named Sydney Smith
Haldimand.

dungeon of the seven pillars, which still seemed to echo the voice of the poor captive. Subsequently, one of a party of eleven, he ascended the Great St Bernard, and visited the convent and the charnel house. Of this excursion Forster furnishes particulars, as he does of everything. What is so very surprising is Dickens's diffidence. He is perpetually asking Forster for advice respecting his creations; and this Forster gives, in his fussy anile way—with much mumbling comment and criticism as a rule leagues wide of the mark.

At the end of August, Dickens was still plodding with *Dombey*. "The difficulty," he says, "of going at what I call a rapid pace, is prodigious; it is almost an impossibility." He attributed this partly to the effect of two years' ease—for that time had elapsed since the close of *Chuzzlewit*—and partly to the "absence of streets and numbers of figures." He is in capital spirits, however, and has such a preposterous sense of the ridiculous, that he constantly requires to restrain his pen from perpetrating extravagances. As regards streets—"For a week or a fortnight," says he, "I can write prodigiously in a retired place (as at Broadstairs), and a day in London sets me up again and starts me." Here, however, a flying visit to London was impossible, and he writes, "My figures seem disposed to stagnate without crowds about them." At Lausanne he got into the habit of reading his story as he wrote it to his little circle there and with "unrelateable success." This furnished him with an idea. Says he: "I was thinking the other day that in this era of lecturing and readings, a great deal of money might possibly be made (if it were not *infra dig.*) by one's having readings of one's own books."

Forster, very sensibly, threw cold water on the suggestion, and subsequently did all in his power to prevent its being carried out. On 20 November, Dickens and his "menagerie" were in Paris.

A pretty little Lausanne incident is narrated by Charles Dickens the younger. He says, "One evening in the twilight when my sister Mamie was sitting at the piano and singing *The May Queen*, Alfred Tennyson unexpectedly

strolled in among us through the window that opened on
to the lawn, as if the odd coincidence were quite a matter of
course." In November 1846 Dickens was anxious about
his sister Fanny, who was consumptive, and had broken
down in an attempt to sing at Manchester. "I am deeply
grieved about it," he says. She consulted his friend
Dr Elliotson, who had previously examined her. On the
earlier occasion he had assured her that her lungs were
not affected and she cried for joy. This time he could
give little hope.[1]

The Christmas story for 1846, *The Battle of Life*, already
referred to, is an unconvincing, rather wearisome narrative
of a young girl who sacrificially surrenders her sweetheart to
her sister. The only good character is Clemency Newcome,
servant to Dr Jeddler. Great was her excitement when
called upon to sign her name.

"In an ecstasy of laughter at the idea of her own importance and
dignity," she "brooded over the whole table with her two elbows,
like a spread eagle, and reposed her head upon her left arm as a
preliminary to the formation of certain cabalistic characters, which
required a deal of ink, and imaginary counterparts whereof she
executed at the same time with her tongue. Having once tasted
ink, she became thirsty in that regard, as tame tigers are said to be
after tasting another sort of fluid, and wanted to sign everything, and
put her name in all kinds of places."

Of the illustrations to *The Battle of Life* Dickens said:
"Except Stanfield's they all shocked me, more or less." [2]

In the lower part of one of the designs "The Night of the
Return," drawn by John Leech, the artist made the mistake
of supposing that Michael Warden, one of the characters,
had taken part in the elopement, and he introduced his figure
with that of the bride, Marion. Rather than hurt Leech's
feelings, however, Dickens good-naturedly let it pass.[3]

---

[1] She died in the summer of 1848.
[2] Letter 25 January 1847. Quoted in the *Dickensian*, 1 December 1934,
p. 50.
[3] F. G. Kitton, *Dickens and his Illustrators*, p. 9.

## § 74. *Victor Hugo. January* 1847

With his "tons of luggage, tons of servants, and other tons of children," it was out of all question for Dickens to attempt to establish himself in an hotel. So he took a house, No. 48, Rue de Courcelles, Faubourg St Honore. The early days were spent in seeing the sights of the city—theatre, museum, and church visiting. It was the last year of the reign of Louis Philippe, and Dickens "saw almost everywhere signs of canker eating into the heart of the people." He says, "It is a wicked and detestable place but wonderfully attractive." French he could never speak very well, but he could write it tolerably.

Late in 1846, Albert Smith had dramatised *The Battle of Life* for Mr and Mrs Keeley, and Dickens left Paris in order to be present at the rehearsal. Writing to Mrs Dickens on 19 December, he describes himself as bothered to death by it. All the actors were bad and the words of the book had been "confused in the copying into the densest and most insufferable nonsense." However, by reading the parts aloud to the actors he contrived to give life to them. It was produced at the Lyceum Theatre on 21 December and, to his gratification, proved a success. Writing to Mrs Dickens he said, "There was immense enthusiasm at its close, and great uproar and shouting for me."

He then returned to Paris, where he was joined by Forster, and they passed a fortnight together sightseeing and in paying their respects to distinguished Frenchmen, including Alexandre Dumas, Alphonse Karr, Eugene Sue, Lamartine, Chateaubriand and Victor Hugo. They found Hugo in a noble corner house in the Place Royale, writing amid gorgeous tapestries, painted ceilings and wonderful carvings. Forster described him as rather under the middle size, of a compact close-buttoned-up figure, with ample dark hair falling loosely over his close-shaven face. He talked of his literary career and of actors and acting, and expressed sympathy in respect to Dickens's dramatic venture—the performance of *The Battle of Life*, mixing his remarks with "very charming flattery in the best taste"; and Dickens, who long remembered the enjoyment of that evening, said when writing to Lady Blessington, "I was much struck by Hugo himself, who looks like a genius as he is every inch of him." [1]

Hugo was just then at the height of his fame, success after success had followed the publication of his *Notre Dame de Paris* and his play *Lucrèce Borgia*, from the rehearsals of which in 1833 had dated his liaison, which was known to everybody, with Juliet Drouet the actress to whom he had given the part of the princess Negroni. It was appropriate that the most popular novelist of France and the most popular novelist of England should meet.

Early in 1847 Dickens left Paris earlier than he had intended owing to the illness of his eldest son, who had been placed with Dr Major, headmaster of King's College School. When convalescent the boy had been taken charge of by his grandmother, Mrs Hogarth. As Devonshire Terrace was still in the possession of Sir James Duke, Dickens took a house in Chester Place, Regent's Park. There, on 18 April 1847, was born his seventh son, Sydney Smith Haldimand. The summer months of 1847 were spent by Dickens and his family at Brighton or Broadstairs. On 22 March 1847, he wrote to tell Beard that John Henry Barrow would be dining with the family on the following Sunday. "Will you," asks Dickens, "come and meet the little man?"

[1] Letter, 24 January 1847.

## CHAPTER XIII

# Spring 1847 to November 1851

I DEVONSHIRE TERRACE, THIRD PERIOD.   FROM LEAVING
CHESTER PLACE TO REMOVAL TO TAVISTOCK HOUSE

§ 75.  *Harold Skimpole.   The Leigh Hunt and
John Poole Benefit.   26 July* 1847

IN 1847 a number of literary men, including Dickens, Jerrold, Lemon and Leech, decided to give a series of dramatic entertainments in order to raise a sum for the benefit of Leigh Hunt and John Poole (1792–1879), author of *Paul Pry* and other farces, both of whom were in financial difficulties.   This intention was scarcely announced when Lord John Russell granted to Hunt a pension of £200 a year.   As, however, there were some long-standing liabilities to efface, it was resolved not to alter the original plan. At Manchester, on 26 July 1847, the pieces chosen were *Every Man in his Humour*, Gore's *A Good Night's Rest*, and Poole's *Turning the Tables*.   At Liverpool, Jonson's play was followed by Peake's farce of *Comfortable Lodgings or Paris in* 1750.

Author of so many charming essays and of that literary gem "Abou Ben Adhem," Leigh Hunt had won a place in the hearts of his countrymen.   Dickens drew him to a hair in *Bleak House*, and everybody recognised the likeness. Harold Skimpole "was a little bright creature, with a rather large head, but a delicate face, and there was a perfect charm in him.   He had more the appearance of a damaged young man than a well-preserved elderly one."   This was when Hunt was about sixty-six.   The Literary Babe, or, to use a prettier, but equally deserved title, the Literary Ariel, knew nothing of business. He had no idea either of time or money, and was unable to repeat the multiplication table. He never kept an appointment, and never knew the value of anything. He was never able to pay his way, or much distressed because he could not. He was one of the most helpless mortals who ever lived.[1]

Said he on one occasion: "I felt my age coming on me, and difficulties not lessened by failing projects; nor was I able, had I been never so inclined, to render my faculties profitable in the market! It is easy to say to a man— Write such and such a thing, and it is sure to sell. Watch the public taste, and act accordingly. . . . There is a great deal of truth in all this. But a man can only do what he can, or as others will let him." No driving a coach and six through a difficulty for Mr Hunt. The gospel according to Ariel was "If you can't, how can you?" Dickens when acknowledging afterwards that he had made Harold Skimpole speak like Leigh Hunt, protested that he had never thought that Hunt "would ever be charged with the imaginary vices of the fictitious creature." The result of the "benefit" was a profit of 400 guineas.

The players had hoped, however, to clear 500 guineas, and the idea then occurred to Dickens, of making up the remaining hundred by means of the publication of a comic history of the trip as if from the pen of Mrs Gamp. It was to be a new "Piljian's Projiss," inscribed to Mrs Harris, and edited by Charles Dickens. Only a fragment, however, was written, and of very poor quality it is.[2]

Still Mrs Gamp's descriptions of some of the members of the company are worth preserving: Cruikshank exhibited a large shirt collar, a hook nose, an eye like a hawk, and "long locks of hair and whiskers." Jerrold was "a fat gentleman with curly black hair and a merry face, standing on the platform rubbing his two hands over one another as if he was washing of 'em, and shaking his head and shoulders very much."

[1] See Chapter V, § 17.
[2] See Forster's *Life*, Ley's ed., pp. 458–63.

Towards Jerrold, for writing *Mrs Caudle's Curtain Lectures* Mrs Gamp naturally felt nothing but detestation. In respect to some of the other performers, Mark Lemon, a corpulent jovial Jew—"my Lemon round and fat," was editor of *Punch*. As Hans C. Andersen once said after seeing Lemon go through some amusing tomfoolery at a garden party, Mr Lemon was "most excellent full of comic"—a striking contrast to that other wag, the grave and almost sepulchral Leech.

In October, Ralph Waldo Emerson revisited England and, at the request of Dickens, Carlyle and others, delivered lectures in London. Another notable event of this year in the literary world was the publication of Thackeray's *Vanity Fair*, held by some to be "quite the greatest achievement in English literature since *Tom Jones*, while Becky Sharp has been ranked with Falstaff, Squire Western, and Uncle Toby. Says Mr Frederic Harrison: "The scene of her husband's encounter with her paramour has no superior, hardly an equal, in modern fiction." Dickens and Thackeray now and again passed each other compliments in public, but in secret they heartily disliked each other. Dickens was jealous of Thackeray, and Thackeray despised nearly all Dickens's latter work. Their public protestations of admiration for each other by no means tally with their private opinions as expressed in their correspondence.

On 1 December 1847, Dickens took the chair at a soirée of the Mechanics' Institution at Leeds. The fact that he would preside had been made known in extremely large letters on posters placed all over the city. Even he, who was used to large advertisement, was startled. He said, "they looked like a leaf from the first primer of a very promising young giant." On 28 December 1847, Dickens opened the Glasgow Athenæum and then proceeded to Edinburgh where he spent the last day of the year and also New Year's Day. The Scott monument he regarded as a failure. He says, "It is like the spire of a Gothic church taken off and stuck in the ground."

§ 76. *"Dombey and Son."  Maclise's Portrait of Mrs Dickens*

*Dombey and Son* was at that time pretty well advanced. The subject of "Chuzzlewit" is hypocrisy, that of "Dombey" pride. As in *The Old Curiosity Shop* the character with which its author took most pains is the least attractive. The original of Paul Dombey was poor little deformed Harry Burnett, one of the children of Dickens's sister Fanny. The mother, who was slowly sinking into her grave, "was particularly troubled at the thought of not being able any longer to take care of her poor afflicted child. Harry, like Paul, had been taken to Brighton, and there, too, like him, had lain for hours on the beach with his books. Some have ridiculed the remarks of Paul Dombey, and said they were unnatural. But Harry was a strange child—meditative and quaint—and Dickens's description of him was realistic. The death of Paul Dombey set open the floodgates of Dickens's friends and acquaintances just as the death of the "divine Nelly" (Jeffrey's phrase) had done. "Oh, my dear, dear Dickens!" cried the susceptible Jeffrey. "What a No. 5 you have given us! I have so cried and sobbed over it last night, and again this morning . . ." and so on. "Read that chapter describing young Paul's death," says Thackeray, "it is unsurpassed—it is stupendous!" [1]

Most readers, however, unless they have a weakness for melodrama, will find little to praise in these passages, and will turn with relief from them to the pages dealing with Susan Nipper and Captain Cuttle. Let it not be supposed, however, that because Dickens sometimes failed so dismally in writing pathos he was insincere. His sorrow for the sufferings of poor little Harry Burnett was unmistakably genuine. When his heart was rent with anguish and he sat down and wrote some unpremeditated sentence, or penned a letter on a sad subject he could be really touching. At

---

[1] The Rev. James Griffin says of Harry Burnett, "The little deformed child was meditative and quaint in a remarkable degree. . . . He was always happy. . . . He died in the arms of a dear nephew of mine since passed away. *Memories of the Past*, p. 209.

times when he simply relieved his bursting heart, and had no thought of anyone else, he forces us to condole with him, but when he lays himself out to produce tears, the person fittest to be condoled with is his reader.

The great character of *Dombey and Son* is Captain Cuttle with his immortal hook, hard-glazed hat, and never-failing well of original precepts. "Turn again Whittington, Lord Mayor of London," we hear him say, "and when you are old you will never depart from it. Wal'r! Overhaul the book, my lad." The second place must be given to Susan Nipper, though it may be doubted whether—with all her virtues— Mr Toots really did marry her; and the third to Mrs Skewton, who, to a person reading the book for the first time, would probably appear the most striking character of all. Mr Gissing well says: "Her paralytic seizure, her death in life, are fine and grisly realism."

One of the most pleasing pictures of cottage life ever drawn is that of the Toodle family. The children, it was declared, would go half wild to see their mother. "That they did, if one might judge from the noise they made, and the way in which they dashed at Polly and dragged her to a low chair, in the chimney corner, where her own honest apple face became immediately the centre of a bunch of smaller pippins, all laying their rosy cheeks close to it, and all evidently the growth of the same tree." It is writing of this kind that draws us to Dickens. He shines with his little Toodles, if he made but indifferent little Dombeys. All the same, Paul Dombey was very real to him, and we learn that "after he had killed him" he walked about the streets of Paris inconsolable all night." [1]

Of the minor characters those best drawn are the Chicken, Mrs Macstinger, and Cousin Feenix. The description of the meeting of Florence and Edith in Chapter 61 is an example of true pathos. The scenes in the church at the christening of Paul are so well sketched that one might almost be there, and the finding of Florence by Walter and the incidents that followed are most prettily told. Dickens

[1] *Dombey and Son* appeared from October 1846 to April 1848. It was the night of 14 January 1847.

seems to have been uncertain whether he had done right in causing Edith to run away with Carker, for he endeavours to shield himself behind a remark of cousin Feenix's, "In point of fact, one does see, in this world—which is remarkable for devilish strange arrangements, and for being decidedly the most unintelligible thing within a man's experience—very odd conjunctions of that sort." Canon Benham, in his *Dickens and Kent*, says, "Unmistakably Paddock Wood Station is the one at which Carker's terrible death occurred." In trying to avoid Mr Dombey, it will be remembered, Carker staggered and slipped on to the line and was killed by a passing train.[1]

The fun circulating round Captain Cuttle has already been noticed. Equally droll is the account of the christening of baby Paul whose crying "so distracted the attention of the ladies that Mrs Chick was constantly deploying into the centre aisle to send out messages by the pew opener, while Miss Tox kept her prayer-book open at the Gunpowder Plot, and occasionally read responses from that service." To the Rev. Melchisedech Howler [2] and Mrs Pipchin [3] reference has already been made. The original of Mrs Skewton is said to have been a Mrs Campbell of Leamington; Captain Cuttle is the same as one David Mainland, master of a merchantman; and the prototype of Sol Gills was a Mr Norie, of the firm of Norie and Wilson of Leadenhall Street, in front of whose small shop stood the Little Wooden Midshipman, subsequently removed to the Minories. In 1848, Maclise painted the well-known portrait of Mrs Dickens, one of the most successful and charming of his productions, for she was still in the hey-day of her beauty. To the sketch of her and Dickens and Miss Hogarth together reference has already been made.[4]

### § 77. *The Shakespeare House Fund*

In 1848, a committee was formed for the purchase and preservation of Shakespeare's house at Stratford-on-Avon.

[1] Cr. ed., vol. 3, p. 624.   [2] Chapter IX, § 32.
[3] Chapter III, § 13.   [4] Chapter XII, § 65.

Dickens threw himself heartily into the scheme, and arranged for a series of performances to take place for the purpose of raising funds, and to assist Mr James Sheridan Knowles, the dramatist. The play chosen was *The Merry Wives of Windsor*, to which was added Kenney's farce, *Love, Law and Physic*. Dickens was Justice Shallow; Lemon, Falstaff; Mrs Cowden Clarke of Concordance fame, Dame Quickly. The first rehearsal was at Miss Kelly's theatre, Dean Street, Soho, on 22 April.

There were two representations at the Haymarket, London, the first being on 15 May. On the 16th, Mrs Cowden Clarke dined at Devonshire House and afterwards she and Mrs Dickens, who had a box at the opera, went to see Jenny Lind in *La Sonnambula* there. The second performance at the Haymarket was on 17 May, when the Queen and the Prince Consort were present, the play chosen being Ben Jonson's *Every Man in his Humour*,[1] Dickens being Bobadil; Forster, Kitely; G. H. Lewes, Wellbred; Augustus Dickens, Thomas Cash; Cruikshank, Oliver Cob; and Mrs Cowden Clarke, Tit, Cob's wife. It was followed by Kenney's *Love, Law and Physic*, in which most of the actors in the previous play took parts, Dickens being Flexible; G. H. Lewes, Andrew; Lemon, Lubin Log.

## § 78. *Mrs Cowden Clarke*

Mrs Cowden Clarke described Dickens at the time as superlatively handsome with rich wavy locks of hair and magnificent eyes.

"In *Love, Law and Physic*," she says, "he used to tuck me under his arm with the free-and-easy familiarity of a lawyer patronising an actress whom he chances to find his fellow-traveller in a stage coach. . . . It is something to remember, having been tucked under the arm by Charles Dickens, and had one's hand hugged against his side! One thinks better of one's hand ever after."

Whether actors ought to conduct themselves towards actresses like that, only persons acquainted with the

[1] Play-bill reproduced in Straus's *Dickens*, p. 112.

191

etiquette of the theatre are, one supposes, competent to decide. Apparently, however, if the actresses like to be squeezed it would be inhuman not to squeeze them. Dickens used to be "in such a state of high spirits" when he played Flexible, that he fell into the habit when he subsequently met Mrs Clarke of addressing her as Flexible addressed Mrs Hilary in the play. "He was very fond," says Mrs Clarke, "of this kind of reiterated joke." The susceptible Dickens certainly was fluttered by the good looks and personal charm of the more mature Mrs Clarke, just as he had been by the good looks and personal charm of the younger Miss Christina Weller. However, he enjoyed himself immensely, she was flattered, and nobody was a penny the worse.

"What times those were!" says Mrs Clarke. "What rapturous audiences a-tiptoe with expectation to see, hear and welcome those whom they had known and loved through their written or delineated productions." At the Manchester Hotel there were flowers for Mrs Dickens, Miss Hogarth and the other ladies of the troupe. "What enthusiastic hurrahs at the rise of the curtain, and as each character in succession made his appearance on the stage! Of course, in general, the storm of plaudits was loudest when Dickens was recognised." On all occasions "his indefatigable vivacity, cheerfulness and good humour from morning till night were delightful. . . . There was a positive sparkle and atmosphere of holiday sunshine about him; he seemed to radiate brightness and enjoyment." In June the players for the Fund commenced their tour in the provinces. They were at Manchester on 3 June, at Liverpool on 5 June. Thence they proceeded on 6 June to Birmingham.

### § 79. *The Actors at Birmingham, 6 June 1848, and in Scotland, 15 July*

After Dickens had returned to London he decided to arrange for a second performance at Birmingham, and to give there in addition to *The Merry Wives of Windsor* and

*Love, Law and Physic,* "the screaming afterpiece of *Past Two O'clock in the Morning.*" In order to cut this last to proper dimensions, he invited Mrs Clarke and Mark Lemon to dinner at Devonshire Terrace.

She thus describes the gathering:

A charming little dinner of four it was—Mr and Mrs Dickens, Mark Lemon and myself. Dickens showed to particular advantage in his own quiet home life; and I infinitely more enjoyed this simple little meeting than a brilliant dinner-party to which I was invited at his house a day or two afterwards when a large company were assembled and all was in superb style, with a bouquet of flowers beside the plate of each lady present. On one of these more quiet occasions, when Mr and Mrs Dickens, their children and their few guests were sitting out of doors in the small garden, I recollect seeing one of the little sons draw Dickens apart and stand in eager talk with him, the setting sun full upon the child's upturned face, and lighting up the father's which looked smilingly down into it, and when the important conference was over, the father returned to us saying, "The little fellow gave me so many excellent reasons why he should not go to bed so soon, that I yielded the point, and let him sit up half an hour later." [1]

During the journey to Birmingham Dickens asked Mrs Clarke to hear him repeat his part in *Past Two O'clock in the Morning,*[2] which, he and Mark Lemon being the only two persons acting therein, was a long one.

"Who," asks Mrs Clarke, "that beheld the convulsive writhes and spasmodic draw-up of his feet on the rung of the chair and the tightly-held coverlet round his shivering body just out of bed as he watched in ecstasy of impatience the invasion of his peaceful chamber by that horribly intrusive Stranger, can ever forget Dickens's playing Mr Snobbington."

When Snobbington enquired whether it rains, Mark Lemon thundered "Pours!" "Who," she asks, "could lose remembrance of Lemon's unparalleled piece of acting" either. The question "Does it rain?" is not in the original play, and consequently Lemon's reply is not in it either.

[1] Mrs Cowden Clarke, *Recollections of Writers,* p. 316.
[2] See §§ 55 and 60.

Dickens no doubt heightened the farcical scenes, and took with them what liberties he pleased.

In July 1848 Dickens made plans for performances in Scotland which were to include, besides the previous pieces, Boucicault's *Used Up*.[1] Mrs Clarke met the rest of the dramatis personæ at Devonshire Terrace on Monday, 3 July, in order to hear this play read, and there was a rehearsal on Friday evening, 7 July, at Miss Kelly's "Temple of Mirth."[2] On the 15th, the company, Mrs Dickens among them, travelled to Edinburgh, and on the 17th they gave there *The Merry Wives of Windsor, Love, Law and Physic,* and *Past Two O'clock in the Morning.* While at Edinburgh the players were in the highest spirits. In reference to Dickens and Lemon an Edinburgh comment was "I never saw anything like those clever men; they're just for all the world like a parcel of schoolboys." On the 18th they played at Glasgow, *The Merry Wives* and *Animal Magnetism.* On the 19th, Dickens organised an excursion to Ben Lomond. They had lunch at a small inn near, and proposed afterwards to take a stroll in order to view the scenery; but Dickens, tired out, stayed in the inn, and Mrs Dickens and Mrs Clarke kept him company. "In the room," says Mrs Clarke, "there was no sofa, so we put together four chairs, on which he stretched himself at full length, resting his head on his wife's knee as a pillow, and was soon in a quiet sleep, Mrs Dickens and I keeping on our talk in a low tone that served rather to lull than disturb him."

There was a second performance at Glasgow on 20 July, one of the pieces being *Used Up.* Dickens as Sir Charles Coldstream was excellent, "but a pre-eminent hit was made by Mark Lemon, who, as one of his 'fop-friends,' invented a certain little ridiculous laugh—so original, so exquisitely inane, so ludicrously disproportioned, in its high falsetto pipe, to the immensely broad chest from which it issued— that it became *the thing* of all the scenes where he appeared."

On 22 July Dickens was back at Devonshire Terrace, whence he wrote to Mrs Clarke, half in jest half in earnest, "I have no energy whatever, I am very miserable. I loathe

---

[1] Chapter 13, § 87.     [2] Mrs Clarke's *Recollections of Writers,* p. 317.

domestic hearths. I yearn to be a vagabond. . . . A real house like this is insupportable after that canvas farm (in *Used Up*) wherein I was so happy." As the proceeds of these entertainments were not after all required for Shakespeare's house the whole of the sum realised was placed in the hands of Mr Sheridan Knowles. In the Royal Academy that year were some pictures illustrating *Dombey and Son*. W. P. Frith told Dickens of them. "Yes," he said, "I know there are; just go and see them and tell me what they are like, I don't care to be caught looking at them myself."[1]

## § 80. *The Illness of Fanny Burnett, July* 1848. *The Haunted Man*

Mrs Burnett whose health had long been declining was in May 1848 taken to London so as to be near the eminent doctor, Sir James Clark. In her last days she often begged her friends to read the 14th of St John—the chapter that has cheered the dying bed of countless Christians. Her death scene is very touchingly described both in the Rev. James Griffin's book, and in one of Dickens's letters. "I asked her," says Dickens, "whether she had any care or anxiety in the world. She said, 'No, none'; it was hard to die at such a time of life, but she had no alarm whatever in the prospect of the change. She said she was quite calm and happy, relied upon the mediation of Christ and had no terror at all." Then comes a sentence which is pathos itself when we remember the lack of harmony in his own home. "Burnett had always been very good to her, they had never quarrelled; she was sorry to think of his going back to such a lonely home; and was distressed about her children." Dickens's Christmas book *The Haunted Man*, written shortly after her death, contains references to her. Poor little deformed Harry died shortly after his mother.

Mrs Burnett was buried in Highgate Cemetery[2] on Friday, 8 September. The Rev. James Griffin went up to London in compliance with her dying request, and officiated

[1] *My Autobiography*, by W. P. Frith, p. 81.
[2] See *Memories of the Past*, by James Griffin, pp. 155–88 and pp. 195–210.

at the funeral. He says, "To me it could not be other than a peculiarly solemn and affecting occasion, Mr Dickens appeared to feel it very deeply. He spoke to me in terms of great respect and affection for his departed sister." Mr Griffin preached her funeral sermon in Manchester from 2 Corinthians v. 5: "Now He that hath wrought us for the selfsame thing is God." Among those who called on Dickens at Devonshire Terrace to condole with him on the occasion of Fanny's death was his old sweetheart Maria Beadnell who had become Mrs Winter.

In September 1848, Mrs Cowden Clarke, assisted by her sister Miss Emma Novello, embroidered a blotting-case for Dickens, and on receipt of it he sent from Broadstairs in September a whimsical letter of acknowledgment, signing it with the various names of parts he had played "written in the most respectively characteristic handwritings"

R. Shallow Cust-alorum ⎫ *Merry Wives of Windsor.*
Abraham Slender ⎭
Robert Flexible[1] (in *Love, Law and Physic*).
(Sir) Charles Coldstream (in *Used Up*).
Doctor Blank (in *Animal Magnetism*).
Young Gas.
Bobadil (*Every Man in his Humour*).
P. Snobbington (*Past Two O'clock in the Morning*).
Charles Dickens.
        The mild manager.

In several letters to Mrs Clarke he refers to himself as "Young Gas."

On Tuesday, 5 December 1848, Dickens's brother Augustus was married. The Christmas Book for 1848, *The Haunted Man*[2] *and the Ghost's Bargain*, is a poor production, having no charms for remembrance except its possession of the Tetterby Baby—the Moloch on "whose insatiate altar" the whole existence of Johnny Tetterby was offered up in daily sacrifice. The presence, however, of the most celebrated of the Dickensian babies does not save

---

[1] The lawyer.
[2] Illustrated by Tenniel, Leech, Stanfield and Frank Stone. See *Letters* of 21 and 23 November 1848; also Cr. ed., xiv., p. 275.

the tale. In December 1848, when the Rev. William Giles of Manchester reached his fiftieth year, a number of his old pupils decided to honour him. A committee, of which Dickens was a member, was formed, and Mr Giles was presented in the Mayor's Parlour, Manchester, on 30 December, with an illuminated address and a silver tea and coffee service.

## § 81. *At Yarmouth, January* 1849

Dickens then commenced the work which is regarded by many as his masterpiece, the delightful *David Copperfield*, which is associated so closely with Yarmouth. It is stated by Forster that Dickens first visited the Yarmouth district in 1849. This, however, is apparently incorrect. An old inhabitant of Yarmouth told Dr Bately of that town that Dickens previous to this date was the guest of Sir Walter Peto, at Somerleyton, and that he several times passed through Blundestone with Sir Morton, who suggested the laying of the plot of the next book in that locality. "Thirty years ago," observes Dr Bately, "there were huts made of boats on Lowestoft beach, the exact counterpart of Peggotty's."

The soft pleasant sands of Yarmouth, its piers used for concerts, its picturesque gardens, its fine wide parade, its handsome streets, its spacious market-place and extensive quays are in the season thronged with holiday-makers; but to many, however, the old-world Yarmouth has at least as many attractions as the new; the venerable church of St Nicholas, which is the largest parish church in the kingdom; its churchyard, where "Ham Peggotty" was buried; the remains of the old town walls, with three of their towers; the ancient and unique Toll house, now used as a free library; the dark and narrow cells of the dungeons below it, where the Royalist poet Cleveland pined; the quaint Dutch houses on the South Quay—all these carry us back centuries, and we hear as it were to-day, the chant of the priest, the moan of poet-prisoner, the clank of chains, and the tender persuasive voice of Yarmouth's fair apostle.[1]  But the most characteristic feature of this fascinating old town is the series of narrow streets or Rows forming, as one writer puts it, a huge gridiron.  They are 145 in number, and narrower than the narrowest London alleys, yet there are houses on both sides, though some stand a little back, being provided with Lilliputian court-yards.  Kitty Witches' Row (No. 95) is at one end so narrow that in passing through you brush both shoulders. For traversing these thoroughfares a special vehicle was invented—a long narrow cart with wheels below its body—the Harry Carry or Yarmouth cart, the driver of which stood upright, urging on his steed like a Roman charioteer.  It was in one of these Rows that Mr Omer's shop was situated, and we can picture little David sitting there, listening to the ceaseless tapping on his mother's coffin.

The connection of Charles Dickens with the Yarmouth neighbourhood commences, however, at Blundestone (Blunderstone) in Suffolk where David was born.  Who does not remember the Rookery (probably the Vicarage) and the sweet-briar fence on the outside of which Mr Murdstone used to stroll, while pretty Mrs Copperfield "walked slowly up and down on the inner side, to keep him company!"  Who cannot see Miss Betsy Trotwood pressing the end of her arbitrary but philanthropic nose against the window pane!  Blundestone Church has no resemblance to Phiz's delightful though fanciful picture of its interior. Not only did Dickens take no pains to describe the church particularly, he was even inartistic enough to give it a commonplace steeple, whereas Blundestone church has a round tower, prettily, like the rest of the edifice, over-run with ivy.  Yonder is the porch through the open door of which David saw a stray sheep—"I don't mean a sinner, but mutton—half making up his mind to come into the church," and that surely is the window through which Peggotty's eye wandered—the window "out of which our house can be seen, and is seen many times during the morning's service, by Peggotty, who likes to make herself

[1] Sarah Martin.

198

as sure as she can that it's not being robbed, or is not in flames." When at Yarmouth the writer did not expect to see a tablet to "Mr Bodgers, late of this parish," but he was bidden to notice a tablet to a young man "who had many virtues all of which, however, were drowned in one vice"—that of gambling; the tablet being none other than the top of the table at which he lost both his time and his money. Mr Murdstone was a smuggler. The incident at Lowestoft, we are told, "exemplifies one of the many tricks of the smuggling trade. The *Skylark*, though to all appearance but a pleasure boat, can have been nothing less than one of those handy craft by which goods, which should have passed the Custom, were often brought ashore without any formalities."

To return to Yarmouth—the wonderful boat, the home of Mr Peggotty, Ham, Little Emly and the sorrowful Mrs Gummidge, is said to have stood on a site east of Black-friar's Tower, on the Blackfriar's Road, but it has long been demolished. Dickens nowhere describes Peggotty's house as inverted. Phiz, however, draws it so, and these in-verted boats were commonly used as habitations on the Norfolk coast. The scenes associated with it are among the best remembered in Dickens; indeed there are no more delightful chapters in fictitious literature.

In February 1849 Dickens took a trip to Brighton where he continued his new story, though he had not yet decided upon a title. The first monthly part of *David Copperfield* appeared early in May 1849. Forster records a dinner on 12 May, at which Carlyle, Thackeray, Mrs Gaskell,[1] Mrs Tagart and Hablot K. Browne were present. When Dickens asked after Carlyle's health, Carlyle, to the amuse-ment of the company, replied in the language of Mrs Gummidge, "I am a lone lorn creetur and everythink goes contrairy with me." On 20 June Dickens, Talfourd, Landseer and Stanfield visited Vauxhall together, in order to view a representation of the *Battle of Waterloo* and they saw the Duke of Wellington himself among the spectators.

[1] Her husband, the Rev. William Gaskell, was minister of Cross Street Chapel, Manchester.

## § 82. *At The Isle of Wight, July* 1849. *The Mannings,* 13 *November* 1849

At the end of July Dickens visited Bonchurch, in the Isle of Wight, having hired for six months a villa called "Winterbourne," the property of one of his friends, the Rev. James White. He was joined there by John Leech and Mrs Leech, a very little woman. At first Dickens was in ecstasies with the loveliness of the situation. There were dinners at Blackgang and hilarious picnics on Shanklin Down. His boys used to play with a golden-haired lad, famous later as Swinburne, the poet. One of these picnics became the subject of a picture by Leech in *Punch* (25 August 1849) with the title "Awful appearance of a wops at a Picnic party." [1]

But the fun was followed by tragedy, for Leech met with an accident while bathing, and an illness followed. Dickens exercised his magnetic powers on him (see § 57) and very quickly sent his patient into a strange sleep. "I talked," said Dickens, "to the astounded little Mrs Leech, across him as if he had been a truss of hay." Though at first so charmed with Shanklin, Dickens subsequently found that it was unsuited for him. It made him drowsy and languorous.

On the 30th the sixth number of *Copperfield* was finished, and on 1 October, the Dickens family once more proceeded to Broadstairs.

One Sunday evening Mazzini, the Italian patriot, dined with Dickens and took him afterwards to see the school established in Clerkenwell for the Italian organ boys. The same year Mazzini left England to throw himself into the Lombard revolt. After the fall of the Roman Republic in 1849 Dickens championed the Italian refugees who came to England, and drew up for them an appeal for funds which appeared in Forster's paper *The Examiner* on 8 September 1849.[2] Dickens's sympathies indeed were with every one who contended on the side of Liberty.

[1] Reproduced in *Charles Dickens by P. and P.*, vol. 1, p. 59.
[2] See the *Dickensian*, December 1914, and Ley's *Forster*, p. 143.

"How well I remember his arched eyebrows and laughing eyes," says Thomas Adolphus Trollope, "when I told him of Garibaldi's proposal that all priests should be summarily executed."

On 13 November 1849, were executed at Horsemonger Lane Jail the notorious Mannings. Mr and Mrs Manning had murdered a gauger in the service of the Customs, named Patrick O'Connor, whose body, covered with quicklime, was found under a flagstone of the kitchen of a house in Minver Place, Bermondsey, which had been occupied by the guilty pair a few days previous. The particulars of the murder are very horrible. Mrs Manning had long turned her hold upon O'Connor to a source of revenue; but, finding that no more was to be got from him, she and her husband resolved on murder. They dug their victim's grave and then invited him to dinner. Mrs Manning asked O'Connor to go downstairs to wash his hands, and as they reached the kitchen she put one arm round his neck, and stabbed him with a stiletto that was in the other. Her husband assisted in the murder, and having possessed themselves of O'Connor's valuables, they took flight. They were tried and sentenced to death.

The night before the execution Dickens conceived the idea of taking an extensive ramble through the resorts of the costermongers, etc., with a view to gathering the impressions of that class regarding the event of the morrow.

"We started," says Mr Henry Manistre, "from Horsemonger Jail—Mr D., Mr William Twelle, a wealthy coppersmith; Mr Cinton, proprietor of a glass factory establishment; John Grant, the London representative of a great Manchester house, myself, and one other. We crossed London Bridge, then through Cheapside, Fleet Street, Strand, clear out to Sterge Lane. We dropped into gin palaces—among filth and vile vapour—a long weary tramp to daybreak, and so back to Horsemonger Jail again."

A day or two later Dickens wrote a history of the trip. He says:

"I never saw a bigger crowd. The housetops were black with people for blocks in every direction, and in the street below the crowd was so dense that it was impossible to move. Men and women were fainting, and then came in the play of the police. On the low building on either side of the street, they were stationed with ropes convenient when a person fainted. He or she was actually passed over the heads of the throng to a point where one of these ropes could be placed under their arms, when the police dragged the limp form up to the roof. Some one threw a basket from a window and it was knocked hither and thither over the heads of the people, as if it were on the bosom of the ocean."

On the morning of the execution Dickens wrote a letter to *The Times* condemnatory of executions in public. Said he: "I believe that a sight so inconceivably awful as the wickedness and levity of the immense crowd collected at the execution this morning, could be imagined by no man and could be presented in no heathen land under the sun." Thanks to the exertions of Dickens and others, the crying evil was, in 1868, done away with. Mrs Manning, who was hanged in black satin, a material that immediately went out of fashion, became the original of Mademoiselle Hortense in *Bleak House*.[1]

§ 83. *In Northamptonshire, 30 November 1849. Mrs. Gaskell, 31 January 1850. "Household Words," 30 March 1850*

When Dickens was in Switzerland in the summer of 1846 he made the acquaintance of a lady and gentleman who subsequently became very intimate friends of his, Mr and Mrs Watson of Rockingham Castle, Northamptonshire. After he and they had parted, numerous letters passed between them, and in November 1849, he accepted an invitation to visit them at their home near Rockingham, which he describes as "a large old castle, approached by an ancient keep, portcullis, etc., filled with company, waited on by six and twenty servants."

The entrance archway and the two bastion towers with curtain walls which flank it, still remained as they did in the Middle Ages. Passing through the archway the

[1] See Chapter XIV, § 92.

great court (thirteenth- and sixteenth-century work) was reached. This house had been the home of the Watsons for over three hundred years. On the beams of the castle hall was the following beautiful sentiment, written in letters of gold. "The house shall be preserved, and never will decaye where the Almightie God is honoured and served daye by daye, 1579."

Among the guests on the occasion when Dickens was there was Mrs Watson's cousin, Miss Mary Boyle, an amateur actress, and she and Dickens got up in the great hall some scenes from the *School for Scandal*, which was followed by conjuring. The servants, headed by an enormously fat housekeeper, occupied the back benches and laughed and applauded without any restraint; and a blushing, sleek-headed footman offered his watch of the good old turnip type for the watch trick. The evening was wound up with dancing, everybody was "uncommonly merry," and no one turned into bed before three in the morning.

Dickens's thoughts had for long played round the idea of a weekly journal, and the fancy at last became reality. The question of title was much debated—"The Robin," "Mankind," "The Household Voice," and many others were suggested, and one after another rejected. Finally his choice fell upon *Household Words*, and among the first whom he asked to contribute to it was Mrs Gaskell, whose personal acquaintance he had made a little before. In a letter to her of 31 January 1850, he says: "I do honestly know that there is no living English writer whose aid I would desire to enlist in preference to the authoress of *Mary Barton* (a book that most profoundly affected and impressed me)." He says he would gladly visit Manchester again to discuss the matter with her, and adds that Mrs Dickens and Miss Hogarth send their love.

As a result, the first number of *Household Words*, 30 March 1850, contained Chapter 1 of Mrs Gaskell's beautiful story, *Lizzie Leigh*, with which Dickens was much struck. She and her husband, the Rev. William Gaskell, a Unitarian minister of Manchester, were friends of the Ternan family with whom Dickens later became intimate.

Mr Gaskell was the translator of Luther's hymn "Ein feste Burg." [1]

Among the other contributors to the Magazine were Richard Hengist Horne, author of *Orion*, which he published at a farthing, Forster, George Meredith, G. A. Sala (who wrote nearly 300 articles for it), Moy Thomas and Miss Martineau; and a number of Dickens's own minor effusions first saw light in its columns.

§ 84. *"David Copperfield." Last number November* 1850. *The Humour of "David Copperfield"*

The last number of *David Copperfield* appeared in November 1850. How real is the whole story! Who does not detest the heartless Murdstone and the crawling, deceitful Uriah Heep! Who does not love Miss Trotwood and Traddles! Who has not been entertained by Micawber! Who does not prefer the silly Dora to the correct Agnes! Some of the minor characters are delightful—for instance the two bird-like aunts, Mr Omer and Mr Barkis. In those days the practice of taking notes on the tilt of a cart was quite common. Ham stands to this day at the public-house, as jovial, as open-hearted, and externally as fishy to the nostrils as ever he was in his canvas jacket and stiff trousers, so stiff that they would have stood quite alone.

The original Micawber is usually thought to be Dickens's father. This, however, is not quite correct, for Mr Thomas B. Gunn tells me that Dickens also availed himself of certain peculiarities of Mr Thomas Powell. "Micawber," says Mr Gunn, "includes both." Powell, who in 1851 quitted England for America (leaving his country for his country's good), was at the age of fifty corpulent and burly, with an oval head, bald in the fore part.

His speech possessed a kind of oratorical unctuousness, he was extremely voluble, and he had a trick of becoming very confidential on small or no provocation. He had a perfect mania for writing

---

[1] When at Manchester, Dickens was occasionally the guest of the Gaskells at 84 Plymouth Grove.

letters for no adequate reason, and requiring no reply. His baby lay in a coal scuttle, he drank porter out of a hyacinth glass, and compounded a very excellent bowl of punch in a soup tureen, over which he became convivial and amusing. He never paid anybody as long as he could avoid it, and resorted to all sorts of stratagems to stave off creditors.

Daniel Peggotty's mysterious imprecation, "May I be gormed," observes Mr Gunn, "had a grim meaning, though Dickens (who in all probability picked it up at Yarmouth, among the boatmen) may not have known it. 'Gorm' was the name of the Scandinavian Cerberus— the dog of Hell (see Gray's *Descent of Odin*)." Miss Trotwood's house with its bit of green in front on which the donkeys used to trespass was not at Dover but at Broadstairs. Canon Benham in *Dickens and Kent* gives his opinion that the spot from which Miss Trotwood drove away the donkeys was the green in front of Fort House—now called "Dickens House." To Salem House and Mr Creakle reference has been made in Chapter 4. Of the people without wits whom Dickens introduces into his stories, Mr Dick easily takes the first place. He is so engaging that it would be a pity if he were sane. Barnaby Rudge must bow to him.

Of the humour of *David Copperfield* we may give the following examples:

*Peggotty Snores.*—"I could not have believed unless I had heard her do it, that one defenceless woman could have snored so much."

*A Polite Fiction.*—"How's your ma, sir?" said Mr Peggotty. "Did you leave her pretty jolly?" I gave Mr Peggotty to understand that she was as jolly as I could wish, and that she desired her compliments—which was a polite fiction.

*Miss Murdstone's Greeting.*—"Is that your boy, sister-in-law?" My mother acknowledged me. "Generally speaking," said Miss Murdstone, "I don't like boys. How d'ye do, boy?"

*Talking through the Keyhole.*—" 'School near London,' was Peggotty's answer. I was obliged to get her to repeat it, for she spoke it the first time quite down my throat, in consequence of my having forgotten to take my mouth away from the keyhole and put my ear there; and though her words tickled me a good deal, I didn't hear them."

Then there is the fun that circulates round Mr Micawber, Dora and Jip—but the mention of this can have only one result, namely to send the reader, eager for a repetition of the merry moments he has so often enjoyed, post haste to his book-shelves, once more to take down from its place of honour—a place it so well deserves—his well-thumbed copy of *David Copperfield*. Of Mr and Mrs Micawber it has been well said, "they live better on nothing than most people do on a little; they fluctuate between tears and smiles; they pass from despair to hot punch." Dickens has conceived nothing more exalted or pathetic than Mr Peggotty's affection for and his wanderings in search of Emily. Edward FitzGerald's comment on *Copperfield* is, "It is very good. . . . But the melodramatic parts, as usual, bad." Carlyle says of Dickens "he is a showman whom one gives a shilling to once a month to see his raree-show and then sends him about his business." [1]

## § 85. *Dickens's Admiration of Defoe. Thomas Adolphus Trollope*

The present is perhaps the most suitable place to draw attention to the immense number of allusions in Dickens's works to *Robinson Crusoe*. That book interested Dickens as did no other work. He describes Miss Trotwood as "sitting on a quantity of luggage, with her two birds before her, and her cat on her knee, like a female Robinson Crusoe, drinking tea."

Writing to Landor 5 July 1856, he says:

"I have just been propounding to Forster if it is not a wonderful testimony to the homely force of truth, that one of the most popular books on earth has nothing in it to make one laugh or cry? . . . . In particular I took Friday's death as one of the least tender and (in the true sense) least sentimental things ever written. It is a book I read very much; and the wonder of its prodigious effect on me and everyone and the admiration thereof, grows on me the more I observe this curious fact."

---

[1] *Letters*, i, 250.

FORT HOUSE, OR "BLEAK HOUSE," IN THE TIME OF CHARLES DICKENS

Occupied by Charles Dickens in 1850 and 1851

*Photo by Swaine & Co., High Street, Broadstairs*

See page 207

MISS GEORGINA HOGARTH BY AUGUSTUS EGG, *c.* 1850

*Photo by T. W. Tyrrell*

There are many other allusions to Defoe in Dickens's works.[1] Dickens sympathised too with the hectic life led by Defoe. He says, "Wellnigh the whole field of the *Vita Activa* was covered by his restless energy, and what he did he did with his might."

Among the later contributors to *Household Words* was Thomas Adolphus Trollope, eldest son of Mrs Trollope the authoress, whom Dickens first met in March 1838, and brother of Anthony Trollope. T. A. Trollope was born on 29 April 1810, and he lived latterly in Italy.

"My contributions," he says, "consisted for the most part of what I considered tit-bits from the by-ways of Italian History. In one instance the article was sent to order. I was dining with Dickens after I had all the remaining hairs on my head made to stand on end by the perusal of the officially published *Manual for Confessors* as approved by the superior authority for the dioceses of Tuscany. I was full of the subject, and made I fancy the hairs of some who sat at table with me, stand on end also. Dickens said with nailing forefinger levelled at me 'Give us that for *Household Words,* just as you have been telling it to us,' which I accordingly did." [2]

T. A. Trollope said of Dickens: "He was perhaps the largest-hearted man I ever knew. . . . He hated a mean action or a mean sentiment."

In reference to this period, Mr Garret Dumas, who was for a time Dickens's amanuensis, says:

Dickens would arrive at his office No. 16 Wellington Street at about eight o'clock in the morning and begin dictating. He would walk up and down the floor several times after delivering himself of a sentence or paragraph. He was generally tired out by eleven o'clock and would then go to his club. Dickens had a very odd habit of combing his hair. He would go through the performance a hundred times a day, and, in fact, seemed never to tire of it. It was invariably the first thing he did on entering the office.

In the autumn of 1850 Dickens succeeded in getting possession of "Fort House," Broadstairs, the tall, bleakly

[1] See also Chapter XI, § 56.
[2] *What I Remember*, by T. A. Trollope. Vol. 2, p. 119.

situated house already mentioned at the top of the cliff, close to the sea. As it was also called "Bleak House," some have imagined that the story so titled was written here. This is a mistake. Much of *David Copperfield* was written at Broadstairs, but *Bleak House* was not begun until after Dickens had left the town for good. Mr Jarndyce's estates, it will be remembered, lay in Herts.

§ 86. *Performances at Knebworth, November* 1850. *"A Christmas Tree," Christmas* 1850

At the end of 1850 there were three private performances (by Dickens, Forster, Egg, Frederick Dickens, Miss Hogarth and others, in the banqueting hall of Lord Lytton's mansion at Knebworth) of Ben Jonson's *Everyman in his Humour*. That on 18 November was followed by Mrs Inchbald's farce *Animal Magnetism*, in which Dickens personified the Doctor; and Lemon, Leech and Egg also took parts.

Two years had elapsed since the publication of *The Haunted Man*, and it occurred to Dickens that an extra Christmas number might be made an annually recurring feature of *Household Words*—the joint contribution of himself and others.

The following are these Christmas Numbers:

| | *Title* | *Dickens's share* |
|---|---|---|
| 1. | 1850. No distinctive title. | A Christmas Tree. |
| 2. | 1851. „       „       „ | What Christmas is as we grow older. |
| 3. | 1852. *A Round of Stories by the Christmas Fire.* | The Poor Relations' Story. The Child's Story. |
| 4. | 1853. *Another Round of Stories by the Christmas Fire.* | The Schoolboy's Story. The Nurse's Story. |
| 5. | 1854. *The Seven Poor Travellers. Richard Double Dick.* | First and Seventh. |
| 6. | 1855. *The Holly Tree Inn.* | Three chapters (Collins the rest). |
| 7. | 1856. *The Wreck of the "Golden Mary."* | First three chapters (Collins the rest). |
| 8. | 1857. *The Perils of certain English Travellers.* | First and third (Collins the rest). |
| 9. | 1858. *A House to Let.* | Going into Society. |

## § 87. *At Rockingham Again, January* 1851

In January 1851 Dickens was at Rockingham again. With the help of the village carpenter he rigged up "a very elegant little theatre." As usual the castle was full of company—friends of the Watsons and of Dickens. The plays acted were *Used Up*, and the farce *Animal Magnetism*. In the latter, Dickens was the Doctor, "in black with red stockings"; Mr Mark Lemon, the valet in blue and yellow, and a chintz waistcoat; Mr Leech, the Marquis; and Mr Egg, the one-eyed servant. Miss Boyle and Miss Hogarth also took parts. As a compliment to the host and hostess Dickens wrote a tag, in which he wished prosperity to them and their race. The first representation took place on 15 January; after the performance there was a dance which lasted till the small hours of the morning, and on the next evening Dickens was in London dining with Lord John Russell, the Prime Minister. The most interesting circumstance appertaining to Rockingham is perhaps the fact that Dickens drew upon it for a description of Chesney Wold, the home of the Dedlocks in *Bleak House* (see letter to Mrs Watson, 27 August 1853), which story was begun at the end of November 1851, the first number being published in March 1852.

Early in 1852 was privately printed a little work entitled, *Rockingham Castle, its Antiquity and History*, by a Mr C. H. Hartshorne. The copy of this book presented by Mrs Watson to Dickens is among the treasures preserved in the Northampton Public Library. Inside the lid is pasted Dickens's book-plate—a recumbent lion, with his name below. Next year, to Dickens's great grief, Mr Watson died, but with the widow he still continued united in close friendship, and several times after visited Rockingham. On 1 March 1851 Macready was entertained at a public dinner. Sir E. B. Lytton presided and among the speakers were Forster, W. J. Fox and Dickens, who proposed the health of the chairman.

§ 88. *Wilkie Collins enters.  The Guild of Literature and Art*

On 8 March 1851, Dickens wrote to "the Colonel," as he called Egg,[1] asking him to approach Wilkie Collins who, he thought, might take the part of Smart, a valet, in Bulwer's play *Not so Bad as we Seem.*  "I knew his father (William Collins, R.A., the painter) well," adds Dickens, "and should be very glad to know him."  Egg complied with the request and a little later Dickens and Collins were introduced to each other at Egg's house, Ivy Cottage, Black Lion Lane (now Queen's Road) Bayswater.  Collins was 29 and dwarfish in stature.  He had very small hands and feet—a woman's slippers were too big for him.  Some of his portraits represent him as shaven; in others he has an ample beard and he wore glasses.  Like Dickens, who was then 41, he loved colour, and was happiest in a red tie and a blue-striped shirt.

His entry into Dickens's life was an important event for both.  Collins had been impressed by the writers of the detective school, and particularly by Edgar Allan Poe with his *Purloined Letter* and *The Murders in the Rue Morgue.*  His first novel *Antonina* had appeared in 1863, and he was to become in England what Gaboriau was to become in France—the leading writer of detective stories.  To equip himself for his work he compiled voluminous commonplace books filled with extracts from the newspapers, but his masterpieces, *The Woman in White* and *The Moonstone,* had yet to be written.  He excelled as a skilful weaver of plots.  His art is to trick, mislead and torture the reader—to lead him breathless through perplexing mazes and finally to exhibit as the villain of the piece one of the least suspected characters.  Thenceforward Dickens and Collins often collaborated, especially in the Christmas stories.  Dickens thought highly of Collins's skill as a novelist, and there is no doubt he would have beaten Collins on Collins's own ground, if he had lived, for the plot of *Edwin Drood* bade fair to be of the best.

[1] Augustus Egg (R.A., 1860).  He died 18 May 1867.

WILLIAM WILKIE COLLINS, 1824-1889, PAINTED BY SIR JOHN MILLAIS

*National Portrait Gallery, London*

See page 210 *et al.*

TAVISTOCK HOUSE (NOW REMOVED)
The Home of Charles Dickens from 1851-1860
*Photo by Catherine Weed Ward*

See page 214

At Egg's house were many jovial gatherings, for here Forster, Leech, W. P. Frith, Lemon and G. H. Lewes used also to meet. Here they dined and gambled for trifling stakes and here Leech told his one story, "The Lawyer who lost his Client." For a time Forster and Collins were friendly, but they came heartily to dislike each other, for Collins, bohemian and fun lover, gradually took with Dickens the place that Forster had previously occupied. Not that Dickens cast off his earlier friend, but he found in Collins a more congenial spirit. This being the case it is not surprising that when Forster came to write the life of Dickens, he took care that Collins should have in it as little prominence as possible. But what of that? Human nature has a weakness for being human nature!

§ 89. *Death of Micawber, 31 March 1851. "A Child's History of England"*

It is very gratifying to remember that Mr John Dickens,[1] Dickens's father, continued to live long after his gifted son had attained fame. That he ever felt hurt on account of the Micawber caricature is unlikely. The probability is that he laughed at it as heartily as anyone. At this time John Dickens was staying at a house in Keppel Street, London, and Dickens, when his father's health began to fail, visited him almost daily. On 30 March, hearing that his father was sinking, Dickens hurried from Malvern (whither he had taken Mrs Dickens, who had been ill) to London, and arrived in Keppel Street on Sunday at eleven in the evening. His father was alive, but did not know anyone. He died, "Oh so quietly," says Dickens, "just before six next morning."

John Dickens was buried in Highgate Cemetery, and the stone placed to his memory by his son bears tribute to his "zealous, useful, cheerful spirit." To Dr Davey, the medical man who had attended his father, Dickens

[1] In the *Dickensian*, vol. 3, No. 2 (February 1907) is a photograph of the bust of John Dickens, by Samuel Haydon. The photograph is by Mr T. W. Tyrrell.

211

sent an elegant silver snuff-box in token of his gratitude for kindness and attention shown to the dying man. Taking his mother in his arms, Dickens told her that for the future she must rely upon him. Mrs Dickens survived her husband twelve years. In a letter to Forster, Dickens, having occasion to refer to his father, said, "I regard him as a better man the longer I live."

During 1851 and the two following years, Dickens published in *Household Words* "A Child's History of England," nearly the whole of which was dictated to Miss Hogarth, Mrs Dickens, owing to family ties and uncertain health, being, of course, unable to give much assistance in this way. It eventually appeared in book form, though it is superficial and has other serious faults. However, Dickens is always on the side of liberty. He does not spare the pedantic James the First, or the frivolous Charles the Second, but he has high praise for the forceful figure of Cromwell. The narrative practically closes with the accession of William III, another of his heroes, when "the Protestant religion was established in England, and England's great and glorious Revolution was complete"; for the rest is a mere summary of the events that followed. In April 1851 Dickens lost his little daughter Dora Annie.

§ 90. *The Speech at Gore House* (10 May 1851). *"Mr Nightingale's Diary,"* 27 *May* 1851

On 10 May 1851 he delivered at Gore House, Kensington, by request of Lady Blessington, a speech on the necessity of Sanitary Reform. It was printed in full for the first time by the Bibliophile Society of Boston, U.S.A., in 1909.[1] Lord Ashley presided and there was a brilliant company. Dickens insisted at the outset "that searching Sanitary Reform must precede all other social remedies and that even Education and Religion can do nothing until the way is paved for their ministration by cleanliness and decency," and it will not escape our notice that the thoughts that were then in Dickens's mind preceded the publication

[1] The MS. was then owned by Mr Edmund D. Brooks of Minneapolis.

of *Bleak House* in which he so earnestly championed the cause of the downtrodden and the oppressed. He already had in mind poor Jo, and the noisy inutility of Mrs Pardiggle. He proposed as a toast the Board of Health, coupling with it the name of Lord Ashley. About the same time he sent to *Punch* (his only contribution to that journal) a paragraph, partly facetious, entitled "Dreadful Hardships" which emphasised the sufferings of the suburbs of London "for want of water."

For some time he had projected the founding of a Guild of Literature and Art, in other words a provident fund and benefit society for unfortunate literary men and artists. It was discussed during the theatrical performances at Knebworth, and Sir E. Bulwer Lytton gave it his support. In order to obtain funds Dickens and his friends decided to give a number of dramatic performances in various parts of the kingdom. Among the pieces to be played were Ben Jonson's *Every Man in his Humour*, Lytton's comedy *Not so Bad as we Seem* and a farce *Mr Nightingale's Diary*, the joint work of Dickens and Lemon.

A commencement was made on 27 May 1851 with *Not so Bad as we Seem* at Devonshire House, Piccadilly, in the presence of Queen Victoria, the Prince Consort, Lord Macaulay, and other notables, Dickens taking the part of Lord Wilmot. At the second performance on 27 May the afterpiece was the one-act farce, *Mr Nightingale's Diary*, but in the course of rehearsal, Dickens, who himself impersonated "Mr Gabblewig" made so many alterations that the piece may be regarded as his rather than Lemon's.[1] In later performances he personated several characters in succession, changing his dress and his voice each time.

[1] An early version of the play before it was touched by Dickens was offered for sale by Messrs Maggs in 1929, Catalogue No. 516, and described as contained on 66 pp. quarto. No date.

## CHAPTER XIV

# November 1851 to March 1856

§ 91. *Dickens removes to Tavistock House, November* 1851.
*"Bleak House" commenced. Mrs Gaskell and "Cranford"*

AT the end of November 1851, Dickens removed to
Tavistock House, Tavistock Square, and here he
commenced a new novel for which no fewer than
ten different titles were proposed previous to the one which
it was destined to bear—*Bleak House*. In *Bleak House*
Dickens assails the Court of Chancery, his object being "to
draw public attention to the enormous waste of time and
money which usually characterised its proceedings." He
was encouraged in this design by receiving about this time
a pamphlet on the subject by Mr W. Challinor of Leek.
One case dealt with was that of a suit affecting a single farm
valued at some £1,200—all that the owner possessed in the
world—against which a bill had been filed for a £300 legacy
left in the will bequeathing the farm. For two years the
lawyers haggled; and the costs incurred amount to three
times the figure of the legacy. Mr Challinor might well
observe, "What a mockery of justice this is!" This case
was the original of that of Gridley, as related in the fifteenth
chapter of *Bleak House*. The suit of Jarndyce and Jarndyce
was based upon the notorious and apparently everlasting
Jennings case—which concerned a vast property that had
belonged to a William Jennings, an old miser of Acton, in
Suffolk.

Dickens's kindness of heart makes its presence known in *Bleak House* perhaps more than elsewhere. He sympathised deeply with the woes of ill-treated women and neglected children—and here we have the Brickmaker's family, the children of "Coavinses," and the most famous of all—the crossing sweeper—Jo.

Mrs Gaskell in her story *Cranford* which commenced in *Household Words* on 13 December 1851 made a number of eulogistic references to Dickens himself. These he, of course, could not allow to be printed in his own journal, so he altered them, putting in place of his own name Thomas Hood's, and substituting for the titles of his own works those by which Hood was best known.

Here are some of the changes:

*Mrs Gaskell* wrote: "Have you seen any numbers of the *Pickwick Papers*—Aren't they famously good?"

*Dickens* altered to "Have you see any numbers of Hood's Own?"

*Mrs Gaskell:* "I prefer Dr Johnson to Mr Boz."

*Dickens:* "I prefer Dr Johnson to Mr Hood."

*Mrs Gaskell:* "She babbled on long enough to get a good long spell at *The Christmas Carol.*"

*Dickens:* "She babbled on long enough for Flora to get a good long spell at *Miss Kelmansegg and her Golden Leg.*"

It will be noticed that Dickens in his haste to alter this reference did not give the title of Hood's poem correctly. It should have been *Miss Kelmansegg and her Precious Leg.*

Mrs Gaskell was very annoyed when she saw the proofs, and in a letter to Wills, wanted to withdraw the story. Wills neglected to show the letter to Dickens at once. When Dickens saw it on 5 December he wrote immediately to Mrs Gaskell and said, after mentioning how delighted he was with the tale, that it had gone to press and that consequently it was too late to make alterations.

In order further to appease Mrs Gaskell, he added, "I would do anything rather than cause you a minute's vexation

arising out of what had given me so much pleasure."
When *Cranford* appeared in book-form she changed the
altered passages to their original state.

On 18 February 1851, at the advanced age of 92, died
at Leith Mrs Dickens's grandfather, George Thomson,[1]
the song-collector and friend of Burns. He and his
daughter, Miss Helen Thomson, had watched with deep
interest the meteoric rise of Dickens; and Mrs Dickens
and the Hogarth family continually corresponded with them.
George Thomson was buried at Kensal Green Cemetery,
London, where his wife had been interred ten years before,
and close to Mary Hogarth's grave.[2]

In a letter written by Dickens to a friend on 7 March
1852, is a reference to Hablot Browne's illustrations in
*Bleak House*. He says, "Browne has done Skimpole and
helped to make him singularly unlike the great original."
In the same letter he expresses himself as very pleased
with the two *Cranford* chapters *Old Letters* and *Poor Peter*;
and exclaims, "Don't you think Mrs Gaskell charming!"
On 13 March 1852, when Mrs Dickens was 37, was born
her tenth child, Edward Bulwer Lytton.

When Dickens became acquainted with Miss Lynn (afterwards Mrs Lynn Linton) is not clear. She says:

"Once when I was staying with Landor he had had a small
dinner party of Dickens, John Forster and myself. I found Dickens
charming and Forster pompous, heavy and ungenial. Forster was
saturnine and cynical. Dickens and Landor were his property—
pocket boroughs in a way—and he resented the introduction of a third
person and a stranger."

All the same Forster had plenty of virtues. He was at
heart a thoroughly good fellow; and Mrs Linton, whose
tongue had a beautiful edge to it, could be as biting as
Lady Lytton. It is quite certain that on this occasion she
gave Forster quite as much as he gave her: Mr Pot and
Miss Kettle. It is impossible, whatever his faults, not to
like Forster.

[1] VIII, §¼24.                    [2] See XI, § 58.

§ 92. *Originals of Characters, etc., in "Bleak House."*
*The Type Evasion*

As already mentioned, Dickens got some of his ideas in
*Bleak House* from Rockingham Castle ["Chesney Wold"] in
Northamptonshire. We also observed that Mrs Manning,
the murderess, was the original of Mademoiselle Hortense.
Her broken English, her impatient gestures, and her
volubility, were all transferred to the destroyer of Mr
Tulkinghorn.

The burial-ground in Russell Court, where Nemo was
laid to rest, was later converted into a playground for
children, who entered at the iron gate which figures in
Hablot Browne's picture "Consecrated Ground." Poor Jo
has moved many.

To the origin of the name "Tom-all-Alone's" we alluded
in Chapter 1. A more graphic description of a London
alley of the wretcheder sort was never penned. But Dickens
excelled in scenes of this kind, and his accounts of Bleeding
Heart Yard, apparently the now transformed Bedfordbury,
leading from St Martin's Lane, and the approach to Mrs
Gamp's home at once occur to the mind. For vividness,
however, we recollect nothing in Dickens to excel that
description in Chapter 2 of *Bleak House*, commencing "The
waters are out in Lincolnshire." A wet day never before
had the honour to be so accurately pictured. Even
Washington Irving's "A wet day at an inn," much as it has
been praised, is less successful. We see the lead-coloured
view from Lady Dedlock's windows. "The vases on the
stone terrace in the foreground catch the rain all day, and the
heavy drops fall, drip, drip, drip, upon the broad flagged
pavement." No wonder Lady Dedlock was "bored to
death."

Lawrence Boythorn, as every one knows, is Walter
Savage Landor, who is said to have taken that presentation
of himself in hearty good humour. On the other hand, the
delineation of Leigh Hunt as Harold Skimpole was justly
resented by Hunt and his family. As Dickens had by his
thoughtlessness brought with his *Nicholas Nickleby* ruin

upon Shaw the schoolmaster, so he by the same fault—for no one imagines that he was actuated by malice—wounded the feelings of the Hunts. We are assured by Mr Edmund Ollier, an old friend of Hunt's, that Dickens personally expressed to Hunt his regret for the Skimpole error.

Dickens on 16 June 1855 wrote a genial paper about Leigh Hunt in *Household Words*, "By Rail to Parnassus." He further made what amends he could in an article "Leigh Hunt: a Remonstrance," which appeared in *All the Year Round* on 24 December 1859.

Caddy Jellyby and Mrs Jellyby are delightful! And can we not sympathise with Richard Carstone for being obliged to wash in a pie-dish, and with Caddy when she wished Africa was dead. To say that Dickens by these scenes and his satirical allusions to Borrioboola Gha, which, by the by, offended Miss Harriet Martineau, wished to discourage the efforts then being made to put down slavery, is of course nonsense. We have all met Mrs Jellyby. Sometimes she neglects her family to write novels, sometimes to attend prayer meetings. There is at fewest one of her sort in every town and village. George Gissing goes into ecstasies over Mr Vholes. "In the whole range of fiction," he declares, "there is no character more vivid than this exhibited so briefly yet so completely." Guster made him "roar with laughter," and he adds truthfully "from a certain point of view everything in this world is laughable." Mr Tulkinghorn's house was that of Forster.

The reiterations in the characters in Dickens's earlier works are not only tolerable but really amusing—as, for example, Mrs Gummidge's oft-repeated declaration that she was a "lone lorn creetur and everythink went contrairy with her." In the later novels Dickens was less successful. Take Mr Vholes, with his three girls at home and an aged father in the vale of Taunton. The trick, however, still occasionally increases the vividness of the narrative—one never, for example, thinks of *Bleak House* without seeing Mr Jellyby's head against the wall.

If Dickens was disturbed by the commotion caused by the identification of Shaw with Squeers, he was infinitely more upset by the likeness everybody saw between Skimpole and Leigh Hunt, and he could escape from the charge only by evasion. He said in respect to the characters in his books they were not portraits of actual persons, they were TYPES. Moreover, the word went round in his family that that was to be the answer to all questioners. His command was studiously obeyed. Curiously enough, Miss Georgina Hogarth, in a letter written to Mr Charles R. Rideal and printed in *Charles Dickens's Heroines*, p. 17, echoes this command. She said:

> "You are quite mistaken in supposing that *every* character in his (Dickens's) books was a portrait of some real person. There were frequent indications of several people in a single character, Mrs Nickleby, for example, I believe was a compound of two or three women, but *all* his characters were *types* and not actual people."

It will be noticed that Miss Hogarth, in her anxiety to defend Dickens contradicts herself. She concedes that only some of the characters were types and then declares that *all* were types. Charles Dickens the younger wrote similarly respecting his father's work.

The truth is that Squeers, Micawber, Mrs Micawber, and Skimpole, and others were *not* types. They were actual persons with embellishments. Dickens was above all an artist, and to understand the artist's attitude to life one cannot do better than study Oscar Wilde's clever "Pen, Pencil and Poison" in *Intentions*. If the characters referred to had not been actual persons with their peculiarities exaggerated, Dickens would not have been an artist. The "Type" theory is pure evasion. Dickens had found himself in a difficulty and he and his circle had to help him out. They did. In other words they didn't; for no common-sense person understanding Literature and Art was hoodwinked. Dickens's forte was not imagination, he was a keen observer. Nothing escaped his photographic eye.

Dickens himself (contradicting himself) declared that he took his more important characters from life. To a friend who asked him if his characters were fancies, he replied with sharpness, "No, sir, they are not; they are copies.

You will not understand me to say, of course, that they are true histories in all respects, but they are real likenesses." The "Type" nonsense was exposed as early as 1898 by George Gissing.[1]

There is humour in *Bleak House*, but (the result of home troubles) the mournful predominates. It is a veritable *Hamlet* for slaughter. Poor Richard reforms only to die, Lady Dedlock, Mr Krook, Nemo and Mr Tulkinghorn, all have tragic dismissals. Dickens was in very, very low spirits during the writing of the larger part of *Bleak House*. The drollest portions are those connected with the Jellybys. To name one of the amenities of the establishment, Esther's bedroom there—was excessively bare and disorderly, and the curtain to her window was fastened up with a fork. Mr Snagsby's comment on the French maid's name is funny enough: Mr Tulkinghorn says: "Oh! Yes, yes. Mademoiselle Hortense." "Indeed, sir?" Mr Snagsby coughs his cough of submission behind his hat. "I am not acquainted myself with the names of foreigners in general, but I have no doubt it would be that." Mr Snagsby appears to have set out in this reply with some desperate design of repeating the name; but on reflection coughs again to excuse himself.

Then a favourite with many readers is "the debilitated cousin"—some relation evidently to Cousin Feenix. When Mr Tulkinghorn is murdered, "the debilitated cousin" only hopes "some fler'll be executed—zample. Thinks more interest's wanted—get man hanged presentime—than get man place ten thousand a year. Hasn't a doubt—zample— far better hang wrong fler than no fler."

The allusions in this tale to marriage and trouble bring to the reader's recollection continually the unhappiness of Dickens's own married life. "My experience teaches me, Lady Dedlock," observes Mr Tulkinghorn, "that most of the people I know would do far better to leave marriage

[1] *Charles Dickens*, by Gissing, who says: "I see in them not abstractions, but men and women; clothed abstractions do not take hold upon the imagination and the memory as these people of Dickens did from the day of their coming into life," p. 16.

alone. It is at the bottom of three-fourths of their troubles."

In optimistic utterances *Bleak House* is not wanting. Thinking of Mr Woodcourt, Mr Jarndyce remarks: "Strange to say, I believe the best man has the best chance."

One of the outcomes of the publication of *Bleak House* was the attack made on Dickens by Lord Chief Justice Denman, who for so long had unremittingly attacked the remnants of slavery both with voice and pen. In the character of Mrs Jellyby he saw an insidious attack on the work to which he had dedicated himself, and he expressed his anger. The attack consisted of a series of articles in the *Standard*, September 1852. After ridiculing Dickens's attack on Chancery abuses which he described as "belated and now unnecessary," he accused Dickens of doing his best to replunge the world into the most barbarous abuse that ever afflicted it. He said, "We do not say that he actually defends slavery or the slave trade, but he takes pains to discourage by ridicule the effort now awaking to put them down." [1] That Lord Denman was in error Dickens's *American Notes* would alone convince any unbiased mind.

§ 93. 4 *May* 1852. *The Guild Company at Birmingham.* *"What shall we have for Dinner"*

Early in May 1852, Dickens had a letter from Mr George Beadnell, father of his old love, Maria, who evidently had persuaded him to write it, for she was continually proud of Dickens's old attachment to her. Mr Beadnell invited him to his country place, Myford, Welshpool; and it is probable that Maria was with her father at the time, and that she awaited the reply with eager curiosity. Many changes had taken place since the old days. Mr Beadnell had grown rich and Maria had long been married. Dickens, pleased to hear from an old acquaintance, replied on Tuesday, 4 May. He concluded his letter with "Give my love to Margaret (Mrs Lloyd) and ask her to give the same to

[1] Lord Denman died in September 1854.

Maria if she should see her. Also remember me to Mr David Lloyd, and believe me ever with ten thousand old recollections, Faithfully yours, Charles Dickens." [1]

On Wednesday, 12 May 1852, Dickens and his company were at Birmingham, and played in the Town Hall, in behalf of the Guild of Literature and Art, Lord Lytton's *Not so Bad as we Seem*. Dickens was again Lord Willmott, Wilkie Collins was Mr Softhead; Forster, Mr Hardman; Mark Lemon, Sir Geoffrey Thornside. In the *Dickensian*, June 1907, is a photograph of the very interesting Ticket of Admission, representing on one side Richard Wilson the landscape artist, and on the other Daniel Defoe. It was designed by Edward Matthew Ward, A.R.A.

Dickens's company also acted, in aid of the Guild of Literature and Art, in the large hall of the Lyceum, Sunderland, on 28 August 1852, Sir Edward Bulwer Lytton's *Not so Bad as we Seem*, followed by *Mr Nightingale's Diary* and *Past Two O'clock in the Morning*—Dickens in the last being again Mr Snobbington and Lemon the Stranger. On 1 September 1852, Dickens and his friends appeared at the Free Trade Hall, Manchester, the play presented being *Used Up*. Next day the new public library in that city was opened by the Queen, Dickens, Lytton and Thackeray being among the speakers. [2]

On Friday, 3 September 1852, they presented Boucicault's play *Used Up* and *Mr Nightingale's Diary* at the Philharmonic Hall, Liverpool. When acting in *Used Up*, Dickens as usual took the part of Sir Charles Coldstream. An illustration from a painting of him in this character by Augustus Egg forms the frontispiece of S. J. Adair Fitz-Gerald's book *Dickens and the Drama*. [3] The play-bill is reproduced in the *Dickensian*, July 1907, and in the *Letters of Dickens to Wilkie Collins*, 1892. In *Used Up* Wilkie Collins was James; Lemon, John Ironbrace, a blacksmith. In *Mr Nightingale's Diary*, Mr Frank Stone was Mr

---

[1] *The Romance of Charles Dickens and Maria Beadnell Winter*, edited by E. F. Payne and H. H. Harper, Boston, U.S.A., 1929, p. 91.
[2] See the *Dickensian*, 1 September 1934.
[3] Chapman and Hall, 1910.

Nightingale, Egg took two characters and Dickens as many as six. Notwithstanding the efforts of Dickens and his friends, the council of the Guild of Literature were not able to carry out their designs though they erected thirteen houses at Stevenage on ground given by Sir Edward Bulwer Lytton, intended as retreats for artists and men of letters. Eventually the guild was dissolved, and its property and assets transferred to the Royal Literary Fund and Artists' General Benevolent Institution. Mr F. Clifford, K.C., the last survivor of the council, died in 1905.

The Christmas number of *Household Words* for 1852 was entitled *A Round of Stories by the Christmas Fire.* Of the ten stories, only two were by Dickens—"The Child's Story" and "Poor Relations." Mrs Gaskell wrote to say how much she enjoyed them; and her encomiums gave him the liveliest pleasure.

Dealing with Dickens's personal habits, his son Charles says: "I wonder how many dinners were begun with a glass of Chichester milk-punch; how many were finished with a dish of toasted cheese." Mrs Dickens published in 1852, under the name of Lady Maria Clutterbuck, a book of her own daily bills of fare with the title *What shall we have for Dinner? satisfactorily answered by numerous Bills of Fare for from two to eighteen persons.* The Introduction runs:

The late Sir Jonas Clutterbuck had in addition to a host of other virtues, a very good appetite and an excellent digestion. My experience in the confidences of many of my female friends tell me, alas! that others are not as happy in their domestic relations as I was. That their daily life is embittered by the consciousness that a delicacy forgotten or misapplied is gradually making the Club more attractive than the Home. I have consented to give the world The Bills of Fare which met with the approval of Sir Jonas Clutterbuck.

This passage reminds us of the title of the poem written by Dickens in his youthful days (see VI, § 18), and that he had a finger in this production may without rashness be presumed. Anyhow, as the only literary venture of Mrs Dickens, it is not without interest. The critics praised the little work, but declared "that no man could possibly survive the consumption of such frequent toasted cheese." [1] On 6 January 1853, a banquet in honour of Dickens was given at Dee's Hotel (later the Old Royal), Birmingham. He was presented with a silver "Iliad" salver and a diamond ring, and when offering thanks he promised to give a public reading at Birmingham in aid of the funds for the building and formation of the Birmingham and Midland Institute. [2]

## § 94. *At Boulogne*

In the spring of 1853, while still engaged upon *Bleak House*, Dickens made a short stay at Brighton. In May he was prostrated by illness, and after his recovery—early in June—he set off for a holiday sojourn at Boulogne, taking up his abode in the charming little Chateau des Moulineaux, Rue Beaurepaire, belonging to the most delightful of landlords—a certain M. Beaucourt. In a droll letter (June 26) one of the happiest pieces of descriptive writing outside his novels, Dickens says:

This house is on a great hill side. It faces the Haute Ville, with the ramparts and the unfinished cathedral. . . . If the extraordinary things in the house defy description, the amazing phenomena in the gardens never could have been dreamed of by anybody but a Frenchman bent upon one idea. Besides a portrait of the house in the dining-room, there is a plan of the property in the hall. It looks about the size of Ireland, and to every one of the extraordinary objects there is a reference with some portentous name. There are fifty-one such references.

Dickens twice after spent his summer holidays at Boulogne, and his description of "our French watering-place" is one of the best remembered of his minor effusions. [3]

Mrs Gaskell's *Ruth* stirred Dickens more than any other of her books. Writing to her on 3 May 1853 he says in reference evidently to two of the characters in it: "I called those two women my dear friends! Why, if I told you the

[1] *Windsor Magazine*, December 1934, p. 23.
[2] See the *Dickensian*, June 1907, which has a photo of the salver.
[3] *Our French Watering Place*. Cr. ed., vol. 17, p. 227.

fiftieth part of what I have thought about them you would write me the most suspicious of notes, refusing to receive the fiftieth part of that." It has been pointed out that there are striking resemblances between certain characters in Dickens's *Hard Times* written a little later and some of the characters in *Ruth*. The influence of Dickens, on the other hand, is seen in Mrs Gaskell's later work.

### § 95. *To Switzerland and Italy with Collins and Egg*

In October 1853, just after Dickens had finished *Bleak House*, he, Collins and Egg, made an excursion through parts of Switzerland and Italy. At the end of October they were at Genoa, whence they took steamer to Naples, where in the company of Layard and Sir Emerson Tennent they spent pleasant hours and explored the neighbouring buried cities.

At Naples there was an occurrence that might have been taken from the sardonic page of Stendhal, who describes the Cavaliere Foscarina "as a perfectly straightforward gentleman, who had consequently been in prison more or less under every régime." [1] Dickens asked a Neapolitan Marchese after a certain gentleman whom he had met and respected when at Naples in February 1845.

"I forget his name," said Dickens.

The Marchese gave it and his face fell directly.

"Dead?" enquired Dickens.

"In exile."

"Oh, dear me!"

"What would you have?" commented the Marchese in a low voice. "He was a remarkable man full of knowledge, full of spirit, full of generosity. Where should he be but in exile!"

"I shall always remember," adds Dickens, "that short dialogue."

From Naples the three friends went to Rome. They were impressed with the desolation of the Coliseum and the Appian Way. On 20 November they were at Florence,

[1] *Chartreuse of Parma*, p. 520.

and on 5 December at Turin, on their way home. It was in reference to this journey that Dickens remarked admirably:

"I am more than ever confirmed in my conviction that one of the great uses of travelling is to encourage a man to think for himself, to be bold enough always to declare without offence that he does think for himself, and to overcome the villainous meanness of professing what other people have professed, when he knows that his profession is untrue."

## § 96. *Readings at Birmingham, 27 and 29 December 1853. "Another Round of Stories by the Christmas Fire"*

As already stated, Dickens, on 6 January 1853, promised to give at Birmingham a couple of readings from his Christmas Books in aid of the New Midland Institute. The dates chosen were 27 and 29 December 1853. In *Speeches Literary and Social, by Charles Dickens*, edited by Richard Herne Shepherd and published in 1870 by John Camden Hotten, it is stated that before reading at Birmingham, Dickens "thought proper to give a trial Reading before a much smaller audience in the quiet little city of Peterborough." Then follows a ten-page account of the Reading by "One who heard it." The memory of the writer, however, must have deceived him, for Mr W. Fickling, B.A., after going through many official documents at Peterborough was able in a lecture delivered there on 7 February 1912 (The Dickens Centenary) to declare "positively and definitely" that there was no Dickens reading at Peterborough at that time. A careful examination of the pages in Hotten proves that they are an account not of any Reading at Peterborough in 1853, but of a Reading which actually took place in that city on Tuesday, 18 December 1855—an event which we shall consider a few pages farther on (XIV, § 100).

Dickens read at Birmingham his *Christmas Carol* on Tuesday, 27 December, and *The Cricket on the Hearth* on Thursday the 29th. On the 30th only working men were admitted. Writing to Mrs Watson of Rockingham, he said: "I never saw nor do I suppose anybody else ever did see such an interesting sight as the working people's night. They lost nothing, misinterpreted nothing, followed everything closely." On the Saturday following, 31 December, he and his friends were entertained at the Hen and Chickens Hotel and Mrs Dickens was presented with a silver flowerstand. The Christmas Number of *Household Notes* for 1853 was *Another Round of Stories by the Christmas Fire.*

§ 97. *"Hard Times." "The Seven Poor Travellers." Christmas* 1854

On 1 April 1854 Dickens commenced in *Household Words* his story *Hard Times*. Speaking of the domestic tragedy of Stephen and Rachel, Dr Ward points out that it has a subdued intensity of tenderness and melancholy of a kind rare with Dickens, upon whom the example of Mrs Gaskell in this instance may not have been without its influence. *Hard Times* has also affinities with Mrs Gaskell's earlier book, *Mary Barton*. This story is singularly unattractive. Indeed it is almost unreadable. Blackpool, Bounderby, Gradgrind and Sleary may be true to life, but all four are insufferable bores. This was his first failure, *A Tale of Two Cities* being the other (see p. 291).

In the meantime, Wilkie Collins had been making a name as a writer. He had published *Basil, A story of Modern Life* in 1852, and *Hide and Seek* in 1854. The latter took Dickens by storm. He says, "I think it far away the cleverest novel I have ever seen written by a new hand." He praises its humour; writing on 22 July 1854 he considered that neither Mrs Dickens nor Miss Hogarth sufficiently appreciated that "very remarkable book." He became the more attached to Collins because he could see in him something that was absent from other young men that he knew. He was original, he was not afraid of toil, he was capable of what was absent from so many others—enthusiasm. Then, too, Dickens was flattered by the extreme deference with which Collins listened to him.

From 2 September 1854 to 27 January 1855, had appeared in *Household Words* Mrs Gaskell's story *North and*

*South.* After Dickens had gone over the proofs with great pains he learnt that Mr Wills had received a letter from Mrs Gaskell stipulating that the proofs were not to be touched "even by Mr Dickens." Dickens gave way to her though he considered that his amendments had improved the story.[1]

Part of the Christmas number of *Household Words* for 1854, which is entitled "Seven Poor Travellers," relates to the ancient and curious Richard Watts's Charity at Rochester. The concluding portion of the story referring to "Richard Doubledick" is one of the most touching instances of Christian forgiveness ever recorded, and hardened indeed must be he who leaves it with dry eyes. At the end of December 1854 Dickens was reading his *Christmas Carol* at Reading. Thence he proceeded to Sherborne. His next destination was Bradford in Yorkshire. On 6 January 1855, his son's birthday, there was played at Tavistock House, Planché's *Fortunio and his Seven Gifted Sons*, Dickens, Wilkie Collins and Mark Lemon taking parts. In January 1855, borrowing an idea from Wilkie Collins, Dickens began a Book of Memoranda in which he set down in a haphazard manner any hints or suggestions that occurred to him. He made use of a number of the entries in it when working at *Little Dorrit* and *Our Mutual Friend*.

## § 98. *Mrs Winter (Maria Beadnell), February and March* 1855

He celebrated his birthday 7 February 1855 by a dinner at Gravesend. Often amid the unhappiness of his home his thoughts wandered to those hectic days when he had hoped to win Maria Beadnell, and one day he walked pensively through Lombard Street just to cast his eyes on the spot where Number 2 (which was pulled down) had stood, while the wonder ran in his mind whether all his success in life could compensate for the loss that had been his when Maria escaped him.

Then, on the evening of 18 February when he was read-

[1] See *Letter to Wilkie Collins,* 24 March 1855.

ing at his fireside and while he was contemplating a week's holiday in Paris with Wilkie Collins, occurred a curious coincidence. Whom should he receive a letter from but, to his surprise, that very Maria Beadnell (who had become Mrs Henry Louis Winter) herself. She referred to the old times in Lombard Street. It will be remembered that Dickens heard from her father in May 1852 (see XIV, § 93). Mr and Mrs Winter, who resided at 12 Artillery Place, London, had a young daughter named Ella. Dickens was 43 and the father of nine children. He replied cordially on Saturday, 10 February 1855, from Tavistock House, declaring that her letter gave him intense pleasure. It had come at a time when the estrangement between Dickens and his wife was particularly acute; and he, momently living again the Lombard Street days, wondered whether union with Maria would have made him happier. He recalled her maiden witchery and the haunting strains of her harp as she sang sweetly to it old-time sentimental ditties. In imagination he once more met her in the moonlight, alone.

"Believe me," he said in reply, "you cannot more tenderly remember our old days and our old friends than I do." After saying that he would be charmed to have a long talk with her, and that he would be most cordially glad to see her after so great a length of time, he went on: "I am going to Paris to-morrow morning, but I purpose being back within a fortnight. When I return, Mrs Dickens will come to you, to arrange a day for our seeing you and Mr Winter."

Then there is a reference to his mother. It appears that Mrs Micawber "had a strong objection to being considered in the least old" and that she usually appeared at Tavistock House in "a juvenile cap" which took "an immense time in the putting on." He mentioned that his address in Paris would be the Hotel Meurice, and that if he could discharge any little commission for Mrs Winter he would be most happy.[1]

Next day (18 February) he journeyed to Paris in the company of Wilkie Collins. In his mind ran recollections of Maria's old attractiveness and his passion for her; and

[1] *The Romance of Charles Dickens and H. B. Winter*, p. 100.

when he was in Paris his thoughts ran far more on his old love than on the theatres and the other amenities of that city. Among the friends whom he met there, were Sir Joseph and Lady Oliffe, and he seems to have shown Lady Oliffe Maria's letter, for she asked him "whether it was really true that he used to love Maria so very, very much." He replied that there was no woman in the world, and there were very few men, who could ever imagine how much.

On Thursday, 15 February 1855, he received another letter from Mrs Winter and he replied to it the same day. In reference to her daughter Ella, he said:

I hope now you know me better you will teach her to tell her children that I loved her mother with the most extraordinary earnestness when I was a boy. . . . This is so fixed in my knowledge that to the hour when I opened your letter last Friday night I have never heard anybody addressed by your name or spoken of by your name, without a start. . . . You may have seen in one of my books a faithful reflection of the passion I had for you, and may have thought that it was something to have been loved so well and may have seen in little bits of Dora touches of your old self sometimes.

Whether she had seen *David Copperfield* or not, Dickens sent her a copy inscribed "Charles Dickens to Maria Winter. In remembrance of old times."

His next letter to her, dated 22 February 1855, was written at Tavistock House just after his return, and he wrote again on 24 February, addressing her as "My dear Maria." Mr H. H. Harper, editor of this correspondence, calls it "one of the greatest love letters of all time." That is excessive eulogy, still it is a very ardent letter.

"Whom can you ever trust," exclaims Dickens, "if it be not your old lover?" It was a long letter full of warmth, for he saw her through the haze of the years, and recalled departed joys. Then occurs a little bit of deceit, the suggestion that Mrs Winter should call at Tavistock House on Sunday and ask first for Mrs Dickens, and then for him. "It is almost a positive certainty," he says, "that there will be no one here but I, between 3 and 4." So she is to ask for Mrs Dickens with the knowledge that Mrs Dickens will not be at home. It was unwise, it was not open, it was running too near a precipice. "In an unguarded moment," to quote Mr Harper, "sober discretion is thrown to the winds and all is forgotten save that he is living again in the old dream!" But then Dickens always acted on impulse. His line of action was invariably unforeseen even by himself, and romantic he had always been, still no harm came from this injudicious letter, though he must have regretted soon afterwards that he had written it.

How or when Dickens and Mrs Winter met is not known, but when they did meet he was enormously disillusioned. The lady of his dreams was unrecognisable. She was stout, finicking and affected, she made up in bulk [1] and flounces for what she had lost in poetry, but she was good-natured to a fault, she had a kind heart. Some women would have traded on his indiscretion. The Dora of *David Copperfield*, however, became the Flora of *Little Dorrit*. She deserved a kinder fate.

One Wednesday evening in March 1855, Dickens called at her house. Her dog Daphne (Dora's Jip) stood stuffed in her hall. Further acquaintance with Mrs Winter increased the disillusionment. She drank brandy in her tea! However, he interested himself in Ella, and presented Mrs Winter with a copy of the two-volume edition of Tennyson's poems.

He received another letter from her on Friday, 9 March, and he replied to it next day, finishing his letter with "You may be perfectly sure that in writing to me, you write to no one else." On Tuesday, 3 April, he wrote again, but his interest in her is seen to be waning. The tone of his subsequent letters is platonic. Her thoughts, however, centred at the time chiefly on her sick baby and when it died in June 1855 Dickens wrote to express his deep sympathy. The correspondence then slackened.

His subsequent letters to her, though kind, friendly and at times affectionate, are thenceforward short, formal and even evasive, and Mrs Winter discovered that her dream of a cordial friendship with her old lover could not be realised. She, however, formed the acquaintance of some of the

[1] Dickens describes Flora as being "tall," but see Chapter VI, § 18.

members of his family, including Miss Hogarth and Kate Dickens; and she was sometimes a guest at Tavistock House; but she found that she was not welcome, and the visits became less frequent.

On 19 March 1855, Dickens was praising and making suggestions concerning Collins's story *Sister Rose* which appeared later that year in *Household Words*. Collins's *After Dark* appeared in its columns in 1856, his *Dead Secret* in 1857.

## § 99. *The Lighthouse*

In June 1855 there was acted at Tavistock House, Collins's play *The Lighthouse*. One of the scenes painted by Clarkson Stanfield represented Eddystone Lighthouse. Dickens, who composed for the play five verses called "The Song of the Wreck," took in it the part of Aaron Gurnock. All concerned in the play thoroughly enjoyed themselves, and astonished the audience. The storm in particular was an immense success. Marcus Stone had charge of the rain, lightning and thunder, the rattle of which was effected by a sheet of iron, Charles Dickens the younger was responsible for the wind, created by "a sort of silk grindstone," and other members of the family dropped heavy articles about "to represent the thud and crash of the billows." Indeed it was as enjoyable as if they had been actually in the storm; and Dickens himself revelled in it.

Carlyle, who was present as a "first nighter," was particularly struck by Dickens's wild "picturesqueness" as the old lighthouse keeper. It was followed by *Mr Nightingale's Diary* and Mrs Inchbald's *Animal Magnetism*.[1] On 14 July it was acted again (this time for the benefit of the funds of the Bournemouth Sanatorium for Consumptive Patients) at Campden House, Kensington, the residence of Colonel Waugh, the advantage being that in this mansion was a miniature theatre complete with pit, boxes, stage and footlights.

[1] See *Kitton*, p. 240; Ley's *Forster*, p. 575.

Later in July Dickens was at Folkestone whence he wrote
on the 17th to Miss Emily Jolly—a contributor to *Household
Words*—from whom he had received the manuscript of *A
Wife's Story*. He told her how in his opinion a story ought
to end. He says of her work: "It displays so much power and
knowledge of the human heart that I feel a strong interest
in you as a writer." But he urges her to reconsider the
catastrophe. "You write to be read of course. The close
of the story is unnecessarily painful." He adds that it will
"throw off numbers of persons who would otherwise read it
and who will be deterred by hearsay from so doing." He
urges her "to spare the life of the husband and of one of the
children." [1]

§ 100. *He returns to Paris. "Little Dorrit," First monthly
part, December 1855. Reading at Peterborough,
22 December 1855. The Holly Tree Inn, Christmas 1855*

In October 1855 Dickens returned to Paris, settling at
49 Avenue des Champs Elysées, and while he was there
appeared the first number of his new story *Little Dorrit*.
About this time he was invited by the committee of the
Mechanics' Institute at Peterborough to give a Reading
in the Corn Exchange in that city. In order to fulfil his
engagement he came direct from Paris and gave his reading
on Tuesday evening, 18 December. He was glad to do
this as a tribute to the memory of his friend the late Member
of Parliament for the city, the Hon. Richard Watson of
Rockingham.[2] The hall was crowded to the doors and
most of the titled and leading people in the neighbourhood
were present, including the Dean and the Hon. Mrs
Watson.

A person who was present on the occasion thus describes
the scene:

At one end of the Corn Exchange Dickens had caused to be
erected a tall pulpit of red baize, as much like a Punch and Judy

---

[1] Maggs's *Catalogue*, No. 590.    [2] He was buried 5 August 1852.

show with the top taken off as anything. This was the reader's rostrum. But as the tall red pulpit looked lanky and very comical stuck there alone, two dummy pulpits of similar construction were placed one on each side to bear it company. When the reader mounted into the middle one nothing was visible of him but his head and shoulders. It was the *Christmas Carol* that Mr Dickens read. As the clock struck the appointed hour, a red jovial face, unrelieved by the heavy moustache which the novelist has since assumed, a broad high forehead and a perfectly Micawber-like expanse of shirt collar and front appeared above the red baize box, and a full sonorous voice rang out the works "Marley-was-dead-to-begin-with——" then paused, as if to take in the character of the audience. No need of further hesitation. The voice held all spell-bound.[1]

"Mr Dickens's reading of his *Christmas Carol*," said the *Peterborough Advertiser* of 22 December, o'ertopped the most lofty expectations. After referring to the "rich veins of beauty and of humour" which run through the *Christmas Carol* the report continued:

To those who heard Mr Dickens, Scrooge will be a life-long and cherished companion, while old Marley's ghost and the Spirits of the Christmas, Past, Present and Future, will most agreeably haunt their minds to their latest day. Nor will Tiny Tim, with his little crutch, ask in vain for a corner in their affections.

The references to Mr and Mrs Fezziwig and their Christmas Eve party were equally enthusiastic. The finish of the Reading "was the signal for the most pro-longed and hearty cheers." A vote of thanks to Dickens was proposed by the Hon. George W. FitzWilliam, M.P., and seconded by the Marquis of Huntly. Dickens after-wards "privately expressed himself as being never more pleased with any audience."

The Christmas Number of *Household Words* for 1855 was *The Holly Tree Inn*, to which Dickens contributed *Myself, The Boots and The Bill*[2] and Collins the rest. On 2 January 1856 Dickens wrote from Paris to Mrs Gaskell in reference to a story which she had been unable to finish for inclusion in the Christmas Number of *Household*

[1] See § 96, also *Speeches by Charles Dickens*, published by Hotten, p. 342.
[2] Cr. ed., vol. 15, p. 24.

234

*Words* . . . "When will it be forthcoming?" he asks. "You have not deserted it. You cannot be such an unnatural mother."[1] While at Paris he was joined by Collins, and they spent many enjoyable hours together.

## § 101. *Scheffer, Ward, Egg, Stanfield*

Before Dickens had been long in Paris he was found out by Ary Scheffer, the painter, "a frank and noble fellow," who had by sheer dint of hard work lifted himself to eminence. Scheffer's early productions were illustrative of the works of Dante and Goethe, and later he had painted religious subjects and portraits. Dickens admired his work, and confessed with reluctance its superiority to that of his friends Ward,[2] Egg[3] and Stanfield.[4] Says he pregnantly: "It is of no use disguising the fact that what we know to be wanting in the men is wanting in their works—character, force, purpose, and the power of using the vehicle and the model as mere means to an end." It was then decided that Scheffer should paint Dickens. The portrait of a man of genius by a man of genius should have turned out a masterpiece, but the fates were unkind, and with "The Nightmare Portrait," as it was called, neither artist nor subject was pleased.

At Paris, Dickens became acquainted with a number of persons of genius, and among them Georges Sand. In the meantime he was proceeding with *Little Dorrit*. Like *Bleak House*, *Little Dorrit* lacks the high spirits and gaiety of the earlier novels; but on the other hand, it possesses a duskiness—a chiaroscuro—that is wondrously seductive.

The most striking character is Mr Merdle, the bloated, speculative, and fraudulent banker. His original was John Sadleir, M.P. for Sligo,[5] who after (his own

[1] Maggs's *Catalogue*, No. 578.
[2] Ward, Edward Matthew, R.A., in 1855 painted "Dr Johnson in the ante-room of Lord Chesterfield," and "The Scene in Change Alley" (South Sea Bubble). See his life, by J. Dafforne, 1879. He committed suicide 15 January, 1879.
[3] Egg, Augustus. See XIV, § 95.
[4] Stanfield, Clarkson. See XIV, § 99.     [5] See XI, § 34.

expression) approaching infamy "step by step, heaping crime upon crime, and ruining tens of thousands," committed suicide in the descending ground just behind Dickens's favourite Jack Straw's Castle, Hampstead Heath. Dickens had his general idea of the society scenes in *Little Dorrit* before the solemn affair, but, says he, "I shaped Mr Merdle himself out of that precious rascality." "Mr Merdle was immensely rich, a man of prodigious enterprise, a Midas without ears, who turned all he touched into gold." He makes his hundred thousand at a stroke. Says Bar, alluding to one of these occasions:

"It was one of those happy strokes of calculation and combination, the result of which it was difficult to estimate. It was one of those instances of a comprehensive grasp, associated with habitual luck and characteristic boldness, of which an age presented us but few."

The very schoolboys had copies set them—"Merdle, Millions."

## § 102. *Flora and Mr F.'s Aunt*

Next to Mr Merdle we must rank that inseparable and entertaining pair, Flora and Mr F.'s Aunt. Some enthusiasts have even gone so far as to give Mr F.'s Aunt the premier place in the novel. Her description is perfection. Dickens never in so few words brought the portrait of any personage so vividly before us:

An amazing little old woman, with a face like a staring wooden doll, too cheap for expression, and a stiff yellow wig perched unevenly on the top of her head, as if the child who owned the doll had driven a tack through it anywhere, so that it only got fastened on. Another remarkable thing in this little old woman was that the same child seemed to have damaged her face in two or three places with some blunt instrument in the nature of a spoon.

Mr F.'s Aunt is indeed an awe-inspiring personage, but though she puts the reader himself out of countenance, he delights in her company, and treasures her table talk— indeed anything that emanates from that formidable oracle. Great too is Mr Pancks who "does, he really does, indeed!"

The original of *Little Dorrit* herself was Dickens's
Chatham playmate, Ann Mitton, who married a prosperous
strawberry grower named Cooper.   Later when she resided
at the Manor Farm, Sunbury, Dickens called on her.   In
1906 she was living at Southgate and had reached the
advanced age of 96.[1]   In respect to the other characters,
Henry Gowan is, one would think, Dickens's precise idea
of what a man ought *not* to be.   The public would not
admire his pictures.   "They had determined to believe
that in every service, except their own, a man must qualify
himself by striving, early and late, and by working heart
and soul, might and main."

Of apophthegms in *Little Dorrit* there are plenty.   To
take one: "We all know how we deceive ourselves—that is
to say how people in general deceive themselves—as to
motives of action" (Chapter 13).   Then in this book we
have Dickens's religion in a nutshell: "Be guided only by
the healer of the sick, the raiser of the dead, the friend of
all who are afflicted or forlorn, the patient Master who
shed tears of compassion for our infirmities. . . .   There
can be no confusion in following Him."

Of the scenes in its pages the one that seems to us
the most vivid is that in the prison, where Blandois (Thomas
Griffiths Wainewright)[2] eats and smokes and wipes his
fingers on the vine leaves—but Blandois with his moustache going up and his nose going down is a very picturesque character.   As in *Bleak House* the Court of
Chancery was assailed, so in *Little Dorrit* "the dilatory
system of conducting public business as adopted by
Government officials" is denounced.   By inventing the
name Circumlocution Office and writing this story, Dickens
gave red-tapeism some ugly knocks, but the reptile is a
hard one to kill.   The Marshalsea which, it will be remembered, was the prison in which Dickens's father was
incarcerated, was demolished in 1887, but its memory is
perpetuated by "Dorrit Street."

It is amusing to recall how frequently the sayings of

[1] *Daily News*, 30 November and 7 December 1906.
[2] See the *Dickensian*, November and December 1906.

Dickens's characters were quoted by his contemporaries. Mr W. R. Hughes, the Treasurer of the City of Birmingham, Swinburne and others were full of them. "The last recorded saying" of Mr F.'s Aunt "Bring him forard, and I'll chuck him out o' winder" was invariably on the lips of William Morris when the name of any person to whom he objected happened to be mentioned.

The humour of *Little Dorrit* circulates mostly round Mrs Plornish (honest soul!) and Cavalletto. Mrs Plornish's Italian, "Me ope you leg well soon," and her habit of translating Cavalletto's replies into the vernacular are delightful; and not less amusing is the little foreigner's habit of lengthening his adverbs, and enriching the language with such amazing words as consequentementally and secrettementally. Mr Sparkler's idea of Dante has always particularly tickled us: "An eccentric man in the nature of an Old File, who used to put leaves round his head and sit upon a stool for some unaccountable purpose, outside the cathedral at Florence." To say that Dickens himself regarded Dante and many another world-famous poet similarly, might be treason: but it would not be far from the truth. One is quite sure that he secretly sympathised with Mr Sparkler's attitude towards the classics. Then we have Mrs General with her "prunes and prisms," the Marshalsea doctor, who took a comb and stuck his hair upright—"which appeared to be his way of washing himself," and Tip, who, when the turnkey advised him to go and serve his country, said that "he didn't seem to care for his country." Tip, by the by, is a wonderfully well-drawn young gentleman. We know how he was got into a "warehouse, into a market garden, into the hop trade, into the law again, into an auctioneer's, into a brewery, into a stockbroker's, into the law again, into a coach office, into a distillery, into the law again"—and so on—the very picture of the useless ne'er-do-well. Dickens's brother Frederick as described in Dickens's letters is wonderfully like Tip. *Little Dorrit*, however, did not please everybody. Thackeray described it to Edmund Yates as "D—d stupid."

CHAPTER XV

# 14 March 1856 to end of year 1857

TAVISTOCK HOUSE, SECOND PERIOD, AND GAD'S HILL PLACE, FIRST PERIOD

§ 103. *Gad's Hill Place Secured*, 14 *March* 1856

FOR long Dickens had coveted Gad's Hill Place, the house that had pleased him in his boyhood. At this time it belonged to the Rev. James Lynn, and he and his daughter, afterwards known as Mrs Lynn Linton, the authoress, resided there. After the death of Mr Lynn in 1855 the property was in the market. Dickens, who was intimate with Miss Lynn, to whom as we have seen he had been introduced by her friend Walter Savage Landor, seized the opportunity and secured it for £1,750. When, however, she asked £40 more for the ornamental timber, Dickens objected, and had recourse to arbitration, as the result of which he had to pay £70. This, however, did not prevent him and Miss Lynn from continuing excellent friends and she contributed both to *Household Words* and *All the Year Round*.

Although Dickens secured the property on 14 March 1856 he did not occupy it for over twelve months, and even then he used it until June 1860 only as a summer residence. The house, a spacious building, with a porch, bow windows and a turret in which hung an alarm bell, was pleasantly situated on the historical spot where Sir John Falstaff committed his robbery; and the lines from Shakespeare, in which Sir John announces his predatory intentions, and bids his lads make suitable preparations,

239

were, by Dickens's direction, hung, illuminated, and framed, in a conspicuous place within:

"But, my lads, my lads, to-morrow morning, by four o'clock, early, at Gad's-hill: there are pilgrims going to Canterbury with rich offerings, and traders riding to London with fat purses; I have vizards for you all; you have horses for yourselves."

The alarm bell, says Mr Edmund Yates, was once, in the early days of Dickens's occupation, rung by way of a freak to see what effect it would have upon the neighbourhood, but not the slightest notice was taken of it.

The grounds were divided by the high road, but Dickens ran a tunnel under, just as Pope had done in similar circumstances at Twickenham, and connected the two portions. At the end of the further garden was subsequently erected a Swiss châlet, presented to Dickens by Charles Albert Fechter, in 1865. A few yards from the house, on the opposite side of the road, can be seen a small inn, the Sir John Falstaff, the surname of whose landlord, Mr William Stocker Trood, may have suggested that of Dickens's last hero, Edwin Drood.

To return to the house, the study—the room on the right side of the entrance—is made familiar by Mr Luke Fildes' picture of "The Empty Chair." Dickens hid the door with counterfeit book backs, lettered "Cats' Lives," 9 vols.; "History of a Short Chancery Suit," 21 vols.; "The Quarrelly Review," 4 vols., etc., etc. There was a similar door at Tavistock House.

In this room were written parts of *A Tale of Two Cities*, *Great Expectations*, *Our Mutual Friend*, and *Edwin Drood*; and as we gaze from its window, and our eyes alight upon the cedars, flower beds, with Dickens's favourite bloom, the scarlet geranium, the shrubbery and the Sir John Falstaff, in the distance—sights upon which Dickens himself so often gazed, we seem almost to be standing face to face with him.

The dining-room looks on to the lawn at the back. Here on Wednesday, 8 June 1870, occurred the sad scene of Dickens's death. Next to it is the conservatory—the

GAD'S HILL PLACE

*Photo by J. Graham, 17 Ordnance Terrace, Chatham*

See page 239

GAD'S HILL PLACE, FROM THE GARDEN AT THE REAR, WITH MEMBERS OF THE DICKENS FAMILY

*From a rare photograph in the possession of J. Graham, 17 Ordnance Terrace, Chatham*

See page 239

last of the many additions made to the house by Dickens. Adjoining the garden is the long-coveted meadow, which at last, in 1868, he, to his great joy, obtained from the governors of Sir Joseph Williamson's Free School; and in which was so frequently played by the guests at "Gads," his favourite game of cricket. Charles Dickens the younger used to say that though his father loved Gad's Hill, he would have loved it less had it been further from the streets of London and his comfortable quarters in the *All the Year Round* office. As always, streets and not lawns or garden-paths, were his passion.

## § 104. *Ellen Lawless Ternan*

For long, Dickens and his wife had, as we have seen, been seriously estranged. At last, a number of events occurred that made the breach between them final. In the first place, Forster was not without blame. He meddled far too much in Dickens's affairs. He had appropriated Dickens. Mrs Dickens naturally disliked him. He did harm with the best of intentions. A wife wants to be consulted whether her counsel is taken or not. Then, too, by this time Miss Georgina Hogarth, who had reached the age of 29, was almost unconsciously and, one must suppose unintentionally, taking the chief place in the home. So between Forster on the one side and Miss Hogarth on the other, Mrs Dickens was being reduced to the position of a nonentity.

At this time or earlier Dickens became acquainted with the Ternan family. The maiden name of Mrs Ternan was Frances Eleanor Jarman.[1] She first appeared as an actress in Edinburgh 3 November 1829, and played afterwards at Covent Garden whence she returned to Edinburgh. She took that city by storm. Christopher North was in raptures over her. In one of his dialogues the Shepherd asks, "Is it possible that Mr Murray is gaun to alloo

[1] She was the daughter of John Jarman. Her mother's maiden name was Maria Mothershed. Thomas Lawless Ternan died 17 October 1846, aged 47.

Miss Jarman to return to Covent Garden?" To which the reply is, "Impossible! a fixed star. The sweet creature must remain in our Scottish sky nor is there now on any stage a more delightful actress."

Then the Shepherd's friend Tickler butts in, describing her "as accomplished, simple and modest in mind and manners—yet lively—and awake to all harmless mirth and merriment. . . . We must love The Jarman." Further on, after praising the other two famous Fannys—Fanny Kelly and Fanny Kemble, Christopher North says:

"Equal to either of them in all things and in some superior to both is our Fanny Jarman. Equal to either in power and pathos and superior to both in grace, elegance and beauty. The three are all as much respected for their virtues in private life as they are admired for their genius on the stage." [1]

On 21 September 1834, Miss Jarman married Thomas Lawless Ternan, the actor-manager of the theatre at Newcastle. In 1843 they were in Dublin and on 1 September 1852 Mrs Ternan played at Sadler's Wells, London, in *All's Well that Ends Well*, taking the part of Countess of Rousillon, as in our illustration, in which appears also Mr Lewis Ball, who figured as the clown. In October 1855 she played, at the Princess's Theatre in Oxford Street, London, Paulina in Charles Kean's revival of Shakespeare's *Winter Tale*. Dickens, an ardent Shakespearian, was intimate with Kean and it may have been that he first saw Mrs Ternan at the Princess's Theatre; or, as already hinted, he may have become acquainted with her through their common friend Mrs Gaskell. Mrs Ternan had three charming daughters—Frances Eleanor, Ellen Lawless and Maria—who were quite as beautiful and almost as gifted as their mother. It was decided that all three,[2]

---

[1] *Noctes Ambrosianæ*, vol. 3, p. 361.

[2] The stage name of Frances Eleanor was "Fanny Ternan." She appeared on 11 June 1855 as Polly Hardup in *Garrick Fever* at the Olympic and on 26 January 1855 as Princess Babillada in *The Discreet Princess* at the same theatre.

Maria appeared as Little Pickle in *The Spoilt Child* at Drury Lane,

following the family tradition, should take to the boards.[1]

Dickens, in those days an habitual frequenter of the green rooms in the theatres, was fascinated by the little actresses or "periwinkles" as he called them. The periwinkle twines round plants just as the human sort takes captive the hearts of mankind. In the words of Culpeper (and he knew everything) "Venus owns this herb." The only comment possible to be made is, "This herb" can't help that. And so we get the word "periwinkling."

## § 105. *Dancing Feet*

In *Little Dorrit*, which appeared in December 1855 to June 1857, is a lively description of the scenes behind the theatre in which Fanny Dorrit acted. Amy Dorrit, her sister, after hearing through darkness the sound of music and dancing feet, found herself at last in a maze of dust where a number of persons moved in a mixture of gaslight and daylight, tumbling over one another amid a confusion of unaccountable shapes of beams, bulkheads, brick walls, ropes and rollers. Fanny Dorrit then conducted her sister to a more open part of the maze, where various golden chairs and tables were heaped together, and where a number of young ladies were sitting on anything they could find and chattering. At that moment a monotonous boy in a Scotch cap put his head through a beam and said, "Less noise there, ladies," and disappeared. Immediately after which, a sprightly gentleman with a quantity of long black hair looked round a beam on the right, and said, "Less noise there, darlings," and also disappeared.

The two sisters conversed and after a while the monotonous boy put his head round the beam on the left and

London, on 8 February 1850. "Her first appearance before a London public." On 28 April 1859 she appeared in Talbourd's classical extravaganza *Electra* at the Haymarket.

said, "Look out there, ladies!" and disappeared. The
sprightly gentleman with the black hair as suddenly put
his head round the beam on the right and said, "Look
out there, darlings!" and also disappeared. Thereupon
all the young ladies rose and began shaking their skirts
out behind.

"Now, ladies!" said the boy in the Scotch cap. "Now,
darlings!" said the gentleman with the black hair. They
were every one gone in a moment and the music and the
dancing feet were heard again. The performers were a
long time gone and during their absence a voice (it appeared to be that of the gentleman with the black hair)
was continually calling out through the music, "One, two,
three, four, five, six—go! One, two, three, four, five,
six—go! Steady, darlings! One, two, three, four, five,
six—go!" Ultimately the voice stopped, and they all
came back again, more or less out of breath, folding themselves in their shawls and making for the streets. The
boy looking round his old beam shouted "Everybody at
eleven to-morrow, ladies!" and the gentleman with the
black hair looking round his old beam delivered himself
of "Everybody at eleven to-morrow, darlings!" each in
his own accustomed manner.

It was in a scene of this kind that Dickens first saw Ellen
Lawless Ternan. She was behind one of the properties
weeping bitterly because she had to appear in very scanty
attire. It was the Victorian period and one can easily
understand the feelings of a young actress on having to
choose between losing her post and appearing in garments
that shocked her modesty. Dickens, whose attitude towards
the stage was more that of the twentieth century than of
the nineteenth, comforted her and overcame her doubts.
But while comforting her his senses took disordered flight.
At the present day when the possession of legs worries
nobody, it is to be presumed that she would not have
troubled. An intimate friendship between the famous
author and the young actress soon followed, a friendship
that daily threatened to become more than friendship.
She was often in his house and he liked to have her in his

MRS. TERNAN AND LEWIS BALL
In " All's Well that Ends Well," Sadler's Wells, 1st September, 1852
See page 242

SCENE FROM "THE FROZEN DEEP"

*Illustrated London News*

See page 248

study when he was writing. How perilous is the rock named Beauty! What havoc may result from a smile, a whiff of scent, a touch—even a tear! Especially when mingled with the sob of violins!

§ 106. *"The Frozen Deep" commenced, May* 1856. *The "Wreck of the Golden Mary," Christmas No. "H.W.,"* 1856

By this time Dickens and Wilkie Collins had become the thickest of friends. Dickens, indeed, preferred the company of the pleasure-loving Bohemian to any other. Writing to Collins a little later he says: "You know I am not in the habit of making professions, but I have so strong an interest in you and so true a regard for you that nothing can come amiss in the way of information as to your well doing."

In March 1856 Dickens was again at 49 Champs Elysées, and Collins, at this time a regular contributor to *Household Words*, dined with him every day. While there, they conceived the idea of a play, *The Frozen Deep*, to be acted at Tavistock House. Later, Macready and Townshend joined them, and the conversation ran chiefly on to the proposed play. Dickens, Mrs Dickens, Georgina, Mary and Katie, then went to the Français theatre to see *Comme il vous plaira*, a version of Shakespeare's *As you like it* by Georges Sand; but it was so absurdly presented that after Jacques had sat on 77 stones and 42 roots of trees they came away. In May, Dickens's thoughts continued to run on *The Frozen Deep*. Writing to Miss Hogarth on the 5th he says:

"I have done nothing yet, except for Richard Wardour (the part he was to play). The extent to which John (Thompson, his butler) and I wallowed in dust for 4 hours yesterday morning getting books and papers put away . . . you may faintly imagine."

It was settled that Stanfield should paint the scenery.

On 13 July Dickens was again at Boulogne, whence he wrote to Collins expressing his admiration of Collins's

*Household Words* story "The Diary of Anne Rodney," the second part of which he had read on the railway as he was returning to Boulogne. He says, "My behaviour before my fellow passengers was weak in the extreme, for I cried as much as you could possibly desire."

Townshend visited Dickens at Boulogne on 6 August and stayed a week. Collins was there on the 15th, and as the result of their conference *The Frozen Deep* made further progress.

On 26 October, Dickens, who had returned to London, took a twenty-mile walk and got up all the Richard Wardour part "to the great terror" of Finchley and the other suburbs through which he passed. On 30 October the manuscript of the play was in the hands of Forster, who made suggestions which did not entirely meet with Dickens's approval.

On Monday, 3 November, Collins dined with Dickens "before rehearsal" to talk over Forster's suggestions, and on the Wednesday following the two friends had a walk together over the fallen leaves in Cobham Park in which one of the scenes is laid. There were further discussions by Dickens, Mark Lemon and Collins "over steak and stout at the Cock in Fleet Street,"[1] and other alterations followed.

*The Frozen Deep* concerns itself with the hatred of a rejected lover (Richard Wardour), a young naval officer, for his successful rival (Frank Aldersley). Clara Burnham, the lady beloved by both, is a clairvoyant, and part of the conversation is between her and her friend Lucy Crayford. By the irony of fate, Wardour and Aldersley, who belong to rival exploring parties, are cast adrift near the North Pole, Wardour from the *Sea Mew*, Aldersley from the *Wanderer*; and Clara, thanks to her clairvoyancy, can see the two men at death grips. Wardour, however, who intended to slay Aldersley, protects and nurses him through storm and hardship, and brings him back alive to Clara and her friends who had conveniently arrived at Newfoundland by a relief ship. Wardour, after giving

---

[1] *Dickens to Collins,* 10 January 1857.

Aldersley and Clara his blessing, dies under the shadow of the Union Jack. Though the play was written in the first instance by Collins, Dickens during the rehearsals made so many changes in it that it may be regarded almost as his. Indeed he had the ruling of everything. Among the interpolations made by him was the part of a ship's cook, John Want—a second Mark Tapley—who provided the comic element.

Most amusing are Dickens's letters describing (while he was in the midst of *Little Dorrit*) the preparations for acting the play. The sounds in the house reminded him of the building of Noah's Ark, from which we may conclude that Dickens was on the spot when that ancient vessel was being constructed. Joiners are never out of the house. All day long a labourer heats size over the fire in a great crucible. "We eat it, drink it, breathe it, smell it. Seventy paint pots (which came in a van) adorn the stage." When not watching Stanfield who was on a plank, splashing himself from head to foot with paint, Dickens tucked himself in any place that would receive him and slaved away, with the smell of size still in his nostrils, in the company of Mr F.'s Aunt and in the hearing of Mrs General's polite references to "Papa, Potatoes, Prunes and Prisms."

The Arctic regions had occupied the public mind a good deal since Dickens's kinsman, Sir John Barrow, had published his book *Voyages of Arctic Discovery* 1846.[1] There are allusions to the Arctic expeditions in several of Dickens's books. For example, Pip says in *Great Expectations* he believes even if he had gone to the North Pole he would have heard from somebody that Pumblechook was the founder of his fortunes.[2]

It is also extremely probable that the clairvoyant idea was supplied by Dickens and that he had it from Miss Ellen L. Ternan. There was clairvoyancy in the Ternan family in whom a particular instance had been handed down. An uncle of Ellen's used to relate:

[1] Sir John Barrow died 23 November 1848.
[2] Cr. ed., vol. 15: p. 175.

One day when I was a child of eight living with my parents in Dublin and my grandmother Mrs Lawless was living in her own house a few miles from Dublin, I saw her or supposed that I saw her. We heard afterwards that she died at the very moment I saw her or supposed that I saw her.

Dickens, as we said, chose for himself the part of Wardour. He allocated that of Aldersley to Collins. His realism at the rehearsals, says his son Charles was "positively alarming—not to say painful. In his demented condition in the last act when he had to rush off the stage he went at it with such a will that the others had to attack him like prize-fighters." Charles, who bore the first brunt, "was tossed in all directions" and was "black and blue two or three times before the first night of the performance." The Christmas Number of *Household Words* for 1856 was *The Wreck of the Golden Mary*.

§ 107. *"The Frozen Deep" first acted at Tavistock House, 6 January 1857. Death of Douglas Jerrold, 8 June 1857*

*The Frozen Deep* was acted at Tavistock House on 6 January 1857, the birthday of Dickens's son Charles, who was 20, and the cast included:

| | | |
|---|---|---|
| Mrs Stevenson | . . | *Miss Helen Hogarth* |
| Clara Burnham | . . | *Miss Mary Dickens* |
| Rose Ebbsworth | . . | *Miss Kate Dickens* |

Writing on 17 January Dickens said, "It has been the talk of all London for these three weeks." [1] The incidental music which accompanied the play was composed by Francesco Berger who saw a good deal of Dickens for many years.

In June 1857 Hans Christian Andersen visited Gad's Hill. With Dickens he was greatly impressed, and with

[1] A printed copy of the play containing stage directions written on the margins was in the possession of the late Mr W. R. Hughes. The narrative was printed in *Temple Bar* in 1874.

PLAYBILL OF THEATRE ROYAL, HAYMARKET, MONDAY, 13TH APRIL, 1857

See page 249

"THE TEMPLE OF HYMEN," FROM THE NEW CLASSIC STORY OF "ATALANTA," OR, THE THREE GOLDEN APPLES," AT THE HAYMARKET THEATRE.—(SEE NEXT PAGE.)

Scene in "Atalanta," 13th April, 1857

In which Ellen Lawless Ternan appeared as Hippomenes

See page 249

Mrs Dickens he was charmed.   He described her as "so gentle, so motherly," adding, "Mrs Dickens I find pretty and her eldest daughter Mary is like her."[1]   In another letter he says:

Mrs Dickens has a certain soft, womanly repose about her; but whenever she spoke there came such a light into her large eyes, and such a smile upon her lips, and there was such a charm in the tones of her voice, that henceforth I shall always connect her and Agnes (in *David Copperfield*) together.

Andersen, says Yates, "was a never-failing source of amusement to all who met him in England, with his old-world gallantry, his pretty speeches, and presentation of little bouquets which he plucked and made up himself, and his extraordinary and childish ignorance of everything that went on around him."   He had not, indeed, the least suspicion of the trouble in Dickens's home.

On 13 April 1857 Ellen Lawless Ternan appeared in the production of Talfourd's play *Atalanta* as Hippomenes at the Haymarket, London.   A notice of the play in the *Era*, 19 April, refers to Miss Ternan as "a debutante with a pretty face and well-developed figure, who when she had gained more confidence would become an acquisition."   A scene in *Atalanta* forms one of our illustrations.

On 8 June 1857 died suddenly Dickens's friend, Douglas Jerrold, who was buried at Norwood Cemetery, Dickens, Thackeray and other prominent men being the pall-bearers. It then transpired that though Jerrold had been a contributor to *Punch* and had, besides, received a large salary as editor of *Lloyd's Weekly Newspaper*, the widow had been left poorly off, so Dickens arranged a series of entertainments on her behalf, including three of his readings of the *Christmas Carol* at St Martin's Hall.   In reference to one of them he said in a letter to Macready, 13 July 1857, "The two thousand and odd people were like one and their enthusiasm was something awful."   He further decided that *The Frozen Deep* should be acted in behalf of the fund, and it gave him great pleasure to learn that the Queen intended to be present at

[1] The *Dickensian*, December 1933.

one of the performances to be given at The Gallery of Illustration. At this time his family first used Gad's Hill Place as a summer residence.

A number of other rehearsals became necessary, for Dickens was very anxious that the company when acting before the Queen should be at its best. "There is a good deal at stake," he said on 26 June, "and it must be done well."

In the Widener Library, Harvard College, is a copy of Dickens's notice respecting these rehearsals.[1] It runs:

## IN REMEMBRANCE OF THE LATE MR DOUGLAS JERROLD

COMMITTEE OFFICE OF THE GALLERY OF ILLUSTRATION
REGENT STREET

*Friday Nineteenth June* 1857

*The Frozen Deep* by WILKIE COLLINS

On the stage here

Friday 26 June at 3 in the afternoon
Monday 29 June at 3 in the afternoon
Thursday 2 July at ¼ past 10 at night
Friday 3 July at ¼ past 10 at night.

On Saturday July 4 the piece will be privately acted here to the Queen. And on Saturday July 11 it will be acted here agreeably to the accompanying programme.

Then followed the names of the players.

§ 108. *"The Frozen Deep" at the Gallery of Illustration before the Queen, 4 July* 1857

The great day for the performance of *The Frozen Deep* at the Gallery of Illustration, 4 July 1857, at last arrived, and the Queen, the Prince Consort and other members of the Royal Family were present, as promised.

[1] See *Mr Dickens goes to the Play*, by Alexander Woollcott. Putnam Sons, 1922.

The Cast was as follows:

| | | |
|---|---|---|
| WARDOUR . . . . | . | *Dickens* |
| ALDERSLEY . . | . | *Wilkie Collins* |
| MRS STEVENSON . | . | *Miss Helen Hogarth* |
| ROSE EBBSWORTH | . | *Miss Kate Dickens* |
| LUCY CRAYFORD | . | *Miss Hogarth* |
| CLARA BURNHAM | . | *Miss Mary Dickens* |
| NURSE ESTHER . | . | *Mrs Francis* |
| MAID . . . | . | *Miss Marley* |

A photograph of the players in *The Frozen Deep* taken in Albert Smith's garden at Walham Green in 1857 was reproduced in the supplement to the *Windsor Magazine*, Christmas 1934. This play was followed by J. B. Buckstone's farce, *Uncle John*, in which Miss Hogarth, Miss Mary Dickens and Miss Kate Dickens took parts. As Miss Hogarth informed Mrs Winter, "The Queen and her party made a most excellent audience." The second performance of *The Frozen Deep* at the Gallery of Illustration took place on Saturday, 11 July, and there was a full report of it in *The Times* for Monday, 13 July. The cast was the same as that on 4 July.

"It was," says Dickens in the Preface to the *Tale of Two Cities*, "when I was acting with my children and friends in *The Frozen Deep* I first conceived the main idea of this story. A strong desire was upon me then to embody it in my own person. . . . Throughout its execution, it has had complete possession of me; I have so far verified what is done and suffered in these pages, as that I have certainly done and suffered it all myself."

—a reference, of course, to the home trouble.

### § 109. *The Gathering at Mr Ouvry's, 12 July 1857*

On Sunday, 12 July, the members of the cast—the "Snow Boys" as Dickens called them—were invited to North End Lodge, Mr F. Ouvry's,[1] and by the kindness

---

[1] Frederic Ouvry was Dickens's friend and solicitor. Besides being a lawyer, he was a gifted antiquary and President of the Society of Antiquaries. Dickens depicted him in *Household Words* as Mr Undery.

of Mr Charles J. Spencer we are able to reproduce the card received by one of them, Mr Marcus Stone. At the back were "Directions for Travellers."

About a quarter of a mile—hardly so much beyond the turn-pike in the Fulham Road, you arrive at the Swan Brewery on your left. Nearly opposite a small road runs to the right, behind the infant Schools to Walham Green Church, the tower of which is before you. Keep straight on passing the church, you will see the chestnut trees over the wall of North End Lodge on the left of the road leading to Kensington.

That same month Dickens's son Walter, then 16, obtained through the kindness of Miss Coutts, a military cadetship which necessitated his proceeding to India; and Mrs Winter, informed of the fact, made on 31 July some valuable suggestions relative to the lad's requirements.

On 29 July the Jerrold Fund was further assisted by the performance at the Adelphi Theatre of Jerrold's play *Black-Eyed Susan*. The character of William was taken by Mr R. P. Cooke; and Dickens, who was present on the occasion, congratulated him on his admirable performance. "It was so fresh and vigorous, so manly and gallant." Dickens's next idea was to have *The Frozen Deep* performed in the Free Trade Hall at Manchester. William Telbin and Clarkson Stanfield were to be responsible for the scenery.

§ 110. *Preparations for acting "The Frozen Deep" at Manchester. The Rehearsals with the Professionals, 2 August 1857*

Writing on 2 August to Wilkie Collins, he said, "It is an immense place and we shall be obliged to have actresses. I am trying to get the best who *have been* on the stage." These "best" were Ellen Lawless Ternan, Maria Ternan and their mother. In a letter of 17 August 1857 from Gad's Hill, Dickens says he is about to proceed to London in order to give "three days' drill" to "the professional ladies who are to succeed the Tavistock girls." [1] These rehearsals

---

[1] *Letters of Charles Dickens*, Macmillan's ed., p. 435.

# IN REMEMBRANCE OF THE LATE MR. DOUGLAS JERROLD.

## GALLERY OF ILLUSTRATION,
### REGENT STREET.

### UNDER THE MANAGEMENT OF MR. CHARLES DICKENS.

On Saturday evening, July 18th, and on Saturday evening, July 25th, 1857, at 8 o'clock exactly, will be presented

**AN ENTIRELY NEW**

ROMANTIC DRAMA, IN THREE ACTS, BY MR. WILKIE COLLINS,

CALLED

# THE FROZEN DEEP.

PERFORMED BY THE AMATEUR COMPANY OF LADIES AND GENTLEMEN WHO ORIGINALLY REPRESENTED IT, IN PRIVATE.

THE OVERTURE COMPOSED EXPRESSLY FOR THIS PIECE BY MR. FRANCESCO BERGER.

*The Dresses by Messrs. Nathan, of Titchborne Street, Haymarket, and Miss Wilson, of Carburton Street, Fitzroy Square. Perruquier, Mr. Wilson, of the Strand.*

| | |
|---|---|
| CAPTAIN EBSWORTH, *of The Sea Mew* | Mr. Edward Pigott. |
| CAPTAIN HELDING, *of The Wanderer* | Mr. Alfred Dickens. |
| LIEUTENANT CRAYFORD | Mr. Mark Lemon. |
| FRANK ALDERSLEY | Mr. Wilkie Collins. |
| RICHARD WARDOUR | Mr. Charles Dickens. |
| LIEUTENANT STEVENTON | Mr. Young Charles. |
| JOHN WANT, *Ship's Cook* | Mr. Augustus Egg. |
| BATESON } *Two of The Sea Mew's People* | Mr. Shirley Brooks. |
| DARKER | Mr. Frederick Evans. |

(OFFICERS AND CREWS OF THE SEA MEW AND WANDERER.)

| | |
|---|---|
| MRS. STEVENTON | Miss Helen. |
| ROSE EBSWORTH | Miss Kate. |
| LUCY CRAYFORD | Miss Hogarth. |
| CLARA BURNHAM | Miss Mary. |
| NURSE ESTHER | Mrs. Francis. |
| MAID | Miss Marlex. |

THE SCENERY AND SCENIC EFFECTS OF THE FIRST ACT, BY MR. TELBIN.
THE SCENERY AND SCENIC EFFECTS OF THE SECOND AND THIRD ACTS, BY **Mr. STANFIELD, R.A.**
ASSISTED BY MR. DANSON.
THE ACT-DROP, ALSO BY **Mr. STANFIELD, R.A.**

To Conclude with the Farce, in Two Acts,

# UNCLE JOHN.

| | |
|---|---|
| NEPHEW HAWK | Mr. Wilkie Collins. |
| HOWARD EASEL | Mr. Frederick Evans. |
| UNCLE JOHN | Mr. Charles Dickens. |
| FRIEND THOMAS | Mr. Mark Lemon. |
| ANDREW | Mr. Young Charles. |
| NIECE HAWK | Miss Hogarth. |
| ELIZA | Miss Kate. |
| MRS. COMFORT | Miss Mary. |

TERMINATING WITH A DANCE BY THE CHARACTERS.

Musical Composer and Conductor of the Orchestra, Mr. **FRANCESCO BERGER**,
WHO WILL PRESIDE AT THE PIANO.

The Audience are respectfully desired to be in their places by Ten minutes to 8 o'clock.

STALLS, ONE GUINEA. AREA, TEN SHILLINGS AND SIXPENCE. AMPHITHEATRE, FIVE SHILLINGS.

Tickets for Stalls, Area, and Amphitheatre, to be had at the Committee's Office, Gallery of Illustration, Regent Street, every day from 12 to 4

**REFRESHMENTS.**—The Audience are respectfully informed that the Committee have made arrangements with Mr. RICHARD GUNTER to supply, during the evening, Tea, Coffee, Creams and Water Ices, Lemonade, Soda Water, &c., &c., at the same Prices as those charged at his Establishment, in Berkeley Square.
The Overture to the FROZEN DEEP, composed by Mr. Francesco Berger, is published by Messrs. Ewer & Co., and can be had in the room.

PLAYBILL, SATURDAY, 18TH JULY, AND SATURDAY, 25TH JULY, 1857
*Photo by T. W. Tyrrell*

See page 251

INVITATION CARD. GATHERING AT MR. OUVRY'S, 12TH JULY, 1857

*Lent by Charles J. Spencer*

See page 251

resulted in serious trouble, for Dickens's infatuation for Ellen Lawless Ternan every time increased.  The cast of *The Frozen Deep* as reorganised for the rehearsals was as follows:

| | |
|---|---|
| CAPTAIN HELDING of the Ship *Wanderer* . . . . | *Alfred Dickens* |
| LIEUTENANT CRAYFORD (who started from England on the *Wanderer* and was only transferred to the *Sea Mew* after they had been locked up in the ice). . . . . | *Mark Lemon* |
| RICHARD WARDOUR on the *Wanderer* | *Charles Dickens* |
| FRANK ALDERSLEY on the *Sea Mew* | *Wilkie Collins* |
| LIEUTENANT STEVENTON . . | *Charles Dickens the Younger* |
| JOHN WANT, Ship's Cook . . | *Egg* |
| BATESON, one of the *Sea Mew's* people . . . . . | *Shirley Brooks* |
| DARKER, one of the *Sea Mew's* people . . . . . | *Charles Collins* |
| LUCY CRAYFORD . . . . | *Ellen Lawless Ternan* |
| CLARA BURNHAM . . . . | *Maria Ternan* |
| NURSE ESTHER . . . . | *Mrs Ternan* |

Marcus Stone also took part in the performance, but he had only one word to say: "Stay!"

It was followed by Buckstone's farce *Uncle John*, the cast for which was:

| | |
|---|---|
| UNCLE JOHN . . . | *Dickens* |
| NEPHEW HAWK . . | *Wilkie Collins* |
| ELIZA . . . . | *Miss E. L. Ternan* |
| MRS COMFORT . . | *Mrs Ternan* |
| DRAWING MASTER . . | *Mr Luard* |
| FRIEND THOMAS . . | *Mark Lemon* |

To Mrs Dickens, however, convinced that her husband was too intimate with Miss E. L. Ternan, the connection of the Ternan family with *The Frozen Deep* was gall and bitterness, and she expressed herself openly, with the result that the trouble in the house rose once more to a height.  It was not that Miss Ternan had very much to say in *The Frozen Deep*.  Indeed she had little beyond the following (though even that little displeased Mrs Dickens):

R

Lucy (*addressing Clara*): Perhaps my own experience might one day help me in guiding you. You have once or twice wondered why I was still a single woman. My dear, I shall always remain what I am now, because the man I loved with all my heart is . . .

Clara: Dead?

Lucy: Dead to me. Married. . . . I don't think he ever suspected how dearly I loved him.

Dickens's feelings at the moment as the result of the family trouble are expressed in Wardour's words: "Hard work, Crayford, that's the true elixir of life! Hard work that stretches the muscles and sets the blood a glowing, that tires the body and rests the mind."

Far more disturbing to Mrs Dickens was the part that Dickens and Miss Ternan took in the farce *Uncle John*. Uncle John an old gentleman having educated a girl of 18, Eliza (Miss E. L. Ternan) the daughter of Mrs Comfort (Mrs Ternan) an elderly widow, is about to marry the girl, and the piece opens with the arrival on the wedding morning of Uncle John's niece, Mrs Hawk (Miss Maria Ternan) and her husband (Wilkie Collins). These two dexterously contrive to make the bride and her drawing-master (Mr Luard) each believe that the other is a prey to the despair of unrequited love. Surprised together as they are separating to meet no more, the young pair are believed to be guilty, and this leads to various exceedingly amusing situations.

## § 111. *The Bracelet*

One day, and apparently while these rehearsals were proceeding, Dickens sent Miss E. L. Ternan a bracelet as a present, but by mistake it fell into the hands of Mrs Dickens, who naturally asked for explanations. Had Dickens and his wife been on good terms, and had he been a wise man, he would have given the explanations required, for there is no proof that he had at the time anything to hide. In a little while the story became public property; and it could not have escaped Mrs Dickens's notice that Uncle John (Dickens) in the farce gives Eliza (Miss E. L. Ternan) "wonderful presents—a pearl necklace, diamond ear-rings."

Miss Ternan accepted the bracelet and other gifts. Yet she was uncomfortable; and Dickens knew it. In Chapter 10 of *Edwin Drood* he writes, "It has been often enough remarked that women have a curious power of divining the characters of men, which would seem to be innate and instinctive." [1] In short he was fully aware of how she regarded him.

There are strong resemblances between the attachment of Dickens to Miss Ternan and that of Victor Hugo to Juliette Drouet, which during Dickens's most recent visit to France was the talk of Paris. Hugo was the most distinguished novelist of France, just as Dickens was the most distinguished novelist of England. Hugo gave an inferior part to Mlle Drouet in *Lucrezia Borgia*,[2] Dickens an inferior part to Miss Ternan in *The Frozen Deep*. It was the acting at the respective rehearsals that gave Hugo and Dickens their respective infatuations. Hugo praised Mlle Drouet in passionate love poems, Dickens eulogised extravagantly Miss Ternan's gifts as an actress. In each case death alone severed the connection. It will be noticed too that there is no real heat in the love scenes in Dickens's stories until we get to those in which Miss Ternan covertly figures. Then too the earlier and tepid and colourless lovers did not quarrel.

§ 112. *"The Frozen Deep" at Manchester,*
*21 and 22 August* 1857

The dates chosen for the performances at Manchester were Friday, 21 August, and Saturday, 22 August. Dickens took every possible precaution to make them a success. For instance, he wrote to his butler John Thompson, telling him to take to Manchester among the properties

---

[1] Cr. ed., vol. 17, p. 70.

[2] Dickens greatly admired this play and knew all about its history. Writing on 24 January 1847 to Lady Blessington, he says, "They are playing *Lucretia Borgia* again at the Porte St Martin . . . a very remarkable and striking play." Writing on 22 July 1854 to Miss G. Hogarth he says, "I saw Grisi the night before last in 'Lucrezia Borgia'—finer than ever."

"the Bell that is struck in *The Frozen Deep*." He adds amusingly, "see that the snow you take is better made than the last. It was very badly cut, and much too large."

The plays at Manchester were a great success. The Press said that the perfection of the acting of *Uncle John* could be conveyed by no verbal description. The humour was chiefly manifested by Dickens and his friend Thomas (Mark Lemon) an old fat and lymphatic fellow. Wilkie Collins's nephew, Hawk, was another bit of exquisite fooling, and the farce was received, we are told, "with that best sort of applause for such pieces—roars and shrieks of laughter." The play as printed evokes little mirth but the antics of Dickens, the would-be bridegroom of 70, and fat Mark Lemon made every scene a success.

On the next day, Saturday, 22 August, the performances were repeated with the same casts. In reference to the latter event, Wilkie Collins says: "This was, I think, the finest of all the representations of *The Frozen Deep*. The extraordinary intelligence and enthusiasm of the great audience stimulated us all to do our best. Dickens surpassed himself. He literally electrified the audience."

The scenery was greatly praised. "William Telbin's interior and landscape with effects of sunset and moonlight was," we are told, "a capital scene." "So was the New-foundland beach and offing," by Stanfield; "but the best scene was the same artist's 'drop' representing Eddystone lighthouse in a storm. It was as fine a piece of seascape as ever adorned a scenic performance." "The applause as the last scene closed was long and loud, and the amateur actors and their professional friends the actresses, in full group, bowed their acknowledgments." Mark Lemon then stepped forward and announced that the performance would be repeated on the following Monday (24 August). The acting of *The Frozen Deep* and other entertainments produced a handsome sum for the Jerrold Fund.

It was while reading the *Christmas Carol* at St Martin's Hall that Dickens made up his mind, we are told, to give a series of public readings for his own benefit.

Mr Walter Wellsman of the well-known Newspaper

Press Directory had, however, in a letter to the author of this book, something to say on this matter.

"My stepfather, Mr C. Mitchell," wrote Mr Wellsman, "was the publisher of Mr Westland Marston's plays and poems. Mr Marston, who had got it into his mind that he was an orator, conceived the idea of reading one of his plays, *Strathmore*, in public, and Mr Mitchell advised him to have a rehearsal before a party of friends. This event took place somewhere about the early fifties, and the reading was given in what, I think, were then called the Grosvenor Rooms. I was quite young at the time, and Mr Mitchell took me with him. Amongst the audience were Charles Dickens and John Forster. The reading was of the most melancholy description. At the end of the first act, Forster, using stronger language than I care to repeat, told Marston it would not do at all; and that he was like a confounded parrot! 'Do,' said he, 'let us know what characters you are personating'; and poor Marston tried again, but it was no good, all he did was to turn his head one way and then another and go on in the old monotone. However, somehow or other, we got to the end, and the company which numbered, probably, from one hundred to one hundred and fifty, departed, leaving only Charles Dickens, Forster, Marston, Mr Mitchell and myself present. I was introduced to Dickens, and presently he said to Marston: 'Give me the book; I will show you how you ought to do it,' and he read a scene, indeed, I think he read an entire act; the characters then all came on the stage and lived, and I shall never forget the impression that reading made upon me. Poor Marston never renewed the attempt.

"Now, as far as I recollect, up to that time Charles Dickens had never read in public, and I always trace to that night the idea that he took from that occasion that he would be able to make a public reader."

Whatever the origin of the idea, this is certain—no madder ever entered the mind of a great writer. Who, however, in life does not make mistakes! All men and some women are liable to err.

## § 113. *The Lazy Tour, September* 1857

On 29 August 1857 Dickens wrote to Collins from Gad's Hill,

Partly in the grim despair and restlessness of this subsidence from excitement, and partly for the sake of *Household Words* I want to cast about whether you and I can go anywhere—take any tour—see anything—whereon we could write something together . . . We want something for *Household Words* and I want to escape from myself . . . my misery is amazing.

The outcome of this letter was that in September Dickens and Collins made a tour together in the north of England, and an account of it appeared in the October number of *Household Words* with the title, "The Lazy Tour of Two Idle Apprentices."

Thomas Idle was Collins, Francis Goodchild, Dickens. Before starting they conversed on the subject of love, brought about by Thomas's singing "Annie Laurie."

"It's no trouble to fall in love," said Goodchild.

"It's trouble enough to fall out of it, once you're in it. So I keep out of it altogether. It would be better for you, if you did the same," [1] retorted Thomas Idle, who was aware of Dickens's infatuation for Miss E. L. Ternan, nor was anyone more competent to give advice than the pleasure-loving and susceptible Collins. Indeed, though his own morals were loose, he was fuller of excellent maxims than the most irreproachable copybook.

Their first stop was Carlisle, whence on 9 September they made their way to Carrock Fell near Hesket Newmarket. This eminence they must needs climb, though it rained continually; and at the top they had, owing to the mist, "a magnificent view of—nothing." On the way down, Collins sprained his ankle, but, dripping wet, they at last regained their inn. Thence in a little covered carriage they proceeded to Wigton, and Dickens carried Collins "melo-dramatically" (Wardour in *The Frozen Deep* to the life) upstairs and to bed. Indeed it was Richard Wardour and Frank Aldersley over again. Collins was kept in bed for some days "enjoying himself by looking at the flies on the ceiling." Thence they proceeded to Allonby, a watering-place which consisted of "five gentlemen in straw hats," four ladies, "three geese in a dirty little brook," "a boy's legs hanging over a bridge," a donkey, "and some fishermen

[1] Cr. ed., vol. 20, p. 5.

who got their living by looking at the ocean"; but "the place was full of children who were always upside down on the public buildings (two small bridges over the brook) and always hurting themselves or one another, so that their wailings made continual noise." "When the donkey got into the brook he was pelted out with stones, which never hit him and which always hit some of the children who were upside down on the public buildings, and made their lamentations louder." On their way back to London the friends were curious enough, as it was race-week, to spend a day at Doncaster, where they found themselves amid all the riff-raff of the country, every other face looking like that of Palmer the murderer.

The Christmas story of 1857 was *The Perils of Certain English Prisoners*,[1] one of the best of Dickens's shorter flights. It is exciting, the reader loses himself—which he rarely does in the other storyettes—and feels genuinely anxious for the safety of the travellers. Dickens's favourite expedient of inordinate reiteration is much resorted to. Mr Commissioner Pordage (a Rochester name, by the way) is always demanding stationery, Mrs Pordage is inseparable from her nightcap, and Charker, one of the most agreeable of the characters, is always bringing "a thing round to what it was not." If Stevenson had not read *The Perils of Certain English Prisoners* previous to writing *Treasure Island*, the coincidence is singular. The pirate captain, Pedro Mendez, with his amiable ways, his guitar, and his influence over his company, is own brother to Long John Silver. Pordage's sitting on the raft and roaring for stationery takes us back twenty years to Mr Tupman's screaming "Fire" when Mr Pickwick went under the ice. It was about as likely to happen. The story, however, contains plenty of capital touches, as, for example, when one of Gill's fellow prisoners recommended him "to take it easy; and if you can't do that, take it as easy as you can."

[1] Cr. ed., vol. 15, p. 74.

## CHAPTER XVI

# January 1858 to June 1860

§ 114. *Speech at the Dinner in behalf of The Hospital for
Sick Children, 9 February* 1858

WHILE Dickens was pondering whether or not to carry out the idea of Readings from his Books, for his own profit, for he still had his doubts, an "occurrence of the time hastened the decision." Want of funds was threatening to arrest the merciful work that was being done in the hospital in Great Ormond Street for sick children. It was decided to try a public dinner by way of charitable appeal, and Dickens, whose philanthropy was well known, was asked to preside. He threw himself into the service heart and soul.

The dinner took place at Freemasons' Hall, Great Queen Street, and his speech was among the best he ever made. He began by saying, "It is one of my rules in life not to believe a man who may happen to tell you that he feels no interest in children." After remarking that adults are themselves "in a child-like state" he went on:

"It is likely that even we are not without our experience now and then of spoilt children. I do not mean of our own spoilt children, because nobody's own children ever were spoilt, but I mean the disagreeable children of our particular friends. We know what it is when those children won't go to bed: we know how they prop their eyelids open with their forefingers when they *will* sit up; how when they become fractious, they say aloud that they don't like us. . . .

And we are perfectly acquainted with those kicking bundles which are carried off at last protesting. . . .

"But, ladies and gentlemen, the spoilt children whom I have to present to you after this dinner are not of this class. The spoilt children whom I must show you are the spoilt children of the poor in this great city—the children who are, every year, for ever and ever irrevocably spoilt out of this breathing life of ours by tens of thousands, but who may, in vast numbers be preserved, if you, assisting and not contravening the ways of Providence, will help to save them."

He then told of some pitiful scenes he himself had witnessed, mentioning particularly a poor little wasted child whom he had seen lying in an egg-box.

"Now, ladies and gentlemen," he continued, "such things need not be, and will not be, if this company, which is a drop of the life-blood of the great compassionate public heart, will only accept the means of rescue and prevention which it is mine to offer."

He then referred to the "courtly old house" that had become a hospital for sick children in Great Ormond Street, which he had himself visited—the old house which had formerly been a gentleman's abode in which happy children pattered up the old oak staircase "and wondered at the old oak carvings on the chimney pieces." He referred to the attentive nurses and the kind medical practitioner, to the trays of toys in front of the little sufferers.

"You may see," he continued, "how the little, tired, flushed cheek has toppled over half the brute creation on its way into the ark; or how one little dimpled arm has mowed down (as I saw myself) the whole tin soldiery of Europe. On the walls of these rooms are graceful, pleasant, bright, childish pictures. At the beds' heads, are pictures of the Figure which is the universal embodiment of all mercy and compassion—the Figure of Him who was once a Child Himself, and a poor one."

He then referred to the large number of out-patients that were brought to that house for relief, and to Charles Lamb's charming essay on Dream Children.

"The dream-children whom I would now raise, if I could, before every one of you, according to your various circumstances, should

261

be the dear child you love, the dearer child you have lost, the child you might have had, the child you certainly have been. . . . Each of these dream children should say to you, 'Oh, help this little suppliant in my name; oh, help it for my sake!' "

There was a simple pathos in his address quite startling in its effect at such a meeting; and he probably never moved any audience so much as by the strong personal feeling with which he referred to the sacrifices made for the hospital by the very poor themselves. That night alone added over £3,000 to the funds of the hospital, and Dickens further helped by reading in its behalf on 15 April his *Christmas Carol*.

And yet, such is the irony of Fate, and so easy is it for a man to deceive himself, at the very time Dickens was moving an audience to tears when pleading, and very rightly, for the sick children, Mrs Dickens was weeping her eyes out because of his insistence on the necessity of a separation from her. That all the blame was on his side, it would not be fair to say, but she certainly did not want a separation. It hurt her terribly and brought about illness after illness. Indeed, while he was softening the hearts of others in behalf of a most worthy cause, he was hardening his own heart against his wife. He brought tears to the eyes of the audience at Freemasons' Hall and they said, "How tender-hearted he is!" but she, for the life of her, could not see that he *was* so tender-hearted. What a higgledy-piggledy world we live in! What a muddle of contradictions is man!

## § 115. *Three in Error*

We are at this point faced with a situation which would be puzzling to persons imperfectly familiar with the weaknesses of human nature. Here are three kindly, well-intentioned persons all convincing themselves that they are doing the right thing, yet all the while doing the wrong.

First, there is Dickens, to the fore in everything for the good of humanity, helping in all sorts of charitable undertakings, yet breaking the heart of a woman who is good, kind and gentle, who is also innocent except of such moods that any other woman might have; who loved her children; who, notwithstanding her husband's attitude to her, still loved him; and who naturally, after twice seeing another preferred to her, felt keenly the preference given to a third person.

Secondly, there is Miss Hogarth, perfectly correct as to her moral conduct, who, while doing her level best in the household and in the interests of Dickens, shuts her eyes to the mistake she is making in permitting herself to take the place in the home which was rightly Mrs Dickens's, and which Mrs Dickens most certainly desired to retain—that is to say the *first* place.[1]

Thirdly, there is Miss Ternan, a girl with puritanical leanings, who allows herself to be dazzled by Dickens's fame and wealth. How easy is self-deception!

Miss Ternan, however, differed in one respect from the other two. Dickens and Miss Hogarth persevered in this course of self-deception. He to the end satisfied himself that no other course could have been taken. She also to the end satisfied herself that no other course could have been taken. Miss Ternan broke entirely from herself and admitted error. She, indeed, is the only one of the three who comes with any sort of credit out of the tangle. Dickens certainly, as his will shows, never repented. He could never see that he had erred. One day someone said to him, "How wicked the world is!" "True," replied Dickens, "and what a satisfaction it is that neither you nor I belong to it."

It has been said against Dickens that in all his movements in behalf of charity he had an eye to his own advantage. But that is not the way to pass judgment. It does not do to probe too deeply into human motives. In every case in which he acted the object was commendable; and at that it should be left.

Dickens's great faults were excess of vanity and excess of self-pity; but there again vanity is not to be condemned. It is really the outward and visible sign of illusion; and illusion is one of the greatest blessings bestowed on mankind. We

[1] Of Miss Hogarth, Dickens's elder daughter speaks with great affection. See letter to F. G. Kitton, *Charles Dickens*, by P. and P., vol. 2, p. 47.

should all be miserable without it. It is when vanity passes all bounds that the trouble comes; and in Dickens, as the result of the incense offered by the multitude, it did pass all bounds, and consequently brought trouble both to others and to himself. As for self-pity, that is altogether harmful. It helps nobody. Dickens at his best was delightful to most people. His high spirits drew men to him. It was good to be in his company. His exuberant vitality, like the perfume of the orange grove, acted on people miles away—wherever, indeed, his books were read.

In March 1858 he wrote to Wilkie Collins:

> The domestic unhappiness remains so strong upon me that I can't write and (waking) can't rest one minute. I have never known a moment's peace or content since the last night of *The Frozen Deep*. I do suppose that there never was a man so seized and rended by one spirit.

On Friday, 26 March 1858, he read the *Christmas Carol* before the members of the Philosophical Institution at Edinburgh, and after the reading the Lord Provost, the Magistrates and Council of the city waited in procession on him at the Music Hall and presented him with a massive silver wassail bowl. Among those who heard the reading were Miss Helen Thomson, Mrs Dickens's aunt and other members of the Thomson family, none of whom had at the time any idea that there was trouble in Dickens's home.

On 29 March Dickens attended the 13th Anniversary of the General Theatrical Fund at the Freemasons' Tavern. Thackeray was in the chair, and Dickens speaking on the English novel said:

> "Every writer of fiction, although he may not adopt the dramatic form, writes in effect, for the stage. He may never write plays, but the truth and passion which are in him must be more or less reflected in the great mirror which he holds up to Nature."

He concluded with a tribute to Thackeray.

About this time, Mrs Dickens, who could bear herself no longer, revealed the state of affairs to her father and mother. Dickens then made various proposals in respect to

CHARLES DICKENS
*Photo by Watkins, probably* 1858
*T. W. Tyrrell's Collection*

CHARLES DICKENS
*Photo by Watkins, 1858*
*T. W. Tyrrell's Collection*

a separate maintenance, all of which were rejected. In the meanwhile Mrs Hogarth and her daughter Helen having heard of his connection with Miss Ternan (innocent at the time though it evidently was) spread the information abroad. Dickens in his exasperation then refused to make any settlement on his wife unless Mrs Hogarth and Helen signed their names to a paper declaring that the separation was not owing to any immorality on his part. This for long they refused to do.

Dickens was further discomposed by the intrusion of Mrs Winter, who had become a more frequent visitor at Tavistock House than he really desired, but Miss Hogarth for some reason encouraged her and made her a confidante. Probably Miss Hogarth was pitting (and blamelessly) the harmless Mrs Winter against the apparently dangerous Miss Ternan. "Flora" used to come to the house and "spread her bonnet and shawl there" with a care indicative of an intention to stay some time, "not that her conversation was interesting, turning as it did on a chaos of subjects in which mackerel became entangled with cockchafers and the wine trade." [1] In truth "poor Flora was in fluctuating expectation of the time when Clennam (Dickens) would renew his boyhood and be madly in love with her again," [2] though, of course, she would have repulsed him—with firmness though with kindness; still the experience would have gratified her. Indeed, when he good-naturedly put a supporting arm round her figure, she, though she understood it to be honourable and gentlemanly in him, hinted that if he pressed her more tightly "she wouldn't consider it intruding." [3]

The Hogarths were at Tavistock House in April, and on the 27th Dickens wrote to Wills:

The Hogarth family don't leave till next Saturday and I cannot in the meantime bear the contemplation of their imbecility any more. . . . The sight of Hogarth at breakfast! I am therefore going to leave here by the mail next Tuesday.

---

[1] *Little Dorrit*, Cr. ed., p. 563.    [2] *Id.*, p. 564.    [3] *Id.*, p. 566.

But Mr Hogarth is described at this time "as an affable, simple-mannered elderly gentleman, free from anything stiff or self-assertive."

§ 116. *First Series of Paid Readings,* 29 *April* 1858, *in St Martin's Hall*

On 29 April Dickens gave the first public reading for his own benefit at St Martin's Hall in Long Acre, a building facing the west end of Bow Street. There were in all five series of Paid Readings—the particulars being as follow:

| | | | |
|---|---|---|---|
| 1st. | 1858 and 1859 under management of | | Arthur Smith |
| 2nd. | 1861 and 1865 first six under management of | | Arthur Smith |
| | the rest under management of | | Mr Headland |
| 3rd. | 1866 and 1867 under management of | | George Dolby |
| 4th. | 1868 and 1869 under management of | | George Dolby |
| 5th. | 11 January 1870 to 15 March 1870 under management of | | George Dolby |

Dickens's objects in giving the readings were two: first, a desire to make money; and secondly, the hope that by flinging himself into a perpetual whirl of excitement he could forget the sad troubles of his home. Said he, a few weeks previous to the first reading: "I have now no relief but in action. I am become incapable of rest. I am quite confident I should rust, break, and die, if I spared myself. Much better to die doing." On another occasion he said: "It is much better to go on and fret, than to stop and fret." Then again, "Poor Catherine and I are not made for each other, and there is no help for it. . . . We are strangely ill-assorted for the bond there is between us . . . I claim no immunity from blame. There is plenty of fault on my side, I daresay, in the way of a thousand uncertainties, caprices, and difficulties of disposition; but only one thing will alter all that, and that is the end which alters everything."

Forster gives as a third reason for the readings—Dickens's apprehension that his powers as a writer were deserting him. This, however, could have had but little weight with him. As a matter of fact, his powers were *not* deserting him. He had lost the vivacity of his earlier days, but out of the ashes of the bygone Dickens had arisen a new Dickens, earnest, rich in invention, sombrous, dusky, fulvous, lurid. Then, he excited the loud, long laugh. Later he holds us with his glittering eye. Besides, even in his least successful productions—his later Christmas contributions to *All the Year Round*, for instance, there are veins of gold.

§ 117. *The Separation, May* 1858

On 1 May 1858 Dickens attended the banquet of the Royal Academy and returned thanks after his health and the health of Thackeray had been proposed by the President, Sir Charles Eastlake. On 8 May he presided at the 48th Anniversary of the Artist Benevolent Fund, which was celebrated at the Freemasons' Tavern. When making speeches Dickens was apt to slip into the sort of language used by Micawber. Thus at this dinner he narrated an absurd story which was, he said, once told him by a dear and valued friend (Douglas Jerrold evidently) who had "passed from this sublunary stage." The story in brief was of a substitute who had to take the part of Reginald in the *Castle Spectre*. The substitute expressed a not unreasonable wish to know in some vague way what the part was about. He thought he should have some slight inkling as to what had really happened to him. They said to him, "Here you are chained in a dungeon. You have been here for seventeen years. You have lived upon bread and water, and in consequence are extremely weak."

When the curtain was rung up the substitute presented to the audience an extremely miserable appearance and was favourably received until, through some mental confusion as to his instructions he stated in pathetic terms that he had been confined in that dungeon seventeen years, during which time he had not tasted a morsel of food, to which circumstance he was inclined to attribute the fact of his being at that moment very much out of condition. The audience, thinking this statement extremely improbable, declined to believe it.

Dickens then said that he had received instructions as to the part he was to take that evening and he hoped he should profit by the terrible warning which he had detailed. The audience certainly had no reason to complain of him, for he straightway delivered a rousing speech in which more humour accompanied an eloquent appeal for the widows and orphans of actors mixed with pleasantries at the expense of the statesmen who had been present at the recent Academy Dinner.

For long, as already stated, the Hogarths held out against signing the paper containing the declaration that the separation of Dickens and his wife was not on account of immorality on his part; but, at last, greatly against their will they consented; and, Mrs Dickens offering no further opposition, Mark Lemon on 22 May was able to inform Forster that she agreed to her husband's terms.

While the Deed of Separation was being drawn up, Mrs Dickens was in a terrible state of distress, and Mrs Hogarth took her to Brighton in the hope of distracting her thoughts. They then visited Mark Lemon and his wife at Crawley. Owing to the worry and anxiety, Mrs Hogarth then fell ill herself, and her life was despaired of. One who knew Mrs Dickens intimately at this time said "she was a sweet and charming woman, good in every sense of the word, and when she left her husband, she left her heart behind." Her daughter Kate, in particular, used to speak most affectionately of her. To Kate's possession came ultimately the miniature of Mrs Dickens by Miss Rose Emma Drummond. It was one of her most treasured possessions.[1]

In a moment of great perturbation Dickens on 25 May then wrote out the statement which is usually referred to as "The Violated Letter" [2] and handed it to his Readings Manager, Mr Arthur Smith, requesting him to show it to anyone, who "wishes to do me right or to anyone who may have been misled into doing me wrong."

[1] See VIII, § 24.
[2] It is dated from Tavistock House "Tuesday, 25 May 1858."

§ 118. *"The Violated Letter,"* 25 *May* 1858.

The following is the letter with the comments on it of the writer of this book.

"Mrs Dickens and I lived unhappily together for many years. Hardly anyone who has known us intimately can fail to have known that we are in all respects of character and temperament wonderfully unsuited to each other. I suppose that no two people, not vicious in themselves, ever were joined together who had a greater difficulty in understanding one another, or who had less in common."

This is true only to an extent. Mrs Dickens did not offer to her husband the perpetual incense that others did, but she was a lovable woman and maintained her affection for him even after their separation—to the end of his life indeed.

"An attached woman servant [1] (more friend to both of us than a servant), who lived with us sixteen years, and is now married, and who was and still is in Mrs Dickens's confidence and in mine, who had the closest familiar experiences of this unhappiness, in London, in the country, in France, in Italy, wherever we have been, year after year, month after month, week after week, day after day, will bear testimony to this.

"Nothing has, on any occasion, stood between us and a separation, but Mrs Dickens's sister Georgina Hogarth. From the age of fifteen she has devoted herself to our house and our children. She has been their playmate, nurse, instructress, friend, protectress, adviser and companion. In the manly consideration towards Mrs Dickens which I owe to my wife, I will merely remark of her that the peculiarity of her character has thrown all the children on someone else."

This is not fair to Mrs Dickens. They had been married twenty-one years. In that period she had given birth to ten children. She had insufficient time to recover after each confinement, as her frequent illnesses prove. She was naturally glad for her sister to help her in the home, but it was unfair to bring against her that "peculiarity of character" to which he refers. Life through she was deeply

---

[1] The Anne who accompanied them to America in 1842.

attached to her children. A mother's love is always stronger than a father's love, and hers was no exception.

"I do not know—I cannot by any stretch of fancy imagine—what would have become of them but for this aunt, who has grown up with them, to whom they are devoted, and who has sacrificed the best part of her youth and life to them. She has remonstrated, reasoned, suffered and toiled, again and again to prevent a separation between Mrs Dickens and me. Mrs Dickens has often expressed to her her sense of her affectionate care and devotion in the house—never more strongly than within the last twelve months."

Mrs Dickens was certainly grateful for help in the household. What woman with so many children would not be? But she was bitterly offended at being relegated to the second place in the home, by one who offered to her husband so much incense, and who though an excellent woman, was by him far too extravagantly praised, for by extravagantly praising her he was reflecting on his wife.

"For some years past, Mrs Dickens has been in the habit of representing to me that it would be better for her to go away and live apart; that her always increasing estrangement made a mental disorder under which she sometimes labours—more, that she felt herself unfit for the life she had to lead as my wife, and that she would be better far away."

It is absolutely untrue, as documentary evidence proves, that Mrs Dickens ever had at any time any "mental disorder." She wished and continually wished to remain at the head of her husband's household. She was sometimes injudicious but she was always absolutely sane.

"I have uniformly replied that we must bear our misfortune, and fight the fight out to the end; that the children were the first consideration, and that I feared they must bind us together 'in appearance.'

"At length, within these three weeks, it was suggested to me by Forster that, even for their sakes, it would surely be better to reconstruct and rearrange their unhappy home. I empowered him to treat with Mrs Dickens, as the friend of both of us for one and twenty years. Mrs Dickens wished to add, on her part, Mark Lemon and did so. On Saturday last, Lemon wrote to Forster that

Mrs Dickens 'gratefully and thankfully accepted' the terms I proposed to her."

All the same, as was subsequently proved, both Forster and Lemon sympathised more with Mrs Dickens than with her husband.

"Of the pecuniary part of them I will only say that I believe they are as generous as if Mrs Dickens were a lady of distinction and I a man of fortune.

"The remaining parts of them are easily described—my eldest boy to live with Mrs Dickens and take care of her; my eldest girl (Mary) to keep my house; both my girls (Kate was the other) and all my children but the eldest son, to live with me, in the continued companionship of their Aunt Georgina, for whom they have all the tenderest affection that I have ever seen among young people, and who has a higher claim (as I have often declared for many years) upon my affection, respect and gratitude than anybody in the world."

The "higher claim" should certainly have been paid to the wife who had borne him ten children and who still preserved her affection for him. The last line shows how hurriedly this document was written, for of course the word "else" was needed after anybody—to make sense.

"I hope that no one who may become acquainted with what I write here, can possibly be so cruel and unjust as to put any misconstruction on our separation so far. My eldest children all understand it perfectly and all accept it as inevitable. There is not a shadow of doubt or concealment among us—my eldest son and I are one as to it all."

Whatever the eldest son may have felt then he felt differently later. He certainly knew in the following year of the Miss Ternan entanglement.

"Two wicked persons, who should have spoken very differently of me in consideration of earned respect and gratitude, have (as I am told, and indeed to my personal knowledge) coupled with this separation the name of a young lady for whom I have great attachment and regard. I will not repeat her name—I honour it too much. Upon my soul and honour, there is not on this earth a more virtuous and spotless creature than that young lady. I know her to be innocent and pure, and as good as my own dear daughters."

The "two wicked persons" were Mrs Hogarth and her daughter Helen. Their wickedness consisted in their expressing their opinions. The young lady was of course Miss Ellen Lawless Ternan; and there is no doubt that Dickens in speaking of her at this time in this way was telling the truth.

He refers to his "own dear daughters," but it is quite certain that Mrs Dickens was as much attached to them as he was.

"Further, I am quite sure that Mrs Dickens having received this assurance from me must now believe it, in the respect I know her to have for me, and in the perfect confidence I know her in her better moments to repose in my truthfulness. On this head, again, there is not a shadow of a doubt or concealment between my children and me. All is open and plain among us, as though we were brothers and sisters. They are perfectly certain that I would not deceive them, and the confidence among us is without a fear."

C. D.

*May 25th* 1858.[1]

To this statement was appended another signed by Mrs Hogarth and her daughter Helen. It runs thus:

"It having been stated to us that, in reference to the differences which have resulted in the separation of Mr and Mrs Charles Dickens, certain statements have been circulated that such differences are occasioned by circumstances deeply affecting the moral character of Mr Dickens, and compromising the reputation and good name of others, we solemnly declare that we now disbelieve such statements. We know that they are not believed by Mrs Dickens, and we pledge ourselves, on all occasions, to contradict them, as entirely destitute of foundation."

Although these ladies signed this statement owing to pressure and in the belief that it would remove the friction in the family, at the same time their statement was evidently the truth, though it was impossible for them to know it was the truth apart from Dickens's word. They were alarmed at Dickens's fury and would have done anything at the time

---

[1] This date may be the date on which Dickens signed the letter or the date of the note signed by Mrs Hogarth and her daughter Helen.

to appease him.   Afterwards they deeply regretted having signed it.

The whole of this document is one long exhibition of Dickens's solicitude to be justified to himself.   Yet he who had written this letter was the same who a few months before had written towards the end of *Little Dorrit*:

"Be guided only by the healer of the sick, the raiser of the dead, friend of all who are afflicted and forlorn, the patient Master who shed tears of compassion for our infirmities. . . .   There is no vengeance and no infliction of suffering in His Life I am sure.   There can be no confusion in following Him." [1]

Despite all Dickens's laudation of Miss Georgina Hogarth he would not have been Dickens if he had not got a little fun out of her name, which reminded Mr Fascination Fledgeby in *Our Mutual Friend* of other words.   "You play—if you can," he says, meditating very slowly, "the concertina.   And you have—when you catch it—the scarlatina."

References to Dickens's matrimonial troubles appeared in the *New York Tribune* of 1858:

June 21, page 6, column 4: "Mr Charles Dickens. From *Household Words* of Wednesday, June 9."

June 21, page 4, column 6: Short editorial paragraph on Dickens's statement.

June 22, page 3, column 5: "Personal."   The first and second paragraphs under this heading contain an item taken from the London *Times* on "The Dickens scandal."

July 24, page 6, column 1: "Affairs in England." The first paragraph of this column gives the "facts of the case" concerning the "scandal."   All these items are small.

A copy of the letter that was handed to Arthur Smith reached America and was printed in full in the *New York Tribune* in August 1858.   Dickens used always afterwards to refer to this as the "violated letter."   Whirl, excitement, heat, glitter, make up the rest of his life.   He flamed it out furiously.   "Does it rain?" asks Mr Snobbington in the play.   "It pours."

[1] *Little Dorrit.*   Cr. ed., p. 653.

§ 119. *The Address in "Household Words," 12 June 1858.*
*The Edmund Yates Article, 12 June 1858*

On 31 May 1858 Miss Hogarth wrote to Mrs Winter, who still haunted Tavistock House, informing her of the separation of Dickens from his wife, mentioning that they had lived unhappily for years. The letter, which is simply an abbreviation of the story as set down in the "Violated Letter," was evidently dictated by Dickens.

The amazement of the public on hearing of the separation can easily be understood, for having read so many tender and realistic descriptions of home life in his novels they had taken it for granted that his own home must have been an earthly paradise.

In the *Manchester Guardian* for 8 June 1858 occurs the announcement, "*The Times* has been requested to anticipate the publication of the following article from *Household Words*." Then follows what is called the "Address," written by Dickens.

The trouble between him and his wife had, he said, "been amicably composed." He then went on:

"By some means, arising out of wickedness or out of folly, this trouble has been made the occasion of misrepresentations, most grossly false, most monstrous and most cruel—involving not only me, but innocent persons dear to my heart. . . . Those who know me and my nature, need no assurance under my hand that such calumnies are as irreconcilable with me as they are in their frantic incoherence, with one another. But there is a great multitude who know me through my writings, and who do not know me otherwise; and I cannot bear that one of them should be left in doubt, or hazard of doubt through my poorly shrinking from taking the unusual means to which I now resort of circulating the truth."

He concludes:

"I most solemnly declare then, and this I do, both in my own name and in my wife's—that all the lately whispered rumours touching the trouble at which I have glanced are abominably false. And that whosoever repeats one of them, after this denial, will lie as wilfully and as foully as it is possible for any false witness to lie, before heaven and earth."

To his wife he wrote:

"Dear Catherine, I will not write a word as to any *causes* that have made it necessary for me to publish the enclosed in *Household Words*. Whoever there may be among the living, whom I will never forgive alive or dead, I earnestly hope that all unkindness is over between you and me."

Dickens then fell out with his publishers, Messrs Bradbury and Evans,[1] because they declined to use their influence to get his *Household Words* address inserted in *Punch*, of which they were proprietors. After, on 17 June 1858, severing his connection with them, he returned to his old publishers Chapman and Hall. With Mark Lemon, the editor of *Punch*, he was equally bitter. He forbade his children to see or speak to their "Uncle Mark" as they called him, and, the trouble with Mrs Hogarth and Miss Hogarth continuing, they were not to speak again to their grandmother or Aunt Helen.[2]

The friends of Mr Hogarth naturally sympathised deeply with Mrs Dickens. Among them was Mr R. S. Rintoul (also a Scotchman), founder and editor of the *Spectator*, who lived in apartments that formed the upper storeys of the publishing office in Wellington Street, Strand. Mr Rintoul was a short sturdy man with a large head well mounted and full of character and resolution and he spoke with the rich Scottish intonation. Mrs Dickens was often seen at the Rintouls'. William Michael Rossetti, who had been, since 1850, on the staff of the *Spectator*, happened to be with the Rintouls one day soon after Dickens had separated from his wife. He says, "I heard the matter canvassed in this family and the verdict went dead against him."[3]

The writer of *Leaves from a Life*, Mrs J. E. Panton, speaking of a time after the separation of Dickens from his wife, says:

[1] The quarrel was subsequently made up. Charles Dickens the younger married in 1861 Mr Evans's daughter.
[2] Letter of Charles Dickens the younger to his mother, 13 July 1858.
[3] *Some Reminiscences*, by William Michael Rossetti, vol. 1, p. 100.

"I well recollect being in a box at a theatre one evening with my mother and Mrs Dickens. The latter burst into tears suddenly and went back in the box. Charles Dickens had come into the opposite box with some friends and she could not bear it. My mother took her back to her house on Gloucester Road, Regent's Park, telling me to sit quiet till she returned. When she did, she said nothing to me, but I heard her tell Papa about it, adding, 'I thought I should never be able to leave her.'"

On 12 June, the very day that the statement in *Household Words* appeared, there appeared in the periodical *Town Talk* an offensive article on Thackeray from the pen of Edmund Yates. This led to a quarrel between Thackeray and Dickens, who had taken Yates's part, and they were not, in consequence of the article, on speaking terms for years.

## § 120. *Landor "in tenebris,"* 12 *July* 1858

To this date belongs that delicious scene in connection with Walter Savage Landor. For many years he and Dickens had been on intimate terms of friendship. His portrait, as Boythorn in *Bleak House*, has already been referred to. Dickens, indeed, never had finer material to work upon, and would, no doubt, have made Mr Boythorn one of his most notable creations, but for fear of wounding the susceptibilities of the original.

On 12 July 1858, Landor, who was fleeing from justice, telegraphed to Forster that he would be at Forster's house, Montagu Square, London, that night, accompanied by one of his nieces. Forster happened to be having a dinner party, among the guests being Sir Alexander Cockburn, the Lord Chief Justice, and Charles Dickens. Presently the door opened, and the servant announced, "as it were, in Cockburn's very teeth," that Landor, a refugee from justice, had come to hide in the house. Says Forster:

"Dickens went out to console him. I thought that Landor would talk over with him the unpleasant crisis, and I shall never forget my amazement when Dickens came back into the room, laughing, and said that he found him sitting on a bed, very jovial, and that his whole conversation was upon the characters of Catullus, Tibullus, and other Latin poets!"

On 21 July Dickens delivered at the Princess's Theatre, London, a stirring speech at a public meeting, presided over by Charles Kean, which was the means of establishing the Royal Dramatic College.[1]

## § 121. *A Provincial Tour*

On 2 August 1858 Dickens commenced a Provincial Tour in connection with his readings. His letters indicate roughly the towns which he visited. Among them were Clifton (2 August), Exeter and Plymouth (5 August). He was very pleased with the audiences at Exeter and Plymouth. He says, however, that all the same he would be glad for quiet, adding "Perhaps it is best for me not to have it just now and to wear and toss my storm away."

On 7 August he was back in London. We next hear of him at Manchester, at Wolverhampton (11 August), Shrewsbury (12 August), Chester, Liverpool and Chester again. On 15 August he returned to London. That month Mrs Winter again wrote to Dickens, telling him that she was staying at her father's house near Liverpool, and asking him to meet her in that city. She included in her letter the verses written by her sister Anne referred to in § 31. Replying on 16 August from Gad's Hill Place Dickens said he had read poor Anne's verses "with great sorrow and with many emotions of sadly affectionate remembrance." It would be impossible, he said, to meet Mrs Winter in Liverpool, but he hoped to see her later in London. His letter concluded with love to Ella and kindest regards to Mr Winter.[2]

[1] Hotten, p. 154.　　　　[2] Payne and Harper, p. 149.

§ 122. *First Visit to Ireland. At Belfast,* 27 *August* 1858

On Friday, 27 August and Saturday, 28 August, Dickens, who had proceeded to Ireland accompanied by his secretary, Arthur Smith, read at the Victoria Hall, Belfast, to a crowded audience. Two rather singular occurrences upset the proceedings on the 27th. Just before the close of the first part a large piece of moulding over the orchestra fell with a crash, but happily nobody was hurt. Later, an amusing incident happened. Dickens was reading *A Christmas Carol* and had reached the description of the festivities at Scrooge's nephew's: "But they didn't devote the whole evening to music . . . Stop! There was first a game at blind-man's buff. Of course there was."

Over and in front of Dickens was a row of gas-lights fed by a flexible tube which lay on the orchestra. Just as he read the words: "blind-man's buff. Of course there was," somebody happened to stand upon the tube and in a moment all was in comparative darkness. The audience was greatly amused, the accident being so opportune. However, ladders were procured and the range of lights being set in order, Dickens was able to continue.[1]

It was the humour in the readings that appealed most to his audiences. "As to the 'Boots'[2] and Mrs Gamp," at Belfast, he says, "it was just one roar with me and them. For they made me laugh so, that sometimes I *could not* compose my face to go on." At Belfast he met a prominent citizen there, Francis Dalzell Finlay, editor of the Belfast *Northern Whig*. In going from one town to another Dickens used an Irish jaunting car, which greatly delighted him.

From Belfast he proceeded to Dublin and thence to Cork and Limerick where he read in the theatre to a "highly sensitive, quick and agreeable audience," and whence he wrote to Finlay, ordering through him a jaunting car like the one he had used at Belfast. While Dickens

[1] *Belfast News Letter*—the leading Belfast newspaper.
[2] "At the Holly Tree."

was reading in Ireland, Mrs Hogarth, who had recovered from her illness, went with Mrs Dickens to Margate, in the hopes that a change of scene would be beneficial to both. But no change could remove the mental trouble of either of them. Among those who deeply sympathised with and tried to console them, were Miss Burdett Coutts, and Mrs Dickens's aunt, Miss Helen Thomson.[1]

As soon as the "Violated Letter" had appeared in the *New York Tribune*, English papers copied it; and on 5 September Dickens wrote to his solicitor expressing his indignation.

The following appeared in *The Liverpool Mercury*[2] of 9 September 1858:

It seems to be thought, by at least one favourite of the reading public, that authors are entitled to submit their private and domestic griefs or grievances to the world, and to ask national sympathy for their family troubles. It further appears to be considered decorous, and dignified, and manly, for a popular writer, whose works are read wherever the English language is read, to use his public position and influence in dragging before the world private individuals whose means of self-defence bear no sort of proportion to his facilities for attack. We consider this practice so outrageously impertinent as regards the public, and so wantonly cruel as regards the private persons whose names are thus forced into a gratuitous and painful notoriety, that we feel called upon to mark it with indignant reprobation.

The words of the *Liverpool Mercury* are not too severe, and the present generation looking back at these occurrences will recall chiefly how well Mrs Dickens comes out of it all. There were two attacks on her (and "attacks" is the only suitable word) in the Press. All the world read them; and she had the dignity to make no reply. There were able pens ready to enter the lists in her favour; but she gave no encouragement to them. Though conscious

---

[1] Letter from Miss Helen Thomson to Mrs Stark, 20 August 1858. Miss Helen Thomson was George Thomson's youngest daughter. She was born in 1795 and therefore at this time 63.

[2] This newspaper was amalgamated in 1904 with the *Liverpool Post*. The full title of the joint paper is *The Liverpool Post and Mercury*.

that the reflections on her were ill-deserved, she maintained a dignified silence. And in so doing she acted rightly and wisely.

When Dickens returned to Gad's Hill Place on 6 September, the jaunting car arrived from Ireland and he used it to convey guests from Higham Railway station to Gad's Hill.[1]

## § 123. *The Apotheosis of Miss E. L. Ternan*

No great while after the separation from his wife and notwithstanding those written protests made to the public, Dickens prevailed upon Miss Ternan to become his mistress; but she gave herself reluctantly. He took for her a house No. 2 Houghton Place, Ampthill Square, near the homes of his boyhood, Johnson Street and the Polygon, for that neighbourhood oddly enough had life through a fascination for him which he could never resist. The house was, as the London Directory shows, in Mrs Ternan's name from 1861 to 1865. From 1866 to 1868 it was vacant. Here he visited her two or three times a week.[2] Thenceforward Dickens had, to quote Lady Tippens's communication to her fan, "two establishments."[3] He imagined that he had entered into a new life and that it would be roses, roses all the way. He forgot that roses have thorns. He thought he was in front of the supremest felicity ever enjoyed by mortal man. He wasn't.

Francisco Berger who had written the music for *The Frozen Deep* was sometimes at No. 2 Houghton Place. He played games of cards there with Mrs Ternan, Ellen and Dickens on Sunday evenings. After the card-playing Ellen and Dickens generally sang duets to Berger's accompaniments.

Miss Ternan was really gifted, but then she came of a gifted family. It is not every one who can bear too much

[1] See the *Dickensian,* September 1934.
[2] Facts supplied by Canon Benham. See also Canon Benham's Life in *D. N. B.*, Second Supplement, vol. 1, p. 142.
[3] *Our Mutual Friend*, Cr. ed., vol. 12, p. 520.

CHARLES DICKENS, BY C. BAUGNIET, 1858
*Photo by T. W. Tyrrell*

MISS ELLEN LAWLESS TERNAN'S HOUSE, 2 HOUGHTON PLACE, AMPTHILL SQUARE (EAST SIDE), LONDON

Second house on the left

*Photo by T. W. Tyrrell*

See page 280

praise, and Dickens overpraised her. "The first thing that tempts young women," Lady Godolphin used to say, "is vanity"; and that was Miss Ternan's weakness, or rather vanity combined with a desire for a competence. If Dickens's conduct spoilt Miss Ternan's life, it certainly went very far to spoiling his own. He could not be happy (how could he!) knowing that Miss Ternan was assailing herself with reproaches and drawing daily further and further from him. They were both of them latterly miserable, and Dickens's unhappiness is reflected in his later books, which can be understood only in the light of this knowledge.

During the time that Dickens was fascinated by Miss Ternan, he wrote *Great Expectations*, *Our Mutual Friend*, and *Edwin Drood*; and his thoughts were largely upon her when he was drawing the characters of Estella Provis (a surname that seems to be not without meaning), Bella Wilfer, and Helena Landless. It is easy to see some of her characteristics in each of these heroines. For instance, all these young ladies were very pretty, all were proud, acting like spoilt children, petulant, difficult to manage and capricious. All were gifted, and each rose from straitened circumstances to a higher position. Estella married Bentley Drummle who has nothing to recommend him but his purse. Bella Wilfer said, "I must have money, Pa, I must marry it"; and Helena Landless apparently meant to have Lieutenant Tartar of the Royal Navy, who had come into the possession of a fortune.

The entry of Miss Ternan into Dickens's life seemed to him its grand event. His previous passions had proved failures. Maria Beadnell had refused him and had degenerated into a Mrs Winter. Mary Hogarth had died, his own wife he had pushed aside as impossible. For Miss Georgina Hogarth he had no tender regard, though he pedestalled her as the immaculate housekeeper. He simply respected her. In Miss Ternan he thought he had found perfection. Life seemed to have begun afresh for him. Never was mortal more disappointed. Here we see five persons—Dickens, Mrs Dickens, Miss Hogarth,

Mrs Winter and Miss Ternan—all disillusioned, and four out of the five unmistakably unhappy.

Dickens was unhappy, for Miss Ternan had proved different from what he had anticipated; the discarded Mrs Dickens was hopelessly unhappy; Miss Hogarth, never entirely at ease in her position, was, as the result of Dickens's passion for Miss Ternan, filled with apprehension; Miss Ternan was gnawed by remorse and yet could not escape from the entanglement, and he understood her feelings, for she thought, as it were, aloud; Mrs Winter, though less affected than the other four, could not help seeing that she had in her turn been pushed aside.

There was affected hilarity in the Dickens's household, but it was make-believe. All save Mrs Winter, and she was chagrined, were palpably unhappy. Dickens had always lived intensely. Thenceforward he lived still more furiously. Of ordinary common sense, he, genius as he was and brilliant as was his output, exhibited not one atom. He thought that hectic movement and the acquisition of gold, more gold and yet more gold could cure him. It could not.

The following incident was related to the writer by the late W. R. Hughes. "The letters of Dickens to Miss Ternan were privately offered for sale in London about 1893. The vendor came to me and putting down the packet said, 'These are Charles Dickens's Letters to Miss Ternan. Will you buy them?' Mr Hughes replied, 'Do you know you are doing a very dangerous thing? These letters cannot have been got honestly. If you'll take my advice you'll go home and burn them.'" Nothing has since been heard of these letters. It is very improbable that the man took Mr Hughes's advice, consequently some day they may come to light.

Most of the facts relative to Miss E. L. Ternan were supplied to the writer of this book by his friend Canon Benham who received them from Miss Ternan herself.

The story of Dickens's intimate association with Miss Ternan was known however not only to Canon Benham, but also to Mrs Dickens, Miss Georgina Hogarth, Mr Edmund Yates, Wilkie Collins, Charles Dickens the younger, and

G. A. Sala. What they did not know was the story of Miss Ternan's remorse as told to the writer by Canon Benham. All these persons, however, wished to keep the knowledge of Dickens's intimacy with Miss Ternan from the public. When therefore long ago it was announced that the writer was collecting material for a biography of Dickens, Miss Hogarth was troubled and Sala furious. Miss Hogarth had recourse to the post, Mr Sala to the Press, making a commencement with the *Manchester Evening News* for 16 September 1893.

After saying "Everybody who was intimate with Dickens is aware that Mr Forster's 'Life' is almost an exhaustive one"—a statement too ridiculous to refute—Sala went on: "I say almost, because there are circumstances connected with the later years of the illustrious novelist which should not and must not be revealed for fifty years to come at the very least." In his *Recollections*, published two years later, Sala says: "I should say that beyond the members of Dickens's own family, there are, now that Wilkie Collins and Edmund Yates are gone, scarcely any custodians of this secret besides myself."

What Sala had to do with the matter, and why he should butt in, the writer does not know. It was no business of his. With Miss Hogarth, on the other hand, one could sympathise; but there was no need for the perturbation of either of them, for the writer had no intention at the time to make the revelations which they feared. It would have been cruel to make them then, and the writer's conscience would have been a greater barrier than Miss Hogarth's letters or Sala's articles. (See preface to this work.) Another member of Dickens's circle, Dickens's daughter, Mrs Perugini, being informed of the line that was to be taken, showed herself reasonable and expressed herself very kindly by letter. With all the members of the Ternan family Dickens continued to be on the most intimate terms and he introduced Miss Frances Eleanor Ternan to his friend Mrs Frances Trollope, little thinking that this action would lead, as it did, to a marriage between her son Thomas Adolphus and the lady. See § 136.

§ 124. *Estella and Helena. The Frith Portrait. "A House to Let," Christmas No. of "H.W.," 1858*

There is much of Miss Ternan in Estella. "I loved her," says Pip, "simply because I found her irresistible. . . . I knew to my sorrow, often and often, if not always, that I loved her against reason, against promise, against peace, against hope, against happiness, against all discouragement that could be"; and then she marries Drummle, an ill-tempered booby who has nothing to recommend him except money. In the end, it is true, she takes for her second husband her old admirer Pip; but Dickens was persuaded unwisely to that by Bulwer Lytton.

An even more life-like picture of Miss Ternan is presented in Bella Wilfer (*Our Mutual Friend*). Here again, money was the attraction. Bella is pictured "seated on the rug to warm herself, with her brown eyes on the fire and a handful of brown curls in her mouth"; and she says, "I love money, and want money—want it dreadfully. I hate to be poor, offensively poor, miserably poor." Miss Ternan was grateful to Dickens for the notice he took of her, flattered by his fame and wealth, and pleased with the presents he gave her, but she did not love him. Notwithstanding that, however, Dickens got great pleasure in her company, and he tried to close his eyes to the fact that she really cared nothing for him; and when (out of gratitude for the ease in life which he had made possible to her) she became really pleasant to him he could say, using the words that close the chapter about Bella's wedding: "And oh, there are days in this life worth life and worth death. And oh, what a bright old song is that oh, 'tis love, 'tis love that makes the world go round!" [1] Certainly Dickens makes Bella with her beauty, her wilfulness, and her high spirits a very attractive young lady.

It may be merely an accident that the name Estella contains the initials of Ellen Lawless Ternan,[2] but the

[1] *Our Mutual Friend*, Cr. ed., p. 557.
[2] See also Chapter XVII, § 129.

name Helena Landless (*Edwin Drood*) was certainly suggested by Ellen Lawless. Helena is Bella, with more strength of character. She too is beautiful—"slender, supple, quick of eye and limb; half shy, half defiant, fierce of look; an indefinable kind of pause coming and going in their whole expression, both of face and form, which might be equally likened to the pause before a crouch or a bound." In other words she sometimes gave way to Dickens and sometimes when the thought of her position came mercilessly upon her, she repelled him.

When Pip, deeply in love with Estella, tells her of his feelings she says calmly, "It seems that there are sentiments and fancies—I don't know how to call them—which I am not able to comprehend. When you say you love me I know what you mean, as a form of words, but nothing more; you address nothing in my heart; you touch nothing there. I don't care for what you say at all." This was precisely Miss Ternan's attitude to Dickens.

Dickens was still in London on 6 September. His wanderings afterwards took him to York (10 September), Scarborough (12 September), Leeds (15 September), Durham, Sunderland, Newcastle-on-Tyne (26 September), Berwick (where he was joined by his daughters), Edinburgh, Dundee, Aberdeen, Perth, London (10 October), Nottingham, Derby (22 October), Wolverhampton (3 November), London (5 November).

In November 1858 came to Mrs Winter a very great blow—the financial failure of her husband. She asked Dickens to aid him to a fresh start in life, but Dickens (who replied on Saturday, 13 November 1858, from Brighton), while expressing sympathy, declined to be drawn into any entangling alliances or responsibilities, and suggested that Mrs Winter's father, who was wealthy, might help.[1] "Poor Papa" didn't want any more indigent relatives or indigent non-relatives to keep.

This year Dickens was nominated for the Lord Rector-

[1] Mr Beadnell died in November 1862. He left £40,000.

ship of Glasgow University. The election took place on
15 November 1858, the poll being:

Sir E. B. Lytton . . . . 217
Lord Shaftesbury . . . . 204
Charles Dickens . . . . 69

Dickens gave the last of his provincial readings this
year at Brighton on 26 November. On 3 December he
presided at the Annual Meeting of the Institutional
Association of Lancashire and Cheshire [1] when he congratulated his hearers upon the progress which "mutual
improvement societies" were then making in that neighbourhood, using "mutual" of course in its correct sense.
Later, when he came to write *Our Mutual Friend* he, as
everyone knows, used it differently. On 4 December he
was at Coventry where he presided at a public dinner in
his honour.

On 13 December Ellen Lawless Ternan was taking the
part of Alice in the play at the Haymarket called the *Tide of
Time*, an original comedy by Bayle Bernard.

In January 1859 Dickens's portrait was painted by
Frith, who on the 22nd says, "Dickens came with Miss
Hogarth and Miss Mary Dickens and remained two
and a half hours. Got in the head in colours. Dickens
most pleasant. No wonder people like him." Between
Maclise's picture and Frith's many portraits of Dickens
had been made—most of them, in Dickens's words,
absolute failures. One of them was not finished and Frith
asked the reason. "The truth is," said Dickens, "I sat a
great many times. The picture bore a strong resemblance
to Ben Caunt (a noted prize-fighter). . . . At last I
thought it was time to give it up, for I had sat there and
looked at the thing till I felt I was growing like it." [2]

Frith's portrait would have been executed before, only
Dickens, who had previously gone clean shaven, had
recently cultivated a moustache; and Forster, for whom

---

[1] Hotten, p. 157. Mrs Winter died at Southsea 20 September 1886.
Mr Winter died in 1871. Their daughter Ella died about 1918.
[2] *My Autobiography*, by W. P. Frith, p. 208.

CHARLES DICKENS IN 1856, BY ARY SCHEFFER
*National Portrait Gallery*

See page 287

CHARLES DICKENS, AFTER FRITH, 1859

*Picture in the Forster Collection, South Kensington*

See page 287

the picture was to be done, wanted to wait till what he called the "hideous disfigurement" was removed. Waiting, however, only made matters worse, for to the offence of a moustache, Dickens added the offence of a beard, so Forster, in fear lest if they waited any longer the whole face would be covered with hair, gave the requisite order. One of Dickens's friends observed facetiously that he highly approved of the change, because he now saw less of him. Frith thus compares Dickens's appearance with that of his earlier days: "The sallow skin had become florid, the long hair of 1835 had become shorter and darker, and the expression settled into that of one who had reached the topmost rung of a very high ladder, and was perfectly aware of his position." While the portrait was being painted occurred the following intensely interesting incident. Says Frith: "On one of the few occasions on which I got to work before him, I saw upon the table a paper parcel with a letter on the top of it. It turned out to be a letter from George Eliot, accompanying a copy of *Adam Bede*. Dickens read the book, pronounced it 'very good indeed,' and declared its author to be a woman."

Frith's portrait was a decided success. Maclise had painted Dickens with "the juvenile head and flowing locks, profuse and rich as Absalom's"; Ary Scheffer had produced a tame portrait, "very brown and flat, with no intellectual fire or force"; Frith, who represents Dickens in an easy coat at his study table, "has caught," to use Mr Yates's expression, "the author's blunt, pleasant, rather defiant look, and the healthy red and yellow of his face." The picture is now in the South Kensington Museum.

The question next was what to do with the scenery which Stanfield had painted for *The Lighthouse* [1] and *The Frozen Deep*. Eventually, Dickens placed the Lighthouse Scene in a single frame and divided *The Frozen Deep* into two—the British Man-of-War showing in one, the Arctic Sea in the other. These also he had framed, and he begged Forster to come and see the result. When he removed to Gad's Hill, the Lighthouse Scene was placed

[1] See Kitton, p. 240.

in the hall. It eventually became the property of Lord Iveagh.

Dickens tells us that it was while he was acting with his children and friends in *The Frozen Deep* that he first conceived the main idea of *A Tale of Two Cities*. Certain it is that while writing *A Tale of Two Cities* he was deeply in love with Ellen Lawless Ternan. Apparently Charles Darney in the story is Charles Dickens, and Lucie Manette is Miss Ternan. The gloom in which the tale is shrouded and its inferiority to all Dickens's other longer stories, reflects the unhappiness in his home and in his heart. The Christmas Number of *Household Words* for 1858 was *A House to Let*. Dickens contributed the chapter entitled "Going into Society." [1]

On 12 March 1859, Ellen Lawless Ternan was acting at the Haymarket in *The World and the Stage*, a play by Palgrave Simpson.

§ 125. *"All the Year Round,"* 30 *April* 1859. *"Tale of Two Cities" begun*

As the result of Dickens's decision to sever his connection with Bradbury and Evans, *Household Words* (with all its rights) was offered for sale on 16 May 1859, when it was purchased for £3,500 by Mr Arthur Smith, acting in Dickens's behalf. The final issue of *Household Words* appeared on 28 May 1859. A few days previous, on the 30th of April, had appeared its successor *All the Year Round*, which contained the opening chapter of Dickens's new story *A Tale of Two Cities* which also appeared in eight monthly parts with sixteen etched illustrations by Hablot K. Browne. A number of those writers who had been connected with *Household Words* contributed to the new periodical. T. A. Trollope, Sir John Bowring, G. A. Sala and others wrote many articles for it.

Before writing *A Tale of Two Cities* Dickens had studied very carefully Carlyle's *French Revolution*. Desirous of being accurate in regard to facts and dates, Dickens asked

---

[1] This was of course the last Christmas No. of *H.W.*

for the loan of the authorities quoted in that work; and it is said that Carlyle in jest sent him all his reference books, "about two cart-loads." In the Preface Dickens says: "It has been one of my hopes to add something to the popular and picturesque means of understanding that terrible time (the French Revolution), though no one can hope to add anything to the philosophy of Mr Carlyle's wonderful book."

Notwithstanding, however, the pains Dickens took with this story it is a mere secondary reflection of Carlyle's masterpiece. It is moreover a hopeless failure. Even Sydney Carton does not save it. Dickens never meddled successfully with history. The historical portions of *Barnaby Rudge* are devoid of interest; and his *Child's History of England* is really hardly worth criticism. It is only fair, however, to mention that our opinion concerning this story is not that entertained by many others. Mr W. R. Hughes, who was among the admirers of *A Tale of Two Cities*, considered Miss Pross "to be the best-drawn character after Carton." Mr Marzials calls it "a powerful book," and insists that Dickens, instead of being a pale copyist of Carlyle. "adds fervour to what he borrows." Professor Ward, who observes that the story contains "several narrative episodes of remarkable power—such as the flight from Paris at the close"—styles it an extraordinary *tour de force*.

In the middle of 1859 Dickens was in touch again with his old friend, W. H. Kolle, whose daughter had written a poem on Joan of Arc. Kolle sent the manuscript to Dickens who replied on 18 June (1859). He read it attentively, but was not impressed by it. Letters continued to pass between the two friends, and later Kolle sent Dickens six more of his daughter's poems. Dickens gave them the praise that was possible, but did not encourage the lady's literary aspirations.[1] The same month Francis Dalzell Finlay was in London and naturally Dickens invited him to Gad's Hill. He said on 28 June: "My station is Higham, on the North Kent railway from

[1] The *Dickensian*, 1 September 1934.

London Bridge. You shall be triumphantly fetched from said station in THE car" (see § 122). By the same train (apparently) Edmund Yates reached Gad's Hill—an additional pleasure for both Dickens and Finlay, for Finlay and Yates were friends, Yates being a regular weekly contributor to the Belfast paper, the *Northern Whig*. On 20 and 27 August and 3 September appeared in the *New York Ledger*, Dickens's tale *Hunted Down*, in which Slinkton (Wainewright) figures.[1]

§ 126. *Reading again at Peterborough, 19 October 1859.*
*Exit Hablot K. Browne*

On Wednesday, 19 October 1859, Dickens was again at Peterborough. Before commencing to read he alluded "to his visit on 18 December 1855 to this city," rendered dear to him by a personal friend (the Hon. Richard Watson), for the benefit of a local institution. The readings chosen on this latter occasion were "The Story of Little Dombey" and the Trial Scene from *Pickwick*. The *Peterborough Advertiser* for 22 October paid a tribute to Dickens's "essentially dramatic genius" which, said the writer,

"appears not only in his works but in his success as an actor, and anyone who has had the good fortune to listen to one of his speeches will be ready to admit that here as well as elsewhere the same power is exhibited. . . . His voice, manners, and features are each in their several ways instruments for the manifestation of this power, and when, as in the reading of his own works, its very highest pitch of development is reached what wonder that the effect is great, and that our emotions seem to be at the command of a potent magician, who, at will, shakes us with laughter or moves us to tears!"

In a letter to Frank Stone, written next day (20 October) but wrongly dated, Dickens says:

"We had a splendid rush last night; I think the finest I have ever read to. They took every word of the *Dombey* in quite an amazing

---

[1] It was republished in *All the Year Round* in 1860, 4 and 11 August in Series No. 67 and 68. See our Chapter X, § 48 and Cr. ed., vol. 15, p. 563.

manner. . . .  Mrs Gamp then set in with a roar, which lasted till I had done. . . .  It was as fine an instance of thorough absorption in a fiction as any of us are likely to see ever again."

On 27 October 1859 Dickens gave the last of his Provincial Tour readings for that year.  All were under the management of Mr Arthur Smith.

With *A Tale of Two Cities* Hablot Knight Browne's connection with Dickens as an illustrator of his books came to an end, and as "Two Cities" was unworthy of Dickens, so the illustrations to it are unworthy of Browne. But it is curious to note that as Dickens rose, culminated, and declined as a humorist, so Browne rose, culminated, and declined as an illustrator of Dickens.  We have the budding humorist and illustrator in "Sunday Under Three Heads," the inimitable humorist and illustrator in *Pickwick, Nickleby, Chuzzlewit, Dombey,* and *Copperfield,* and the decadent humorist and illustrator in *Bleak House, Little Dorrit* and *Tale of Two Cities.*  The first was published in 1836, the last in 1859, thus embracing a period of twenty-three years.  It is easy to understand why Browne excelled only in humorous situations, for he was himself a born humorist.  When inspired, his conception often bettered that of the author he illustrated.  An enthusiastic fox-hunter, he delighted in horses, which he drew so well as to excite the envy of Leech.  Browne outlived Dickens twelve years, dying at Brighton on 8 July 1882.[1]

*A Tale of Two Cities* [2] was finished in the number of *All the Year Round* for 26 November 1859.  On the same page began Wilkie Collins's masterpiece *The Woman in White,* which ran on till 25 August 1860.  Dickens in a letter to Collins of 7 January 1860 praised this story highly.[3]  *The Woman in White* was, Mr S. M. Ellis tells us, the lady who became Collins's mistress.  His house, 12 Harley Street, and his later residences were in ill repute,

---

[1] An excellent article on Browne as an illustrator of Dickens appeared in the *Dickensian,* vol. 2, No. 7, from the pen of Mr W. A. Fraser.

[2] *A Tale of Two Cities* was dramatised by Fox Cooper and first performed at the Victoria Theatre 7 July 1860.

[3] *Letters,* p. 492.

but Collins—a Bohemian to the finger-tips—was quite indifferent to what anybody thought. Dickens regarded the description of the Woman in White's first appearance on the Hampstead Road as one of the most dramatic bits of descriptive fiction that he knew.

§ 127. *"The Haunted House," First Christmas No. (1589) of "A.Y.R." "The Uncommercial Traveller,"* 1860

The first extra Christmas number of *All the Year Round* was published this year, the title being *The Haunted House*.[1]

Two of the chapters in it by Dickens are partly autobiographical, with allusions to his childhood at Chatham, to his belief in apparitions ("I once," said he, "saw the apparition of my father at this hour"); to his bloodhound Turk, and to his friend and solicitor, Mr Frederick Ouvry ("Mr Undery"), who "played whist better than the whole Law List."

The following are the nine sets of Christmas Stories of *All the Year Round*.

| | | Dickens wrote: |
|---|---|---|
| 1859. | The Haunted House | Three Chapters |
| 1860. | A Message from the Sea (scene laid at Clovelly) | First chapter, second chapter and parts of others |
| 1861. | Tom Tiddler's Ground | |
| 1862. | Somebody's Luggage | |
| 1863. | Mrs Lirriper's Lodgings | |
| 1864. | Mrs Lirriper's Legacy | |
| 1865. | Dr Marigold's Prescriptions | Three Chapters |
| 1866. | Mugby Junction | Four chapters |
| | | Barbox Brothers |
| | | Barbox Brothers & Co. |
| | | Main Line, The Boy at Mugby |
| | | No. 1 Branch Line |
| | | The Signal Man |
| | | The Overture |
| 1867. | No Thoroughfare | First and fourth acts (portions) |
| | | Act 3 |
| | | *Collins* the rest. |

[1] Cr. ed., vol. 15, p. 121.

CHARLES DICKENS IN 1859, AGE 50
*From a photo by Mason & Co.*

CHARLES DICKENS, BY RUDOLPH LEHMANN, 1861
*Photo by T. W. Tyrrell*

# JANUARY 1858 to JUNE 1860

On 28 December 1859 died Macaulay, who was buried on 9 January. Dickens was present at his funeral. Says an onlooker: "He walked among the subdued-looking clericals and staid men of mark; there was a stride in his gait and a roll: he had a seafaring complexion and air, and a huge white tie."

In 1860, appeared in *All the Year Round* a series of detached papers entitled *The Uncommercial Traveller* which contains autobiographical passages. One of the most vivid chapters is that on the wreck of the *Royal Charter* off Anglesea on 26 October 1859 when nearly 500 persons lost their lives. In chapter 4, "Two Views of a Cheap Theatre," Dickens criticises the Rev. Newman Hall who, in 1854, had succeeded the Rev. Rowland Hill at Surrey Chapel, and who sometimes on a Sunday night preached to huge congregations at the Surrey Theatre. Dickens praised Mr Hall in respect to the large Christianity of his general tone and to his renunciation of all priestly authority.[1]

With the Trollope family Dickens at this time and later became very intimate.

"I used to see him frequently," says Thomas Adolphus Trollope, "in his latter years. I generally came to London in the summer, and one of the first things on my list was a visit to 20 Wellington Street (the office of *All the Year Round*). Then would follow visits to Tavistock House and Gad's Hill and at Verey's in Regent Street, a place he much patronised. I remember one day meeting C. H. Townshend at Tavistock House and thinking him a very singular and not particularly agreeable man. Of course we had much and frequent talks about Italy. I have in my possession a great number of letters from Dickens."

---

[1] Later, the Rev. Newman Hall became associated with Christ Church, Westminster Bridge Road, opened 4 July 1876.

CHAPTER XVII

# June 1860 to 9 November 1867

GAD'S HILL ALONE, FIRST PERIOD

§ 128. *Marriage of Kate Dickens to C. A. Collins.*
*Death of Alfred Dickens,* 27 *July* 1860

IN July, Dickens's younger daughter Kate, who had great personal charm and in many respects resembled her mother, was married to Charles Allston Collins, brother of Wilkie Collins, and also a writer. Among the guests at Kate Dickens's wedding were Holman Hunt, Chauncey Hare Townshend, Charles Kent, Miss Mary Boyle, Percy Fitzgerald, who was a special favourite of Dickens, Fechter (of course), Edmund Yates, Dickens's old friend Thomas Beard, W. H. Wills,[1] Mrs Wills, Henry Fothergill Chorley[2] the musical critic and Mr Frederic Lehmann and his wife, whose sister, Miss Chambers, was one of the bridesmaids. Speaking of Chorley, Edward FitzGerald said, "Dickens loved him,"[3] and that, in Fitz-Gerald's opinion, was sufficient evidence of his worth.

The carriages passed under triumphal arches to the church. The scarlet geranium, Dickens's favourite flower, flamed in the garden. All was gay. And yet all was not quite gay, for one who ought to have been there—the bride's mother—was not there. Her name, like the bride's, was Kate. Yet it seems the bells rang merrily.

As regards the bridegroom, none has spoken of him more highly than John Payne, who was strangely fascinated with

[1] Sub-editor of *All the Year Round.*
[2] He bequeathed £200 a year to Dickens's daughter, Mary.
[3] *Letters to Fanny Kemble,* p. 54.

his works, which he often praised in conversation with the author of this book. In the fine sonnet "Charles Allston Collins" [1] (*Carol and Cadence*, p. 174) he ranks C. A. Collins above his brother Wilkie and takes the opportunity to pay likewise a tribute to Dickens:

> Collins, the credit which thou mightest claim
> Hadst thou on honour's bederoll stood alone,
> Was shadowed by a brother better known,
> Though less deserving than thyself of name,
> And more yet by the world-involving fame
> Of one,[2] to whom thou stood'st, though not his own,
> In son's stead; he who dwelleth near the throne
> Must needs be cast in shadow by its flame;
> But I, that am "a borrower of the night" [3]
> And more to those who shun the garish light
> Incline than those who in the full noon-sheen
> Of public favour bask, too oft by chance,
> With thee "on wheels" to wander love and e'en
> A-horseback, through the wilder ways of France.

The last two lines are a reference to what Payne called Collins's "delightful books"—a *Cruise upon Wheels*, *The Bar Sinister* and a *New Sentimental Journey*. Payne once said to the author of this book, "Dickens is the second English writer. He comes next to Shakespeare. We go to Dickens for pathos as well as for humour." Payne added:

Humour is the salt of life. A man who has it can face the world without fear. It is wit and love combined. The difference between Dickens and Thackeray is that Dickens laughs *with* people, Thackeray laughs *at* people. *Martin Chuzzlewit* is Dickens's greatest book.

Payne's admiration for Dickens is also expressed in several of his other poems, notably "Trinitas Anglica" (*Vigil and Vision*, p. 65)—a tribute to Shakespeare, Dickens and Turner, which commences,

> Three names o'er all do glorify our land.

---

[1] C. A. Collins died in 1873 at the age of 45. His wife became Mrs Perugini.

[2] Dickens, of course.

[3] A reference to Payne's habit of writing and reading half the night. See the *Life of John Payne*, by Thomas Wright, 1919.

On 27 July Dickens lost his brother Alfred, who died at Manchester, leaving a widow and children to be relieved by Dickens.

Writing to a friend, Mrs Dickenson, on 19 August 1860, Dickens, after referring to his brother's death, says:

"My mother, who was also left to me when my father died (I never had anything left to me but relations), is in the strangest state of mind from senile decay, and the impossibility of getting her to understand what is the matter, combined with her desire to be got up in sables like a female Hamlet, illumines the dreary scene with a ghastly absurdity that is the chief relief I can find in it. Well, Life is a fight, and must be fought out.[1] Wilkie has finished his White Woman (if he has done with his flesh-coloured one,[2] I should mention that too) and is in great force."

In October 1860 Dickens was rather worried because a tale by Charles Lever [3] which was appearing in *All the Year Round* "had disappointed its readers"; he therefore "struck in" with a new story of his own—that translucent and well-nigh flawless gem—that epic of the marshes—*Great Expectations*, the first chapter of which appeared in its columns on 1 December 1860.

### § 129. "*Great Expectations*," 1 *December* 1860

What Tennyson was to the pine woods, Wordsworth to the mountain tarns, Cowper to elmy fields and whispering avenues, Dickens is to the "meshes." We have said that there was no poetry in Dickens; but by that we meant that he customarily looked at everything from a matter-of-fact, utilitarian point of view. When he attempts to write verse the effect is dismal; when he lays himself out to write poetical prose, we get the ludicrous sing-song of *The Old Curiosity Shop*; but when he forgets himself and talks lovingly of the Kentish marshes—the haunt of his boyhood

---

[1] Maggs's *Catalogue*, No. 548, p. 108.
[2] A reference to Collins's mistress.
[3] Dickens's *Letters to Charles Lever* were published in 1933 by Humphrey Milford. Reviewed in the *Dickensian*, 1 December 1833, p. 60.

and of old exciting days—he catches the divine afflatus, and even Saul is numbered among the prophets. As for the reader—to borrow that beautiful word first used, perhaps coined, by Sir Richard Burton—he is ensorcelled!

The story opens vividly. Even *Treasure Island*, with its "Old Sea Dog" and its "Fifteen Men on the Dead Man's Chest," does not more quickly rivet the attention. We stand in Cooling churchyard among the nettles. Beyond is the dark, flat wilderness, intersected with dykes, mounds and gates, with scattered cattle feeding on it. At our feet lie the quaint, lozenge-shaped stones to Pip's little brothers. Then comes Magwitch in coarse grey with a great iron on his leg. We are turned upside down, the church—"the lonely church right out on the marshes, with the graves round it"—goes head over heels before us, and when we come to ourselves we are seated on a high tombstone, while Magwitch is devouring ravenously the crust snatched from our pocket. Truly, we have all trembled with poor little Pip. The stones at Cooling may still be seen. Pip speaks of only five, but in reality there are thirteen—ten in one row and three close by another. Children of one family— Comport, of Cowling Court—who were buried about 1770. The marshes also figure in the dialogue between Trooper George and Phil Squod in *Bleak House* (Chapter 26). Hard by Cooling Church stand the picturesque Gate Towers of Cooling Castle.

*Great Expectations* differs from Dickens's other novels in the fact that the hero and heroine are really live and interesting characters with human faults and failings. Pip and Estella are neither nonentities nor angels. They are not drawn so pale that one can scarcely see them, and they are not too good for the world into which they happened to be precipitated. *Great Expectations* is the only book by Dickens in which the hero and heroine are the most interesting characters in it.

And there was a reason for this. Pip is to some extent Dickens himself as a boy in the dame school, and as a youth with ambitions. The year 1859, when this book was commenced, Dickens had for long been infatuated with Miss

Ellen Ternan and he was quite unable to keep out of his books persons in whom he was deeply interested. Estella is Ellen Lawless Ternan. Dickens was fond of twisting names in order to create those of characters. Thus Micawber was certainly "My father"; Edwin Drood was his correspondent, Edwin Drew mixed with the name of the landlord of the Sir John Falstaff inn whose name was Trood; and as already noticed,[1] though it may be merely a coincidence, the name chosen for the lady, Estella, contains the initial letters of Ellen Lawless Ternan, El la and Te. In any case, Estella's attitude to Pip was exactly that of Miss Ternan to Dickens. "You know," says Pip to her, "that I have loved you long and dearly."[2] In the "Violated Letter" he had referred to her as "a young lady for whom I have a great attachment and regard." His thoughts were continually upon her at this period and he was powerless to exclude her from his writings. But Estella does not return Pip's love. She says, "I have no heart. . . . I have no softness there, no—sympathy—sentiment—nonsense."[3]

"Yet," says Pip, "I loved Estella. . . . I loved her simply because I found her irresistible. Once for all; I knew to my sorrow, often and often, if not always, that I loved her against reason, against promise, against peace, against hope, against happiness, against all discouragement that could be."[4]

He says to her, "You have been the embodiment of every graceful fancy that my mind has ever become acquainted with."[5] She says, "Say no more. We shall never understand each other."[6]

He said to himself "I love her! I love her! I love her!" hundreds of times.[7] She was indeed his grand passion, compared with which all his previous passions were palenesses. He said again "I love—I adore Estella.[8] And yet when I think of Estella"—

"And when don't you, you know!" Herbert threw in, with his eyes on the fire.[9] "Can't you detach yourself?"

---

[1] Cr. ed., Chapter XVI, p. 59.    [2] Cr. ed., vol. 16, p. 273.
[3] *Ibid.*, p. 180.    [4] *Ibid.*, p. 176.    [5] *Ibid.*, p. 275.
[6] *Ibid.*, p. 274.    [7] *Ibid.*, p. 185.    [8] *Ibid.*, p. 187.    [9] *Ibid.*, p. 188.

GRAVES OF THE COMPORTS, COOLING

*Photo by J. Graham, 17 Ordnance Terrace, Chatham*

See page 297

"TOM TIDDLER'S GROUND"—THE COMMITTEE OF CONCOCTION

The figures, going from left to right, are A. Sala, Wilkie Collins, Charles Dickens, John Hollingshead.
The one with hair erect is either Wills or Moy Thomas

*From "The Queen," 21st December, 1861*

See page 305

"No; impossible!"

"You can't try, Handel!" [the name given by Herbert to Pip, who is certainly Dickens].

"No; impossible."

Forster, Collins, Sala knew of this passion, and these very words may have been used by Forster; certainly he frowned on it, as did Collins, Bohemian though he was. Reference was made earlier in these pages to the ease with which human beings deceive themselves. Dickens was not unaware of this weakness, for he puts into Pip's mouth the words, "All other swindlers upon earth are nothing to the self-swindlers, and with such pretences did I cheat myself."

Extreme in everything, Dickens in the presence of Ellen Ternan entirely lost his head. Her beauty sent him into a frenzy. Consciously or unconsciously he drew exactly in this book the condition of his own soul. Of unpremeditated pathos this story affords several striking examples, the most notable being the account of the death of Magwitch. The original of the river-side Inn to which Magwitch was taken by boat from London was the Lobster Smack, Canvey Island. "This boat journey," says Alex J. Philip, "is minutely and circumstantially described and is as accurate as a guide book." [1]

Mr Jaggers is cleverly done. He wrenched the weakest part of our dispositions out of us. "For myself," adds Pip, "I found that I was expressing my tendency to lavish expenditure, and to patronise Herbert, and to boast of my great prospects, before I quite knew that I had opened my lips." Of the minor characters the most pleasing is "the Aged," so comfortably provided for on Mr Wemmeck's toy estate at Walworth. Was ever a sullen fire more happily described than in Chapter 33: "A scorched leaf of a copy-book under a bushel of coal dust.[2] Who cannot see Joe in Pip's room—holding his hat "carefully with both hands, like a bird's nest with eggs in it," and refusing to hear of parting with it!

As Mr Andrew Lang says: Pip, Pumblechook, Mr Wopsle and Joe Gargery, are all immortal and cause laughter

[1] *A Dickens Dictionary*, by Alex J. Philip.    [2] Cr. ed., vol. 16, p. 59.

inextinguishable. Happy indeed is Dickens when dealing with a scene like that in which Joe and the "Strange man" figure.[1]

"Son of yours?" asked the strange man, looking at Pip.

"Well," said Joe, meditatively—not, of course, that it could be in any wise necessary to consider about it, but because it was the way of the Jolly Bargeman to seem to consider deeply about everything that was discussed over pipes; "well—no. No, he ain't."

"Nevvy?" said the strange man.

"Well," said Joe, with the same appearance of profound cogitation, "he is not—no, not to deceive you, he is *not*—my nevvy."

That is the kind of writing in which Dickens excels and which draws every reader to him.

Humour is not the salient characteristic of *Great Expectations*, but it is more to the fore than in several of the previous stories. One finds it notably in all that is said or done by that beautiful and noble character—that true gentleman, Joe Gargery. The hit where Magwitch gobbles mincemeat, meat, bone, bread, cheese, and pork pie all at once, reminds us of the different flavours detected by David Copperfield when his aunt succoured him at Dover. Then we call to mind the evening school where Mr Wopsle's great-aunt "went to sleep from six to seven every evening in the society of Youth, who had paid twopence per week each for the improving opportunity of seeing her do it." And Biddy's answer to Pip's enquiry whether he would have been good enough for her—

"Yes, I am not over particular," replied Biddy. "It scarcely sounded flattering, but I knew she meant well."

Excellent too is the dialogue between Pip and Wemmick.

"A man should never——" commences Pip.

—"Invest portable property in a friend," follows Wemmick. "Certainly he should not. Unless he wants to get rid of the friend—and then it becomes a question of how much portable property it may be worth to get rid of him."

The droll sketch of Bill Barley,[2] ex-ship's purser and

[1] Cr. ed., vol. 16, p. 58.
[2] Cr. ed., vol. 16, Chapters 46, 55, 58, pp. 285, 340, 363.

drunken old rascal, was a favourite with Swinburne, and he used to quote Bill as his contemporaries quoted the Bible, or as he himself quoted Mrs Gamp.

What an exquisite thumb-nail picture is that of Bill Barley's daughter Clara!

"As we were thus conversing while old Barley's sustained growl vibrated in the beam that crossed the ceiling, the room door opened, and a very pretty, slight, dark-eyed girl of 20 or so, came in with a basket in her hand; whom Herbert tenderly relieved of the basket, and presented blushing, as Clara."

The theme of Chuzzlewit was hypocrisy, of Dombey, pride. That of *Great Expectations*[1] is "ingratitude"— Pip's ingratitude, of which he at last bitterly repented, to honest, forgiving Joe. *Bleak House* assailed the Court of Chancery; *Little Dorrit* the Circumlocution Office; *Great Expectations* lunges at the ridiculous funeral customs of the time. Dickens admirably and derisively describes the mutes as "two dismally absurd persons, each ostentatiously exhibiting a crutch done up in a black bandage, as if that instrument could possibly communicate comfort to anybody." The six bearers were "stifled and blinded under a horrible black velvet housing with a white border," the whole looking "like a blind monster with twelve human legs, shuffling and blundering along under the guidance of two keepers." But he adds, with fine, though good-natured sarcasm, "the neighbourhood highly approved of these arrangements." "Dickens once," says Mr W. R. Hughes, "described a funeral as 'an army of black beetles.'"

§ 130. *Originals of Persons and Places in "Great Expectations"*

The original of Satis House, the residence of Miss Havisham, is the picturesque, ivy-clad Elizabethan mansion standing near the Vines—a Rochester public pleasure ground—called Restoration House. The Three Jolly Bargemen, Joe's house of call at Cooling, was literally The Three Horseshoes, and Mr Pumblechook's house may have

---

[1] *Great Expectations* was dramatised by Shafto Scott, and performed with the title *My Unknown Friend* at Wallack's Theatre, New York, 1872.

been a portion of the picturesque row of tenements, one of which was "Mr Sapsea's House," opposite Eastgate House, in Rochester High Street. Dickens's first intention had been to make the tale end sorrowfully, but at Lord Lytton's suggestion he altered it, and allowed Pip and Estella to marry.

Canon Benham sets down Joe Cargery's forge as the one at Cliffe-at-Hoo, near Cooling.[1] The original of Joe is said to have been a John Cayford; a blacksmith who often did jobs for Dickens in the Tavistock House period.[2] Some idea for Miss Havisham's manner of living may have been taken from the well-known incident in connection with Dirty Dick's, a famous tavern of bygone times, situated in Bishopsgate Street Without. Dirty Dick (Nathanial Bentley) lost his bride on the morning they were to be wedded, and the room containing the banquet was ordered by the bridegroom to be closed and sealed, and so it remained during his lifetime. The incident is related in one of the numbers of *Household Words*, consequently Dickens must have been acquainted with it. The Blue Boar is no doubt The Bull, Rochester.

Few of Dickens's books are capable of furnishing the textuary with more numerous or more striking aphorisms. Take that beautiful saying regarding our tears. "Heaven knows we need never be ashamed of our tears, for they are rain upon the blinding dust of earth, overlying our hard hearts."

Mr Wemmick says: "It's a good rule never to leave documentary evidence if you can help it, because you don't know when it may be put in." "Our worst weaknesses and meannesses," says Pip, "are usually committed for the sake of the people whom we most despise." *Great Expectations* contains eight drawings by Marcus Stone, the best being the frontispiece "With Estella after all." Not only did Dickens dedicate this story to his friend Chauncey Hare Townshend, he also presented him with the manuscript.

[1] *Dickens and Kent.*
[2] See *Daily Chronicle*, 21 June 1904. Dickens's amanuensis at that time was a man named Meadows.

§ 131. *Second Series of Paid Readings.  Death of Arthur Smith, October* 1861.  *"Tom Tiddler's Ground"*

The Christmas Number of *All the Year Round* for 1860 was entitled, *A Message from the Sea*, of which Chapters 1, 2 and 5 were written by Dickens.    It tells how an American Captain Jorgan, much given to slapping his leg, turns up at a north Devonshire village and upsets the equanimity of a young affianced couple (Alfred and Kitty) by producing a bottle recovered from the sea, containing the statement that the money, £500, which the young man had inherited from his father, and on the strength of which he hoped to marry, was stolen.    Alfred is resolved that, if possible, the money shall be restored to its rightful owner, and as it is not his, decides, regretfully, that the marriage must be put off. The owner turns out to be Kitty's father, who refuses the money; so the lovers are able to marry after all.

The tale, poor as it is, contains some agreeable Dickens touches.    Captain Jorgan's advice, "If ever you come— or even if ever you don't come—to a desert place, use your eyes and your spy-glass well; for the smallest thing you see may prove of use to you," commends itself to all, and we endorse his remarks on "doing nothing"—"Any fool or fainting heart can do that, and nothing can come of nothing."    Some time in 1860, Dickens burnt "in a great holocaust" all the private letters that had been received by him.

In March 1861 he commenced his second series of Public Readings.    The first six were given at St James's Hall—St Martin's Hall having been burnt down.    They were superintended by Mr Arthur Smith, and the success that attended them was as conspicuous as that of the first series; but towards the end Dickens's exertions told upon him seriously.    He slept "horribly" and with "head dazed and worn out by gas and heat."

His praise as a reader was sung far and wide.    Sir Squire Bancroft thus describes one of these occasions, the scene being St James's Hall:

"Two vast audiences thronged the large hall.  We were seated in the front row of chairs, and plainly saw the tears provoked by the wonderful reception given to Dickens directly he stepped upon the platform. Those who had heard him often said he read as if inspired—certainly he never had a finer audience. We all seemed spell-bound under his varying powers, and, after the lapse of many years, the emotions he so quickly in their turn aroused live in the memory, and will be there quite vividly while we have life."

In order to confer with Lord Lytton, whose *Strange Story* was to appear in *All the Year Round*, Dickens, accompanied by Miss Georgina Hogarth and his daughter Mary, passed a week at Knebworth, where he met Lord Orford and Mr Arthur Helps. In their company and in the company of the two ladies, he called at Elmwood, Redcoats Green, near Stevenage in order to see Mr James Lucas, a man of ample means who had gained notoriety by voluntarily spending, in a house which he had allowed to fall into decay, a life of wretchedness and filth. People spoke of his matted hair and staring eyes. Wearing nothing except a "blanket and a skewer," and crouching all day long among heaps of ashes in his foul kitchen, he had also obtained a name for generosity, owing to his habit of bestowing coppers and gin on tramps, and sweets—pecks of which he kept by him— on children. He had even, in Dickens's words, "blanketed and skewered and sooted and greased himself into the London papers."

In September 1861, Mr Arthur Smith fell ill. He died on 9 October, and Dickens attended the funeral. The next day Dickens heard of the death of his brother-in-law, Henry Austin, who was buried on 14 October. In losing Smith, Dickens felt as though his right arm had gone. Mr Headland, who succeeded him, did his best, but the readings at Norwich, which followed, were not a success. It was then discovered that Austin had been in straitened circumstances, and Dickens generously came forward and paid his brother-in-law's debts. Indeed the debts of some relative or other "Poor Papa" seemed to be perpetually called upon to pay.

On 25 November 1861, Dickens was at Berwick-on-Tweed on his way to Edinburgh. He read in Queen Street Hall, Edinburgh, on 27, 28 and 30 November and 2

JOHN HOLLINGSHEAD, TAKEN ABOUT 1859

*Photo by Herbert Watkins, Regent Street*

See page 305

"THE FIVE BELLS," NEW CROSS ROAD, LONDON

Previous to 1841

"THE FIVE BELLS," NEW CROSS ROAD

Erected in 1841

See page 310

December 1861.[1]  The Christmas Number of *All the Year Round* was *Tom Tiddler's Ground*, an account of the visit to Mr James Lucas the Hertfordshire hermit.

Lucas, who was presented by somebody with a copy, used to asseverate that Dickens's uncomplimentary story was false from beginning to end—no such traveller having visited him, no such conversation as reported having ever taken place.  He also sent an article to the Press.  No doubt the story has some of Dickens's embellishments, but the description of the monomaniac and his surroundings must have been substantially correct.

In a letter to Mr F. D. Finlay (27 March 1862) Dickens says in reference to the article written by Mr Mopes [Lucas], "There is not a syllable of truth in it.  It is sheer invention of the wildest kind." [2]  Lucas died in April 1874 at the age of 63, and was buried in Hackney Churchyard.

On 3 December 1861 Dickens, in a letter to Thomas Adolphus Trollope, refers to a capital story in *All the Year Round*, the "Two Sea Born Babies."  "Wonderfully droll, I think.  I may say so without blushing, for it is not by me.  It was done by Wilkie Collins."

In *The Queen* for 21 December 1861, appeared a large and amusing picture entitled *Tom Tiddler's Ground, The Committee of Concoction, Extraordinary Proceedings in Wellington Street*.

Dickens, George Augustus Sala, Wilkie Collins and John Hollingshead are round a table, all in a stage of excitement.  At the back is Moy Thomas with his hair on end.  A boy is bringing in two big bottles of ink.  On the wall are two sketches "Jupiter and his satellites" and "Collins Wilkie ye modern Frankenstein."  The letterpress is as amusing as the picture.  It runs:

Mr Charles Dickens having unanimously moved himself into the chair remarked that the eyes of Europe were upon them.  (A laugh.) The eyes of America had something else to look out for, in fact they

---

[1] There are advertisements and notices in the *Scotsman* of that time.
[2] The *Dickensian*, 1 September 1934, p. 276.

were black eyes.[1] (Roars of laughter.) Sala wanted descriptions of low life, Wilkie Collins desired murder. Hollingshead's chief thought was on the £ s. d. likely to come in. Moy Thomas entirely concurred in the views "Holly" had so well expressed. Collins read large extracts from a manuscript which he pulled from his pocket. Eventually it was decided that the next number of *All the Year Round* should consist of seven chapters, entitled "Tom Tiddler's Ground," three to be by Dickens.[2]

On 20 September 1862, Dickens tells Wilkie Collins that he finds his story *No Name* "wonderfully fine"; "far before and beyond *The Woman in White*."[3] I was certain from the *Basil*[4] days that you were the writer who would come ahead of all the field—being the only one who combined invention and power, both humorous and pathetic, with that invincible determination to work, and that profound conviction that nothing of worth is to be done without work, of which triflers and feigners have no conception."

Early in November 1862, died Mr George Beadnell, Mrs Winter's father, at the age of 89. Mrs Winter sent Dickens a touching account of his last moments, and Dickens, who replied from Paris, Rue du Faubourg St Honoré 27, on Monday, 17 November 1862, after mentioning that he had read of the event in Galignani sent condolences, along with kind regards to her and her sister Margaret (Mrs Lloyd). Later, Mr Winter took holy orders and became in 1866 curate at Little Eversham, Cambridge. He was afterwards vicar of Alnmouth, Northumberland, where he died on 22 March 1871. The Christmas Number of *All the Year Round* for 1862 was *Somebody's Luggage*.

At what date Dickens first became acquainted with Charles Albert Fechter the actor is uncertain, but from 1863 to 1867 Fechter was lessee of the Lyceum theatre, London, and Dickens assisted him financially. On 10 January 1863 Fechter appeared in *The Duke's Motto*; and

[1] A reference to the Civil War then being waged between the North and South.
[2] Cr. ed., vol. 15, p. 170.
[3] *Letters to Wilkie Collins*, p. 125.　　[4] *Basil*, by Wilkie Collins, 1852.

he and Dickens became the most intimate friends.    Indeed he was praised by Dickens extravagantly.


§ 132.  *Dickens on the Mormons.   Death of Mrs Hogarth,*
*5 August* 1863.   *Death of Dickens's mother,*
*September* 1863.   *Mrs Lirriper's Lodgings, Fifth*
*Christmas No.* (1863), *"A.T.R."*

Dickens remained in Paris in January and February 1863, and after his return the second series of his readings was continued.

In April 1863 he lost his friend Egg.    Mourning the loss of friend after friend—for he had already parted from his brother Alfred, Arthur Smith, his brother-in-law, Mr Austin, and others—he recalled again a sad passage from *The Frozen Deep*, and then added—"However, this won't do.    We must close up the ranks and march on."    In July he hears with pleasure that Mr Percy Fitzgerald was engaged upon a Life of his old favourite Lawrence Sterne.

We get a peep at Dickens at this time in an undated letter written by (Sir) George Grove.    "On Thursday we went to a great dinner at Westbourne Terrace."    Dickens and his sister-in-law (Miss Georgina Hogarth) Browning and others were present.    "Dickens," says Grove, "was very amusing, but not in the least forced.    He was full of a ship of Mormon emigrants which he had been seeing, 1,200 of the cleanest, best conducted, most excellent looking people he ever saw."    This recalls Dickens's article in *The Uncommercial Traveller* entitled, "Bound for the Great Salt Lake." [1]

On 5 August 1863, died at the age of 68, Mrs Dickens's mother, wife of Mr George Hogarth, and in September Dickens lost his own mother, who was 73.

Although Dickens had to answer hundreds of letters he was ever willing to encourage young and ambitious correspondents.    Thus on 14 October 1863, he tells Miss Grace Barrow—with the spirit of whose letter he was pleased, "Through the practical steady, quiet course that

[1] Cr. ed., vol. 16, p. 518.

you have taken lies the road to self-respect and self-made independence. . . . In every art there would be far less misery and bitterness if many more began as wisely." In the middle of February 1864, Dickens took a house in London, 57 Gloucester Place, Hyde Park, where he stayed till June.

On Christmas Eve, 24 December 1863, occurred the death of Thackeray, when Dickens, giving to oblivion, as a wise man should, all bygone petty jealousies and animosities, penned to the memory of his great and gifted rival a warm and touching tribute (see *Cornhill Magazine*, February 1864). In February 1864 Dickens received another terrible shock in the death at Calcutta of his son Walter.

On 3 June 1864, died Dickens's friend William Johnson Fox, and on 2 July appeared in *All the Year Round* a review of Percy Fitzgerald's *Life of Sterne*, called by Dickens "Two volumes of lively biography." On 29 October 1864 Dickens, to his great sorrow, lost his friend John Leech. The Christmas Number of *All the Year Round* for that year was *Mrs Lirriper's Legacy*. Collins, who by this time had become Dickens's right hand, was then living in Harley Street, whence he removed to Melcombe Place, Dorset Square, and afterwards to 90 Gloucester Place near Portman Square.[1]

At the end of the year, Dean Hole, who purposed writing Leech's biography, wrote to ask whether Dickens possessed any letters from Leech, and Dickens, replying in the negative (20 December 1864) remarked: "A year or two ago, shocked by the misuse of the private letters of public men, which I constantly observed, I destroyed a very large and very rare mass of correspondence."[2]

§ 133. *Dickens at the Five Bells, Hatcham*

In May 1864, appeared the first number of another long story by Dickens, *Our Mutual Friend*, which he commenced in Gloucester Place. No one nowadays would use the expression "Our Mutual Friend" when the term required

---

[1] Collins died at 82 Wimpole Street.    [2] See § 131.

is "Our Common friend," but previous to the issue of this tale it seems to have been current even among persons of education. Mr Rokesmith, as will be seen in Book I, Chapter 9,[1] is the common friend of Mrs Wilfer and Mr Boffin. Dickens himself had used the term previously in *Little Dorrit*, for instance, Book I, Chapter 10, where Mr Meagles is the "mutual friend" of Doyce and Clennam,[2] and in Book I, Chapter 24, where Flora boldly defends the term, calling it "that very proper expression."[3] To have an error in English stereotyped in the pages of one great book and in the title of another is a unique curiosity. The attention thus drawn to this error was the means of accomplishing its quietus. Not even Flora, with all her charm, was able to save it. Still it was very bold of her and of Dickens, too, for as early as 1852 (three years before the appearance of *Little Dorrit*) Macaulay had castigated Croker for using "the vulgarism of 'mutual friend' for 'common friend'." It rather looks as though Dickens shouted it out in defiance of Macaulay; just as naughty boys will shout things and then run away, only Dickens didn't run away.

The members of Dickens's family, curious to say, knew far less than other persons respecting his real life. Several of them wrote books about him, but they tell us practically nothing worth knowing. The truth is that he, like his father, but for a different reason, was in the habit of disappearing entirely from time to time from his home. To this habit there are references in *The Old Curiosity Shop*. His favourite retreat (and this is mentioned in no other work) was an apartment close to the Five Bells, an inn situated at the corner of Hatcham Park Road [4] and New Cross Road. He appears to have been there in 1853 just before he wrote *The Schoolboy's Story*.[5] He was certainly there in 1861, and later from time to time. It was evidently at Hatcham that "Old Cheeseman" in *The Schoolboy's Story*

[1] Cr. ed., vol. 12, p. 91.    [2] *Ibid.*, p. 110.    [3] *Ibid.*, p. 233.
[4] Formerly Five Bells Lane.
[5] Cr. ed., vol. 17, p. 266. It appeared in *Household Words*, December 1853.

entertained his schoolfellows so magnificently, "Fowls, tongues, preserves, trifles, crackers—eat all you can and pocket what you like," the masters being feasted afterwards at the Seven Bells, which evidently did duty for the Five Bells. "And didn't our fellows go down in a body and cheer outside the Seven Bells! Oh no!" This is the most charming of Dickens's short stories. It is better even than Maupassant's considerably later *La Question du Latin*, which has a similar theme, for it has humour as well as pathos.

In the Old Kent Road, a continuation of New Cross Road, stood the Deaf and Dumb establishment to which "Dr Marigold" took his Sophy for tuition (*Dr Marigold's Prescriptions*, Christmas Number, 1865, of *All the Year Round*). Dickens's most important connection with this neighbourhood was at the time (1864) he was writing *Our Mutual Friend*, a number of the scenes in it being laid there. The present Five Bells was erected in 1841. The whole neighbourhood was built over about 1850, and is part of a charity estate which was then largely agricultural land.[1]

Among Dickens's nieces was a pretty girl, Emily Barrow, who had as a particular friend another pretty girl, Charlotte Elizabeth Lane, whose parents lived at Lewisham, not far from Hatcham. Both girls attended a private school in Lewisham High Street, where they learnt French, Music and Dancing together. Soon after leaving school they heard that Dickens was in apartments near the Five Bells; and Emily resolved to call on her famous kinsman. Charlotte Elizabeth accompanied her. Dickens, who loved a pretty face even more than he loved apples (and Charlotte noticed that whenever possible there was a pyramid of apples on his table), was much taken with his callers and he invited them to Gad's Hill Place. He gave them a good time there and then took them to the Bank of England to see "the gold being shovelled up with shovels."

It will be remembered that Bella Wilfer in *Our Mutual Friend* "thought, as she glanced at the mighty Bank, how

[1] A drawing of the original Five Bells inn from a water colour dated 1837, is preserved in the British Museum, and was reproduced in *Reminiscences of Old Deptford*, by Thankfull Sturdie in 1895.

agreeable it would be to have an hour's gardening there with a bright copper shovel, among the money." The Barrow girls (for Emily had a sister) and Charlotte Elizabeth were often at Gad's Hill Place afterwards. Emily's brother Thomas Frederick, who also sometimes accompanied them, fell in love with Charlotte and sent her valentines. She was secured, however, not by Thomas Frederick, but by John Mantel, a young schoolmaster of Deptford; while Emily married Charlotte's uncle, George Frederick Lawrence, whom she had met when he was a pupil at the Lewisham School. Charlotte Elizabeth's and John Mantel's was a run-away marriage like John Rokesmith's and Bella's. Roke-smith and Bella ran away because Mrs Wilfer was "wearing," and John Mantel and Charlotte ran away because Mr Lane's second wife was "wearing." The Rokesmith wedding took place at the neighbouring Greenwich.

The schools described by Dickens "for they were two-fold as the sexes"—were "down in that district tending to the Thames, where Kent and Surrey meet. . . . The schools were newly built," but Dickens's whole description of the neighbourhood tallies precisely with the description of those who knew it in the fifties and sixties; and it is most likely that the droll dialogues between Miss Peecher and Mary Anne originated from the chattering of Emily and Charlotte about their school experiences—and perhaps one of the two was the Mary Anne who when answering a question "stretched out her arm as if to hail a cab or an omnibus."

When Charlotte and Emily were at Gad's Hill Place they noticed that Dickens was often moody. "He would sit at the table oblivious of all seated near him and it was difficult at such times to get him to enter into any conversation. It would almost appear as though he was in a temper if anyone spoke to him. Then he would suddenly push back his chair; leave the table while in the middle of a meal, hurry off to his writing, and sit for an hour or two. Members of his family would afterwards go and peep at his manuscript, often coming away laughing at what they had read. John Mantel and his wife settled in after years at Olney, where the author of this book often conversed with them about

311

Dickens.[1]  Dickens's sarcastic references to Joanna South-cott also link him with Deptford.  In Church Street stood the chapel (later a theatre) in which she preached.  Her connection with it was local talk and in Dickens's time she had followers here though she had died in 1814.

## § 134. *The Staplehurst Accident, 9 June 1865.*
### *The Characters in "Our Mutual Friend"*

In the spring of 1865 Dickens took a house in Somer's Place, Hyde Park, and in May he made, for his health's sake, a journey to Paris.  On his way home on 9 June, he very nearly lost his life in a terrible railway accident near Staple-hurst.  The bridge over the river was broken down, and all the carriages except that in which Dickens had been seated were in the water.  His carriage "caught upon the turn" by some of the ruin of the bridge, hung suspended and balanced in an apparently impossible manner.  After help-ing out his fellow passengers, and assisting, to the best of his ability, those who were injured, he suddenly remembered having had with him a portion of the MS. of *Our Mutual Friend*; consequently he clambered back for it.  The rescued number was that describing the reception of Mr and Mrs Lammle by Mr and Mrs Boffin, who had invited this precious pair to breakfast, and the wedding of Miss Bella Wilfer.  Indeed he exhibited great presence of mind.  Mrs Dickens wrote to congratulate him on his escape.  In reply he said he was "glad to receive her good wishes." He told her that he was shaken "not by the shock but by the two or three hours' work among the dead and dying."

For some weeks after, he could not bear the thought of railway travelling, and in order to avoid it, he (for he had given up Gloucester Place) left Gad's Hill and took up his abode temporarily in the town house of his friend, Mr Milner Gibson, 5 Hyde Park Place.  He never after entered a railway carriage without enduring mental suffering.

Some of the characters in *Our Mutual Friend* fail to

[1] From notes supplied by Mrs Mantel and her daughter Mrs Nancy Adkinson of Wolverton.

interest us. Podsnap, Veneering, Twemlow (though "a well conducted old female who does no harm"), Riah and Miss Wren, whatever their virtues only weary us. Not so the petulant Bella and her cherubic Pa. They would have irradiated any work of Dickens's, but in *Our Mutual Friend* they are supreme—Miss Bella "so insolent, so trivial, so capricious, so hard to touch, and yet so pretty," and "R.W." who recalls that other pink of clerks, Mr Bob Cratchet.

The humour enveloping Mr Silas Wegg is usually of so cheap a kind that we find ourselves sometimes enquiring whether it can be Dickens's at all. Wegg, however, whatever may be said against him, is, with his wooden leg—the "other one"—as Mr Venus oddly calls it, an undoubtedly picturesque figure; and but for him, that delightful scene in which he badgers Mr Boffin (Bk. IV, chap. 3) and the equally delightful sequel to it (Bk. IV, chap. 13) would have been impossible.

Bradley Headstone is a strikingly lifelike portrait of the machine-made, mechanical schoolmaster. "He had acquired mechanically a great store of teacher's knowledge. He could do mental arithmetic mechanically, sing at sight mechanically, blow various wind instruments mechanically, even play the great church organ mechanically," but there was not a rag of imagination or an original idea in his head. Until recently it was supposed to be a virtue in the state to manufacture such men; who in their turn manufactured mechanical pupils. The fact is now being grasped that so far from its being a virtue, it is a useless absurdity to attempt to grind all children in the same mill. Is not that scene droll in which Miss Peecher catechises Mary Anne, who kept "stretching out her arm, as if to hail a cab or omnibus!"

The columnar Mrs Wilfer "with a condescending stitch in her side which was her company manner," is also true to nature, and most folk have met her double. Podsnap was Forster. Riah, the benevolent old Jew, was created to gratify a Jewish lady who complained that in the character of Fagin an injustice had been done to her race. The saint, however, is not worthy to black the devil's boots. Most people are evil-minded enough to prefer Fagin. Two

313

years later the lady presented Dickens with a copy of Benisch's Hebrew and English Bible, with the inscription, "Presented to Charles Dickens, in grateful and admiring recognition of the noblest quality man can possess, that of atoning for an injury as soon as conscious of having inflicted it."

Mr Boffin's prototype was a wealthy dust contractor and philanthropist named Henry Dodd, who owned a huge dust heap in Shepherdess Fields, Islington. The death-bed of Little Johnny owed its origin to Dickens's visit to the Children's Hospital in Great Ormond Street.[1] The original of Mr Venus's establishment was No. 42 St Andrew Street (near Seven Dials), kept by a taxidermist named Willis. After referring to it, Percy Fitzgerald said to Dickens, "I have found out the original of Venus," on which Dickens said, "You are right." *Our Mutual Friend* was issued in twenty monthly parts at one shilling each. It was illustrated with forty woodcuts by Marcus Stone.[2]

As before stated, much of the humour of *Our Mutual Friend* is unworthy of Dickens.

The description of Mr Boffin's visit to Mr Lightwood's is really amusing and Mr Lightwood's boy who mostly spent his time "chopping at the flies on the window sill" was an original young gentleman who quite deserved "the couple of pound" which Mr Boffin gave him for nothing.

There is a piquant reference to the quarrels of authors in Book I, Chapter 15. "Lor," cried Mrs Boffin, "What I say is the world's wide enough for all of us!" "So it is, my dear," said Mr Boffin, "when not literary. But when so, not so." The election at Pocket Breeches pales before that at Eatanswill, but what an excellent thumbnail picture is that of the "feeble little town hall on crutches, with some onions and bootlaces under it, which the legal gentleman says are a market." Unforgettable is the reference to the begging letters received by Mr Boffin, among the corre-

---

[1] See Chapter XVI, § 114.
[2] Dickens supplied instructions. Thus on September 30 1865 he suggests as frontispiece for the second volume, a picture of Mr Boffin digging up the Dutch bottle—Wegg and Venus in the distance.

spondents being "several daughters of general officers long accustomed to every luxury of life (except spelling)."

If, however, *Our Mutual Friend* has little real humour, it has much heart, Dickens's amiable disposition exhibiting itself in almost every chapter. He is here as he was in the *Christmas Carol* the children's kind and sympathetic friend. The appearance of *Our Mutual Friend* was followed by an appreciative review of it, from the pen of Mr Edward S. Dallas,[1] in *The Times*, and Dickens as proof of the pleasure it gave him presented Mr Dallas with the manuscript of the story, which found its way to America.

Says one who has seen it, "Almost always writing on thick blue note-paper, and with blue ink, Dickens has been faithful to his rule in this MS. The blue ink is not always of the best and the fineness and closeness of the writing are enough to render the most amiable of experienced printers insane."

Dickens's contempt, often displayed in his stories, for the man who has, or thinks he has no field in which to exert his energy, is conspicuous in the conversation between Eugene and Mortimer (Bk. I, chap. 3). "The pair of preserved frogs, sword in hand with their point of honour still un-settled," which adorned the window of Mr Venus, were no doubt the pair that always stood on Dickens's desk.

It is only the first half of the story that is dull, even though that is here and there agreeably illuminated by sparkles which never fail to be produced when Bella and her Pa come into contact. The second half is in the very best vein of the later Dickens, and abounds in delightful scenes, among which stand prominently out "The Golden Dustman at his worst" (III, 15); the Feast where Bella, her Pa, and Roke-smith dine so charmingly in Veneering's office (III, 16), and Mrs Boffin laying bare the plot (IV, 13) with its touches of genuine pathos.

To give his stories a verisimilitude and to increase their vividness, Dickens often paints minutely. Of this habit we have many examples in *Our Mutual Friend*. This is con-spicuous on the occasion in which Wegg (accompanied by

[1] He married Miss Glyn the actress. Mr Dallas was a Scotchman.

Mr Venus) found himself for the last time in Boffin's mansion. "They were shown into a waiting-room, where the all-powerful Wegg wore his hat and whistled, and with his forefinger stirred up a clock that stood upon the chimney-piece, until he made it strike." This is a small matter, but how real it makes the whole of the succeeding interview! Mr Wegg's impudence could not possibly have been brought more startlingly before us. In Mr Wegg, with his "Miss Elizabeth, Master George, Aunt Jane, and Uncle Parker" we have again the reiterative trick, but here it is not objectionable, and in the last scene, where Wegg actually puts money value upon these nonentities, the effect is really rich. After all deductions *Our Mutual Friend* still remains a wonderful work.

In April 1865 Charles Albert Fechter appeared at the Lyceum in *Belphegor, the Mountebank*, a play adapted from the French by Charles Webb. One of the characters was Henri, a child, a part taken previously by a girl. According to Miss Kate Field, author of *C. H. Fechter* (Boston, U.S.A., 1882),[1] the version in which Fechter appeared was

---

[1] Brit. Museum, 11794, g. 34.

Four versions of Belphegor are known:

(1) *Belphegor, or The Marriage of the Devil*, a tragi-comedy acted at Queen's Theatre in Dorset Garden as early as 1691. (Works of John Wilson, published in 1874. Brit. Museum, 2302, b. 7.)

(2) *Belphegor, or the Mountebank and his Wife*, adapted from the French by J. Courtney. Produced at the Adelphi, 13 January 1851. There was an illustrated notice of it in the *Illustrated London News*, 18 January 1851. It is said also to have been produced at the Royal Surrey Theatre, 20 January 1851, by J. Courtney. (Lacy's Acting Plays, Brit. Museum, 2304, d. 7.)

(3) *Belphegor*, adapted from the French (the authors being Marc Fournier and M. Dennery) by Thomas Higgie and T. H. Lacy. (Lacy's Acting Plays, Brit. Museum, 2304, i. 1.) First performed at the Royal Victoria Theatre, 27 January 1851.

(4) *Belphegor, the Mountebank; or, Woman's Constancy*. Translated from the French (the authors being Fournier and Dennery) by Charles Webb. Volume 103 of French's Acting Plays. A continuation of Lacy's Acting Plays. Brit. Museum, 2304, g. 21. This was no doubt the Fechter-Dickens play.

A notice of the Fechter-Dickens play appeared in the *Illustrated London News*, 22 April 1865. Another notice appeared in the *Despatch* for 18 June 1865.

"entirely re-written by Charles Dickens, with a child's part introduced to display the great dramatic ability of Fechter's son, Paul, then a child of seven."

§ *135. Dickens on Clare, 15 August 1865. The Châlet, Third series of Paid Readings, George Dolby. "Dr Marigold's Prescriptions," Seventh Christmas No. (1865), "A.Y.R."*

In May 1865 appeared *The Life of John Clare* by Frederick Martin, a really delightful book. Dickens's comment on it, written on 15 August 1865, is worth quoting in order to show how little he understood that poet. "You read that life of Clare?" he says. "Did you ever see such preposterous exaggeration of small claims. And isn't it expressive, the perpetual prating of him in the book as *the Poet*." Clare, thanks to the labours of Edmund Blunden and others, has long since come to his own. The world will ever be indebted to the photographic eye and the ready pen of him who sang the primrose, asking:

> With its little brimming eye
> And its yellow rims so pale,
> And its crimped and curdled leaf
> Who can pass its beauties by!

But what cared Dickens for the scent of the bean-field or the scarlet of the clock-a-clay in the pip of the cowslip![1]

About this time—in 1865—Charles Albert Fechter presented to Dickens the Swiss châlet mentioned in § 103. This was his favourite retreat in summertime, and in it he wrote a great part of his later works. On 12 November 1865, died at the age of 55 at Holybourne, Alton, Hampshire, Mrs Gaskell. She was buried in the graveyard of Brook Street Chapel,[2] Knutsford, the place of worship so beautifully described in her story *Ruth*. There is a tablet

[1] Clare's 1820 volume was reviewed by William Gifford in the *Quarterly Review*, No. 45, May 1820.

[2] See *Brook Street Chapel*, by Rev. George A. Payne, 1934, *Banbury Guardian* office.

to her in Cross Street Unitarian Chapel, Manchester. Her husband died in 1884.

The Christmas Number for 1865 was *Dr Marigold's Prescriptions*, to which Dickens contributed three out of the eight chapters. The comment of probably every reader has been "Dickens had a tender heart." Preparations were then made for a third series of Public Readings. Dickens has on a previous page been described as the Literary Crœsus—with his perpetual cry Gold! Gold! Gold! But in the new campaign he was to outdo even himself. To quote Forster, "His task of the next three years, self-imposed, was to make the most money in the shortest time without any regard to the physical labour to be undergone."

Dickens hired No. 6 Southwick Place, Hyde Park, in March 1866, and during the third series of readings, made it his headquarters. He arranged to read there on Sunday, 12 March, his "Doctor Marigold," which he purposed to include in the Public Readings. Among those whom he invited to hear him were Forster and Robert Browning.

His health was declining, he had lost much of his buoyancy; but flash and glitter—flattery and gold together egged him on. Like the dazed moth he dashed again and again at the fascinating and deadly lamp. The business of the readings was managed by Mr George Dolby, who proved himself an invaluable aid, and did everything within his power to lighten his chief's burden. For weeks the two were constantly on the whirl. It was a perpetual round of railway carriage, reading-desk and weariness. It would have been a severe strain for a strong man, but Dickens's bodily vigour had long been failing him. His success was unabated. We read of tremendous halls, of thousands being turned away, vociferous cheering, enthusiastic crowds; but we also read of severe pains in the left eyeball, distressing seizures in the heart, attacks in the left foot, and sleepless nights.

In May 1866, his old friend, John Hullah, wrote to say that he would like to republish the songs in *The Village Coquettes*. Dickens replying on 8 May, from 6 South-

PRIOR'S GATEWAY, ROCHESTER

*Photo by J. Graham, 17 Ordnance Terrace, Chatham*

See page 347

CHARLES DICKENS

*Photo by Gurney, New York, 1868*

*T. W. Tyrrell's Collection*

wick Place, Hyde Park, said he was quite willing for their republication, only he did not wish his name to be associated with them. He preferred "to blush anonymously"— not being proud of his share in that play.[1] On 13 August he congratulated B. W. Proctor on his biography of Charles Lamb. "It is not," he wrote, "an ordinary triumph to do such justice to the memory of such a man. And I venture to add, that the fresh spirit with which you have done it impresses me as being perfectly wonderful." Later Percy Fitzgerald, who was collecting material for a biography of Garrick, wrote to ask Dickens about the actor's connection with Rochester. Dickens was unable to supply the information required, but he asks Fitzgerald: "How on earth do you find time to do all these books?"

On 10 May 1866, Dickens was billed to read "Dr Marigold" and "The Trial Scene from Pickwick" at Birmingham. He had a tremendous hall, but made the mistake of reading *Nicholas Nickleby* instead of "The Trial." He discovered the accident, however, at ten o'clock, and said if they liked he would give them "The Trial" too. He commented, in a letter written next day to Miss Georgina Hogarth, "They *did* like and I had another half-hour of it in that tremendous place."

§ 136. *Mrs Ternan returns to the Stage. Marriage of Frances Eleanor Ternan to T. A. Trollope,* 29 *October* 1866

Mrs Ternan, who had quitted the stage in 1858, returned to it again on 11 January 1866, to take the part of "Blind Alice" in the representation by Dickens's friend Fechter, at the Lyceum, of Scott's *Bride of Lammermoor* ("The Master of Ravenswood"). She was evidently given this part by Dickens, who was financially behind Fechter in his ventures at that theatre.[2] Forster tells us that

---

[1] See the *Dickensian*, December 1933, p. 22.

[2] Ley's *Forster*, p. 660; also p. 698. Dickens became Fechter's "helper in disputes, adviser on literary points, referee in matters of management, and for some years no face was more familiar than Fechter's at Gad's Hill or in the Office of *All the Year Round.*"

Dickens was moved to take this step "quite as much by generous sympathy with the difficulties of the position of an artist who was not an Englishman, as by genuine admiration of Fechter's acting.[1] To Fechter, who in the above-mentioned play took the part of Edgar Ravenswood, Dickens was a true friend and for "some years," to quote Forster again, "no face was more familiar than Fechter's at Gad's Hill, or in the office of *All the Year Round*."

On 27 October 1866, *The Frozen Deep* was billed to be acted at the Olympic Theatre, London. Henry Neville played Richard Wardour, Lydia Foote Clara Burnham. On 29 October Thomas Adolphus Trollope married Frances Eleanor Ternan, sister of Ellen Lawless Ternan. Writing to Trollope on 2 November, Dickens says:

"I should have written immediately to congratulate you on your then approaching marriage and to assure you of my most cordial and affectionate interest in all that nearly concerns you had I known how best to address you. No friend that you have can be more truly attached to you than I am. I congratulate you with all my heart. . . . As to your wife's winning a high reputation out of your house. . . . I have not the least doubt of her power to make herself famous. . . . I little thought what an important master of the ceremonies I was when I first gave your present wife an introduction to your mother." (See § 123.)

He expressed himself delighted when they both signified their intention of continuing to contribute to *All the Year Round*.

T. A. Trollope and Miss F. E. Ternan had both lived in Italy and had been close friends long before their marriage. Both spoke Italian fluently and both were authorities on and wrote upon Italian literature. It is probable that most of the articles on Italian subjects in both Dickens's periodicals were supplied by "The Italian Trollopes," as Percy Fitzgerald calls them. It was natural that Dickens should be drawn towards the sister of his friend Ellen Lawless Ternan, and when Mrs F. E. Trollope sent him her story *Aunt Margaret's Trouble*, he gladly accepted it. The

[1] Ley's *Forster*, p. 698.

first chapter appeared in *All the Year Round* on 14 July 1866, and the last on 18 August 1866.

"To the Italian Trollopes," says Percy Fitzgerald, "Dickens was always partial. I well remember the earnest admiration with which he spoke of that short pathetic tale *Aunt Margaret's Trouble*—the rapturous way in which he praised it. It seemed to me rather of the goody-goody or household pattern, but I have no doubt he was right in his view." It is evident, however, that Dickens's friendship with Miss Ellen Lawless Ternan had something to do with his partiality for her sister's work. However, the public took to the story, for when in 1866 it was published in book form, it went into seven editions. Dickens further showed his appreciation of Mrs Trollope's work by giving her a commission for a long and serious story to be called *Mabel's Progress*. She and her husband often collaborated.

Her other novels were *Veronica* (1870), see § 145; *A Charming Fellow* (1876); *Black Spirits and White* (1877); *Like Ships on the Sea* (1883); *The Sacristan's Household* (1884); *The Unfortunate Marriage* (1888); *Madame Leroux* (1890); *Among Aliens* (1890); *How it Strikes a Contemporary* (1892); *That Vita Wheel* (1892). She was also the author, with her husband, of *The Homes and Haunts of the Italian Poets* (1881). She translated P. Cossa's *Nero* (1881) and C. Streter's *Italy from the Alps to Mount Etna*.[1] Mrs Frances Eleanor Trollope must not be confused with her mother-in-law, Mrs Frances Trollope, who died in Florence on 6 October 1863, in the house of Mr T. A. Trollope. Frances Eleanor Trollope published a biography of her in 1895.

§ 137. *"Mugby Junction." Second Visit to Ireland. Hoghton Tower*

During the autumn there were cricket matches in the field adjoining Gad's Hill Place, and Dickens, encouraged by their success, organised in the winter foot races and

[1] See *What I remember,* by T. A. Trollope, 3 vols., 1887–9.

rustic sports there. As many as two thousand persons attended, every competitor was furnished with a list of rules, and put upon his honour to assist in preserving order; everything went rapturously.

The Christmas Number of *All the Year Round* for 1866 was *Mugby Junction*, and Dolby tells us the origin of it. He says, that during one of their journeys, upon their arrival at Rugby, it was found that the carriage in which they were travelling was on fire, and while the burning carriage was being detached from the train, Dickens and Wills went in search of coffee. "The appurtenances of the refreshment room were wretched and the manners of the woman in charge deplorable. A cup of coffee having been passed to him, Dickens extended his hand for the sugar and milk, when the woman snatched them back and told him he shouldn't have any milk and sugar till he had paid for the coffee. A page in buttons was so tickled that he burst out into an uncontrollable fit of laughter." In the next Christmas Number, he appeared as the Boy at Mugby in *Mugby Junction*. The first chapter is called "Barbox Brothers," derived, no doubt, from Tarbox, a well-known Rugby surname.

Dickens, writing in reference to his next batch of Readings, says: "I start on Wednesday afternoon, 15 January, for Liverpool, and then go on to Chester, Derby, Leicester and Wolverhampton. On Tuesday, 29 January, I read in London again, and in February I read at Manchester; then go on into Scotland."[1] While taking a rest at the Bridge of Allan he wrote to Collins chiefly in order to give his opinion of Charles Reade's new novel *Griffith Gaunt*. He says:

"I regard it as the work of a highly accomplished writer and a good man, a writer with a brilliant fancy and a graceful and tender imagination. . . . . I am staying in this quiet, pretty place to recruit a little. To-morrow night I am in Glasgow again, and on Friday (22 February) and Saturday in Edinburgh. Then I turn homeward for Tuesday (26 February) night at St James's Hall. Enormous crowds everywhere."

---

[1] Kitton's *Charles Dickens*, p. 340.

In March he proceeded to Belfast (this was his second visit to Ireland), where he read in the Ulster Hall on Wednesday, 20 March 1867, and where he met again his friend Francis Dalzell Finlay. There were special trains from surrounding districts, and so great was the crowd that numbers were unable to obtain admission. Dickens spoke not from the usual platform, but from an extemporised one near the floor. A eulogistic account of the Readings appeared in the Press, with only one faint note of adverse criticism. "His voice," said the reporter, "appears somewhat uniform."

From Belfast he proceeded to Dublin whence on 22 March he wrote to Miss Georgina Hogarth, telling her that he hoped to be in London next day. On 25 April he was at Preston, and finding that his next engagement was at Blackburn, distant only twelve miles, he sent his men with the effects on by rail, and he and Dolby did the journey on foot. On the way they came upon the picturesque ruins of Hoghton Tower [1] and Dickens, who, just then, had on the anvil a short story which he had undertaken to write for America, was curious enough to make an inspection. As a result Hoghton Tower became the scene of *George Silverman's Explanation*.[2] He read at Blackburn on 26 April.

On Wednesday, 1 May 1867, he was able to write from Stoke-upon-Trent to Collins, "To-morrow night at Warrington will finish my present course—with the exception of one night at Croydon, and one more night at St James's Hall. I shall be at Gad's from Saturday (4 May) to Monday." Everywhere the Readings continued to be received with tumultuous applause, and Dickens often exhibited the high spirits of his early manhood. In an account of one of the journeys we read of Wills and Dolby whistling in the train while Dickens danced the sailor's hornpipe; but the most ludicrous incident of all occurred at Southsea near Portsmouth. Here, as Dickens, Wills and Dolby were passing through one of the streets,

[1] Since restored. It is the residence of the De Hoghton family.
[2] Cr. ed., vol. 15, p. 617. See our Chapter XVIII, § 139.

Dickens took upon himself to imitate the frolics of a clown of the Grimaldi type, and having mounted three steps leading to one of the houses, was proceeding to lie down, clown fashion, on the upper step, when the door opened, and, to the intense amusement of Dolby and Wills, a stout woman appeared. While all three were running away like naughty schoolboys, the wind lifted Dickens's hat, and the chase for it rendered the incident all the more ludicrous. A parting glance at the scene of action showed every doorstep and window occupied by amused onlookers.

Dolby describes Dickens, who wore a pea-jacket or "reefer," and a broad-brimmed hat, worn jauntily on one side, as upright and sinewy with wiry moustache, grizzly beard, face deep lined and bronzed, and large eyes. He had "the iron will of a demon, and the tender pity of an angel— his whole mien reminding of nothing so much as a Viking." On 18 May 1867 died Dickens's friend Clarkson Stanfield. Both Dickens and Mark Lemon were present at the funeral, and the quarrel that had taken place between them was made up. On 5 June 1867, Dickens presided at the Ninth Anniversary Festival of the Railway Benevolent Society at Willis's Rooms, London. During the year Wilkie Collins was contributing to *All the Year Round* his novel *The Moonstone*. Dickens after reading the first three numbers wrote to Wills 13 June 1867: "It is a very curious story—with excellent character in it. . . . It is in many respects much better than anything else he has done."

The ninth and last Christmas Number of *All the Year Round* was *No Thoroughfare*.

§ 138. *"Holiday Romance," January to May* 1868

A little earlier he had sent Messrs Ticknor and Field, American publishers, for insertion in their magazine *Our Young Folks*, a contribution entitled *Holiday Romance* [1]—a

---

[1] Cr. ed., vol. 15, p. 583. It appeared in *Our Young Folks*, January to May 1868.

story of children pretending to be grown up.[1]  Writing to Fields on 25 July 1867, he expressed the hope that the Americans would "see the joke" of it.  He got huge pleasure himself out of the Pirate portion (Part III).  "It made me laugh," he says, "to that extent that my people here thought I was out of my wits."  The public, however, liked best the chapter entitled "The Magic Fishbone."  Edward FitzGerald after reading this letter commented, "One thinks what a delightful thing it is to be such an author."

How full Dickens's life was at this time, is shown by a letter written at Gad's Hill Place, 12 September 1867. He says:

"I have to fix my disturbed mind on the Christmas story (*No Thoroughfare*) I am doing with Wilkie (Collins) and to hammer it out bit by bit as if there were nothing else in the world; while the regulation of my personal affairs—the six months' prospective management of a great periodical published every week, the course to be taken in America (for he had decided to go there again on 9 November), the apportionment of 100 nights of hard work—tug at my sleeves and pull at my pen every minute in the day." [2]

On 9 July 1867 Dickens wrote to Thomas Adolphus Trollope:

"My readings secretary (Dolby) whom I am despatching to America at the end of this week will dine with me at Verey's in Regent Street at 6 exact to be wished God-speed.  There will be, besides Wills, Wilkie Collins and Mr Arthur Chappell.  Will you come?  No dress."

Of course Trollope went and the God-speed party was a very pleasant one.

In September Dickens gave Collins some assistance in making a stage version of *No Thoroughfare* for Fechter. His letters in September and October are mostly on this subject.  Fechter took the part of Obenreizer and made a great success of the play not only in London, but also later in Paris and the United States.

---

[1] Dickens had amused himself with this idea as early as 1855—in the Christmas Book *The Holly Tree*.
[2] Maggs's *Catalogue*, 538.

## CHAPTER XVIII

# 9 November 1867 to 31 December 1869

GAD'S HILL ALONE, SECOND PERIOD. FROM HIS SECOND
VISIT TO AMERICA TO END OF YEAR 1869

§ 139. *Second Visit to America. Opposition of Forster.*
*Mountains of Green Backs*

AS regards the temptation to make a second visit
to America Forster strongly opposed it, but as
a compromise it was decided to send Dolby in
order to ascertain to what extent the Readings were likely
to be a success. Dolby went, and, being a very capable
man of business, soon did everything required and reported
favourably. He also visited some of the celebrities, and
among them Longfellow, whom he found to be a patri-
archal-looking man with beautiful long white hair, but not
at all like a poet. Dolby had apparently expected to see
him nursing a lyre. When Dolby returned to England,
he made his way to Ross in Herefordshire which was his
home. There he met Forster, who very wisely had come
to the conclusion that the American Tour ought not to be.
There were many reasons, he said, why there should not
be a visit to America, and two in particular. In the first
place, Dickens's health had declined ever since the Staple-
hurst accident; and in the second, Dickens's desire to
increase his property to such an extent in so short a space
of time and in such a way, was unworthy of him, or in
fact of any man of genius.

"I shall write," continued Forster, "and tell him he
must give up the idea." Thereupon Dolby telegraphed
to Dickens: "I can make nothing of Forster; he is utterly

unreasonable and impracticable. Come down here and stay at my house, and we will tackle him together." So Dickens went, Forster finally gave way, and arrangements were made for the voyage.

On Friday, 1 November 1867, before Dickens started for America, a party of his friends met and dined at Wilkie Collins's, their object being to wish him God-speed. Dickens wore an extra large cravat and in it "a most wonderful scarf-pin, large in size, strange in form, an object of inevitable attraction." He said: "I hope you all like my pin; it is uncommon, I think. I hope there is no such pin as this in America. I have invested in it for the whole and sole purpose of pleasing my friends over the water." Next day, a banquet took place in his honour at the Freemasons' Tavern, Great Queen Street, Lord Lytton presiding.[1] Never to author was so much incense offered. Dickens was giddy with delight.

The vessel chosen was the *Cuba*. The voyage was rough, and Dickens in his description of a service on board speaks of the clergyman being conducted into the saloon by two stalwart stewards supporting him, as if they were "bringing him up to the scratch for a prize-fight." When Dickens arrived in New York he found the city billed with his favourite colour, light orange. It seems that two tons of paper were used, but subsequently it was found unnecessary during the whole of the tour to advertise in this way. The first Reading was on 2 December 1867. Dolby was worried almost to death by speculators, and by persons pretending to be deaf, blind, etc., in order to avoid the trouble of purchasing tickets in the usual course. The price of the tickets was two dollars. Speculators sold them for twenty-six dollars. The queue before the ticket office was half a mile long. The crowd assembled the day preceding the sale of tickets and kept their places all night, having supplied themselves with straw mattresses, blankets, food and drink.

Among the men of note met by Dickens (and his wonderful scarf-pin was duly admired) were Emerson, Agassiz,

[1] *Speeches . . . by Charles Dickens*, Hotten, p. 219.

Holmes and Longfellow. Photographs, wonderfully unlike him, adorned the shop windows; and then he was
prevailed upon to have his portrait taken by Mr Ben
Gurney, of New York, who produced a likeness, declared
by many to be the best photograph of him ever done.
When Fields heard him read, he said: "You have given
me a new lease of life, for I have been so looking forward
to this occasion, that I have had an idea all day that I
should die at five minutes to eight to-night, and be deprived
of a longing desire I have had for the last nineteen years to
hear you read in my country." Much of the money taken
was in green-backs, and Dickens was hugely tickled at
seeing Dolby drawing them by handfuls from his pockets
until the immense heap piled on the table looked "like a
family wash." Then we read of his hotel catching fire,
when Dickens stuffed himself with paper money, and made
his escape in "a pea jacket, blue sailor trousers, and a
thick muffler round his neck, looking more like a pilot than
ever." At Christmas Mrs Fields decorated his rooms with
English mistletoe and holly "with real red berries"—
procured from England for the purpose; and his table was
supplied with roast beef and turkey and an English plum
pudding.

The most trying part of the tour was the travelling—
the Americans being terrible sinners in the matter of
over-heating their cars, and excluding fresh air. Dickens
tried to evade the difficulty by riding outside with the
brakeman, but the cold almost slew him. Insomnia and
loss of appetite followed and finally came an attack of
influenza. Dickens, however, always endeavoured to keep
appointments—his maxim being "No man has a right to
break an engagement with the public if able to be out of
bed."

The people of New York, who were not altogether
pleased with Dickens's manager, called him "Pudding-
headed Dolby"; and as Dolby had never before had a title
conferred upon him, he and Dickens thought they might
as well retain it—and they did—making it, however, P.-H.
Dolby, for short. Dickens was at Philadelphia on 23

January 1868. The people there advised him to go to Chicago. They said, "If you don't read in Chicago the people will go into fits!" "Well," answered Dickens, "I would rather they went into fits than I did."

The reason he did not wish to visit that city was because his brother Augustus was living there "with a very handsome woman." In the house also were two children whom Augustus rather believed to be his own. When it was suggested to Dickens that he should assist "this very handsome woman" he mentioned that he was already supporting the only genuine Mrs Augustus Dickens who was living in England and was a frequent guest at Gad's Hill Place. He could truthfully have added that he was also supporting the only genuine Mrs *Charles* Dickens, who was *not* a frequent guest at Gad's Hill Place.

Among the amusements of the tour was a walking match between Mr Dolby—a very big man—and the American tour-manager, Mr Osgood, a very little man. It came off in a biting wind, through deep snow wreaths—hair, beard, eyelashes, and eyebrows were frozen hard and hung in icicles. Osgood was victor, though "Dolby did very well indeed." A splendid dinner crowned the day, and the whole affair was a grand success.

With the president of America (Andrew Johnson) Dickens was much struck. He describes him as a man not to be turned or trifled with, "A man (I should say) who must be killed to be got out of the way." Then the influenza got worse, and Charles Sumner, calling one day on Dickens, found him hidden in mustard poultices and almost voiceless. Dolby was indefatigable in his attentions. Said Dickens, "He is as tender as a woman and as watchful as a doctor." Owing to loss of appetite, Dickens established this system: "At seven a.m. a tumbler of new cream and two tablespoonfuls of rum. At noon a sherry cobbler and a biscuit. At three a pint of champagne. At five an egg beaten up with a glass of sherry. At ten, soup, and anything to drink I can fancy," but whether all this rum, sherry and champagne acted beneficially on him is doubtful.

Being desirous of leaving behind him in a substantial form some trace of his second visit to America, Dickens had his *Old Curiosity Shop* produced in raised letters for the use of the blind, and presented a copy to every asylum in the Union. On 21 March 1868, he wrote from Springfield to Mr Frederick Ouvry, his friend and solicitor: [1]

"You can hardly imagine what my life is with its present condition—how hard the work is, and how little time I have at my disposal. It is necessary to the daily recovery of my voice that I should dine at 3 when not travelling; I begin to prepare for the evening at 6; and I get back to my hotel, pretty well knocked up at half-past 10. Add to this, perpetual railway travelling in one of the severest winters ever known." [2] Then too he had become lame of one foot.

The thaw that followed the severe frost was still harder to endure. They travelled through water, at four or five miles an hour, "seeing nothing but drowned farms, barns adrift like Noah's arks . . . and all manner of ruin."

His tour was drawing to an end. The work had been hard, the climate hard, the life hard, but the gain had been enormous. In New York there were five farewell nights, and a public dinner at Delmonico's with Horace Greeley in the chair, during which Dickens testified to the remarkable improvement of America in all things since his visit twenty-five years previous. The day fixed upon for commencing the return voyage, on board the *Russia*, was 22 April, and among those who assembled to bid him adieu, was, to his pleasure, Anthony Trollope.

The parting scene was thus described by an eye-witness: "It was a lovely day—a clear blue sky overhead—and he stood resting on the rail, chatting with his friends. It seemed hard to say the word 'Farewell.' Yet the tugboat screamed the note of warning, and those who had to return to the city went down the side."

"All left save Fields. 'Boz' held the hand of the publisher within his own. There was an unmistakable look in both faces. The

---

[1] See Chapter XV, § 109.
[2] Ley's Forster, p. 791.

lame foot came down from the rail, and the friends were locked in each other's arms. Fields then hastened down the side, and the lines were 'cast off.' A cheer was given for Dolby, when Dickens patted him approvingly upon the shoulder, saying 'Good boy.' Another cheer for Dickens, then the tug steamed away.

" 'Good-bye, Boz.'

"Good-bye, from Fields, who stood the central figure of a group of three, Du Chaillu and Childs being the others. Then 'Boz' put his hat upon his cane, and waved it, and the answer came 'Good-bye' and 'God bless you every one.' "

On 4 January 1868 commenced in *All the Year Round* Wilkie Collins's story *The Moonstone*. *George Silverman's Explanation* [1] appeared in the *Atlantic Monthly* in January to March 1868, and in *All the Year Round* in February of that year.

Some have seen in *George Silverman's Explanation* an allegory of Dickens's own life; and it does seem to be a reflection of parts of it, particularly of the Christiana Weller affair. [2] Dickens liked to introduce little bits of his own experience into his stories. Indeed he could hardly help doing so. In respect to Adelina Fareway, George said to Granville Wharton, "I doubt if you have ever yet so much as seen Miss Fareway."

"Well, sir," returned he, laughing, "you see her so much yourself, that you hardly leave another fellow a chance of seeing her." And there the subject dropped for that time. But George so contrived as that Adelina and Granville should come together shortly afterwards. "For years," after he had surrendered Adelina to Wharton, "a cloud," he says, "hung over him, and his name was tarnished. But," he says, "my heart did not break, if a broken heart involves death; for I lived through it."

There may be some who see no connection between this incident and incidents in Dickens's life. It does not matter. Certainly both George and Dickens were greatly given to self-pity; and George's scorn of Verity Hawkyard has autobiographical interest.

[1] Cr. ed., vol. 15, p. 615.     [2] See Chapter XII, § 67.

§ 140. *June* 1868. *Longfellow in England. Death of Townshend*

The return voyage from America had done Dickens good; and he jokingly described himself as "causing the greatest disappointment in all quarters by looking so well." He had arranged with Messrs Chappell of London to give one more series of Readings in town and country, and that was really to be the last. His clear profits from the American tour had been £20,000; by the prospective readings he anticipated gaining £13,000; making a total of £33,000 in two years.

In June among the visitors at "Gads" was the poet Longfellow. In the autumn Dickens had to part with his youngest son Edward, who was to set out for Australia to join his brother Alfred, who had succeeded as a sheep-farmer. The ship sailed on 26 September 1868, and Dickens felt the parting keenly.

"I put," said he to his son, "a New Testament among your books . . . because it is the best book that ever was or will be known in the world, and because it teaches you the best lessons by which any human creature, who tries to be truthful and faithful to duty, can possibly be guided. . . . Never abandon the wholesome practice of saying your own private prayers night and morning. I have never abandoned it myself, and I know the comfort of it."

In the meantime Fechter who, with the aid of Collins, had dramatised *No Thoroughfare* [1] had made a great success of it at the Adelphi in London. It was equally successful in Paris, where it was produced in June. Fechter himself always took the part of Obenreizer.

While Dickens was in America he lost his old friend the Rev. Chauncey Hare Townshend. Anxious that Dickens should edit and publish his religious opinions, Townshend bequeathed to him a large sum of money. To this uncongenial task Dickens thereupon set himself; and Dolby calling one day found him "nearly distracted by the conglomeration of ideas he had to deal with, of which he could make neither head nor tail." On being asked whether he

[1] Christmas Number of *All the Year Round*, 1867.

CHARLES DICKENS

*Photo by Gurney,* 1868

*T. W . Tyrrell's Collection*

MISS GEORGINA HOGARTH
*Photo by T. W. Tyrrell*

had decided upon a title he replied that the only one that had so far occurred to him was *Religious Hiccoughs*. However, the work was finally published with the title *The Religious Opinions of Chauncey Hare Townshend*.

On 20 October 1868 Dickens lost his last surviving brother Frederick. "It was a wasted life," commented Dickens, "but God forbid that one should be hard upon it or upon anything in this world that is not deliberately and coldly wrong." In the Powysland Museum at Welshpool is preserved a letter from Dickens to Frederick dated 5 February 1857.[1] He says he cannot lend his brother £50, because he could not trust him and also because it would do him "no real good." At last, however, on that 20 October 1868 Frederick ceased to want to borrow anything from anybody. He was buried in West Cemetery, Darlington.

In 1868 appeared Forster's *Life of Landor* and Mrs Lynn Linton, who had been intimate with Landor, was asked to review it for *All the Year Round*. But not liking Forster, she commenced her article with, "*The Life of Walter Savage Landor* has yet to be written." Dickens paid for the review, but would not insert it, and wrote another himself in its place. In a letter to Mrs Lynn Linton he said, "I find that you do not think well of this book—I do." The writer of the present work when a young man, once deservedly drew upon himself the wrath of Mrs Lynn Linton by signing himself "Yours fy, Thomas Wright" instead of "Yours faithfully." She was a rather exacting lady, and found it hard to forgive anybody who was sparing in ink. Forster saw Dickens frequently that summer, but "never without the impression that America had told heavily upon him. There was manifest abatement of his natural force." One day, too, as he walked from his office with Miss Hogarth he could read only the halves of the letters over the shop doors.

[1] See *Daily Chronicle*, 2 April 1907.

## § 141. *Fourth Series of Paid Readings*

Dickens's fourth series of Paid Readings began in October 1868. Dolby again acted as his business manager. He was well received at Manchester, but even better at Liverpool, where he read on 25 October. There he had an audience of over two thousand, and the door money, besides the proceeds of the tickets, amounted to over £200. Hundreds of persons were turned away. Dickens's staff "rolled on the ground" of his room "knee deep in cheques, and made a perfect pantomime of the whole thing." Similar scenes followed. Everywhere he was greeted with furore —the money poured in in cataracts. People fought to shake hands with him, and after his reading scrambled on to the platform to secure the showered leaves of his scarlet geranium. His net profits amounted to £300 a week. All this was tremendously gratifying; but, to a man who already had more than enough, of what advantage was it to him! Had it, however, ended here, there would have been little harm done. But this was only the beginning. Already his friends were anxious. Said Sir E. Landseer: "I wish he looked less eager and busy, and not so much out of himself or beyond himself. I should like to catch him quiet now and then." But how could a man be "quiet now and then" with a wife separated from him and known to be unhappy, and a mistress cold and indifferent to him! What a hash, with all his success, he managed to make of life!

While at Liverpool he purposed to include among his Readings the murder scene in *Oliver Twist*. Forster having objected, it was decided to give on 14 November a trial Reading before a select company at James's Hall. The audience, consisting of about one hundred and fifty persons, chiefly representatives of literature and art, were awe-struck. One visitor said he was doubtful as to the advisability of giving the Reading before a mixed audience, he himself having felt an almost irresistible desire to scream. "If only one woman cries out," said another, "when you murder the girl, there will be contagion of hysteria all over the place." But a distinguished actress, on being asked her opinion, said, "Why, of course do it! The public have been looking out for a sensation these last fifty years, and now they will have it." Dickens still hesitated, but finally resolved to give the Readings a trial in public. Unfortunately for his own welfare, they were received with acclamation; and an enormous amount of labour, with additional fatigue was the result. In the opinion of his best friends nothing did more to aggravate his sufferings and hasten his end than the repeated delivery of the Murder.

In a letter to Frith on 26 November 1868 inviting him to listen to this unfortunate reading, Dickens says, "It is horribly like, I am afraid." He added that he had a vague sensation of being "wanted" by the police as he walked about the streets.[1] By one person he was *not* "wanted"— Miss Ternan. The only woman he loved he didn't love— so to speak—for he could not hide from himself that her attachment to him was artificial—that she merely endured him; and her attitude to him is plainly revealed in the descriptions of the various wooings to be found in his last novels. Dickens as an endeavourer to mould a woman's destiny was not a success.

## § 142. *In Scotland again*

In December he was in Scotland, where he was cordially received and had the pleasure of meeting again some of his old friends. He wrote from Edinburgh to his Belfast friend F. D. Finlay on 12 December 1868.

The excitement of the public during the last Scotch Readings was past description, and it had the effect of causing Dickens to make even greater exertions than usual. When with difficulty he reached his retiring-room, he was often so utterly prostrate that rest was necessary on a sofa before he could regain sufficient strength to utter a word. And yet he did not care to shelve this Reading, or to combat with what he called his "murderous instincts." Dolby wanted him to reserve the "Murder" for the big towns, substituting elsewhere the Carol or some other, and thus avoid the pain

[1] *Further Reminiscences*, Vol. 3, p. 234.

"of tearing himself to pieces every time for three nights a week, and suffering unheard-of torments afterward." This remonstrance of his faithful companion brought to Dickens's lips hot words.

"I left the table," says Dolby, "and proceeded to put my tour list in my writing-case. Turning round, I saw he was crying (my eyes were not so clear as they might have been), and coming towards me, he embraced me affectionately, sobbing the while—'Forgive me, Dolby! I really didn't mean it; and I know you are right.'" From that time the "Murder" was given less frequently.

Æsop, who is always wrong, says that when the frogs (the Dickenses and Dolbys of those days) petitioned Jupiter he thundered down a log. But it was not a log. What really descended was a shower of American green-backs. Those not sufficing, Jupiter despatched a stork, in other words the success that attended the Reading of the Murder scene. The petitioners found out their mistake when it was too late.

Dickens left Scotland on 18 December, and on the 21st read again in St James's Hall. There was no Christmas Number for *All the Year Round* that year. He read the Murder scene for the first time publicly in London on 5 January 1869. Mr Edmund Yates says:

"Readers of the old editions of *Oliver Twist* will recollect how difficult it was to fight against the dreadful impression which Mr George Cruikshank's picture of Nancy left upon the mind, and how it required all the assistance of the author's genius to preserve interest in the stunted, squab, round-faced trull whom the artist had depicted. Accurately delineating every other character in the book, and excelling all his previous productions in his etching of 'Fagin in the condemned cell,' Mr Cruikshank not merely did not convey the right idea of Nancy, which would have been bad enough, but conveyed the wrong one which was worse. No such ill-favoured slut would have found a protector in Sikes. . . . In the reading we get none of the common side of her character, which peeps forth occasionally in the earlier volumes. She is the heroine, doing evil that good may come of it."

§ 143. *His Third and Last Visit to Ireland,* 7 *January* 1869. *Dickens Reads at Blackburn,* 19 *April* 1869

On 7 January Dickens made for Belfast, Miss Georgina Hogarth, Percy Fitzgerald and Dolby accompanying him. They put up at the old-fashioned Royal Hotel in Donegal Street. It was his third and last visit to Ireland. The first Reading was to be at the Ulster Hall on Friday, 8 January. It was a vast place and Fitzgerald climbed to the far-off gallery to report how Dickens's voice carried. After dinner Dickens reclined on a sofa and Dolby went through various gymnastics, including standing on his head on a chair, in which he was not very successful. Dickens, then, in spite of his weariness was piqued into competing. "I'll show you how to do it, Dolby," he said—and he actually did it. When Dolby told the story, however, his hearers did not believe him. They said, "It can't be done"—just as if that was any argument when Dickens set his mind to do anything.

*The Belfast News Letter,* commenting next day on the Reading, gave Dickens high praise for "his power of evoking the physical scene," adding:

"We regret to say that the hall was by no means well filled. When Mr Dickens last read here there was much disappointment, owing to the fact that he was unheard by many of those in attendance, and this may have had something to do with limiting the extent of the audience. However, better arrangements had been made for this occasion. . . ."

With all these devices, the extent of the Hall taxed his voice considerably, and it was sometimes difficult accurately to distinguish the words. On 14 January Dickens and Miss Hogarth dined with his old friend Finlay and Lord Dufferin.

He read again at Belfast on Friday, 15 January, and this time there was an enormous company. The Press said "The readings were marked by all Mr Dickens's verve and genius, and the farewell of the audience was a most regretful one." From Belfast he proceeded to Dublin. On 15

February he was back in London for another Reading at St James's Hall.

Early in 1869 Collins and Fechter wrote a play called *Black and White*, and Dickens, who took a lively interest in everything that concerned these two intimate friends, prophesied on 25 February a great success for it. It was acted in the London Adelphi in March. Dickens's excessive admiration of Fechter puzzled the rest of his friends. "He was not," says Mr Ley, "personally worthy of the regard bestowed upon him." Marcus Stone and others of Dickens's circle, while they admitted his gifts as an actor, heartily disliked his company. They said he was no gentleman.

During the whole of March, Dickens unwisely continued the scenes from *Oliver Twist*. He was at Manchester on 7 March, at Hull on 8 March, back in London on 13 March and at Manchester again on 20 March, whence he sent his love to his sister Letitia, and Harriette his brother Augustus's wife, both of whom he still had to keep or partially to keep. "Poor Papa" indeed was always having some distressed or insolvent relative to relieve. After the second evening at Manchester, he caught the London train (with two minutes to spare) in order to attend the funeral of his old friend Sir James Emerson Tennent. He dressed, supped and slept during the journey, and finally, says Dolby, "stepped out at Kings Cross bright and elastic," and Dickens's gas man commented, "The more you want out of master, the more you'll find in him." To Forster, however, who was also present at the funeral, he appeared "dazed and worn."

He read at Birmingham on 1 and 2 April 1869, and the Town Hall was filled to overflowing. On 10 April a public dinner was given to him at Liverpool, with Lord Dufferin in the chair, Anthony Trollope, Lord Houghton and G. A. Sala being also among the speakers. What pleased him most during that visit was his being stopped in the streets by working men who wanted to shake hands with him and to tell him how they enjoyed his books. On 19 April he read at the Exchange Hall, Blackburn.

§ 144. *At Blackpool. Kicking his Hat about*

On 21 April 1869 he was relaxing at Blackpool where he "had a delicious walk by the sea." The Reading at Preston arranged for 22 April had to be abandoned by order of Mr F. Carr Beard, Dickens's doctor. Next morning as Dickens was walking to the railway station, his hat happened to blow off, and some ill-natured Preston men caused "County Court summonses to be served on him for compensation and disappointment, on the ground that they had seen him on the sands at Blackpool 'kicking his hat about as if he had been a boy.'" This alleged ridiculous procedure was so like Dickens in his earlier and more rollicking days that we wish it had been true.

Having brought his patient to a stand, Mr Beard consulted Sir Thomas Watson, and the two doctors decided that the course of Readings would have to be abandoned—and Reading combined with travelling stopped for ever.

Dickens then gave four final "Farewell" Readings in the Free Trade Hall, Manchester. Dolby says, "We had passed an enjoyable and quiet Sunday at the Queen's Hotel and as by a wonderful circumstance it did not rain, we drove to Alderley Edge, the fresh air reviving the chief amazingly."

Early in May, Dickens, so as to be near Dr Beard, secured apartments at the St James's Hotel, Piccadilly. Another object was that he might be able to show greater attention to his American friends, Mr and Mrs Fields, and Mr and Mrs Childs, who were on their way to London, and for whose entertainment he had drawn out a Brobdingnagian programme, which included excursions in the city and visits to Gad's Hill. Under the escort of a Scotland Yard detective they visited the rat-ridden opium dens by Ratcliffe Highway, utilised in *Edwin Drood*, and Tiger Bay, a resort of Lascars and Chinamen. They came away with the memory of disagreeable sights and incoherent jargon. Later they visited surrounding pleasant spots, including Cobham Park, Cooling and Canterbury. For the last, a journey of twenty-nine miles, "two post carriages were turned out with postilions in the red jackets, buckskin breeches, and top

339

hats, of the old Dover Road—for Dickens (and he was bubbling over with wit and merriment) did the thing well.

Canterbury was entered just as the bells of the cathedral were ringing for morning service. The congregation was small, the visitors were disappointed at the careless, half-hearted manner in which the service was performed, and Dickens, accustomed to do everything so thoroughly, said he could not conceive how persons accepting an office or trust so important as the proper rendering of a beautiful cathedral service could go through their duties in so perfunctory and slip-shod a fashion.

Later there was a gathering at Gad's Hill provided in honour of Mr W. H. Palmer of Niblo's Theatre, New York, who had come to England in order to secure the services of Fechter for a season. The chief feature of the gathering was a game of billiards between Mr Benjamin Webster, who represented England, and Mr Palmer, on whom devolved the responsibility of standing for America. To Dickens's delight, Mr Webster, though aged and infirm, obtained the victory. When Fechter proceeded to America Dickens heralded the event with an article in the Boston *Atlantic Monthly*. Fields, who published his reminiscences in *Yesterdays with Authors*, tells us that Dickens once said to him, concerning Gray, "Never did a poet come down to posterity with so little a book under his arm."

The breech between Cruikshank and Dickens appears to have been repaired at the time of the Leigh Hunt benefit, but they were not friends long. In 1869 Mr Richard Heathcote Gooch, who had written a story *An Old Man-o'-War's Man's Yarn*, asked Cruikshank, whom he knew very well, to introduce him to Dickens. But Cruikshank declined, saying, "When I and Mr Dickens meet on the same side of the way, either Dickens crosses over or I do." Mr Gooch, however, subsequently applied to Dickens direct. Dickens was all kindness, and accepted the dedication of several of Mr Gooch's stories.

Had not Dickens's health given way, it is probable that he would about this time have visited Australia, for his two sons were doing well there and he longed to see them again.

There was also the possibility of finding over sea a new subject for a book. He was unable to go, however, so we have no Australian Martin Chuzzlewit, or Mark Tapley or John Want.[1] Late in 1869 he lunched with George Eliot, and at table told the story of the dream of President Lincoln, the last night of his life. The President thought he was alone on a boat on a great river, and the dream ended by his exclaiming: "I drift—I drift—I drift." "Dickens," adds George Eliot, "told this very finely. I thought him looking dreadfully shattered."

§ 145. *"Veronique" and "Veronica."*   *Percy Fitzgerald's "An Experience"*

In the middle of the year Mrs F. E. Trollope sent Dickens a story entitled *Veronica*, which commenced in *All the Year Round* on 7 August. It then transpired that Florence Marryat (daughter of Captain Marryat) had, before Mrs Trollope began her story, hit upon *Veronique* as the title of a novel—the publisher of which was Richard Bentley; and the "fraudulent butler,"[2] as Dickens called Bentley, "wouldn't change it." So the two stories came out about the same time, *Veronique* and *Veronica*. The last chapter of *Veronica* appeared on 30 April 1870. "It is perfectly understood," wrote Dickens to Percy Fitzgerald, "that you write the long serial story next after Mrs Trollope's" and in the same number that *Veronica* ended, appeared the announcement that *The Doctor's Mixture*, the title (suggested by Dickens himself) of Fitzgerald's story, would commence on 4 June.[3] Dickens thought as highly of Fitzgerald's work as he did of Mrs Trollope's. He indeed, according to Mr Kitton, altered the plot of *Edwin Drood* entirely, after reading *An Experience*,[4] a story which Fitzgerald contributed to *All the Year Round*. "It is," says Dickens, on 19 August 1869, "according to my thinking one of the most remarkable pieces I ever saw." Writing

[1] See pp. 160 and 247.
[2] Letter to Percy Fitzgerald, 19 August 1869.      [3] See p. 320.
[4] Published in the 37th number of the new series.

to Forster, Dickens says: "I laid aside the fancy I told you of, and have a very curious and new idea for my new story. Not a communicable idea (or the interest in the book would be gone), but a very strong one, though difficult to work." [1] Whoever, therefore, wants to understand *Edwin Drood* and Dickens's attitude to it should not neglect Percy Fitzgerald's *An Experience*.

On 27 September 1869, when Dickens delivered at the Town Hall, Birmingham, his inaugural address as President of the Birmingham and Midland Institute, he took the opportunity to discharge his conscience of his political creed. "My faith," he said, "in the people governing is, on the whole, infinitesimal, my faith in the people governed, is on the whole, illimitable." A little later Thomas Adolphus Trollope invited him to Florence. Dickens replied on 10 November, "Whenever (if ever) I change 'going' into 'coming' I shall come to see you."

[1] See Ley's *Forster*, p. 807; also Maggs's *Catalogue*, No. 530, p. 61.

CHAPTER XIX

# The Year 1870

§ 146. *Fifth Series of Paid Readings,* 11 *January* 1870 *to*
15 *March* 1870

ON 6 January 1870 he was at Birmingham again, his
object this time being to deliver the prizes to the
successful students at the Birmingham and Midland Institute. Among the winners was a lady named
Winkle. At the mention of her name the audience became
convulsed with laughter. Dickens, after indulging in a
little conversation with her, turned to them and said amid
more amusement, "I have recommended Miss Winkle to
change her name." Next day he visited the works of
Messrs Elkington's in New Street, and then returned to
London, where he had arranged to give a series of Farewell
Readings at St James's Hall; for his health had improved
and he thought he might safely venture. In order to be
near the hall he hired No. 5 Hyde Park Place.

These Readings were twelve in number and his medical
attendant was present on every occasion. The first was
given on 11 January, but it was unwise to make the attempt,
for on the second night of the "Murder" Reading his pulse
rose to 124, and he was obliged to quit the platform for a
while and lie on a sofa. For several moments he was
utterly prostrate. After about ten minutes he drank some
brandy and water and then rushed on to the platform again
in order to finish. Charles Dickens, the younger, said that
his father during the last Readings found it impossible to
pronounce "Pickwick" correctly, calling it "Pickswick,"
"Picnic" or "Peckwicks."

On 12 February 1870 died, as the result of a fall down-stairs, Mr George Hogarth, Mrs Dickens's father, at the age of 86. He is buried in Kensal Green Cemetery. The same tombstone commemorates the death of Mary Scott Hogarth,[1] 7 March 1837, and that of his wife Georgina, who died on 5 August 1863. Hogarth, who had marked literary as well as musical tastes, left a fine library consisting chiefly of scientific and musical works.

The final of the Farewell Readings took place on 15 March, the *Christmas Carol* and the Trial from *Pickwick* being the pieces selected. When Dickens appeared, book in hand, and greatly agitated (his pulse indeed was 108) the whole assemblage rose to greet him and cheered again and again. The Reading over, he retired for a few minutes. Then he returned and with a voice full of emotion he delivered his farewell address. Amid repeated acclamations on the part of the audience and the waving of handkerchiefs he left the platform with tears on his cheeks, for he was moved to the depths, but he was recalled and again met with rapturous applause. He kissed his hand and retired. The total number of Readings given between 29 April 1858, when he read for the first time for his own benefit, and 15 March 1870, was 423. Of these 111 were under the management of Mr Arthur Smith, 70 of Mr Headland, and 242 of Mr Dolby. In all he cleared by them something like £45,000.

In March, in compliance with a request of the Queen, he paid a visit to Buckingham Palace, with the result of an interview that gave him great pleasure. The Queen showed particular interest in his American experiences and presented him with an autographed copy of her *Journal in the Highlands*. On 21 March he told Forster that when walking down Oxford Street the same incident had occurred that he had noticed on a former occasion. He had not been able to read, all the way, more than the right hand half of the names over the shops. His left hand was usually in a sling.

[1] See §§ 41, 58, 91.

344

# THE YEAR 1870

§ 147. *"Edwin Drood," First Number,* 1 *April* 1870

On 1 April appeared the first number of *Edwin Drood*, which had been commenced the previous October. Of the twelve monthly parts of which the work was to consist only six were finished. The title of it was most likely taken from the name of a young man, Edwin Drew (a correspondent of the writer of this book), who at the time the story was in hand happened to be in communication with Dickens. Mr Drew, who was later well-known in journalistic and musical circles in London, was engaged on the *Hampshire Chronicle*; and, recollecting Dickens's early struggles and ultimate success, he had written to Dickens to ask respecting the possibility of gaining a livelihood by the pen in London, by one without money or friends. In reply, Dickens said, "On no account try literary life here. Such an attempt must lead to the bitterest disappointment." Like most other advice, however, it was not taken. Mr Drew did make his way to London and had no reason to regret the course he took. It has also been pointed out that the landlord of the Sir John Falstaff inn just opposite Gad's Hill Place was named Trood. It was not Edwin Trood, however, but William Stocker Trood. The story is very briefly as follows. A young man, Edwin Drood, who often visits his uncle Mr Jasper, at Cloisterham, is betrothed, in accordance with his father's dying wish, to a pretty girl, Miss Rosa Bud, who attends the school of Miss Twinkleton. But neither Rosa nor Edwin is satisfied with the arrangement. By and by another young man, Neville Landless, and his sister Helena appear on the scene. The youths take a dislike to each other and quarrel violently. Subsequently Landless confesses to his tutor Mr Crisparkle that he is himself in love with Rosa; but it is soon evident that Mr Jasper is also in love with her.

Shortly after, Edwin Drood disappears, and foul play is suspected. Landless, who was supposed to have been last in his company, is arrested, but owing to insufficient evidence, is quickly set at liberty. Mr Jasper dogs the steps of Landless, and declares he will ferret out the murderer,

345

but the reader is led to believe that Mr Jasper himself had done the deed. After the death, or supposed death, of Edwin, he visits Rosa and declares his passion, promising to forgo his pursuit of Landless, for whom she evidently feels some affection, if she will give him encouragement. Both Rosa and Mr Grewgious, her guardian, believe Mr Jasper to be the murderer—and there the story is broken off. Other characters are Mr Sapsea, a conceited auctioneer, Mr Datchery, a mysterious old man, who comes to watch Mr Jasper, and Lieutenant Tartar, a handsome sailor who makes Miss Bud's acquaintance. Dickens, as we have seen, obtained some ideas for his story from Percy Fitzgerald's short tale entitled *An Experience* published in the 37th Number of *All the Year Round*, new series.

§ 148. *Originals of the Characters and Places, "Edwin Drood"*

The following are some of the originals of persons and places in *Edwin Drood*:

Opium Sal—the old woman to whom Jasper used to resort—was a real character and lived in a "den" at Blue Gate Fields in the East End. In 1877 she still occupied the room in which Dickens found her; and still got her living by supplying opium to Chinese sailors. The Nun's House is the fine old Elizabethan structure in High Street, Rochester, called Eastgate House. Opposite, with its overhanging storeys and picturesquely timbered gables, is the residence of Mr Sapsea. The writer of this book when at Rochester, at Christmas 1893, had the satisfaction of being conducted over the cathedral by Mr William Miles, the verger, who regarded himself as responsible for the character of Mr Tope—"chief verger and showman" who was "accustomed to be high with excursion parties." [1]

Minor Canon Row, called by Dickens "Minor Canon Corner," where Mr Crisparkle lived, still stands, and is, of course, an object of interest to all visitors to Rochester. There are three Gate-houses near the cathedral, all of which

[1] Miles died at Rochester 23 March 1908, aged 91. See *Daily Chronicle,* 24 March 1908.

seem to have been drawn upon by Dickens in his description of Jasper's house—College Yard Gate, abutting on the High Street; Prior's Gate, an ivy-covered castellated structure, south of the cathedral; and the Deanery Gatehouse. "Of all the Gatehouses," observes Mr W. R. Hughes, "the last is the only one suitable for the residence of a person in the position of Jasper, who was enabled to offer befitting hospitality to his nephew and Neville Landless." The College Yard Gate, however, must be regarded as the typical Jasper's Gatehouse. Durdles in the flesh was a "drunken old German stonemason, much addicted to prowling about the cathedral trying to pick up little bits of broken stone ornaments, carved heads, crockets, finials, etc. These he carried about in a cotton handkerchief," which may have suggested to Dickens the ever-present dinner bundle.

The conversation between Edwin and Rosa took place in the "Vines"—the Monks' Vineyard of *Edwin Drood*—under a fine clump of old elms called "the Seven Sisters." It was in the Monks' Vineyard too that Datchery and the Princess Puffer conferred. And one could still go on, for almost every spot referred to in *Edwin Drood* can be identified—in the cathedral in particular where one can have but little imagination, who does not see Jasper and the choir enter, and hear the intoned words "When the wicked man" —"rising among groins of arches and beams of roof, awakening muttered thunder," or see, after the service, the choir scuffling out again and crossing the close, or hear the cawing of the rooks near Minor Canon Corner.

*Edwin Drood* had wonderful possibilities. Mr Jasper, Mr Crisparkle and Durdles are drawn with the cleverness of Dickens's best days—especially Durdles, who is the pink of the story: but Mr Sapsea, Mr Grewgious and Edwin Drood himself are all notable characters in the Dickens Valhalla. As regards the ladies, apparently had Dickens been able to finish the book Helena (to an extent Miss E. L. Ternan) would have become the principal character —Rosa taking the second place.

There is little humour in *Edwin Drood*. Durdles, however, is responsible for gleams. We may notice, for

347

example, the paragraph relative to his dinner. "Durdles leads a lazy gipsy sort of life, carrying his dinner about with him in a small bundle, and sitting on all manner of tomb-stones to dine. This dinner of Durdles's has become quite a Cloisterham institution; not only because of his never appearing in public without it, but because of its having been, on certain renowned occasions, taken into custody along with Durdles (as drunk and incapable) and exhibited before the Bench of Justices at the town hall." Then there is the remark of Lieutenant Tartar who chose a particular room as his dormitory because having served last in a little corvette, he knew he should feel more at home where he had a constant opportunity of knocking his head against the ceiling.

After the death of Dickens, Longfellow wrote to Forster expressing the hope that *Edwin Drood* was finished. "It is certainly," he added, "one of his most beautiful works, if not the most beautiful of all. It would be too sad to think the pen had fallen from his hand, and left it incomplete." Forster, too, felt the power of *Edwin Drood*. He admired the subtlety with which the characters were touched, and the necromancy of the magician which set before us places the most widely contrasted, enabling us to see "with equal vividness the lazy cathedral town and the lurid opium-eater's den." The design for the monthly wrapper of the story was prepared by Charles Allston Collins.[1] The twelve wood engravings for it were from the pencil of Luke Fildes.

§ 149. *The Newsvendors' Dinner, 5 April* 1870. *Death of Maclise, 25 April* 1870. *Death of Mark Lemon, 23 May* 1870

On 5 April Dickens presided at the Annual Dinner in aid of the funds for the Newsvendors' Benevolent and Provident Institution held at the Freemasons' Tavern. He was sup-

[1] Dickens, on 14 January 1870, expressed himself charmed with this cover. The design is reproduced on the cover of the *Dickensian*, vol. 1, No. 12.

ported by the Sheriffs of the City of London and Middlesex. After he had given the toast "The Corporation of the City of London," Mr Alderman Cotton, in replying, reminded the company that Mr Dickens did really once go through a Lord Mayor's Show in a Lord Mayor's carriage, so if he had not felt himself quite a Lord Mayor, he must have at least considered himself next to one. Dickens, who then rose, was obliged to correct Alderman Cotton. He said, "I never had that honour. Furthermore, I beg to assure you that I never witnessed a Lord Mayor's Show except from the point of view obtained by the other vagabonds upon the pavement." [1]

After paying compliments to newsvendors in general, he said he was once present at a social discussion when the question was asked, "What is the most absorbing and longest-lived passion in the human breast?" Later, on a country road during a shower and under an umbrella, he propounded this old question to a sprightly and vivacious newsman, who replied without the slightest hesitation that it was the passion for getting your newspaper before anyone else. Dickens, after expressing his belief that the newsman was right and paying compliments to John Lothrop Motley, the American Ambassador, and Henry Wadsworth Longfellow, supporters of the Institution, proposed the toast of the evening, "Prosperity to the Newsvendors' Benevolent and Provident Institution."

On 7 April 1870, he wrote to J. S. Le Fanu, author of *In a Glass Darkly*, in reference to a proposed contribution by that writer for *All the Year Round*. On 25 April died Daniel Maclise. Writing to Forster, Dickens said, "I at Higham had the shock of first reading at a railway station of the death of our old dear friend. What the shock would be, you know." On 2 May, he, though far from well, attended the Royal Academy Dinner (held in the large central hall of Burlington House), his last public appearance, and he seized the opportunity to pay a feeling tribute to Maclise's worth and genius, while before him hung on the wall that artist's last work "The Earls of Desmond and

[1] See Hotten, p. 322.

Ormond." The 200 guests included the Prince of Wales, the Duke of Cambridge, Mr Childers, Lord Elcho, Mr Motley, Mr Gladstone, the Archbishop of York and Dean Stanley. Dickens acknowledged the toast to Literature. He recalled, he said, the dear friends of his— members of the Royal Academy, who, its grace and pride— had dropped from his side one by one. He was thinking of Egg and Stanfield as well as Maclise. "They have so dropped from my side one by one," he said, "that I already begin to feel like the Spanish monk whom Wilkie tells of who had grown to believe that the only realities around him were the pictures which he loved, and that all the moving life he saw, or ever had seen, was a shadow and a dream." He then paid a tribute to Maclise's "prodigious fertility of mind and wonderful wealth of intellect," . . . and "made bold to say that no artist of whatever denomination, ever went to his rest leaving a golden memory more pure from dross." Mr Blanchard Jerrold, who a few days later met Dickens limping across the Strand, thought he had aged very much.

On 15 May Dickens wrote to J. B. Buckstone, the play-wright, stating that he was disabled, owing to foot trouble, from attending a meeting in connection with the General Theatrical Fund. On the 18th he replied to W. J. O'Griscoll, who was writing the *Life of Maclise*. He was obliged to admit that he had in the great holocaust burnt all the letters he had received from that artist (see § 131). On 20 May he wrote to his son Alfred in Australia, who it will be remembered (§ 140) had been joined there in September 1868 by his brother Edward. The letter, however, did not reach them until after they had heard by telegraph the news of their father's death.

Subsequently he met Mr Disraeli [1] at a dinner at Lord Stanhope's, and breakfasted with Mr Gladstone. Referring to Disraeli, Dickens said afterwards to Yates: "What a delightful man he is! What an extraordinary pity it is that he should ever have given up literature for politics." Disraeli having spoken once of the charm of Dickens's

[1] Created Earl of Beaconsfield in 1876.

conversation, his brightness, and his humour, Yates remarked, "I had always held that Dickens was an exception to the general rule of authors being so much less interesting than their books."

About this time a Liverpool gentleman who attributed much of his prosperity to the beneficial effects of Dickens's works, wrote, sending for his acceptance a cheque for £500. Says Forster : "Dickens was greatly touched by this, and told the writer, in returning the cheque, that he would certainly have taken it if he had not been, though not a man of fortune, a prosperous man himself." Any small memorial in another form, however, the donor was informed, would be gladly received. Subsequently came a richly-worked and suitably inscribed basket of silver, accompanied by a handsome centre-piece for the table ornamented with figures representing the seasons. The last time Dickens and Forster met was on 23 May, when they dined together in Hyde Park Place. The news which had just come in of the death of Mark Lemon cast, however, a gloom over the evening, and Dickens talked of the crowd of friends who, one by one, had been cut off—most of them in their prime—Maclise, Watson, Egg, Clarkson Stanfield, Talfourd, Townshend, Channing, Arthur Smith.

§ 150. *The Acting at Lady Freake's, 2 June* 1870.
*His Will*

At the end of May, Dickens and his friends were rehearsing plays almost every day at Hyde Park Place. Dickens undertook the entire stage management, and though suffering from his lameness, directed everything "with a boy's spirit and a boy's interest." The plays were for a dramatic entertainment to be given on 2 June by Lady Freake at Cromwell House, the pieces selected being *A Happy Pair, Prima Donna* and *Le Myosotis*.

Miss Mary Dickens, Mrs Charles Collins (Kate Dickens) and Herman C. Merivale, took parts. In the morning, Merivale, who was gloomy about his share, asked Dickens whether he thought it was comic or serious. With a twinkle

351

in his eye, he replied, "My dear boy, God alone knows. Play it whichever way you feel at the time." It was a stifling night but Dickens himself was behind the scenes the whole of the time—his face worn and haggard, yet he went through it all with infectious enjoyment. Percy Fitzgerald, who was present, noticed particularly the acting of the ladies, which he said was "exceedingly touching and clever." [1] Indeed, both Miss Dickens and Mrs C. Allston Collins were born actresses, and that evening they outdid themselves.

Dickens made his will on 2 June 1870, that is seven days before his death. He left £1,000 free of legacy duty to Miss Ellen Lawless Ternan. His references to Miss Georgina Hogarth are "I give to my dear sister-in-law Georgina Hogarth, the sum of £8,000 free of legacy duty . . . and I leave her my grateful blessing as the best and truest friend man ever had. . . . I solemnly enjoin my dear children always to remember how much they owe to the said Georgina Hogarth, and never to be wanting in a grateful and affectionate attachment to her." His references to his wife were, unhappily, self-applauding, cold and unfeeling—without one loving, one forgiving word. When she read them, how they must have stabbed her! He leaves her the annual income derived from the sum of £8,000, adding, "I desire here simply to record the fact that my wife, since our separation by consent, has been in the receipt from me of an annual sum of £600, while all the great charges of a numerous and expensive family have devolved wholly upon myself." To his children, to John Forster, and to his servants he also made bequests. The will closes with the following oft-quoted words: "I commit my soul to the mercy of God through our Lord and Saviour, Jesus Christ, and I exhort my dear children humbly to try to guide themselves by the teaching of the New Testament in its broad spirit, and to put no faith in any man's narrow construction of its letter here or there." This is all very well, but example is better than precept; and, as William Blake used to say, "the whole of Jesus Christ's teaching is summed up in

[1] Percy Fitzgerald's *Recollections*.

352

the words, 'I forgive you, you forgive me. This alone is the Gospel.'"

Admirable as was the corollary, it left the body of the will a lamentable production. Charity bids us assume that had Dickens known that his death day was so near, he would have worded it differently. As it was, he duped himself to the last.

Dickens left a little under £100,000. He was in Town on 2 June, for the usual Thursday meeting on the business of *All the Year Round*, and Dolby's last interview with him took place there. Instead of returning to Gad's Hill on that day, Dickens remained over night, and was at work again in his room at 26 Wellington Street on Friday, 3 June.[1]

## § 151. *Death, 9 June* 1870

On Monday the 6th he was out with his dogs, and walked as far as Rochester; on the Tuesday he drove to Cobham Wood, and in the evening he fixed some Chinese lanterns in the conservatory which he had recently added to his house. On Wednesday the 8th he received a letter from the Rev. John M. Makeham, a Nonconformist minister who protested against a passage in *Edwin Drood* (then appearing in monthly parts). The passage, which is in the tenth chapter, reads: "Would the Reverend Septimus submissively be led, like the highly popular lamb, who has so long and unresistingly been led to the slaughter, and there would he, unlike that lamb, bore nobody but himself"[2]—the objection being that it was suggested by the verse in Isaiah liii. 7, "which is greatly reverenced by a large number . . . as a prophetic description of the sufferings of the Saviour." Dickens, in reply, said that he had merely used a much-abused social figure of speech impressed into all sorts of service on all sorts of inappropriate occasions, adding, "I have always striven in my writings to express veneration for the life and lessons of our Saviour." This letter and three others (one of which was to Charles Kent)

---

[1] *Windsor Magazine*, December 1934.     [2] Cr. ed., vol. 17, p. 74.

were the last he wrote. He then worked at *Edwin Drood* in his châlet.

At six that evening when he seated himself to dinner he told Miss Hogarth that for an hour he had been very ill. Rising from the table he would have fallen but for her support. When she endeavoured to get him to the sofa he said "On the ground," and these were the last coherent words he spoke. Early next morning his son Charles telegraphed to Mr Holsworth, the manager at the office of *All the Year Round*, instructing him to obtain further medical advice without a moment's delay. A few hours after the despatch of this urgent message, that is to say a little after six in the evening, Dickens died.

The sensation caused by his death, not only through England, but throughout the whole world, has perhaps never been equalled in the annals of our literature. The news was so sudden and so unexpected—and the great author had been held in esteem and honour in every English-speaking household. It was as if people had lost one of their own kin. All men mourned. Dickens's wish was to be buried in the graveyard of Rochester Cathedral, but this could not be carried out because the churchyard had been closed as a place of interment. It was the wish of the public that he should be buried in Westminster Abbey.

The decision remained with Dean Stanley, who had not known Dickens till the year of his death. In that year he had met him three times—once at a private party, where he had been greatly struck by his conversational powers; once at the Academy Dinner; and once when Dickens dined at the Deanery. As soon as possible Forster and Dickens's son Charles called on Stanley, and it was arranged that the body should be brought from Rochester to London that night and that the mourners were to arrive at nine next morning. The coffin was carried to the Poets' Corner, accompanied by ten or twelve persons, none of whom, in accordance with the wishes of the deceased, wore "scarf, cloak, black bow, long hatband, or any other revolting absurdity."

354

THE GRAVE OF CHARLES DICKENS, WESTMINSTER ABBEY

*Photo by Catherine Weed Ward*

See page 354

MARY WELLER AND HER HUSBAND
(Mr. & Mrs. Thomas Gibson)
*Photo by J. Graham, 17 Ordnance Terrace, Chatham*

See page 366

The stone placed over the spot is inscribed:

CHARLES DICKENS.
Born February the Seventh 1812.
Died June the Ninth 1870.

Though in accordance with Dickens's wishes there had been as little formality as possible, crowds afterwards flocked to view the grave. Many flowers were strewn by unknown hands. Tears flowed from unknown eyes. From the scene at the Abbey the mind naturally turns again to Gad's Hill, and one thinks of the well-known picture, "The Empty Chair," drawn by Mr Luke Fildes, the illustrator of *Edwin Drood*. This picture shows the interior of the study at Gad's Hill Place with the dummy books, and the desk with the various objects that were so familiar to the dead writer, including the two bronze duelling frogs already alluded to, and a bottle of his favourite blue ink. Before the desk stands "The Empty Chair" and in the distance, through the open window, one can see the roof top of the Sir John Falstaff.

When Forster's *Life of Charles Dickens* appeared, Edward FitzGerald's comment was, "Very good, I think; only he has no very nice perception of character. . . . But there is enough to show that Dickens was a very noble fellow as well as a very wonderful one. . . . I for one worship Dickens." Elsewhere, 22 September 1879, he says: "I am here (at Lowestoft) re-reading Forster's *Life of Dickens* which seems to me a very good book, though people say there is too much of Forster in it. At any rate, there is enough to show the wonderful daemonic Dickens: as pure an instance of genius as ever lived; and it seems to me, a man I can love also."

§ 152. *Last Days of Mrs Dickens*

Mrs Dickens, after her husband's death, resided at 70 Gloucester Crescent, London. In Shirley Brooks's Diary under date 11 July 1870, is the entry:

E. (Mrs Shirley Brooks) called on Mrs Dickens, first time since the death. Describes her as looking well, being calm, and speaking of matters with a certain becoming dignity. Is resolved not to allow Forster, or any other biographer, to allege that she did not make Dickens a happy husband, having letters after the birth of her ninth child, in which Dickens writes like a lover. . . . The affair is to the honour of Mrs Dickens's heart.

Mrs Dickens died at 70 Gloucester Crescent on 22 November 1879 at the age of 64. She had survived her husband a little over nine years.

Miss E. L. Ternan continued, after Dickens's death, to brood over her connection with him. At last she disburdened her mind to Canon Benham. She told him the whole story [1] and declared that she loathed the very thought of this intimacy.

[1] The Author of this work received it from Canon Benham.

# APPENDICES

## Summary of Dickens's Character and Life Work

Dickens's place among the immortals is assured. He reigns with Cervantes, with Swift and with Sterne. *Pickwick, Nicholas Nickleby* and *David Copperfield* have taken their place among the classics, and men will no more part with them than with *Don Quixote, Gulliver's Travels, Tristram Shandy* or *The Sentimental Journey*. Scarcely below the three masterpieces falls *Great Expectations*—some passages of which indeed seem more real to us, even than the best work in *Copperfield*. These four are easily first. To the second rank belong *Oliver Twist, The Old Curiosity Shop, Martin Chuzzlewit, Dombey, Bleak House, Little Dorrit, Our Mutual Friend* and the unfinished *Edwin Drood*; to the third *Sketches by Boz, The Christmas Books* and *Hard Times*.

Concerning *Barnaby Rudge* and *A Tale of Two Cities*—which belong to quite a different order of story—the most opposite opinions are held. These—Dickens's only essays into the realm of historical fiction—are in the opinion of many complete failures. Others, however, will not have it so, and *A Tale of Two Cities* has by some been ranked among his best stories. Swinburne, for instance, called it "a faultless work of tragic and creative art."

Dickens is most successful in dealing with grotesque characters, Micawber, Dick Swiveller, The Marchioness, and others. We remember their idiosyncrasies, and, in the words of Mr Arthur Rickett, "their favourite tricks of speech, how they looked; we can hear the inflection of the voice: in fact we know as much about the outward man and as little about the inward man as we do about the people to whom we are introduced from time to time. Few characters in fiction dwell so vividly in our recollection as do these queer, uncouth personages."

Edward FitzGerald's praise of Dickens is unstinted. He says in a letter to Fanny Kemble (24 August 1874): "I have been sunning

357

# THE LIFE OF CHARLES DICKENS

myself in Dickens—even in his later and very inferior *Mutual Friend* and *Great Expectations*. Very inferior to his best, but with things better than anyone else's best, caricature as they may be. I really must go and worship at Gad's Hill, as I have worshipped at Abbotsford, though with less reverence, to be sure. But I must look on Dickens as a mighty Benefactor to Mankind."

Of Dickens's attitude towards his wife enough has been said in these pages. It cannot be defended, and there the subject must be left. Referring to Dickens's friends, Yates observes: Forster, "partly owing to natural temperament, partly to harassing official work and ill-health," was older than his years. Dickens was closely associated with him, but he was more intimate with Thomas Adolphus Trollope and Wilkie Collins. "Of the warm-hearted hero-worship of Charles Kent he had full appreciation." Though in his later years Dickens was aggressive, imperious and intolerant to outsiders, to his friends, his temper was always of the kindest and the sweetest. Yates considered him the best after-dinner speaker he had ever heard.

He was thorough in everything he did. He put his whole soul into the work in hand, and endeavoured at all times to do his level best. "He had," observes one of his circle, "the volcanic activity, the perturbed restlessness, the feverish excitability of genius." In his passion for bright colours he does not stand alone among men of letters. His crimson waistcoat and yellow gloves are as much a matter of history as Goldsmith's plum-bloom coat. Carlyle could speak of him as a "most cordial, sincere, clear-sighted, quietly decisive, just, and loving man." He was fond of animals and particularly of dogs of the larger breeds, several of which usually accompanied him in his walks. No dog, however, looms very large in any of his stories. For hitting off in few words the leading characteristics of man, woman or animal, he had no equal except Thomas Carlyle.

Swinburne, in a fine and radiant sonnet, ranks Dickens's spirit with that of Shakespeare and the soft bright soul of Sterne, and declares that he had "Fielding's kindliest might and Goldsmith's grace."

Dickens was no student, and in this fact lay his power. "A student," as Gissing says, "is commonly unobservant of outward things"; but in this fact also lay his weakness, for he is no chronicler of the movements of the soul—as for example was George Eliot, a student to the finger-tips. But who would have Dickens other than what he is? His humour pardons almost everything. It has been abundantly dealt with in these pages, but it is not wanting in his short stories.   It shines particularly in "The Schoolboy's Story" (see p. 309) in which the boys, repentant for being unkind to Old Cheeseman, "gave him two white mice, a rabbit, a pigeon and a beautiful puppy.   Old Cheeseman cried about it, especially soon afterwards when they all ate one another."   How munificently was Old Cheeseman treated when he became second Latin Master! Did he not receive £2 10s. a quarter "and his washing!"

Forster's *Life of Dickens*, which appeared in 1872–4, pleased nobody except G. A. Sala.   At the same time all Dickens students must be grateful to Forster, for his work, though it omits very much that is of first importance in Dickens's life and has many inaccuracies, is a storehouse of facts.   The chief trouble in reading it is that you never know where you are in respect to the dates. It is a muddle, but a very useful muddle.   George Henry Lewes, Wilkie Collins and Mrs Lynn Linton especially hated it.   She calls it "a cold, carping and unsympathetic biography."

# APPENDIX NO. 2

## Dickens as a Textuary

It is improbable that Dickens, extensive as is his cult and devout as are his worshippers, has ever been used, like Virgil and some others of old, for purposes of divination; but containing as he does so many sentiments bold, noble, sensible, and humane, he forms an admirable textuary or text mine.  We have already quoted many of his sayings.  Let us take a few more.

"There is some victory gained in every gallant struggle that is made."  This was said in one of his speeches; and in another speech we have the same sentiment, worded differently: "To strive at all involves a victory achieved over sloth, inertness, and indifference."

The following quotations are also noticeable and suggestive:

"Ah! poetry makes life what light and music make the stage."—*Pickwick Papers.*

"There never were greed and cunning in the world yet, that did not do too much and over-reach themselves."—*David Copperfield.*

"Probably every new and eagerly expected garment ever put on since clothes came in, fell a trifle short of the wearer's expectations."—*Great Expectations.*

"In every service . . . a man must qualify himself by striving early and late, and by working heart and soul, might and main."—*Little Dorrit.*

"Of all fruitless errands, sending a tear to look after a day that is gone is the most fruitless."—*Nicholas Nickleby.*

"The things that never happen are often as much realities to us in their effects as those that are accomplished."—*David Copperfield.*

"Any man may be in good spirits and good temper when he's well dressed.  There ain't much credit in that.  If I was very ragged and very jolly, then I should begin to feel I'd gained a point."—*Martin Chuzzlewit.*

360

## How did "Edwin Drood" End?

In the final instalment of *Edwin Drood* appeared the following Postscript by Messrs Chapman and Hall: "All that was left in the manuscript of *Edwin Drood* is contained in the number now published —the sixth." Subsequently Forster discovered among the leaves of Dickens's other manuscripts some papers which proved to be a scene in which Mr Sapsea and new characters, a dancing master named Kimber, and a Mr Peartree, appear; but what Dickens intended to do with these persons is not clear.

The question has often been asked: How did *Edwin Drood* end? From remarks let fall by Dickens, Forster concluded that Edwin Drood was really murdered by Jasper, and that the last chapters were to be written as if from the condemned cell. The body apparently had been buried in lime, somewhere in the cathedral, but the tell-tale was to be the gold ring which was in Edwin's possession the last time he and Rosa met. In support of Forster's theory, which was also upheld by Mr Fildes, the illustrator of *Edwin Drood*, it may be mentioned that Mr Charles Dickens, junior, informed Mr W. R. Hughes, that Edwin Drood really died.

What Forster and Fildes said, however, stands for very little. Dickens gave them a few hints, but he certainly did not tell them definitely how the tale was to end. Nor need the younger Dickens's evidence have much weight. Dickens when commencing the tale may have intended to kill Edwin Drood, and he possibly said so to his son, but, as the tale advanced, that idea may have been abandoned in favour of one far more artistic, and more in keeping with his usual methods of procedure.

This subject was thoroughly thrashed out by Mr Richard A. Proctor (the astronomer) in *Watched by the Dead*. He points out that the idea which more than any other had a fascination for Dickens was that of a wrong-doer watched at every turn by one of whom he has no suspicion, for whom even he entertains a feeling of contempt; and that there are watchers and watched in nearly every one of

Dickens's longer stories. He then attempts to prove that Edwin Drood did not die, and it may be noticed that in *No Thoroughfare* occurs a murder, some of the circumstances of which are akin to those in *Edwin Drood*; the man whom we have given up for dead turning out not to have been dead after all. *Hunted Down* also presents an analogous case.

Mr Proctor made much of the ghost of a shriek heard by Durdles —observing—"The shriek fore-heard by Durdles was Jasper's own"; and he ends the story as follows: "Jasper obtains from Durdles the key of Mrs Sapsea's monument, to which he conveys quicklime. He strangles Edwin with the silk scarf, drags his body to the monument and shuts it in." Later, Durdles, going tapping about, discovers that Mrs Sapsea's tomb sounds less hollow than formerly. He opens it—and there lies Edwin Drood. "The body is removed to the Traveller's Rest. Edwin Drood, who is not dead, recovers, and those acquainted with the affair resolve to keep it secret. Disguised as Datchery, he watches Jasper in order to bring him, at a suitable time, to punishment. On Edwin's finger was a ring. Mr Grewgious, in order to get Jasper more into his toils, would seek for this ring. Jasper would remember that it was still on the finger of the corpse, and that he had unwittingly left a fatal witness of his crime, within the very tomb of his victim." He is forced to the tomb itself, nay to the very dust of his victim, that he may there grope in fear and horror for the "evidence of his crime." He creeps down the crypt steps, reaches the tomb, raises his lantern. And what sees he? There clearly in the gloom, stands Edwin Drood, with stern look fixed on him—pale, silent, relentless. With a shriek of horror (the "ghost" of which had been heard before by Durdles) Jasper casts down the lantern and flies to the winding staircase of the tower. Neville, Tartar, Drood and Crisparkle follow him and Jasper is captured, not, however, before he has killed Neville, and he ends his life by suicide in prison. What gives colour to this idea is that on the cover of the original issue of *Edwin Drood* is a series of pictures by Fildes foreshadowing the story. One of these represents Jasper with his left hand on the lock of an open door and his right hand raising a lantern, while before him stands a young man, who is doubtless Edwin. Tartar marries Rosa, Crisparkle Helena; Edwin Drood remains a bachelor.

A different view of the story was taken by J. Cuming Walters in *Clues to Dickens's Mystery of Edwin Drood* (1905). Mr Walters was convinced that Edwin Drood really died. Canon Benham wavered. At first he agreed with Proctor. Later he said, "I have no doubt, after long reflection, that Jasper murdered Edwin Drood and that Datchery is Helena Landless." Sir William Robertson Nicoll, whose study, *The Problem of Edwin Drood*, appeared in October 1912, also agreed with Mr Walters. An article, "Was Edwin Drood Murdered?" written by Sir Frederic Maughan, a judge of the High Court, appeared in the *Daily Mail* for 30 and 31 October. 1928. He said, "I am quite convinced that John Jasper failed to murder Edwin Drood, and that Dick Datchery is Drood in disguise. . . . It is quite plain that John Jasper attempted at midnight on Christmas Eve to murder Edwin Drood, and thought he had succeeded in the attempt."

"Jasper," Sir Frederick points out, "removed the watch and the only jewellery which he knew Edwin wore, but omitted to remove the engagement ring in Edwin's breast pocket." It seems more than a conjecture to suggest that Grewgious or some of the other persons who are watching Jasper let him know of the ring having been on Edwin's person on Christmas Eve in order to trap him, and that Jasper goes to the place where he left the body in quick-lime on Christmas Day, intending to get the "one wanting link" by which he purposes to destroy Landless by "planting" it in his rooms at "Staple Inn." The centre picture at the bottom of the cover of *Edwin Drood* apparently represents Datchery (Edwin Drood in disguise) confronting Jasper.

### List of Attempts to answer the Question, "How did 'Edwin Drood' End?"

The following is a fairly complete list of the attempts to answer the question, How did *Edwin Drood* end?

1870. R. H. Newell. Orpheus C. Kerr. *The Cloven Foot.* English edition. *The Mystery of Mr E. Drood.* 1871.

1871. (America) Henry Morton and Others. *John Jasper's Secret; being a Narrative of Certain Events following and explaining The Mystery of "Edwin Drood."* With 20 illustrations.

1872. The same (*London*) first issued in 8 parts, 8vo., blue wrappers, October 1871 to May 1872.

1873. A Spirit Solution. Brattleborough, Vermont, U.S.A. *The Mystery of "Edwin Drood" Complete.*

1878. Gillan Vase, a lady. *A Great Mystery Solved.* Reviewed in the *Examiner,* 5 October 1878.

1878. "Thomas Foster" (Richard Proctor the astronomer) *Belgravia Magazine* article signed Thomas Foster (see Appendix No. 3). This and other articles published as *Watched by the Dead.*

1884. Anonymous Article in the *Cornhill Magazine* (March).

1905. J. Cuming Walters. *Clues to Dickens's Mystery of Edwin Drood,* 1905. Reviewed by B. W. Matz in the *Dickensian,* vol. 1, No. 7, p. 184 (July 1905).

1905. Andrew Lang. *The Puzzle of Dickens's Last Plot.*

1905. George F. Gadd. "The History of a Mystery," the *Dickensian,* vol. 1, No. 9, p. 240, No. 10, p. 270, No. 11, p. 293; No. 12, p. 320.

1905. Letter of Luke Fildes, R.A., *The Times,* 3 November 1905; *Dickensian,* vol. 1, No. 12, p. 319.

1907. Canon Benham, article "Dickens and Kent" in *Memories of the Counties of England.* (Bemrose and Sons.)

1908. Edwin Charles. *Keys to the Drood Mystery.*

## APPENDICES

1912. *The Problem of "Edwin Drood": a Study in the Methods of Dickens*, by W. Robertson Nicoll. New York and London, 1912.

1914. *The Mystery of the Drood Family*, by Montagu Saunders. Cambridge University Press, 1914.

1914. *The Mystery of "Edwin Drood," completed in* 1914, by W. E. C. New Text Drawings by Zoffany Oldfield. New Text Review and edited by Mary L. C. Grant, London, N.D. (Brit. Mus. 012602, h.2.)

1919. Mary Kavannagh. *A New Solution of the Mystery of "Edwin Drood."*

1928. Sir Frederic Maughan, a judge of the High Court. "Was Edwin Drood Murdered?" Articles in the *Daily Mail* 30 and 31 October, 1928, agrees for the most part with Proctor.

1934. "A Suggested Solution of the Mystery of Edwin Drood" is reviewed in the *Dickensian*, Summer No., 1934, p. 231. It is by Canon W. J. Phythian-Adams.

# APPENDIX NO. 5

## Events Subsequent to the Death of Dickens

1871.  Mr Winter died.

1872.  Publication of first volume of Forster's *Life of Charles Dickens.*

1873, Jan. 18.  Death of Lord Lytton.

1873, Apr. 27.  Macready (William Charles) died at age of 80.

1873, Oct. 30.  Mrs Thomas Lawless Ternan, mother of Ellen Lawless Ternan, died at The Lawn, 89 Banbury Road, Oxford, in the house of her son-in-law, W. Rowland Taylor, at the age of 71.

  W. Rowland Taylor is mentioned in the Burgess Rolls of the Banbury Road, and he is also referred to in T. Adolphus Trollope's *Autobiography.* See *Jackson's Oxford Journal* (weekly issue), 8 November 1873.

1876, Feb. 1.  John Forster died at the age of 63.

1879, August. 5.  Charles Albert Fechter died aged 56.

1879, Nov. 22.  Mrs Charles Dickens died at her residence, 70 Gloucester Crescent, at the age of 64, having survived her husband nine years.

1882, July 8.  Hablot Knight Browne died at Brighton, aged 67.

1886.  Death of Thomas Gibson, husband of Mary Weller.

1886, Sept. 20.  Mrs Winter died at Southsea.

1888, Apr. 22.  Sunday, Death of Dickens's old nurse, Mary Weller (Mrs Gibson).

1889, Sept.  Death of Wilkie Collins.

1890, Dec. 1.  Helen Isabella Hogarth (Mrs Roney), died at Liverpool.

1892, Nov. 11.  Thomas Adolphus Trollope, husband of Frances Eleanor Ternan, died at Clifton, aged 82.

1893.  Henry Burnett, husband of Dickens's sister Fanny, died at Titchfield, Hants.

1893, June 19.  Mrs Frances E. Trollope (Frances Eleanor Ternan) in consideration of the literary merits of her husband the late

# APPENDICES

Mr Thomas Adolphus Trollope was granted a Civil List Pension of £50.

1894, May 19. Edmund Hodgson Yates died.

1896, July. Charles Dickens the younger, died.

1897, June 2. Mrs Elizabeth Dickens, widow of Charles Dickens the younger, was granted a Civil List Pension of £100. She died 18 April 1907.

1899, Nov. 19. W. R. Hughes died at Birmingham.

1900, Oct. George Dolby died in Fulham Infirmary.

1901, Jan. 3. Letter in the *Daily Chronicle* from Thomas Wright of Olney advocating the establishment of a Dickens Museum in London.

1902, Feb. Death of Charles Kent.

1902. *Life of Charles Dickens*, by F. G. Kitton, published.

1902, Nov. 5. The Dickens Fellowship founded. Among the presidents have been Percy Fitzgerald and Sir Henry F. Dickens. The Dickens House, 48 Doughty Street, was secured in 1924.

1904, Sept. Frederic George Kitton died, aged 48. See the *Dickensian*, vol. 1, No. 1, p. 7.

1904, Nov. 15. Mr Samuel R. Starey died.

1917, Apr. 19. Georgina Hogarth aged 90, died at her house, 72 Church Street, Chelsea, Thursday evening, 19 Apr. 1917. Buried at Mortlake cemetery, 23 April.

1933, 21 Dec. Sir Henry Fielding Dickens, K.C., died.

# APPENDIX NO. 6

## Thomson, Hogarth, Barrow, John Dickens and Charles Dickens Families

### CHILDREN OF GEORGE THOMSON

1. Katharine: born 1783; died young.
2. Alsie: born 1785; died young.
3. Robert: born 1786; died 1886.
4. Margaret: born 1787; died at a very advanced age.
5. Anne: born 1788; died at a very advanced age.
6. William: born 1790; died 7 April 1894.
7. Georgina: born 1793; married George Hogarth. She died 10 April 1917
8. Helen: born 1795 (see p. 279, footnote); she died at an advanced age.

### CHILDREN OF GEORGE AND GEORGINA HOGARTH

1. Catherine Thomson: born 19 May 1815. Married Charles Dickens. She died 22 November 1879.
2. Mary Scott: born 26 October 1819. Died 7 March 1837.
3. Georgina: born 22 January 1827. Died at her house, 72 Church Street, Chelsea, Thursday evening, 19 April 1917. Buried in Mortlake Cemetery 23 April.
4. Helen Isabella: born 1833: married Richard Roney. She died at Liverpool, 1 December 1890.

### CHILDREN OF CHARLES BARROW, LIEUTENANT IN THE NAVY

1. John Henry.
2. Thomas Culliford.
3. Edward.
4. Mary: married —— Allen, and afterwards, Dr Lamert.
5. Elizabeth: married John Dickens. She died in September 1863.

### CHILDREN OF JOHN DICKENS

1. Frances Elizabeth (Fanny): born 1810; married Henry Burnett.
2. Charles John Huffam: born 7 February 1812; died 9 June 1870.

APPENDICES

3. Alfred: born 1813; died in childhood.
4. Letitia Mary: born 1816; married Henry Austin.  She died 1893.
5. Harriet Ellen: died in childhood, 3 September 1819.
6. Frederick William: born 1820; died at Darlington, 20 October, 1868.
7. Alfred Lammert: born 1822; died at Manchester, 27 July 1860.
8. Augustus: born 1827; died probably in America.

When Charles Dickens died in 1870, Letitia (Mrs Austin) was the sole survivor of the family.

CHILDREN OF CHARLES DICKENS

1. Charles Culliford Boz: born 6 January 1837; died 1898.
2. Mary (Mamie): born 12 March 1838; died 1896 (unmarried).
3. Kate Macready: born October 1839; married (1) in 1860, Charles Allston Collins.  He died in 1873.  Married (2) C. E. Perugini.  He died in 1919.
4. Walter Landor: born 1841; died at Calcutta, 1863.
5. Francis Jeffery (Frank): born 1844; died at Illinois, 1886.
6. Alfred Tennyson: born 28 October 1845; died at New York, 1912.
7. Sydney Smith Haldimand: born 18 April 1847; died 1872.
8. Henry Fielding: born 16 January 1849; died 21 December 1933.
9. Dora Annie; born 16 August 1850; died 1851.
10. Edward Bulwer Lytton: born 13 March 1852; died in New South Wales in 1902.

Charles Culliford Boz, Dickens's eldest son, for long assisted his father in the conducting of *All the Year Round*.  The Magazine was left to him, and he threw himself into the congenial work of carrying on its traditions.  His paper, *Reminiscences of my Father*, appeared as a supplement to *The Windsor Magazine*, Christmas 1934.  He had eight children.  Mary Angela Dickens, his eldest daughter, is known as a novelist.  Henry Fielding Dickens, who was 21 when his father died, had a brilliant career.  He was knighted, and became a K.C. in 1922.  He was at one time Recorder of Deal and afterwards Recorder of Maidstone.  Captain Gerald Charles Dickens, C.M.G., Naval Instructor, Imperial Defence College since 1927, who was born 13 October 1879, is his second son.

369

# APPENDIX NO. 7

## The Early Illustrators of Dickens

Compiled from articles in the *Dickensian*, by W. A. Fraser; *Dickens and his Illustrators*, by F. G. Kitton; and *The Dickens Picture Book*, *A Record of the Dickens Illustrators* (Charles Dickens Library, vol. 18), by J. A. Hammerton (Brit. Mus. 012602, K.2).

*Browne, Hablot K.*
The Strange Gentleman, Acted
29 Sept. 1836, Published in
1837 . . . . . . 1 (etched frontispiece)
Pickwick . . . . . 36
Sunday under Three Heads . 4 designs
Nicholas Nickleby . . 39 „
Sketches of Young Couples . 6 „
Sketches of Young Gentlemen . 6 „
The Old Curiosity Shop . . Figure pieces
Barnaby Rudge . . . „ „
Martin Chuzzlewit . . . 40 designs
Dombey and Son . . . 40 „
David Copperfield . . . 40 „
Bleak House . . . . 40 „
Little Dorrit . . . . 40 „
A Tale of Two Cities . . 16 „

*Cattermole, George.*
Master Humphrey's Clock . . 14 designs
Barnaby Rudge. . . . 15 „
The Clock Chapters . . . 10 „

*Collins, Charles Allston.*
Edwin Drood . . . . The Monthly Wrapper

# APPENDICES

*Cruikshank, George.*

| | | | | |
|---|---|---|---|---|
| Sketches by Boz | . | . | . | 38 designs |
| The Mud Fog Papers | | . | . | 3 „ |
| Oliver Twist | . | . | . | 23 „ |
| The Lamplighter's Story | . | | . | 1 design |

*Doyle, Richard,* contributed to all the Christmas Books with the exception of the *Carol* and *The Haunted Man.*

*Fildes, Luke.*

Edwin Drood . . . . 12 designs

*Landseer, Sir Edwin.*

The Cricket on the Hearth . 1 design (Boxer, the dog)

*Leech, John.*

| | | | | |
|---|---|---|---|---|
| A Christmas Carol | . | . | . | 8 designs |
| The Battle of Life | . | . | . | 3 „ |
| The Chimes | . | . | . | 5 „ |
| The Cricket on the Hearth | | . | . | 7 „ |
| The Haunted Man | . | . | . | 5 „ |

Thus he contributed to *all* the Christmas Books and he alone supplied the eight illustrations to *A Christmas Carol.*

*Maclise.*

| | | | |
|---|---|---|---|
| The Cricket on the Hearth | | . | 1 design |
| The Battle of Life | . | . | 4 designs |
| The Chimes | . | . | 3 „ |
| Master Humphrey's Clock | | . | 1 design |

*Seymour, Robert.*

Pickwick . . . . . 7 designs

*Stanfield, Clarkson.*

| | | | | |
|---|---|---|---|---|
| The Chimes | . | . | . | 1 design |
| The Cricket on the Hearth | | | | |
| The Battle of Life | | | | |
| The Haunted Man | . | . | . | 2 designs |

Thus he contributed to all the Christmas Books except the first.

*Stone, Frank*

The Haunted Man . . . 3 designs

*Stone, Marcus.*

| | | | | |
|---|---|---|---|---|
| Pictures from Italy | . | . | . | 4 designs |
| American Notes | . | . | . | 4 „ |
| Our Mutual Friend | . | . | . | 40 „ |
| Great Expectations | . | . | . | 8 „ |

A Tale of Two Cities. Frontispiece to first cheap edition in 1864.

*Williams, Samuel.*

Master Humphrey's Clock, vol. 1, p. 46, 1 design

*Tenniel, J.*

The Haunted Man . . . 2 designs

*Walker, F.*

Hard Times (Library Edition) . 4 designs

## APPENDIX NO. 8

### Percy Fitzgerald's Articles, Boz and his Publishers. Dickensian, Vol. 3

No. 1. Macrone and others.          January 1907, p. 10.
   2. Richard Bentley and his Miscellany   February 1907, p. 33.
   3.          ditto             March 1907, 70.
   4. From Richard Bentley to Chapman &
       Hall                      April 1907, 93.
   5.          ditto             May 1907, 126.
   6. Bradbury and Evans and some others   June 1907, 158.

## APPENDIX NO. 9

### Some of the Principal Dickens Collections

1. The Pierpont Morgan Library, New York. (*Dickensian*, No. 229, p. 63.)
   (A) *Manuscripts:*
   A Christmas Carol.
   The Cricket on the Hearth.
   The Battle of Life.
   Holiday Romance.
   Hunted Down.
   Sketches of Young Gentlemen.
   O'Thello, 2 pages.
   Opinion. Essay dated 8 January 1859 and signed J. Buzfuz.
   Reflections of a Lord Mayor, 7 pages, *Household Words*.
   That Other Public, 11 pages, *Household Words*.
   Prologue to Marston's The Patrician's Daughter, 2 pages, 1842.
   The Frozen Deep, original draft of Wilkie Collins, with names of actors in Dickens's hand.
   (B) Letters. Correspondence with Macrone, etc.
   (C) Other Items. Many.
2. The Library of Mr W. M. Elkins, Philadelphia. (*Dickensian*, No. 229, p. 64.)
   (A) *Manuscripts:*
   Poem of 8 lines To Ariel, 26 October 1838, in an album of Miss Priscilla Horton (Mrs German Reed).
   Two pages regarding the Fund to be raised for the benefit of Mrs George Cattermole and her family.
   (B) Other items. Many.

374

3. Count de Suzannet's Library at La Petite, Chardière, Lausanne.
    (*Dickensian*, No. 230, p. 112.)
    (A) *Manuscripts:*
    > A Fable, verses composed by Dickens, for album of
    > Miss Ellen Beard.
    > The Ivy Green.
    > The Pickwick Papers, 1 page.
    > Nicholas Nickleby, 39 pages.
    > The Schoolboy's Story, Christmas Number of *House-
    > hold Words*, 1853.
    > A Little Dinner in an Hour.
    > All the Year Round, 2 January 1869.
    > The Uncommercial Traveller.
    > Tom Tiddler's Ground. *All the Year Round*, 1861.
    (B) 550 Autograph Letters of Charles Dickens.
    (C) Other Items.
4. The Henry E. Huntington Library, San Marino, California.
    (*Dickensian*, No. 231, p. 204.)
    (A) *Manuscripts:*
    > Drafts for four of the Christmas Stories.
    > A Child's History of England.
    > The Demeanour of Murderers.
    > Dreadful Hardships (Dickens's rejected contribution
    > to *Punch*.)
    > Ecclesiastical Registers. An attack on the abuses
    > attending the various registries of wills.
    > Protesting against the prison Laws of England.
    > Supposing.
    (B) Other Items. Many.
5. The Dickens House, 48 Doughty Street. (*Dickensian*, No. 231,
    p. 205.)
    (A) *Manuscripts:*
    > Various.
    (B) *Letters.*
    (C) Other items. Many.
6. The Harry Elkins Widener Library at Harvard University.
    (*Dickensian*, No. 232, p. 292.)
    (A) *Manuscripts:*
    > Cash account kept by Dickens at Ellis and Black-
    > more's.
    > The Frozen Deep, one page of MS. in Dickens's
    > hand.

Parody on Gray's Elegy apparently sent to Mary
Boyle, 3 December 1849.
(B) Other Items. Many.
7. The Forster Collection at the Victoria and Albert Museum,
South Kensington. (*Dickensian*, No. 233, p. 31.)
(A) *Manuscripts:*
Oliver Twist (Chapters 12 to 43).
The Lamplighter.
Sketches of Young Couples.
Master Humphrey's Clock (The Pickwick and Weller
Chapters).
The Old Curiosity Shop.
Barnaby Rudge.
American Notes.
Martin Chuzzlewit.
The Chimes.
Pictures from Italy.
Dombey and Son.
David Copperfield.
Bleak House.
A Child's History of England.
Little Dorrit.
A Tale of Two Cities.
The Mystery of Edwin Drood.
(B) Miscellaneous Writings. Many.
(C) Other items. Very many.
8. The Museum, Wisbech. Manuscript of *Great Expectations*.
9. Messrs Maggs's Collection, 34, 35 Conduit Street.
10. Drexil Institute, Philadelphia. MS. of *Our Mutual Friend*.
Presented by E. S. Dallas.
11. Mr W. C. Edwards's Collection, 3 Victoria Road, Clapham
Common. Letters to Macrone, etc.
12. The British Museum. Letters, etc.
13. The Walter T. Spencer Collection, 27 New Oxford Street,
London W.C.

# APPENDIX NO. 10

## Bibliography

(See Chapter VII, p. 58)

(1) Seven sketches in the *Monthly Magazine*.
  1833. Dec. A Dinner at Poplar Walk.
  1834. Jan. Mrs Joseph Porter.
    Feb. Horatio Sparkins.
    Apr. The Bloomsbury Christening.
    May. The Boarding House.
    Aug. The Boarding House, No. 2.
    Oct. The Steam Engine.
(2) Four sketches in the *Morning Chronicle*, all signed Boz.
  1834. Sept. 26. Omnibus.
    Oct. 10. Shops and their Tenants.
    Oct. 23. The Old Bailey.
    Nov. 5. Shabby Genteel.

DECEMBER 1834 TO 2 APRIL 1836
*Furnival's Inn, First Period*

(See Chapter VIII, p. 70)

(3) 1835. Two more sketches in the *Monthly Magazine*.
    Jan. Mr Watkins Tottle, chapter 1.
    Feb. Mr Watkins Tottle, chapter 2.
(4) Twenty sketches in the *Evening Chronicle*, 1835.
  Jan. 31. Hackney Coach Stands.
  Feb. 7. Gin Shops.
    „ 19. Early Coaches.
    „ 28. The Parish.
  Mar. 7. The House.
    „ 17. London Recreations.

377

Apr.  7.  Public Dinners.
  ,,  11.  Bellamy's.
  ,,  16.  Greenwich Fair.
  ,,  23.  Thoughts about People.
May  9.  Astley's.
  ,,  19.  Our Parish, No. 1.
June  6.  The River.
  ,,  18.  Our Parish, No. 2.
  ,,  30.  The Pawnbroker's Shop.
July  14.  Our Parish, No. 3.
  ,,  21.  The Streets.
  ,,  28.  Our Parish, No. 4.
Aug.  11.  Private Theatres.
  ,,  20.  Our Parish, No. 5.

(5) Twelve sketches in *Bell's Life in London*, signed "Tibbs."

Sept. 27 (1835).  Seven Dials.
Oct.  4.      Miss Evans and the "Eagle."
  ,,  11.      The Dancing Academy.
  ,,  18.      Making a Night of it.
  ,,  25.      Love and Oysters (Misplaced attachment of Mr John Dounce).
Nov.  1.      Some account of an Omnibus Cad.
  ,,  22.      The Vocal Dressmaker (The Mistaken Milliner).
  ,,  29.      The Prisoner's Van.
Dec. 13.      The Parlour (The Parlour Orator).
  ,,  27.      Christmas Festivities (A Christmas Dinner).
Jan.  3 (1836).  The New Year.
  ,,  17.      The Streets at Night.

(6) Two sketches in the *Library of Fiction*, edited by Charles Whitehead, announced 26 March 1836. London: Chapman & Hall.

The Tuggs's at Ramsgate.  2 illustrations by Seymour.

A Little Talk about Spring and the Sweeps.  1 illustration by Robert William Buss.

In Sketches by Boz, entitled the "First of May."

(7) "Sketches by Boz," 2 vols.  16 illustrations by Cruikshank. Preface dated February 1836. London: John Macrone.

# APPENDICES

2 APRIL 1836 TO MARCH 1837
*Furnival's Inn, Second Period*
(See Chapter IX, p. 83)

(8) "Sunday under Three Heads," by Timothy Sparks. Illustrated by Hablot K. Browne. London: Chapman & Hall. June 1836.

(9) Two sketches in the *Carlton Chronicle*.
Aug. 6 (1836). The Hospital Patient.
Sept. 17 (1836). Hackney Cabs and their Drivers.

In October appeared in its columns two further sketches reprinted from the *Morning Chronicle* (see the *Dickensian*, 1 March 1934, article by Walter Dexter).

(10) Four sketches in the *Morning* and *Evening Chronicle*, 1836.
Meditations in Monmouth Street, *M.C.*, 24 September; *E.C.*, 26 September.
Scotland Yard, *M.C.*, 4 October; *E.C.*, 15 October.
Doctor's Commons, *E.C.*, 12 October. Vauxhall Gardens by Day, *M.C.* and *E.C.*, 26 October.

(11) "The Pickwick Papers," 20 monthly numbers. First number, April 1836; last number, November 1837.

(12) "The Strange Gentleman." First performed 29 September 1836.

(13) "Village Coquettes," Played privately 23 July 1836.
First performed 6 December 1836.

(14) "Sketches by Boz," 2nd series. Preface dated 17 December 1836; published by Macrone.
The first complete edition (containing both series) was issued by Chapman & Hall in monthly parts in 1837 to 1839.

(15) *Bentley's Magazine*, 1837. Contributions chiefly concerning Mudfog.

MARCH 1837 TO END OF 1839
*Doughty Street Period*
(See Chapter X, p. 113)

(16) "Oliver Twist" appeared in *Bentley's Magazine* from February 1837 to September 1838.

(17) "Is she his Wife?" A comic Burletta. Performed at St James's Theatre, 6 March 1837.

(18) "Nicholas Nickleby." In 20 monthly numbers, April 1838 to October 1839.
(19) "The Memoirs of Joseph Grimaldi." 2 vols. London: Richard Bentley. Preface dated February 1838.
(20) "Sketches of Young Gentlemen." London: Chapman & Hall, 1838.
(21) "The Lamplighter." A farce, 1838.
(22) "The Loving Ballad of Lord Bateman." London: Charles Tilt, Fleet Street, 1839.
(23) Notice of John Gibson Lockhart's pamphlet, "The Ballantyne Humbug Handed," *Examiner*, 31 March 1839.

END OF 1839 TO JUNE 1842
*Devonshire House, First Period*
(See Chapter XI, p. 135)

(24) "Sketches of Young Couples." London: Chapman & Hall, 1840.
(25) "Master Humphrey's Clock." First number, 4 April 1840. "The Old Curiosity Shop" (begun in No. 4 of *Master Humphrey's Clock*).
(26) "Barnaby Rudge." First number, January 1841.
(27) "The Fine Old English Gentleman"—A squib.—*Examiner*, 7 August 1841
(28) "The Quack Doctor's Proclamation"—A squib.—*Examiner*, 14 August 1841.
(29) "Subjects for Painters"—A squib.—*Examiner*, 21 August 1841.
(30) "The Lamplighter's Story." Printed in the Pic-nic Papers. By various hands, edited by Charles Dickens. London: Henry Colburn, 1841.

JUNE 1842 TO SPRING 1847
*Devonshire House, Second Period*
(See Chapter XII, p. 155)

(31) "Circular Letter" on International Copyright with America. Devonshire Terrace, 7 July 1842.
(32) "Prologue" to Mr Westland Marston's Play, "The Patrician's Daughter." *Sunday Times*, 11 December 1842.
(33) American Notes. London: Chapman & Hall. 2 vols. 1842. 18 October.

# APPENDICES

(34) "Letter to the Editor of *The Times.*" Devonshire Terrace, 15 January 1843. Appeared in *The Times* next day. It refers to a criticism of American Notes.

(35) "Martin Chuzzlewit." In 20 monthly parts. January 1843 to July 1844.

(36) "Christmas Carol." Illustrations by Leech. London: Chapman & Hall. Christmas Book, 1843.

(37) "A Word in Season." Verse. Printed in *The Keepsake*, 1844.

(38) "Letter to the Committee of the Metropolitan Drapers' Association." Devonshire Terrace, 28 March 1844.

(39) "Threatening Letter to Thomas Hood." Printed in Hood's Magazine. May 1844.

(40) "Evenings by a Working Man." By John Overs. Preface by Dickens. London: T. C. Newby, 1844.

(41) "The Chimes." London: Chapman & Hall. Christmas Book, 1844.

(42) "The Cricket on the Hearth." London: Bradbury & Evans. Christmas Book, 1845.

(43) Contributions to the *Daily News.* Many, including:
    (1) "The British Lion." Signed Catnach.
    (2) "Crime and Education." 4 February 1846.
    (3) "Hymns of the Wiltshire Labourers." 14 February 1846.
    (4) "Letters on Capital Punishment." Three Letters— 9 March, 13 March, 17 March, 1846.

(44) "Pictures from Italy." London: Bradbury & Evans, 1846.

(45) "The Children's New Testament." An abstract of the narrative of the four gospels for the use of juvenile readers written by Charles Dickens exclusively for his own children, in June 1846. First published in the *Daily Mail*, 5 March to 17 March as "The Life of Our Lord."

(46) "Dombey and Son." In 20 monthly parts, October 1846 to April 1848. London: Bradbury & Evans.

(47) "The Battle of Life." London: Bradbury & Evans. Christmas Book, 1846.

SPRING 1847 TO NOVEMBER 1851
*Devonshire House, Third Period*
(See Chapter XIII, p. 185)

(48) "Mrs Gamp's Account of the Leigh Hunt Benefit." A fragment. Written in August 1847. Preserved in Forster's *Life of Dickens.*

(49) Notice of "The Drunkard's Children," in 8 plates, by Cruik-shank. *Examiner*, 8 July 1848.

(50) Notice of "The Rising Generation," a series of twelve drawings by Leech. *Examiner*, 30 December 1848.

(51) "The Haunted Man." London: Bradbury & Evans. Christmas Book, 1848.

(52) "David Copperfield," 20 monthly parts, May 1845 to November 1850. London: Bradbury & Evans.

(53) "Two Letters to *The Times*." 14 November and 19 November 1850.

(54) *Household Words*. First number published 30 March 1850. Many articles, including those indicated below by the letters *H.W.*

(55) "A Christmas Tree." Christmas (1850) No. of *H.W.*

(56) "The Guild of Literature and Art." *H.W.* 10 May 1851.

(57) "One Man in a Dockyard." Dickens and R. H. Horne. *H.W.* 6 September 1851.

(58) "What Christmas is as we grow older." Christmas (1851) No. of *H.W.*

(59) "A Child's History of England." *H.W.* January 1852 to December 1853.

(60) "Mr Nightingale's Diary." A Farce. 1851. Joint work of Dickens and Lemon.

NOVEMBER 1851 TO MARCH 1856
*Tavistock House, First Period*

(See Chapter XIV, p. 214)

(61) "Bleak House" (March 1852 to September 1853).

(62) "To be Read at Dusk."

(63) "Trading in Death." 27 November 1852. *H.W.*

(64) "A Round of Stories by the Christmas Fire." Christmas No. (1852) of *H.W.*

(65) "Frauds on the Fairies." 1 October 1853. *H.W.*

(66) "Another Round of Stories by the Christmas Fire." Christmas No. (1853) of *H.W.* Dickens contributed "The Schoolboy's Story" and "The Nurse's Story."

(67) "The Late Mr Justice Talfourd." 25 March 1854.

(68) "Hard Times." 1 April to 12 August 1854, in *H.W.*

(69) "Seven Poor Travellers." Christmas No. (1854) of *H.W.*

(70) "By Rail to Parnassus." *H.W.* 16 June 1855 (*re* Leigh Hunt).

APPENDICES

(71) "The Holly Tree Inn." Christmas No. (1855) of *H.W.*
(72) "Little Dorrit." In 20 monthly parts. December 1855 to June 1857.
(73) "A Nightly Scene in London." 26 January 1856, *H.W.*

14 MARCH 1856 TO END OF YEAR 1857
*Tavistock House, Second Period. Gad's Hill, First Period*

(See Chapter XV, p. 239)

(74) "Proposals for a National Jest Book." 3 May 1856, *H.W.*
(75) "Child's Hymn." Christmas 1856.
(76) "The Wreck of the *Golden Mary.*" Christmas No (1856) *H.W.*
(77) "Curious Misprint" in the *Edinburgh Review*, 1 August 1857.
(78) "The Lazy Tour." October 1857.
(79) "The Perils of Certain English Prisoners." Christmas No. (1857) of *H.W.*
(80) "Vie et Aventures à Nicholas Nickleby." This translation contains an address by Dickens to the French Public. Paris: Hatchette, 1857.

JANUARY 1858 TO JUNE 1860
*Tavistock House, Third Period, and Gad's Hill, Second Period*

(See Chapter XVI, p. 260)

(81) "The Violated Letter." *New York Tribune.*
(82) "Personal—Household Words," 12 June 1858. (This is the statement Dickens published respecting his separation from his wife, and the rumours circulating in connection with it.)
(83) "Reprinted Pieces" (31 sketches from *Household Words*).
(84) "A House to Let." Christmas No. (1858) of *H.W.*
(85) "A Tramp's Wallet." By William Duthie. Revised by Dickens. 1858.
(86) "Old Leaves." By W. Henry Wills. Revised by Dickens.
(87) "All the Year Round." 30 April 1859. Many articles, including those indicated below by the letters *A.Y.R.*
(88) "A Last Household Word." 28 May 1859.
(89) "The Poor Man and his Beer." *All the Year Round*, 30 April 1859.
(90) "The Blacksmith": A Trade Song. *All the Year Round*, 30 April 1859.

(91) "A Tale of Two Cities." 30 April 1859 to 26 November 1859, in *All the Year Round*.
(92) "Hunted Down." 1859.
(93) "Leigh Hunt": A Remonstrance. 24 December 1859.
(94) "The Haunted House." First Christmas No. (1859) *A.Y.R.*
(95) "A Message from the Sea." Second Christmas No. (1860) *A.Y.R.*
(96) "Uncommercial Traveller." *All the Year Round*, 28 January 1860.

JUNE 1860 TO 9 NOVEMBER 1867
*Gad's Hill Alone, First Period*

(See Chapter XVII, p. 294)

(97) "Great Expectations," in *All the Year Round*, December 1860 to August 1861.
(98) Letter to *The Times*. 12 January 1861.
(99) "The Election for Finsbury." 23 November 1861. Letter to the *Daily News*.
(100) "Tom Tiddler's Ground." Third Christmas No. (1861) *A.Y.R.*
(101) "Somebody's Luggage." Fourth Christmas No. (1862) *A.Y.R.*
(102) "The Earthquake." 8 October 1863. Letter to *The Times*.
(103) "Mrs Lirriper's Lodgings." Fifth Christmas No. (1863) *A.Y.R.*
(104) "In Memoriam" (A Notice of Thackeray). *Cornhill Magazine*. February 1864.
(105) "Our Mutual Friend." May 1861 to November 1865.
(106) "Mrs Lirriper's Legacy." Sixth Christmas No. (1864) *A.Y.R.*
(107) "Dr Marigold's Prescriptions." Seventh Christmas No. (1865) *A.Y.R.*
(108) "Legends and Lyrics," by Adelaide Anne Procter, Introduction by Dickens.
(109) "History of Pickwick." 31 March 1866. Letter to *Athenæum* respecting Seymour and "The Pickwick Papers."
(110) "Mugby Junction." Eighth Christmas No. (1866) *A.Y.R.*
(111) "The Late Mr Stanfield." *All the Year Round*, 1 June 1867.
(112) "To *The Times*." 4 September 1867. Referring to reports regarding his health.

384

# APPENDICES

9 NOVEMBER 1867 TO 31 DECEMBER 1869
*Gad's Hill Alone, Second Period*
(See Chapter XVIII, p. 236)

(113) "No Thoroughfare."   Ninth and last Christmas No. (1867) *A.Y.R.*

(114) "Uncommercial Traveller," with eleven new papers from *All the Year Round*, 1868.

(115) "George Silverman's Explanation." *Atlantic Monthly*, January to March 1868.

(116) "Holiday Romance." *Our Young Folks*, U.S.A. January to May 1868.

(117) "A Debt of Honour." Postscript to the later editions of American Notes and "Martin Chuzzlewit," May 1868.

(118) "New Uncommercial Samples." *All the Year Round*. New series.

(119) "Notice of Forster's *Life of Landor*." *All the Year Round*, 24 June 1869.

(120) "On Mr Fechter's Acting." *Atlantic Monthly*, Boston, August 1869.

(121) "Religious Opinions of Chauncey Hare Townshend," 1869.

THE YEAR 1870
*Gad's Hill Alone, Third Period*
(See Chapter XIX, p. 343)

(122) "Edwin Drood," First number published 1 April 1870. Three parts out of the proposed twelve were published before Dickens's death, and three were left in manuscript.

*Note.*—A fairly complete Bibliography of Charles Dickens will be found in Vol. 18 of Charles Dickens Library, edited by J. A. Hammerton. Educational Book Co., 1910. (British Museum Cat. 012602 K, 2.) It omits, however, our No. 9, The Sketches in the *Carlton Chronicle*.

# INDEX

Address in *Household Words*, The, 274
Ainsworth, Harrison, 75
*All the Year Round*, 288
"Alexis," 143
Alpington, cottage at, 133
America, Dickens's first visit to, 148; his second visit to, 326
American Notes, 156
Andersen, Hans C., 187
Austin, Henry, 67

Bank of England, 310
*Barnaby Rudge*, 140
Barrow, Edward, 61, 132
Barrow, Mrs Edward, her miniature of Dickens, 53
Barrow, Emily, 310
Barrow, Grace, 307
Barrow, John Henry, 28, 47, 57, 132
Barrow, Thomas Culliford, 23; loses a leg, 37; Dickens's letter to him, 81
*Battle of Life, The*, 182
Beadnell, Anne, 54, 65; dies, 89
Beadnell, George, 54, 221; dies, 285
Beadnell, Margaret (Mrs Lloyd), 54, 221, 306
Beadnell, Maria Sarah [Mrs Winter], 54, 59, 61, 229, 230, 265
Beard, Dr F. Carr, 339
Beard, Thomas, 66, 83, 170, 294
*Belphegor*, 316
Benham, Canon, 190, 205, 302, 356
Bentinck Street, 58
*Bentley's Miscellany*, 104, 132

Bibliography, 377
*Bill of Fare, The*, 55
Binney, Rev. Thomas, 125, 162
Birmingham, Dickens's Readings at, 226
Birmingham, Dickens acts at, 192
Black, John, 71, 163
Blackburn, Dickens at, 338
Blackpool, Dickens at, 339
*Bleak House*, 214, 217, 220
Boulogne, Dickens at, 224
Bracelet, The, 254
Braham, John, tenor singer, 84
Bridgman, Laura, 156
Broadstairs, 115
Brown, Hablot Knight, 87; with Dickens at Bowes, 124; his last Dickens illustrations, 291; dies, 366; list of his Dickens Illustions, 370
Burnett, Fanny, 24, 43, 84, 167; illness of, 195; dies, 195
Burnett, Harry, 188, 195
Burnett, Henry, 83
Byas's Asylum at Bow, 128

*Carlton Chronicle*, The, 91
Cattermole, George, 135
Childs, Mr, 339
*Child's History of England*, 211
*Chimes, The*, 173
Christmas Books, 169
Christmas Carol, 169
Christmas Stories, 169
Clare, John, 317
*Clari*, 60

387

Clarke, Mrs Cowden, 191

Clutterbuck, Lady Maria (Mrs. Dickens), 223

Collier, John Payne, 64

Collins, Charles Allston, marries Kate Dickens, 294; John Payne on, 295; dies, 295; his wrapper illustrations to *Edwin Drood*

Collins, Wilkie, 210, 225, 227; and *The Lazy Tour*, 258; his *After Dark*, 232; *Woman in White*, 296, 306; *No Name*, 306; *The Moonstone*, 324; dies, 366

Cornwall, the trip to, 158

Count de Suzannet's collection, 375

Coutts, the Baroness Burdett, obtains a cadetship for Walter Dickens, 252; sympathises with Mrs Dickens after the separation, 348, 279

Creakle's School (Jones's), 44

Cruikshank, George, 95, 105, 117, 118, 119, 120; stands on his head in a phaeton, 154

*Daily News* founded, 238

Dallas, Edward S., 315

*David Copperfield*, 197, 204

*Deaf as a Post* (John Poole's play), 154

Defoe, 142, 206, 207; Denman, Lord Chief Justice, 221

Dickens, Augustus, born, 369; in Chicago, 329, 338

Dickens, Mrs (Charles Dickens's wife), 73; her portrait by Maclese, 73, death, 356

Dickens, Charles, birth, 23; comes of age, 58; engaged to Miss C. T. Hogarth, 73; as a Letter-Writer, 162; separates from his wife, 267; his reference to Miss E. L. Ternan in the "Violated Letter," 271; his will, 252; dies, 353; as a Textuary, 360

Dickens, Charles Culliford Boz (Charles Dickens's eldest son), born, 97

Dickens, Edward Bulwer Lytton, 369

Dickens, Fanny, 24, 43. See Burnett, Fanny

Dickens, Frederick, born, 27, 74; dies, 333

Dickens, Francis Jeffery, born, 170; dies, 369

Dickens, Sir Henry Fielding, 369; dies, 367

Dickens, John (Charles Dickens's father), 23, 178; dies, 211

Dickens, Mrs John, 23; dies, 307

Dickens, Kate, born, 133; marries (1) C. A. Collins, 294; (2) C. E. Perugini, 369

Dickens, Letitia, 25, 59, 61, 62

Dickens, Mary (Mamie), born, 130; dies, 369

Dickens, Sydney Smith Haldimand, 180, 369

Dickens, Walter Landor, 148, 252; dies, 369

Dickens Collections, 374

Dickens House (48 Doughty Street) secured, 367

*Doctor Marigold*, 157

Dolby, George, 266, 325, 326; has a title conferred on him, 328; in a walking match, 329; and the "Murder scene," 334, 335; dies, 367

*Dombey and Son*, 188

Drummond, Miss Rose E., her miniature of Dickens, 72

Eden, City of, 151

*Edwin Drood*, 345, 346

Egg, Augustus (artist), 211, 225, 235, 361, 364

Election for Lord Rectorship of Glasgow University, 286

Ellis and Blackmore's, 46

388

Events subsequent to the death of Dickens, 366

Fannys, the three, 175
Fechter, Charles Albert, 306, 316; writes with Wilkie Collins the play *Black and White*, 338
Fechter, Paul (a child), 317
Fildes, Luke, artist, illustrates *Edwin Drood*, 371
Finlay, Francis Dalzell, 278, 323
Fitzgerald, Percy, his *Life of Sterne*, 308, 314; his *Life of Garrick*, 319; his story *An Experience*, 341, 346; in Ireland with Dickens, 337; articles by, 373
"Five Bells," Hatcham, 308
"Flora," 236
Forster, John, 111, 174, 197, 211, 268, 326, 351
Forster Collection, South Kensington, 376
Fox, William Johnson, 56, 155, 159; dies, 308
Frith, William Powell (artist), 111, 211, 287
*Frozen Deep, The*, 251
Furnival's Inn (No. 13), 70
Furnival's Inn (No. 15), 78

Gad's Hill Place, 33, 239
Gamp, Mrs, 160, 186
Gaskell, Mrs, 159 215, 223; her story *Ruth*, 224; dies, 317
Gibson, Thomas, marries Mary Weller, 25; dies, 366
Giles, Rev. William, Junior, 28, 123, 197
Giles, Rev. William, Senior, 28
Gissing, George, 189, 220
Gooch, Richard Heathcote, 118, 340
Gore House, Dickens's speech at, 211
Grant brothers, 128
*Great Expectations*, 296

Great Ormond Street Hospital for Sick Children, 260
Griffin, Rev. James, 146, 188, 195
*Grimaldi, Memoirs of*, 131
Guild Company, 221
Guild of Literature and Art, 213

Hall, Rev. Newman, 293
*Hard Times*, 227
Harley, John Pritt (comedian), 92, 114, 132
Harry Elkins Widener Library, 375
*Haunted House, The*, 292
*Haunted Man, The*, 196
Henry Huntington Library, 375
Hogarth, Catherine Thomson. *See* Dickens, Mrs Charles
Hogarth, Georgina, 73, 158, 163, 219, 227, 263, 322; dies, 367
Hogarth, George (Mrs Charles Dickens's father), 71, 105, 265
Hogarth, George (Mrs Charles Dickens's brother), dies, 147
Hogarth, Mrs George (Mrs Charles Dickens's mother), as Mrs Jeniwin, 131, 184; illness of, 268; dies, 307
Hogarth, Helen Isabella, 73, 272, 275; dies, 366
Hogarth, Mary Scott, 73, 81, 84; calls at Macrone's, 96, 106; dies, 109, 159
Hoghton Tower, 323
Hole, Dean, 308
*Holiday Romance*, 324
*Holly Tree Inn*, 234
Holocaust, The, 303, 308
*Household Words*, 203
Huffam, Christopher, 24, 38; dies, 133
Hughes, W. R., of Birmingham, 102; dies, 367
Hugo, Victor, 183; and Juliette Drouet, 184, 255
Hullah, John Pyke (composer), 92, 318

Hunt, Leigh, 217, 218

Illustrators of Dickens, 370
Ireland, Dickens's first visit to, 278; second visit to, 323; third visit to, 337
Irving, Washington, 97, 138, 217
*Is She his Wife?*, 106
Isle of Wight, Dickens at, 200
Italy, Dickens in, 173, 225
"Ivy Green, The," 53, 375

Jarman Case, The, 48
Jarman, Frances Eleanor, 241. *See also* Ternan, Mrs
Jaunting car, The, 278, 280
Jeniwin, Mrs, 85, 131
Jerrold, Douglas, 174; dies, 249, 250

Kemble, Fanny, 143
Kent, Charles, 353; dies, 367
Kettering Election, The, 76
Kitton, F. G., 167; dies, 367
Kolle, Henry, 54; marries, 63; his daughter's poems, 289

Landor, Walter Savage, 136, 175, 217, 276
Lane, Charlotte Elizabeth (Mrs John Mantel), 310
Lane, M. R., 128
Laurence, Samuel (artist), 123, 134
*Lazy Tour, The*, 257
Le Fanu, J. S., 349
Leather Bottle, The (Cobham), 101
Leech, John, 200; illustrates the Christmas Books, 371; dies, 308
Leigh, Marianne, 56, 59, 63
Lemon, Mark, 211, 253, 275; dies, 351
Lever, Charles, 296
Lewes, George Henry, 113, 191, 211
*Life of Christ*, Dickens's, 155
*Lighthouse, The* (play by Wilkie Collins), 232

Linton, Mrs Lynn, 216, 239
*Lirriper's Legacy, Mrs*, 307
*Lirriper's Lodgings, Mrs*, 307
*Little Dorrit*, 233, 238
Longfellow, Henry Wadsworth, 158, 348
*Loving Ballad of Lord Bateman*, 113
*Love, Law and Physic* (Kenney's play), 191, 193
Lytton, Lord, 75, 223, 304

Macaulay, T. B., 309; dies, 293
Maclise, Daniel, 104; his pencil drawing of Dickens, Mrs Dickens and Georgina Hogarth, 116; his picture "The Girl at the Waterfall," 158; dies, 349; his portrait of Dickens, 130; his portrait of Mrs Dickens, 73, 190
Maclone, John, 75; dies, 115
Macready, William Charles, 114, 133; dies, 366
"Magic Fishbone, The," 325
Mannings, execution of the, 201
Marston, Westland, 257
*Martin Chuzzlewit*, 159
*Master Humphrey's Clock*, 135
Mathews, Charles, 51
Matthews, Rev. Timothy Richard, of Bedford, 90
"Micawber," 27, 68, 131, 146; dies, 211
Mr F.'s Aunt, 236
Mitton, Mary Ann, 27
Mitton, Thomas, 59, 61, 133
Mormons, Dickens and the, 307
*Morning Chronicle*, The, 66
*Mudfog Papers*, The, 105
"Mutual" used for "common," 309

*Nellyad, The*, 139
*New York Tribune*, 279
Newsvendors' Dinner, The, 348
*Nicholas Nickleby*, 123, 129

390

*Not so Bad as we Seem* (Lord Lytton's play), 222

Old Curiosity Shop (Fetter Lane), 64
*Old Curiosity Shop* (the story), 107, 110, 135, 137, 139
*Oliver Twist*, 105, 116
*O'Thello, The*, 62
*Our Mutual Friend*, 308, 312
Ouvry, Mr Frederic, the gathering of the *Frozen Deep* party at his house, 251

Paid Readings, first series, 266; second series, 303; third series, 318; fourth series, 334; fifth series, 343
Panton, Mrs J. E., 275
Paris, Dickens at, 183, 233
*Past Two O'clock in the Morning* (Mathews's play), 140, 153, 193, 222
Payne, John, on C. A. Collins and Dickens, 295; on Humour, 295
*Perils of Certain English Prisoners*, 259
Peterborough, Dickens at, 226, 233; his second visit to, 290
*Pickwick Papers*, 80
Plays by Dickens: *The Strange Gentleman*, 92; *Village Coquettes*, 93; *Is She his Wife?*, 106; *The Lamplighter*, 108
Polygon, The, 51

"Q" (Francis Alexander), 150
Quilp, 131
"Quiz," E. Caswell, his *Sketches of Young Ladies*, 131

Ragged Schools, 164
Reade, Charles, 322
Riah, the benevolent Jew, 313
Rintoul, R. S., 275
Rockingham Castle, 202, 209
*Roland for an Oliver, A* (T. Morton's play), 153

Ross, Georgina, 53

Sadleir, John, M.P. ("Mr Merdle"), 96, 235
Sala, G. A., 283
Sala, Madame, 93, 106
Scheffer, Ary, 235, 287
Separation, The, 267
Seymour, Robert, 80; his suicide, 85
Shakespeare House Fund, 190
Shaw, William [Squeers], 124
Shiers, Richard, 44
*Sketches by Boz*, 79
*Sketches of Young Couples*, 131
*Sketches of Young Gentlemen*, 131
*Sketches of Young Ladies*, 131
Skimpole, Harold [Leigh Hunt], 185
Smith, Arthur, 291; dies, 304
*Somebody's Luggage*, 306
Stanfield, Clarkson, 232, 235; dies, 324
Staplehurst accident, 312
Starey, S. R., 164; dies, 367
Stendhal quoted, 225
*Strange Gentleman, The*, 92, 93
*Sunday under Three Heads*, 89
Stone, Frank, 117, 222, 290, 371
Stone, Marcus, 252, 253, 372
Switzerland, Dickens in, 179, 225

Tagart, Rev. Edward, 159
*Tale of Two Cities, A*, 51, 288
Talfourd, Thomas Noon "Traddles"), 50, 204
Tavistock House, 214
Tennyson, Alfred, 181
Ternan, Ellen Lawless, 241; Dickens sees her weeping, 244; appears as "Atalanta" at the Haymarket, 249; Dickens in love with her, 253; plays in *The Frozen Deep*, 253, 256; Dickens sends her a bracelet, 254; apotheosis of, 280; becomes Dickens's mistress, 262, 280; she is troubled, 282, 283; takes the part of Alice in *The Tide of Time*,

288; regrets her connection with Dickens, 356; Dickens leaves her a thousand pounds, 352

Ternan, Mrs Frances Eleanor (Miss Jarman), 241; returns to the stage, 319; dies, 366

Ternan, Frances Eleanor (daughter of Mrs F. E. Ternan), 242; marries T. A. Trollope, 320; her works, 321

Ternan, Maria (daughter of Mrs F. E. Ternan), 242

Ternan, Thomas Lawless, 241

Thackeray, William Makepeace, 134, 199, 264, 276; dies, 308

Thompson, T. J., marries Mrs C. Weller, 171

Thomson, George, 73; dies, 216

Thomson, Helen, 73, 264; her letter to Mrs Stark referred to, 279

Three in Error, 262

Tom-all-Alone's, 33, 168

Tom Tiddler's Ground, 168, 304

Townshend, Rev. Chauncey Hare, 143; dies, 332

Trollope, Mrs Frances Eleanor (daughter of Mrs F. E. Ternan), 320; list of her works, 321; has a Civil List Pension, 367

Trollope, Mrs Frances (mother of Thomas Adolphus and Anthony), 175, 283, 320, 321

Trollope, Thomas Adolphus, 121, 201, 207, 288; his Autobiography, 366; marries Miss F. E. Ternan, 320; dines with Dickens at Verey's, 325; dies, 366

Type evasion, The, 217

Uncle John (J. B. Buckstone's play), 251, 253, 254

Unitarianism, Dickens and, 155

Uncommercial Traveller, The, 293, 307

Used Up (Boucicault's play), 194, 195, 196, 222

Verey's in Regent Street, 293

Veronique and Veronica, 341

Vholes, Mr, 218

Village Coquettes, The, 93

Violated Letter, The, 269

Wainewright, Thomas Griffiths, 121, 237

Ward, Edward Matthew (artist), 235

Watson, Hon. Richard, M.P., 202, 209; dies, 233, 290

Weller, Christiana, 170

Weller, Mary (Mrs John Dickens's servant), 25; dies, 366

Whitehead, Charles, 79, 80

Winter, Mr, 229; his financial failure, 285; dies, 306

Winter, Mrs (Maria Sarah Beadnell), 196, 229; Dickens's letter to her, 230; at Tavistock House, 265; dies at Southsea, 366

Wright, Thomas of Olney (author of this work), advocates establishment of a Dickens Museum, 367

Yarmouth, Dickens at, 197

Yates, Edmund, 276, 283

P76 - Damn the Tories — will win
P118 exposed the most hateful evils of
his day!

P173 New Testament, in its broad spirit....
" Orss — Evenings by a Working Man
200 Roman republic Dickensia 1914 (note
212 A Child's History of England liberty Commn
213 Bleak House, championed the down trodden
221 Dickens accused of supporting slavery. see American Notes
238 Mrs Sparkler's attitude to Classics —
262 Childrens hospital lecture ... hardening his heart again
305 Jupiter and his satellites in microscope
308 Self-made independence
332 New Testament to son (for Australia)
352-3 Gospel essence Wm Blake
342 — politics Birmingham 27 Sept 186

CPSIA information can be obtained
at www.ICGtesting.com
Printed in the USA
BVHW041342030619
549989BV00020B/458/P

9 781163 179611